INCREASING FACULTY DIVERSITY

INCREASING FACULTY DIVERSITY

THE OCCUPATIONAL CHOICES OF
HIGH-ACHIEVING MINORITY STUDENTS

Stephen Cole

Elinor Barber

with

MELISSA BOLYARD AND ANNULLA LINDERS

HARVARD UNIVERSITY PRESS

Cambridge, Massachusetts

London, England

2003

Library of Congress Cataloging-in-Publication Data

Cole, Stephen, 1941–
    Increasing faculty diversity : the occupational choices of high-achieving minority
students / Stephen Cole, Elinor Barber with Melissa Bolyard, Annulla Linders.
        p.   cm.
    Includes bibliographical references and index.
    ISBN 0-674-00945-2 (alk. paper)
    1. Faculty integration—United States.   2. Minority college teachers—United States.
3. Minority college graduates—Employment—United States.   4. Vocational interests—
United States.   I. Barber, Elinor G.   II. Title.
LB2332.6.C65 2003
378.1′2′089—dc21   2002027331

To the memory of Elinor Barber:
coauthor, colleague, friend

CONTENTS

TABLES AND FIGURES

TABLES

FIGURES

This project began in discussions between the late Elinor Barber and Neil Rudenstine, then president of Harvard University. All of the Ivy League institutions had a common interest in doing whatever they could to increase the ethnic and racial diversity of their faculties. Elinor Barber, a research associate in the Provost's Office at Columbia University, volunteered to conduct a research project with its aim being to develop policy recommendations that would help the Ivy League and other interested colleges and universities increase the ethnic and racial diversity of their faculty. Elinor Barber then recruited me to join her in the project.

The research would be sponsored by the Council of Ivy Group Presidents, an association of the eight Ivy League institutions, headquartered in Princeton, that helps its members deal with common problems. Ours was the first research project sponsored by the Council, and it was enthusiastically supported by Jeffrey Orleans, Executive Director of the Council. We thank him for the help and advice he provided throughout this project.

The Council of Ivy Group Presidents provided an initial seed grant, which paid for our review of the literature, the qualitative research that was done before the surveys were conducted, and the preparation of a formal proposal. The proposal was then submitted to the Andrew W. Mellon Foundation, which agreed to provide the majority of the funds ultimately used to conduct this research. We thank William Bowen and Harriet Zuckerman of the Mellon Foundation for their support and advice.

When it became clear that we needed to increase the sample of schools studied, we submitted a grant for supplementary funding to the

Ford Foundation. We thank Edgar Beckham of the Ford Foundation for his support. During the last stages of the research the Russell Sage Foundation appointed me a Visiting Scholar at the Foundation. The year I spent there allowed me to complete the data analysis and write the report. We thank Eric Wanner of the Russell Sage Foundation for his support. Jonathan R. Cole, Provost of Columbia University, was the Principal Investigator for this research, and we thank him for his support and advice. Columbia University administered the grant, with subcontracts administered by the Research Foundation at the State University of New York at Stony Brook.

While we were conducting the research, we received a request from Brown University and the Leadership Alliance, a group of private universities and historically black colleges and universities (HBCUs) that work together to further the educational attainment of African Americans, for help with a qualitative research project on the problems faced by minority graduate students. The focus groups we conducted for them provided useful supplementary data for our own project. We thank Vartan Gregorian, then president of Brown University, and James Wyche, Executive Director of the Leadership Alliance, for their support.

The research reported in this book could not have been done without the help of many colleagues and friends. The two most important are Melissa Bolyard, a graduate student in the Department of Sociology at Stony Brook, and Annulla Linders, a former graduate student at Stony Brook and now an Assistant Professor at the University of Cincinnati. Annulla was Project Director for the research and was heavily involved in every aspect, from the writing of the proposal to the completion of the initial report prepared for the Council of Ivy Group Presidents. Her help was crucial during the data collection phase, which she supervised. When the mail and phone surveys were being conducted, I was a Visiting Professor at the University of Queensland in Australia. Without Annulla's devotion to this project well beyond the call of duty, it could never have been completed.

Melissa Bolyard joined the research team when we were beginning our analysis of the quantitative data. She did all the computer programming for the data analysis. A true collaborator, she was heavily involved in all the data analysis and interpretation. In the last two years of the project, she continued to work virtually full time on this research without any compensation. Melissa is coauthor of Chapter 7 and a major part of Appendix C, and she contributed significantly to all of the other data analysis chapters. Without Melissa's skills as a data analyst and methodologist this book would not have been completed.

Andrea Tyree, Professor of Sociology at Stony Brook, served as the methodological consultant to the research team. She weighted the data and was constantly available as a consultant as we interpreted the data, through the final drafts of the data analysis chapters. In addition, Andrea wrote several key sections of Appendix C. We thank her for her ability to think through difficult methodological issues and come up with elegant solutions.

Chapter 9, on the pipeline into academia, makes heavy use of census data. Elizabeth Arias, at the time Assistant Professor of Sociology at Stony Brook, currently a demographer at the National Center for Health Statistics, was a coauthor of this chapter and conducted all of the analysis of the census data on which the chapter was based. Elizabeth also wrote a section of Appendix C.

Two others who were essential to the completion of this research were Michael Aguilera, a postgraduate fellow at Stony Brook, and Mary Moycik-Aguilera. They formatted the entire document, including all the tables and figures. Their dedication allowed us to deliver the manuscript in the correct format and on time.

In conducting this research we were fortunate to have the support of the following members of our Advisory Committee: Helen Astin, Higher Education Research Institute, UCLA; Richard Light, Kennedy School of Government, Harvard University; Daniel Solorzano, Department of Education, UCLA; and Claude Steele, Department of Psychology, Stanford University. We thank them for their advice during all phases of the project. Thanks also to Norman Bradburn, National Opinion Research Corporation, University of Chicago, for helping us develop a convincing cover letter for our mail survey.

During the academic year 1997–98, while I was a Visiting Scholar at the Russell Sage Foundation, I received invaluable assistance from all of my colleagues. Gary Field, Department of Economics, Cornell School of Industrial and Labor Relations, was more than generous, spending many hours going over methodological problems with me. Others who gave important advice were Reynolds Farley, University of Michigan; Aurora Jackson, University of Pittsburgh; Lawrence Katz, Harvard University; Lissandro Perez, Florida International University; Anne Preston, Haverford College; Ruben Rumbaut, Michigan State University; and Mark Schneider, SUNY at Stony Brook.

We also owe a substantial debt to the people who served as liaisons at the thirty-four schools included in our main survey and the three schools included in our pretest survey: at Amherst College, Sarah Sutherland; at Bowdoin College, Christine Brooks; at Brown University, Karen Roemer; at Carleton College, Christine Otis Skinner; at Colgate University, Michael Cappeto; at Cornell University, Michael Matier; at Dartmouth College, Margaret Dyer-Chamberlain; at Florida A&M, Malcolm Barnes; at Hamilton College, Louise Peckingham; at Harvard University, Martha Homer; at Haverford College, Randie Milden; at Howard University, Charles Jarmon; at Middlebury College, Don Wyatt; at North Carolina A&T, Paula Young; at Oberlin College, Mary Durling; at Ohio State University, Joan Huber; at Pomona College, Richard Fass; at Princeton University, Hal McCulloch; at Rutgers University, Godfrey Roberts; at Stanford University, Kathryn Gillam; at Swarthmore College, Ngina Lythcott; at SUNY at Stony Brook, Annulla Linders and Emily Thomas; at Tufts University, Dawn Terkla; at UCLA, Raymund Paredes; at the University of Maryland at College Park, James Newton; at the University of North Carolina, Angell Beza; at the University of Pennsylvania, Kent Peterman; at the University of Texas, Gary Hanson; at the University of Virginia, Rick Turner; at the University of Washington, Fred Campbell; at the University of Wisconsin, Charlene Tortorice; at Vassar College, Clare Graham; at Wesleyan University, Billy Weitzer; at Williams College, David Booth; at Xavier University, Dereck Rovaris; and at Yale University, John Goldin.

The following people helped facilitate the focus groups: at Columbia University, Kathleen McDermott; at Dartmouth College, Susan Wright; at Howard University, Linda Jones; and at Princeton University, David Redman.

The following people helped conduct the focus groups: Richard Barba-Reyes, SUNY at Stony Brook; Jacob Heller, SUNY at Old Westbury; Annulla Linders, University of Cincinnati; Raymond Maietta, SUNY at Stony Brook; Vera Phillip-Evans, SUNY at Stony Brook; Frank Shih, SUNY at Stony Brook; and Richard Williams, Rutgers University. The following undergraduate students at Stony Brook helped with the focus groups: Orlando Montan, Paul Morea, Jeff Petruzzeli, James Pimpinella, and Corey Williams. Andria Cooke and Patrice Fouron, also Stony Brook undergraduates, provided valuable clerical assistance. Dannielle Hartmann, another Stony Brook undergraduate, completed an independent research project in which she analyzed the differences between African Americans at different types of schools. Her work is utilized in Chapter 8. Jane Ely and Chinatsu Maeda, SUNY at Stony Brook, served as my assistants during the last three years of this project.

Bernard Barber and Maria Cole provided thoughtful advice on all phases of the research throughout the seven years of this study. I thank them for both their wisdom and their patience. Bernard Barber played a particularly important role after the death of Elinor Barber. He read all of the chapters with an eye toward pinpointing anything in the text he felt Elinor might have been uncomfortable with.

Perhaps most of all, we owe thanks to the 7,612 students who took the time to fill out and return our questionnaire.

Prior to the completion of this book a substantially longer version of the manuscript was sent out for peer review. We would like to thank the following for reading all or parts of the manuscript, and for providing comments that served to improve this book: Walter Allen, Professor of Sociology, UCLA; Helen Astin, Higher Education Research Institute, UCLA; Bernard Barber, Professor Emeritus of Sociology, Columbia University; Jonathan R. Cole, Provost, Columbia University; Ronald Ehrenberg, Professor of Economics, Cornell University; Kenneth A. Feldman, Professor of Sociology, SUNY at Stony Brook; Douglas Massey, Professor of Sociology, University of Pennsylvania; Jeffrey Orleans, Director, Council of Ivy Group Presidents; and Ernest Pascarella, Professor of Education, Iowa State University. Three readers in particular went well beyond the call of colleagueship in providing detailed comments on a page-by-page basis. These were Jonathan R. Cole, Elizabeth Arias, and James A. Davis of the National Opinion Research Corporation. Jim Davis deserves special thanks. Not only did he provide detailed critical comments on an earlier draft of the manuscript, but he also read a later draft. His additional comments helped make this a better book. It is rare to find a colleague who is willing to put in the kind of time that such comments require, and who does not hesitate to be strongly critical when he believes such criticism is warranted. We tried to make use of most of the suggestions provided by our readers, but of course I alone am responsible for any remaining errors. None of the opinions expressed in the book are necessarily those of any of the sponsors or any of the advisors.

Thanks to Donna Bouvier at Harvard University Press for helping to make the text more readable and lucid. It was a pleasure working with her, and her suggestions for editorial changes were always right on the mark.

Finally, I would like to thank my editor, Michael Aronson, who has shown confidence in my work for more than twenty-five years.

Elinor Barber died in the winter of 1999, just as this manuscript was begun to be written. Without her this project never would have been initiated, much less completed. Finishing the manuscript without her help and advice was a difficult task. This book is dedicated to her memory.

Stephen Cole

1

THE PROBLEM

The United States is becoming an increasingly multicultural society. The Census Bureau estimates that within the next thirty to fifty years whites will no longer make up more than half of the population, as the number of Asians, Latinos, and other immigrants continues to increase. Much of this diversity already exists. The 2000 Census shows that Latinos now represent approximately 12 percent of the population, roughly equivalent to the size of the African American population. As our society has become more multicultural so have our institutions of higher education. Over the past thirty years, American colleges and universities have attempted to make their student bodies reflect the racial and ethnic characteristics of the general population. Many colleges, particularly the most prestigious and most selective ones, have initiated affirmative action programs or "racial preferences" in admissions, aimed at increasing the number of enrolled students who are members of underrepresented racial or ethnic minority groups, specifically African Americans, Latinos, and Native Americans.[1] Using racial preferences in admissions means that race is taken into account as one factor in making the admissions decision. The result is that some members of the underrepresented racial and ethnic groups are admitted in preference to white applicants who have higher academic qualifications—specifically, higher scores on the Scholastic Aptitude Test (SAT) and higher high school grade point averages (GPAs). In terms of student representation, significant progress in increasing diversity has been made in the last thirty years.

The overwhelming majority of the academic community believes that racial and ethnic diversity of both students and faculty is a desirable goal. There are many potential benefits of diversity. Ethnic diversification among students is widely approved, because it suggests that successful efforts are being made to overcome the educational and financial disadvantages that have prevented especially African American, Latino, and Native American students from taking full advantage of the educational and career opportunities that come with an undergraduate education. A baccalaureate degree is a passport to a set of occupations whose earnings potential considerably exceeds those that require only a high school diploma. Although the specific differential in earnings potential between those with and without a college degree has varied over time, there is a large body of literature that shows that education, particularly the achievement of a college degree, is a key determinant of both occupational status and earnings.[2] Scholars do not agree on what specific mechanisms create this association, but there is no disagreement on its existence. Thus, whether education has this effect because it increases the relevant job skills ("human capital") of its recipients (Becker 1975) or because it provides a credential necessary for access to privileged positions (Collins 1979), or both, education, and particularly a college degree, is an important contributor to the achievement of occupational and economic success. Beyond that, a baccalaureate degree is a requirement for access to various kinds of postbaccalaureate education, including graduate education leading to master's and Ph.D. degrees and professional education leading to law, medical, and other degrees.

With increasing diversification of the undergraduate student body has come the expectation that the faculty teaching this student body will become similarly diverse. There are several reasons why supporters of diversity believe that it would be desirable to have an ethnically diverse faculty.[3] First, having representation of African Americans and Latinos on faculties roughly proportionate to the representation of students from these groups would suggest that long-standing discrimination is being abandoned and that the ability of these minorities to fill faculty positions in all fields has been recognized.[4]

Second, faculty diversity is believed to be necessary to afford minority students the kind of teachers who will be sympathetic to their special problems, give them the kind of encouragement they need to succeed in college and beyond, and demonstrate to them that in the academic sphere, at least, full recognition of the ability of minority group members is possible. It is assumed that the traditional advantages of white students, both in college and beyond, will persist as long as African American, Latino, and Asian students are taught by faculty who are predominantly, if not exclusively, white.

2

Third, faculty diversity, its supporters believe, will ensure that in the social sciences and humanities appropriate attention will be given to the creativity of African Americans, Latinos, Asians, and Native Americans and to the contributions they have made to every aspect of American society. In addition, informed attention is more likely to be paid to the persistent racial and ethnic conflicts within the society.

Fourth, proponents of diversity assume that the academic performance and career aspirations of minority students will be enhanced if minority faculty serve as role models for them, even though until now no adequate evidence has been available to determine whether this assumption is indeed true. The influence of such role models is thought to derive from their exemplification of a successful career in academia and from the special impact they have on minority students as teachers and mentors.

And finally, the argument is made that in the humanities and social sciences, at least, and perhaps even in some of the natural sciences, faculty diversity ensures that theories and empirical data will be informed by the special perspectives that, by virtue of their own experience, only members of certain racial and ethnic groups and women can bring to research and teaching.[5] On this point, there is far from perfect agreement in the academy; moreover, currently all of the benefits of ethnic and racial diversity remain in the realm of conjecture rather than empirically demonstrated facts.

Although many agree that the achievement of racial and ethnic diversity in both student bodies and faculties is a desirable goal, there is no agreement on the means that should be used to attain this goal. Particularly, there is substantial disagreement over the use of affirmative action, which in practice ranges from having quota systems or "set-asides"[6] for minority students and faculty to including race as one criterion in the admission and hiring process.[7] The administrations of virtually all major universities and colleges and the educational establishment appear to be almost uniformly committed to racial preferences as a tool to achieve diversity. However, a series of surveys have brought into question the extent to which both faculty and students support the type of affirmative action in which a minority student with lower qualifications than a white student is admitted while the more qualified white student is rejected or a minority faculty member is hired in preference to a more qualified white candidate (Wood and Sherman 2001). These surveys suggest that the ma-

3

jority of both students and faculty are opposed to policies in which race trumps qualifications. Of course, the content of both student and faculty opinions on this issue varies greatly from one campus to another.

Opposition to racial preferences is based on the belief that this system of admissions or hiring violates the rights of white individuals who are protected under the Fourteenth Amendment, which guarantees everyone equal protection of the law regardless of their race, and Title VII of the 1964 Civil Rights Act, which states: "No person in the United States shall on the grounds of race, color, or national origin . . . be subjected to discrimination under any program or activity receiving Federal financial assistance." In 1978, in the case of University of California Regents v. Bakke (438 U.S. 265) the Supreme Court ruled in a 5 to 4 decision that a quota system employed by the University of California at Davis's medical school was illegal and violated the civil rights of the plaintiff, Allan Bakke, who was retroactively admitted to the school. The decision, however, was narrow in scope, and the opinion of one justice, Lewis Powell, left open the possibility of using racial preferences if they were necessary to create diversity that was educationally beneficial. Powell looked for constitutional justification for his opinion in the First Amendment, which he saw as allowing institutions of education to pursue their goals without government interference and allowing them to take race into account as one of several factors considered in the admissions process. No other justice joined Powell in this part of his opinion—but since that time universities supporting affirmative action have used the Powell opinion as constitutional legitimation for their action.

There is one way in which universities would be able to achieve racial and ethnic diversity of its faculty without resorting to the use of racial preferences in hiring. This alternative route to diversity would be to increase the number of high-achieving African American, Latino, and Native American college graduates who are equivalent in academic skills to white and Asian college graduates and who decide to select academia as their career. The aim of the research reported in this book is to find what factors influence highly talented minority students to select academia as a career and to suggest policy that might increase the number going into academia. The challenge is to increase the pool of minority candidates for academic positions to such an extent that suitable candidates will be available for openings at all levels of the higher education hierarchy, from the elite research universities seeking highly productive scholar-teachers to those in four-year and two-year colleges demanding good teaching skills.

If the racial distribution of Ph.D. recipients who wanted to be professors was the same as either the proportion of students in each racial group or—better—the proportion of the population in each racial group, there would be a large enough pool of candidates in each racial group so that faculty diversity could be attained without the use of racial preferences. This would be especially true if the distribution of talent in each racial group was the same.

Desirable as the diversification of faculty may be, at this time it is far from being achieved. The discrepancy between the representation of minority students and that of minority faculty is large. Our data indicate that at the present time, in many of the thirty predominantly white schools that we studied, the proportion of African American and Latino faculty is below that of undergraduates, while the proportion of Asian and white faculty is above that of undergraduates. Data from other sources lead to the same conclusion. As of 1996, according to data published by the National Center for Educational Statistics (NCES) of the U.S. Department of Education (1998, Table 206), of the total undergraduate student population, 10.8 percent were African American, 8.3 percent were Latino, 6.0 percent were Asian, and 1 percent were American Indian/Alaskan Native. In 1992 (the last year for which NCES data were available) 5.2 percent of full-time instructional faculty were African American; 2.6 percent, Latino; and 5.2 percent, Asian (NCES 1998, Table 230).[8] In public and private research universities, the percentages of African American and Latino faculty were even lower: in the public universities, the faculty was 2.8 percent African American and 2.2 percent Latino; and in the private universities, 5.0 percent African American and 2.1 percent Latino. At private liberal arts colleges 5.4 percent of the faculty were African American and 1.3 percent Latino.[9] Only the percentage of Asian faculty was closely comparable to the percentage of undergraduate Asian students; in the case of African Americans the percentage of students was just about double that of faculty, and for Latinos the percentage of students was triple that of faculty. In the period 1976–1993, the proportion of minority graduate students increased from 10.8 percent to 15.4 percent (approximately a 50 percent increase), whereas in the same period the proportion of minority undergraduates increased from 16.6 percent to 24.5 percent (again an approximately 50 percent increase) (NCES 1995, Table 201). But the graduate enrollment of minorities continues to substantially lag the undergraduate enrollment.

The figures just given are all overall percentages; breakdowns show where greater discrepancies exist. In the natural sciences (NCES 1995, Table 222), for example, the percentage of African American faculty is much lower, 3.4 percent, but so also is the percentage of African American undergraduates. In the case of Asian faculty, the percentage in the humanities is only 3.2 percent and in the social sciences, 3.3 percent. Yet our data reveal that more than half of Asian students in the schools we studied are majors in the humanities or the social sciences.

There is, to be sure, the difficult question of what constitutes the optimal proportion of minority faculty: should it correspond to the proportion of the general population, or the proportion of students of that ethnicity, or the proportion of students of that ethnicity in a particular field? We cannot determine the best answer to this question; for practical purposes, it seems sufficient to state that there is need for more minority faculty. Ultimately, if true racial and ethnic equality is attained, the race and ethnicity of neither faculty nor students would matter.

Before reviewing the factors influencing the career choices of high-achieving minority students, we want to make clear that our concern with faculty diversity is a systemwide concern rather than an individual campus concern. Thus we are not concerned with how a particular institution can increase its diversity; rather, we want to know how to increase the average degree of racial and ethnic faculty diversity at all institutions of higher education. Currently minority faculty diversity is a zero-sum game. There is only a relatively small number of minority members who have the Ph.D.s (the minimum qualification for hiring at most four-year colleges and universities) and want to work in academia. As long as this number remains stable, if university A recruits a minority faculty member who is currently working at university B, university A becomes slightly more diverse and B slightly less diverse. But considering the system as a whole there is no change in the level of faculty diversity. The only way that systemic change can be produced is to increase the overall pool of minority members who are interested in and have the necessary qualifications to be professors at all levels of our system of higher education. We argue (and present data in Chapter 9 in support of this argument) that the reason for the small numbers of minority faculty at various universities is almost exclusively a result of the small number of minority Ph.D.s being produced and not a result of prejudice or discrimination on the part of institutions of higher education. In fact, given the existence of hiring practices privileging race at a wide range of colleges and universities, these schools are "prejudiced" or "discriminate" in favor of hiring minority faculty members.

In a recent essay on diversity, sociologist Neal Smelser makes a similar point about the attempt of universities to diversify their faculty with members of underrepresented minorities:

> [I]n faculty hiring policies universities have likewise committed themselves to increase the numbers of women and minorities in an absolute sense. Particularly with respect to certain minorities— Native Americans, blacks, and Hispanics—this is currently a collectively impossible goal because of the small pool of doctoral candidates that appear in the market in any given year. The resultant situation is a heady competition for scarce minority candidates, including the practice of one institution pirating such candidates from another. Individual minority candidates may benefit from this process, but it does not seem to address the general problem of improving access for all minorities. (p. 44)

Let us turn to a brief summary of some possible influences on occupational choice of high-achieving minority students, particularly the factors that may influence these students to select academia as a career over other rewarding careers and thus increase the pool of Ph.D.s from which minority faculty can be drawn.[10]

Demand and Supply for Professors

When college students consider what job they will try to obtain after finishing their education they are likely to be influenced by two broad general considerations. First, the majority of students are likely to enter jobs that they see as best allowing them to achieve their own particular goals. Thus, if the most important thing to a student is how much money she can earn in a job, that student will probably try to enter a high-paying occupation. Students are also likely to select jobs they believe will be the most enjoyable or interesting to them. Occupational choice, however, is also likely to be influenced to some degree by the second general consideration: the student's perception of the chances of obtaining a particular job given current economic conditions. Thus, a student might want to be a college professor but her knowledge that it is hard to get a job as a professor might influence her to change her career aspiration.

There are two factors that influence the number of people who become professors in colleges and universities. One is the students' interest in this job; the other is demand for these positions. The number of open positions at institutions of higher education, or (perhaps better) the number of new people hired to be professors is a measure of demand. This number, which has varied quite substantially since World War II, is heavily influenced by the number of people in the population who decide to attend college, the average class size at educational institutions, and the financial condition of the hiring colleges.

During the 1960s, as the first part of the postwar baby boom entered college, the demand for academics soared. This increase was also fueled by the cold war and the decision by the federal government that in order to compete with the Soviet Union it was necessary to spend more money on higher education and research. In the 1970s the demand for professors began to decline.[11] Throughout the 1980s and 1990s the overall supply of Ph.D.s interested in working in academia has substantially exceeded the demand despite the predictions of some that the 1990s would see a shortage of college professors (Bowen and Sosa, 1989).

The real level of demand for academics can be at least roughly measured. College students may or may not accurately perceive the level of demand. To our knowledge no study has been done that shows the influence of changing demand for professors on the number of students entering graduate programs and completing Ph.D.s. There can be little doubt, however, that there is such a relationship.[12] The strength of this relationship and the lag time between supply and demand remain to be determined.[13] Such a study would have to be done over a considerable time period. Our study does not consider demand-side factors as influencing students wanting to become professors. We examined students who were graduating at one point in time (the spring of 1996); changes in supply over time thus were not pertinent.[14]

Although James Davis's study *Undergraduate Career Decisions* (1965) is now almost forty years old, it is useful in suggesting that in the 1960s demand for academics was substantially higher than what our survey found for the mid-1990s. In a random sample of seniors who returned self-administered questionnaires in 1961, 12 percent of the respondents stated that they intended to work at some type of institution of higher education (Davis 1965, p. 203). This is a higher percentage than we found in our sample, which is very substantially more elite than the random sample of Davis. Given the relationship between wanting to be a professor and academic performance (see Chapter 5), the more elite the sample, the higher the proportion of students we would expect to select academia as their first-choice occupation. Davis's findings suggest that had a sample similar to ours been interviewed in the early 1960s a substantially higher proportion of students than what Davis found would have selected college professor as their first-choice occupation.[15] Assuming this assertion to be true, the most obvious reason for the decline over time would be changes in demand. Alexander Astin (1993) reports that among a random sample of college seniors studied in 1985 only 1.9 percent selected college teacher as their career choice.[16] If both the Davis sample and the Astin sample were indeed random, this suggests an extremely dramatic decline in the proportion of college students wanting to be college professors between the early 1960s and the mid-1980s.

It is possible that the sample studied by Davis (1965) may have represented a somewhat more elite group of students than that studied by Astin (1993). This is not because of any flaws in the Davis sample but is a result of the increase in the proportion of high school graduates who are attending college that occurred between 1961 and 1985. In 1985 the average college student may have been less well academically prepared than was the average college student in 1961. This underscores the importance of the sample in determining the proportion of seniors who want to be college professors. The more elite the sample, the higher the proportion of students who want to be college professors. We explicitly designed our study to be a sample of high-achieving college graduates because we thought that they would be the students most likely to want to be college professors. Random-sample studies of occupational choice invariably show an increase in the proportion of students wanting to be college professor between the freshman and senior year. Our study of elite students, however, revealed a significant decline in the proportion selecting college professor as their first-choice occupation in their senior year compared to the freshman year. In fact, in our sample college professor was the career with the highest percentage of freshman interest. (See Chapter 3, Tables 3.4 and 3.6.)

Ronald Ehrenberg (1992) may have suggested one reason for the decline in interest in an academic career. He noted changes in the number of doctoral degrees granted over time and related significant declines in the 1970s and 1980s to the increasing relative attractiveness of careers in competing professions, such as medicine and law.

Before concluding this discussion of demand, it is important to note that the demand for professors of different ethnicities is not necessarily the same. The strong interest of a large number of institutions of higher education in increasing the racial and ethnic diversity of their faculty members creates a situation in which the demand for minority professors is probably substantially greater than the demand for white professors. Given this likely higher level of demand, it might be possible to implement policies that would increase the proportion of high-achieving minority college graduates who are interested in academic careers to a level significantly above the proportion of high-achieving white college graduates who decide to go into academia. An important question is the extent to which minorities are aware of the relatively high demand for underrepresented minority members in academia.

The Logic of Studying Occupational Choice

In general there are three categories of variables that have been found to influence the occupational choices made by college students.[17] First are the characteristics of the individual students when they enter college. Examples of such variables would be race or ethnicity; gender; socioeconomic status of their family of origin; occupational and educational aspirations; performance in high school; measures of academic preparation or "ability," such as scores on the Scholastic Aptitude Test (SAT); and personal values and interests acquired prior to college. Because the students have these characteristics prior to entering college, they are called "input" factors.

The next two sets of variables concern the nature of the college experience. The first of these may be called institutional characteristics—differences in the type of college that students attend. The single most-studied variable in this category is the quality, or "selectivity," of the school. As explained below, there are differing hypotheses about how this variable influences career selection. Other school characteristics that are sometimes considered are the size of the school, the location of control (whether the school is public or private), and whether the school has a predominantly white or predominantly African American student population. The three variables used in our design and analysis are selectivity, size, and whether the students are predominantly white or African American. (See Chapter 2.)

Size is supposed to affect occupational choice because of the level of faculty contact. Presumably in small schools students have greater opportunity to interact with faculty; this interaction is assumed to influence their career choice, with a positive effect on the selection of academia as a career.

There are varying theories about how the racial composition of the student body may influence African American students and white students in predominantly white schools. These theories will be discussed later, when we consider this variable in more detail.

The third set of variables that is believed to influence career choice is the students' differences in college experience. For example, within a given college the following factors will vary from student to student: grades earned, amount of faculty contact, service as research or teaching assistant, major selected, courses taken, participation in extracurricular activities, socializing, employment, living arrangements, and participation in various advisory programs. All of these and many other experiences that students have while attending college can influence their occupational choice and their future lives.

Input variables, school characteristics, and within-school experiences are all considered to be potential influences on "outcome" measures, such as career choice. There is general consensus about the methods that must be used in order to determine the independent effects of school characteristics or within-college experiences on outcomes. Virtually all researchers agree that before one can assess the impact of college characteristics or within-college experiences, however, one must control for input factors. For example, let's say we were to find that minority students who attend Ivy League schools are more likely than those attending any of the other type of school we study to decide to become college professors. With this knowledge alone, it would be incorrect to conclude that this outcome is a result of something particular about the Ivy League colleges. We must first examine the possibility that the Ivy League colleges attract a different type of student and that it is these input characteristics that account for the outcome (choice of college professor as a career) rather than the characteristics of the school. The fact that virtually everyone who discusses the methodology of studying the effects of college on students agrees that one must control for input factors does not mean that all studies that have been conducted have actually done so.[18]

There is a massive amount of literature on the effects of college on students. This research is summarized in two classic review volumes. Kenneth Feldman and Theodore Newcomb's *The Impact of College on Students,* published in 1969, summarizes and synthesizes the results of more than 1,500 articles and books published mostly between the 1950s and the time of the book's publication. Ernest Pascarella and Patrick Terenzini's *How College Affects Students,* published in 1991, summarizes and synthesizes the results of about 2,700 works, most of them published after the publication of Feldman and Newcomb (1969).

Most of the outcome measures, or dependent variables, that researchers studying the effect of college on students concentrate on are either irrelevant or only tangentially relevant to our concerns. There are relatively few studies that focus on the dynamics by which college affects the occupational choices of students, and there are even fewer studies that consider in detail the possible effects of attending various types of college on the selection of academia as a career. Those studies that do exist on the influences on selection of academia as a career generally have relatively small samples of minority students and do not analyze how the selection dynamics of one ethnicity differ from another. Our study is the largest ever conducted of the occupational choices of minority college students with the dependent variable being the selection of specific occupations, particularly academia.

Input Characteristics Influencing Occupational Choice
Occupational Choice on Entering College

Virtually all of the research done on occupational choice comes to the conclusion that the first or second most important influence on the occupational choice of college seniors is their occupational choice when they entered college as freshmen. For example, Alexander Astin and Robert Panos (1969) conducted regression analyses to predict the choice of twelve separate career categories. They found that initial career choice carried the largest weight in seven of the regression equations and the second largest weight in five of the regression equations (p. 98). Pascarella and Terenzini (1991) cite a study by Astin and conclude that "for a substantial number of students, career development during college is more a process of implementing career than of choosing one. There is substantial evidence to support this claim that initial career choice at the beginning of college tends to be the single best predictor of career choice

12

at the end of college and the career or occupation actually entered" (p. 424). They then go on to cite five different sources supporting this assertion.

Most studies of student occupational choice point out that students frequently change their career plans between the freshman and senior year, but if one had to select only one variable to predict the occupational choice of seniors, the best predictor would be their occupational choice as freshmen. Davis (1965) reports that about half of the graduates end up in the same career as they indicated was their freshman preference. This of course suggests the importance of discovering how students make occupational choices prior to entering college.

We are unaware of any studies that focus on how students develop their occupational interests prior to entering college. There are analyses, however, in the studies mentioned above of the correlates of freshman choice. As far as the selection of high-status careers goes, including that of academia, the single most important variable identified has been academic performance in high school as measured both by high school grade point average (GPA) and scores on standardized tests, such as the SAT. (In Chapter 4 we analyze the correlates of freshman choice of academia—with a special emphasis on why African American students are less likely than other students to be interested in academia when they enter college. Including a retrospective question on freshman choice allows us to conduct a pseudolongitudinal study, comparing freshman interests with senior choice and attempting to discover the variables that influence persistence or change.)

Academic Preparation or Ability

Students who enter college who have done well academically in the past are more likely to select high-prestige careers, including academia, as freshmen. We use SAT scores as an indicator of preparation or high levels of academic ability (depending on how one interprets the meaning of the SAT). The SAT is the same for all students, and a large majority of the students in our sample took it and reported their scores. We do not use high school grades as a variable in this study because of the difficulty of interpreting them as a result of widely varying grading practices. Also, since our study is confined to high-achieving students, a substantial majority (as indicated by the results of a pretest survey to be discussed in Chapter 2) had high GPAs in high school.

All of the research leads to the commonsense hypothesis that those students who do well academically in college will be substantially more likely than those who do not do well to be interested in college professor as a career. This finding was so well established and intuitively sensible that we used it in designing our study. At nonselective schools we did not interview arts and sciences graduates who had GPAs of less than 2.8.[19]

Given the importance of GPA as an influence on occupational choice and the selection of college professor in particular, it is important to consider what the determinants of GPA are. Presumably GPA would be heavily influenced by a student's level of academic preparation and academic ability, characteristics that are supposed to be measured by the SAT. For many years there have been critics of the SAT, which along with high school GPA is probably the most important criterion used by most colleges in making admissions decisions. Recently this criticism has intensified as a result of the debate over racial preferences in admission. African American and Latino students do worse than Asians and whites on the SAT, and no matter what variables are controlled for, this "SAT gap" persists. Thus, for example, among African American and white students who come from families with similarly high levels of socioeconomic status (SES), white students still outperform African American students by a substantial margin. Christopher Jencks and Meredith Phillips argue that this gap is one of the most important factors preventing greater equality among ethnic groups, and their collection *The Black-White Test Score Gap* (1998) presents research that attempts to explain this difference.

Racial preferences in admissions frequently amount to admitting African American and Latino students who have considerably lower SAT scores (approximately 200 points on the combined tests for the Ivy League) than admitted white students.[20] Because the SAT is the only criterion that is universal (virtually all applicants to selective schools take it) and allows comparison between virtually all applicants to selective schools, it highlights the gap in academic preparedness between African American and Latino students on the one hand and white and Asian students on the other. Thus, those university officials who want to maintain racial and ethnic diversity even in situations where the use of racial preferences in admissions to public colleges has been made illegal have lobbied to drop the SAT as a requirement or introduce other criteria of admissions that will indirectly preference African American and Latino applicants.

There has recently been much criticism of the SAT as a predictor of how an applicant will do in school and in later life.[21] Some argue that the test measures only certain aspects of academic ability and ignores others equally important. That the test does not measure all aspects of human intelligence and creativity is obvious; but most colleges do not rely solely on SAT scores and high school GPAs. Thus, if a concert pianist applied to a school it would be clear that that student had a skill that the school might value and that would not be reflected in the SAT score.

There are two common criticisms of the SAT that research has suggested may not be valid. First, some argue that the test is inherently biased against minority groups and women (women as a group score consistently lower on the quantitative part of the test than do men as a group). Psychometricians have evaluated the "bias" claim thoroughly and have concluded that there is no evident bias in the test. Jencks (1998) reviewed the literature on cultural bias in many types of tests, including the SAT, and concluded "that the size of the gap [between blacks and whites] does not depend in any simple, predictable way on the nominal content of the test." (p. 69). Jencks sums up the results of his analysis of cultural bias in the SAT and other tests in the following words:

> Blacks score lower than whites (and Asians) on a wide range of tests that cover both subjects taught in school and skills that are not taught in school. The gap is no greater on tasks that appear to measure familiarity with the content of "white" or "middle class" culture than on tasks that appear to be more culturally neutral. Furthermore, the gap on IQ tests is similar to that on many tests of academic achievement. This means that the black-white differences go far beyond such apparently trivial matters as knowing who wrote *Faust* or what a sonata is. (p. 83)

Critics also claim that SAT scores do not predict how well students will actually do in college and later in life. Most studies of the relation between SAT scores and GPA show only a moderate correlation of around .30, which means that SAT scores explain only about 9 percent of the variance of GPA and are therefore not a particularly good predictor of how students will do in college.[22] There is, however, an important problem in most of these studies: the restriction of range on the independent variable (SAT scores). A restriction of range on a variable means that there is not much variation on that variable in the sample being studied. Thus, for example, among students admitted to Harvard there will be much less variation on SAT scores than we would find among everyone who takes the SAT. The lower the variance on a variable the harder it is to find a high correlation between that variable and any other. As an example of restriction of range and how it can limit correlations, consider all those men who play center on National Basketball Association (NBA) teams. Suppose we find that there is only a .30 (or even lower) correlation between their height and measures of how well they perform. We would not then conclude that height is not an important requirement to play center in the NBA and proceed to recruit players under six feet for the position. The reason the correlation is so low is that in order to play center in the NBA at all requires being of a certain height. Thus virtually all centers are around seven feet tall, and relatively small differences in height among those who play may not explain differences in their performance. Most studies on predicting success in college examine the correlation between SAT scores and GPA of students attending a single school, such as Harvard. However, because acceptance into Harvard requires a very high score on the SAT, a serious restriction of range on the independent variable results. In the case of a study of the correlation between SAT scores and GPA of Harvard students (or other elite schools) there would also be a serious restriction of range on the dependent variable (GPA), since at elite schools usually over 90 percent of the students achieve GPAs of B− or better. The less variance on the dependent variable there is, the harder it is to explain it. Thus, to conclude from the fact that SAT scores are only correlated .30 with the GPA of students at Harvard that the school could therefore safely admit students with substantially lower SAT scores than it does without lowering the quality of its student body would be an error.

Another important error made in virtually all the studies of the correlation between SAT scores and GPA is that they fail to take into account the difficulty of the courses taken. Students with lower SAT scores may select courses with higher grade distributions than students with higher SAT scores, and this would reduce the difference in their GPAs. Leonard Ramist, Charles Lewis, and Laura McCamley-Jenkins (1994) conducted a study for the College Board that examined the correlation between SAT scores and grades in particular courses, controlling for the difficulty of the course and taking into account restriction of range. They found an adjusted correlation close to .70. In short, despite the contention of some critics, SAT scores turn out to be the best single predictor of how well students will do in college.[23]

Researchers studying the relationship between the academic performance of various racial and ethnic groups and the SAT have discovered an important phenomenon called "underperformance" (Klitgaard 1985; Ramist, Lewis, and McCamley-Jenkins 1994; Bowen and Bok 1998; Vars and Bowen 1998). Underperformance applies to African Americans and less to Latinos. It means that if we take two groups of students with the same SAT scores, one white and the other African American, the white students will earn higher grades in college. Since grades are so important in determining career choice, the fact that African Americans (and to a lesser extent Latinos) achieve lower GPAs than their level of academic preparation predicts is a serious problem. The reasons for this phenomenon are not well understood. The most cogent explanation is the theory of Claude Steele (1997), who argues that African Americans who identify with the realm of school (those who care about how well they do in school) are affected by the negative stereotype of African Americans as being less intelligent than whites. The fear of confirming this negative stereotype creates test anxiety in African Americans, which serves to lower their performance on tests such as the SAT. In a series of experiments Steele has provided some evidence to support his theory.

Steele takes groups of relatively high-achieving African American students (presumably students enrolled at Stanford University, where he teaches) and randomly divides them into two groups. He gives both groups the same test, which is made up of difficult questions taken from the achievement tests administered by the Educational Testing Service (ETS). He tells one group of students that the test is aimed at measuring academic ability. The other group he tries to desensitize to the fear of stereotyping, telling them that the test is not one of academic ability and that there generally is no racial or ethnic difference in how students score. His results show a significant difference between the control group and a group of white students (when SAT scores are controlled).[24] But for the experimental group, the one that has been desensitized, there is an insignificant difference between their performance and that of white students (again, with SAT scores controlled). Thus Steele explains the underperformance phenomenon.[25] His theory is a very important one for our research, and we discuss its utility for understanding our data in Chapters 6 and 8.

Gender

A relatively high degree of occupational sex segregation exists in the United States (Jacobs 1989). In fact sociologists have concluded that the main reason why men earn more money than women is that they are in different jobs. Past studies of occupational choice such as those conducted by J. Davis (1965), Astin and Panos (1969), and Leonard Baird (1973) all found gender to be an important influence on career choice. In our sample we found no difference in the proportion of women and men wanting to be college professors. Therefore gender did not play a significant role in our analysis.[26]

Socioeconomic Status

Although the socioeconomic status (SES) of a student's family of origin (usually measured by parental education and income) is significantly related to whether that student will complete college or not, it tends to be either weakly related or not related at all to postgraduate educational attainment (Stolzenberg 1994). Although SES seems to be predictive of entering some occupations, such as business, studies of the predictors of students selecting college professor as an occupation have found SES of family of origin to be unimportant. These studies, however, were usually studies of random samples, the overwhelming majority being white.[27]

Our study focuses on the influences on career choice of minority college students. We hypothesized that SES might have a significant influence on the likelihood of minority students wanting to become college professors. Compared with other high-status jobs (particularly physicians, lawyers, and business executives), college professors have relatively low earnings. We thought that minority students who came from families with relatively low SES might have a greater interest in entering an occupation with high financial rewards than minority students who came from families with relatively high SES. Students from middle-class or upper-middle-class backgrounds might be less intent on maximizing earnings in order to achieve middle-class status and more influenced by personal interests.

In general, studies of occupational choice have shown that students' interests and values are more important influences on their career choices than the desire to maximize financial rewards (Rosenberg 1957; J. Davis 1965).[28] In one of the few studies we know of in which students were specifically asked their feelings about the occupation of college professor, James Davis (1965, p. 200) found that only 6 percent of his sample agreed with the statement: "I probably couldn't make as much money at this type of work [college professor] as I'd like to make." We thought, however, that high-achieving minority students from low SES backgrounds might have a different attitude.[29] We emphasize high achieving because these are the kind of students who have the opportunity to enter other occupations, such as law, medicine, and business, in which they might end up earning substantially higher incomes than they could as college professors.

Values

Some studies of occupational choice have emphasized the significance of values and personal interests in the selection process. Perhaps the most thorough of these was the 1950s study of Morris Rosenberg (1957). Although values may play an important role in the occupational choice process, we decided not to emphasize them in our research. We made this decision primarily because our study is policy driven, and we believe that there is little that institutions of higher education can do to change the values that Rosenberg discusses, most of which the students have developed prior to entering college. We do deal with values insofar as they relate specifically to a choice of academia as a career.

Culture

Some researchers have expressed concern that among African American youth a subculture exists that downplays the significance of academic achievement and defines doing well in school as "acting white." If true, this could be a serious impediment to the overall educational achievement of African Americans. Alejandro Portes and Kenneth Wilson (1976), in a study of black and white high school students, found that the correlation between ability and academic performance is twice as strong for whites as it is for African Americans. This suggests that African Americans may go to high schools where the student subculture does not put a premium on academic achievement, so the students who get the highest grades are not necessarily those with the most ability (Coleman 1960).

Law professor Adeno Addis (1996) quotes an article appearing in the June 17, 1994, *San Diego Union-Tribune* by Ernesto Portillo, Jr.:

> What is even more depressing are the reasons that young African Americans gave for choosing not to go to college: that it is not "cool" to appear brainy and studious, that they will become outsiders in the community of people that surround and matter to them . . . One African American high school student said that another African American student called him a "white boy" because

he was seen to be intelligent and studious. As this student put it, "You can't be cool if you're smart. That's the kind of thing I grew up with." (p. 1378)

Another aspect of this subculture has been stressed in Signithia Fordham's (1988, 1996) research on the values and aspirations of African American high school students. She argues that whereas the dominant culture sees success in individualistic terms, the African American subculture increasingly views success in collective terms:

> Increasingly, . . . Black Americans are rejecting the older generation's attitude towards social mobility: they do not view the accomplishment of individual members of the group as evidence of the advancement of the entire group . . . Black children who grow up in predominantly Black communities, then, are raised in the collective view of success . . . But since an individualistic rather than a collective ethos is sanctioned in the school context, Black children enter school having to unlearn, or at least, to modify their own interactional or behavioral styles and adopt the styles rewarded in the school context if they wish to achieve academic success. (Fordham 1988, pp. 54–55)

In other words, African American youngsters have to become what Fordham calls "raceless," and this produces strong ambivalence and conflict in adolescents who are oriented to high academic performance. They cannot be "bicultural"; they must choose between the culture of their peers and academic success. Fordham believes that it is easier for female students to become "raceless"; males are more confused and ambivalent. In her book *Blacked Out* (1996), a qualitative study of a large all-black high school in Washington, D.C., Fordham describes the problems of high-aspiring African American male students, who may find themselves denigrated as effeminate or gay. Given the importance of academic achievement in the decision to become a college professor, if such an anti-academic achievement culture exists among African Americans it is a substantial impediment to the production of more minority Ph.D.s.[30]

The Influence of School Characteristics

Educational researchers, regardless of what level of the system they have studied, have shown great interest in comparing the influence of characteristics of schools as opposed to the characteristics of students on various outcome measures. For example, they ask: What are the effects of variables such as class size, the amount of money spent per pupil, and the type of training received by the teachers on how much students learn in elementary school? Do students learn more in highly selective private colleges than they do in less selective state universities? There is a vast amount of literature on these questions and, like other areas in educational research, there is considerable disagreement over the answers. It is, however, possible to reach a broad generalization: The preponderance of research, especially the more methodologically sophisticated research, suggests that school characteristics have relatively little influence on the various outcomes that have been studied.[31]

In order to determine if a school characteristic is influencing students in some way, one must control for all the input characteristics that might influence the outcome.[32] Otherwise a conclusion that a school characteristic was a cause of an educational outcome could be spurious, an artifact of the correlation of both the outcome and school characteristics with input variables. Thus, if we were to find that students who attend highly selective and expensive private colleges and universities score higher on achievement tests at the end of college than do students who attend less selective and expensive state universities, we could not immediately conclude that the students at the private schools had received a better education. It is possible that the observed relationship between type of school and how much students learn is an artifact of the academic ability levels of students admitted to each of the two types of school. What one would have to do is to control for students' ability prior to entering college (by use of their SAT scores, perhaps) and then, with this variable held constant, see if type of school has an effect. When Alexander Astin (1968) conducted just such a study, he concluded that smart students learn a lot no matter what type of college they go to and less well prepared students learn less no matter what type of school they go to. This is just one of many studies illustrating that input variables and within-school experiences are more important than school characteristics as influences on outcome variables.

At the beginning of his career Astin's research suggested that institutional characteristics of colleges had very little effect on all the outcome measures he studied. His later research suggests that college environmental characteristics are more important than originally thought. But an examination of results presented in one of his more recent monographs

(Astin 1993) raises some questions as to how well college characteristics can help one understand outcomes once input variables are controlled. In an appendix to his 1993 monograph Astin reports the multiple R for 84 outcome variables using only input variables.[33] He then shows how much the multiple R (not the amount of variance) increases when all 192 environmental variables are entered into the regression equations. A hand count reveals that for 20 of the outcome variables R did not increase at all; for 22 it increased by one point; for 13 by two points; for 7 by three points; for 10 by between four and seven points; and for 12 by more than seven points. Most of these latter 12 variables were measures of satisfaction. The fact that the 192 environmental variables studied by Astin generally do not increase R by very much does not mean that some of them will not be statistically significant influences on some outcomes, including career choice. It does mean that, in general, variables characterizing college environments are unable to explain much variance on most outcome measures.

Institutional Quality or Selectivity

We had a strong interest in several college characteristics, and our study was designed to see how these characteristics influenced the interest of minority group students in entering academia. Perhaps the most important of these is the selectivity of the school. As discussed in detail in Chapter 2, our study included four types of institution: Ivy League schools, selective liberal arts colleges, large state universities, and historically black colleges and universities (HBCUs). The first two types of school are highly selective. Selectivity varied among the schools in the latter two categories but, in general, was substantially lower than in the first two, which we call the "elite" schools. Basing our thinking on a classic paper of James Davis ("The Campus as a Frog Pond," 1966), we believed it possible that minority students might be less likely to decide to become college professors if they attended elite schools than if they attended less selective schools.

Davis's paper tested the theory of relative deprivation as applied to college graduates' choice of high-performance careers. The concept of relative deprivation was first introduced by Samuel Stouffer et al. (1949) and systematically developed in two articles, one by Robert K. Merton (1957) and the other by Merton and Alice Rossi (Merton and Rossi 1957). The theory of relative deprivation is based on the concept of "comparative reference group." The theory is that when individuals assess how well off they are they make this judgment by comparing themselves with particular reference groups, and these comparisons can have greater influence than actual, objective conditions. The famous example described by Stouffer dealt with satisfaction with promotion opportunities of two groups of soldiers: those in the Air Force and those in the Military Police. The objective rates of promotion were much higher in the former group than in the latter. Yet when asked to assess how satisfied they were with promotion opportunities, soldiers in the Military Police were substantially more satisfied than were the soldiers in the Air Force. The only way that this paradoxical finding could be explained was to employ the concept of comparative reference group and the theory of relative deprivation—that satisfaction with a particular life condition will be based less on objective conditions than on a comparison with those with whom one comes into contact. Members of the Air Force compared themselves with other members of the Air Force. They saw that many of their fellow soldiers were promoted. Therefore, if they had not been promoted they were dissatisfied with promotion opportunities. Members of the Military Police compared themselves to other members of their own group. Since very few of them were promoted, those who had not been promoted did not feel deprived and therefore expressed satisfaction with promotion opportunities.

James Davis (1966) applied this theory to the career choice patterns of college students. He began his argument with an observed fact: the distribution of grades in colleges of differing selectivity tended to be the same.[34] Thus, if you take two groups of students who have the same academic ability, with one group going to a highly selective school and the other to a less selective school, the latter group is likely to obtain higher grades, because in the less selective school the competition for grades will be less stiff than in the more selective one. Using the data from his 1965 monograph, David (1966) conducted a test of this theory. He found that in making career choices grades are more important than academic ability. Students who get the highest grades are the most likely either to maintain a commitment to a high-achievement career or to switch into a high-achievement career. The inverse is also true. Those with low grades are the least likely to maintain a commitment to a high-achievement career and the least likely to switch into such a career. Controlling for a rough measure of academic self-confidence reduced the effect of grades on career choice, thus offering support to his theory that when students attend highly selective schools they are forced to compete with other high-ability students, are less likely to earn high grades, and therefore develop lower levels of academic self-confidence, which in turn leads to a decline in the selection of high-performance careers. Given the data available to Davis his argument is relatively convincing.[35] Although there has been some debate over the validity of this argument (see Pascarella and Terenzini 1991, pp. 186ff) it seems reasonable to hypothesize that if students attending highly selective colleges become less confident of their academic abilities, they will find the path to academic success daunting.

The Davis theory might be particularly relevant in examining the career choices of minority college students. Given the admissions criteria utilized at the most selective schools (including "race sensitive" admissions criteria), that African American and Latino students admitted under these programs are likely to have somewhat lower levels of academic preparation or ability than Asian and white students. Having to compete with students of higher academic preparation at the most selective schools might serve to lower the academic self-confidence of these minority students and thus lower their career aspirations, making them less likely to choose college professor as a career.

This argument is essentially the "fit hypothesis" as put forth by opponents of affirmative action, including some prominent African American scholars. Among these scholars are Thomas Sowell (1972, 1993) and Shelby Steele (1994). Sowell, in his book Inside American Education (1993), argues that as a result of affirmative action the best African American students are forced to compete with white students who are better prepared and as a result the African American students get lower grades and develop lower levels of academic self-confidence. The skimming off by the top schools of the brightest African American students means that these students are not available to be admitted to the next lower level of schools—where the best African American students would do much better academically because of the lower level of competition. The effect ratchets down throughout the hierarchy of schools, so that at every level the African American students are forced to compete with better-prepared white students. Sowell argues that without affirmative action there would be a better fit between the level of academic preparation of African American students and the schools they attend. This in turn would result in African American students performing better in school, which would lead to better occupational outcomes for these students.

Shelby Steele makes a similar argument: "The effect of preferential treatment—the lowering of normal standards to increase black representation—puts blacks at war with an expanding realm of debilitating doubt, so that the doubt itself becomes an unrecognized preoccupation that undermines their ability to perform, especially in integrated situations" (quoted in Bowen and Bok 1998, p. 261). This quote is reminiscent of the theory of Claude Steele, discussed earlier. It is possible that affirmative action might serve to activate the fear of negative stereotyping, which Claude Steele claims is responsible for the underperformance of African American students.

A recent study by William Bowen and Derek Bok (1998), which the authors claim demonstrates that racial preferences in admissions are crucial in creating a black middle class, raises the question of the effect of institutional selectivity on future educational attainment and income, if not directly on occupational choice. The authors followed the career outcomes of African American students who graduated from twenty-eight schools, which the authors claim are "highly selective." In fact, as the authors recognize, there is a good deal of variation in selectivity among these twenty-eight schools. Bowen and Bok found that African Americans who attended the most selective schools in the sample were more likely to attain advanced degrees and to earn higher incomes when other relevant variables were controlled. Given the importance of controlling for relevant input factors (as pointed out above) it is not clear that the outcomes Bowen and Bok attribute to attending highly selective schools as a result of racial preferences are indeed a school effect rather than the result of uncontrolled selectivity. In fact, a further analysis of the Bowen and Bok data set by Stacy Dale and Alan Krueger (1999) showed that uncontrolled selectivity did influence some of the outcomes that Bowen and Bok attributed to attendance at highly selective schools. Dale and Krueger are able to eliminate uncontrolled selectivity by matching students to the type of schools they applied to and were accepted or rejected by. After taking into consideration the selection bias in the Bowen and Bok data set, Dale and Krueger conclude that the effect of school selectivity argued by Bowen and Bok to demonstrate the efficacy of racial preferences is an artifact of student input characteristics.[36]

Institutional Size and the Mystique of the Liberal Arts College

Most educational researchers have hypothesized that institutional size should be negatively related to the choice of academia as a career. The explanation for this is faculty contact. At smaller colleges students presumably come into more contact with faculty members outside of the classroom, and this contact is believed to influence students to select an academic career. As a result of high levels of faculty contact it has been assumed that small, selective liberal arts colleges are most likely to produce the highest portion of graduates who go on to earn Ph.D.s, particularly in the sciences.

This hypothesis was first put forth in 1952 by Robert Knapp and Hubert Goodrich in a book entitled Origins of American Scientists; the following year Knapp, with Joseph Greenbaum, published *The Younger American Scholar*. The gist of these books was that certain types of colleges, essentially the small, selective liberal arts colleges such as Reed, Antioch, and Oberlin, produced a disproportionate number of American scientists.

The work done by Knapp and others trumpeting the benefits of attending small liberal arts colleges has been criticized strongly, especially by Astin (1962), as not paying sufficient attention to the importance of input variables. Was attending the liberal arts college the crucial factor that led to the decision to become an academic, or did these colleges attract students who were already predisposed to an interest in academia? Contrary to the assertions of some of their critics, Knapp and his fellow researchers were aware of the necessity of controlling for input characteristics and in one study used early SAT data to do so. Yet Knapp and Goodrich insisted that in addition to any input factors that might be influencing choice of career, the climate at the liberal arts colleges was a significant contributor to such a decision. They concluded that the larger colleges suffered from impersonality, which in turn reduced the probability that their students would select academia as a career, while "the smaller [schools] admit of an intimacy in human contacts and a pervasiveness of personal influence that is qualitatively different . . . Thus the highest productivity is found in those institutions which are small enough to preserve their community atmosphere yet large enough to assure the adequacy of their faculty and facilities" (Knapp and Goodrich 1952, pp. 47–48).

After having demonstrated that student characteristics (input) were of greater importance than institutional characteristics, Astin (1963) reported that certain northeastern men's colleges (such as Amherst, Dartmouth, and Yale, which were all male at the time), were "under productive"—that is, their actual Ph.D. output was below what was expected on the basis of gender, ability, and major field of study, while certain coeducational liberal arts colleges (such as Carleton, Oberlin, and Pomona) were "over productive." Faced with these findings, Astin resorts to the explanation that "climate" (unmeasured) at these different types of schools made the difference.

In a more recent study, Astin and Helen Astin (1992) set out to determine why some students pursued science-related careers and came to the conclusion that independent of all other variables, small colleges, particularly liberal arts colleges, are more likely to produce students interested in science. They explain this by the greater possibility for faculty contact at these institutions and by the fact that the faculty members seem to be more student oriented as opposed to research oriented. The research we conducted enabled us to examine the extent to which liberal arts colleges have an independent effect upon producing Ph.D.s when input variables are controlled. (This issue is addressed in Chapter 8.)

Predominantly White or Predominantly Black Student Body

In our study one of the most important college characteristics is the racial composition of the student body. Here too, as in so many other areas of educational research, both the hypotheses that have been put forth and the results of empirical research are contradictory. Some have hypothesized that African American students would do better and be more likely to pursue high-status careers like academia if they attended historically black colleges or universities (HBCUs), in which the student body is usually close to one hundred percent black. The argument is that at these institutions African Americans would not face prejudice or the negative effects of pervasive institutional racism, which is said to exist at the predominantly white schools. Also, being taught by a larger proportion of African American instructors is believed to be beneficial to African American students, since these instructors will better understand the interests of African American students and be more likely to serve as role models for the students. Others have argued that African American students would do better in predominantly white schools because these schools on average have higher level of resources and generally offer a superior education.

It is worth quoting in full the argument expounded by Pascarella and Terenzini (1991) for the differential effects on African American students of attending predominantly black, as against predominantly white, institutions. They write that a strong case has been made . . . that black students who attend predominantly black institutions benefit from a supportive social, cultural, and racial environment that enhances their successful adaptation to the academic demands of undergraduate life. Thus, black students perform better academically at black institutions not because getting good grades is easier but because the social environment enhances their successful academic adjustment. Consistent with this perspective, Pascarella, Smart, and Stoecker (1989) found that black students performed better academically at predominantly black institutions even when statistical controls were made for the academic selectivity, financial resources, size, and control of the institution attended. (p. 382)

Although earlier research had suggested that African Americans who attend HBCUs were more likely than those who attended primarily white schools to complete college, Astin's 1982 study on minorities reaches the opposite conclusion:

[I]t would appear that black undergraduates will tend to get higher grades at a black college than at other colleges, but they will also be less satisfied and less likely to persist to the completion of a baccalaureate. This pattern of effects contrasts with the pattern found earlier for Blacks who entered college in 1968 (Astin, 1977b). Conceivably, the relatively more favorable effects of white versus black colleges observed in the current study reflect the white college's increasing sensitivity to the special needs of black students. (p. 101)

In 1991 Walter R. Allen, Edgar G. Epps, and Nesha Z. Hanif edited *College in Black and White: African American Students in Predominantly White and in Historically Black Universities,* which focuses on the effects of attending a predominantly black as opposed to a predominantly white school. Unfortunately, like virtually all the research we have been able to locate on this topic, very little of it deals directly with the question of occupational choice, although there is significant attention paid to variables that the literature suggests are correlated with occupational choice.

In his introduction to the book, Allen summarizes some of the main findings of past research on the differences between African American students who attend HBCUs and those who attend predominantly white schools:

> Black students on predominantly white campuses continue to be severely disadvantaged relative to white students in terms of persistence rates . . . academic achievement levels . . . enrollment in advanced degree programs . . . and overall psychosocial adjustments . . . Black students on historically Black campuses are disadvantaged relative to students (both Black and white) on white campuses in terms of family socioeconomic status . . . and high school academic records . . . caliber of university instructional faculty and facilities . . . academic specializations selected . . . and enrollment in advanced study . . . are also lower for Black students on Black campuses. (p. 4; the ellipses represent sources cited by Allen)

"In sum," writes Allen, "the evidence suggests that Black students on Black campuses are more disadvantaged in socioeconomic and academic terms than are Black (or white) students on white campuses" (p. 6). Allen concludes his introduction by discussing the role of values in the study of race and education. He claims that values often influence the results obtained and that many researchers who have studied African American students might not have fully recognized the severely disadvantaged position of African Americans in the general society and the impact that this has on their educational performance and outcomes (pp. 11–13).

More recently, economists Ronald Ehrenberg and Donna Rothstein (Rothstein and Ehrenberg 1994) carefully compared the effects of attendance at an HBCU with those of attendance at predominantly white institutions on such factors as graduation rates, early career labor market success, and the probability of attending graduate school, using data from the National Longitudinal Survey of the High School Class of 1972 (NLS72). Their analysis shows that a total of 33 percent of African American students who had earned a bachelor's degree by 1979 were enrolled in graduate programs by 1979. Among African American graduates of HBCUs 27 percent were enrolled, and among African American graduates of predominantly white institutions 38 percent were enrolled. However, when academic ability and family background were taken into account, Ehrenberg and Rothstein found that whether or not an African American student attended an HBCU was not a significant factor.

29

Within-College Effects

Given the desirability of recruiting high-achieving minority students to academic careers, carefully considering the possible effects of within-college experiences is especially important. About these experiences Pascarella and Terenzini (1991) conclude that "[w]ith some exceptions, the research on the effects of between-college differences on students' academic and social self-concept is reasonably consistent in indicating that when various pre-matriculation characteristics are held constant, what happens to students after they enroll has greater influence on them than where they enroll" (p. 205).

Academic Performance

How students perform in school, usually measured by GPA, has been found to be an important determinant of career choice. Students who do well are more likely to select high-prestige careers, particularly medicine and academia, more likely to persist with freshman interest in these two careers, and more likely to be recruited into an interest in these two careers (J. Davis 1965; Astin 1993). It is not at all surprising that academic performance in college should turn out to be an important influence on the decision to select academia as a career. If a student is not academically successful and has not received rewards for his or her academic performance, it would make little sense for that student to think of spending the rest of his or her life in a job where "being good in school" is a prerequisite. People want to stay in environments in which they have been highly rewarded and to leave environments in which they have not received rewards but instead have suffered negative experiences.

Faculty Contact

Among researchers who have studied the effects of college on occupational choice there seems to be universal agreement that faculty contact is an extremely important variable, particularly as an influence on the decision by students to become college professors. Feldman and Newcomb (1969) report the results of studies on the influence of faculty contact on the career choices of college students. They write, "Faculty appear to be of greater influence in certain career areas than in others. Not surprisingly, faculty are a particularly crucial influence in the decisions of students to become teachers, especially college teachers" (p. 253).

As discussed at greater length in Chapter 2, determining cause and effect in studies of faculty influence on students' plans is difficult. Does faculty encouragement move students, regardless of their academic performance, to consider academic careers? Do faculty tend to encourage their good students, who may be more likely to choose academic careers in any case? Do good students who may plausibly consider academic careers attach themselves to faculty, who therefore appear to influence them? One way to handle at least part of the problem is to control for freshman occupational interests and examine the effect of faculty contact net of initial interests.

Astin and Astin (1992) report that student contact with faculty members through such activities as acting as a research or teaching assistant to a faculty member or visiting a faculty member in his or her home had independent significant influences on students' decisions to pursue careers in science-related fields. They also report that these variables influenced persistence or defection from the same fields.

Role Models

Related to the variable of faculty contact is the influence of faculty members as role models. There has been consistent speculation that having role models affects students' decisions to pursue high-prestige careers, particularly careers in academia. It is also commonly believed that the gender and the race or ethnicity of the role model makes a difference. Supposedly minority group members and women will do better in school and be more likely to aspire to academic careers if they have role models that match their own gender and ethnicity.[37] This belief is so widespread that it is frequently used as one justification for the utilization of racial preferences in the hiring of university and college faculty members. The empirical research on role models, particularly on the extent to which same-race, same-gender role models influence both career choice and academic performance, is reviewed in some detail in Chapter 7. Let it suffice here just to summarize: We have found no methodologically adequate study that empirically demonstrates that same-gender, same-ethnicity role models are more important than role models in general. In fact, the empirical literature on the effect of any type of role model is very thin.

The very concept of role model, however, is far from clearly defined. Our own study is based on a thorough review of the concept by Adeno Addis, who published a paper in the *University of Pennsylvania Law Review* in 1996 entitled "Role Models and the Politics of Recognition."

Addis gives much evidence that there is a widely held belief that the absence of minority role models is a reason for the lower levels of minority academic achievement and for the scarcity of African Americans and Latinos in many professional careers.[38] He relates in detail the battle that occurred at Harvard Law School in the early 1990s when African American professor of law Derrick Bell resigned because of the Harvard Law School's refusal to appoint an African American woman to a faculty position. "Professor Bell felt that neither the male African American professors nor the white female professors could be role models for female African American students" (p. 1379, n. 4). Addis recognizes that the claims made about role models are not based on empirical evidence: "Quite often the discourse (and controversy) concerning role models, popular and scholarly, does not revolve around empirical claims. Rather the term is invoked as a means of making and contesting normative claims about the desirability of certain activities and as a rhetorical device to defend desired objectives or to attack unacceptable commitments" (p. 1380).

The primary purpose of the Addis article is to point out the varying ways in which the concept of role model has been used and to introduce his idea of the importance of role models in what he calls the "politics of recognition." First, he points out that the terms "role model" and "mentor" have often been used interchangeably. But to be a mentor requires close personal contact between the mentor and the person being mentored. To be a role model does not necessarily involve close personal contact between the role model and those being influenced. Addis also points out that the terms "role model" and "hero" have been used interchangeably, but they too refer to different functions: "One of the distinguishing features of a role model is that he or she inspires the possibility of emulation. On the other hand, a hero instills admiration and respect for the qualities he or she displays and the achievements he or she has attained" (p. 1389).

Basing his argument on research and theory in sociology on roles, Addis delineates the definition of role model that emerged from this literature. The idea is to illuminate "the processes by which an aspiring role occupant learns the virtues and commitments associated with that role from a role occupant" (p. 1390). He then quotes Robert Merton's discussion of the differentiation between the concepts of role model and "reference individual." According to Merton (1957), emulation of individuals "may be restricted to limited segments of their behavior and values and this can be usefully described as adoption of a role model. Or, emulation may be extended to a wider array of behaviors and values of these persons who can then be described as reference individuals" (quoted in Addis 1996, p. 1391).

Thus, the concept of role model refers to influence restricted to behavior relevant to a specific role rather than a more general influence on many aspects of one's life. Assuming this definition of role model, Addis then asks whether it is necessary for effective role models to be of the same race or gender as the aspiring role occupant. Although at the time he wrote there was no reliable empirical evidence on this point, he argues that there is no reason in principle why a white role model might not be just as effective as a minority role model in socializing role aspirants into a role they desire to occupy. He quotes Judith Jarvis Thomson as saying that as a student she did not feel that she learned any more from female professors than from male professors and that as a teacher she feels that she is not necessarily more effective with female students than with male students. Although Thomson does not claim to be generalizing, Addis concludes that she is correct in at least arguing that there is no evidence to support the belief that in order to be effective a role model must be of the same gender or race as a role aspirant: "There is no evidence that aspiring role occupants master a specific role faster or better when the role occupants are of the same race or gender" (p. 1406).

But Addis then points out that there is another way in which the concept of role model can be used. Rather than conceptualizing role models as people who socialize role aspirants into a new role, role models can simply demonstrate to excluded groups the possibility of one of their members attaining a particular role. According to Addis, "given the dearth of minorities and women in certain professions, it might be necessary for aspiring minority and female role occupants to see minorities and women in those roles to reassure themselves that they can indeed occupy those roles and perform those functions and to show them how those who share similar historical and institutional vulnerabilities can best occupy, perform in, and redefine those roles" (pp. 1409–1410). We would only point out that whether role models work in this way or whether they work in the more delimited way is an empirical question. Is it true that minority students will be more likely to think they can be professors, and therefore aspire to the occupation of professor, if they have minority role models as opposed to white role models?

Addis introduces his notion of the value of role models in the "politics of recognition." According to this argument it does not matter if it is untrue that students may learn more about a particular role from same-race, same-gender role models. Having members of minority groups or women in positions of importance and authority (such as professors) serves a basically symbolic function. As Addis puts it, "the presence of members of traditionally excluded groups will provide visible reassurance to the aspiring role occupants that the dominant group does not devalue them and their horizons of significance . . . In other words, the presence of supposed role models of the same race or gender provides a counter narrative to the dominant narrative that has reinforced the exclusion of these marginalized groups" (p. 1430). This is a good argument for faculty diversity even if the evidence should show that having same-sex, same-race role models does not increase the probability of women and minorities' aspiring to be professors.[39]

Extracurricular Activities

Studies that have attempted to examine the effect of participation in extracurricular activities on occupational success have resulted in conflicting findings. Pascarella and Terenzini (1991, pp. 475–478) examine various such studies, which show the influence of participation in a wide range of extracurricular activities on a series of outcome measures. In general, they conclude that such activities have small to nonexistent effects. They do not mention, nor are we aware of, any studies that show the effects of extracurricular activities on choice of specific careers, particularly that of college professor. Our empirical evidence suggests that students who participate in athletics underperform academically (Chapter 5). The qualitative research we conducted (described in Chapter 2) suggests that participation in extracurricular activities might have a negative effect, particularly on African American students. The African American students whom we interviewed who had relatively high SAT scores and relatively low GPAs were asked to explain the discrepancy. One of the more frequent reasons given was that the students had become too heavily involved in extracurricular activities, particularly those associated with minority affairs.

Peer Groups

Several studies suggest the importance of peer interests as an influence on individual career choice. None of these studies, to our knowledge, look at specific friendships and social ties of college students, but rather treat peer influence as more of an environmental variable. Thus, Astin and

Astin (1992), in a study of the factors influencing students to pursue careers in science, show that the number of peers in a given field influences whether or not a student majors in that area.

James Davis, in his 1965 study, also argues that the changes students make in their occupational choices during college are influenced by the characteristics of their peers. Students tend to move from occupations where the other students in that occupation are dissimilar to them to occupations in which the other students are more similar to them. Thus, "birds of a feather flock together." Our own data enables us to determine whether the selection of academia as a career is influenced by the proportion of freshman at a school who say they are interested in academia as a career (see Chapter 8).

Participation in Programs Aimed at Encouraging Students to Become Academics

A series of both government- and foundation-sponsored programs have as their aim to encourage participants to pursue careers in either academia or some science-related field. To our knowledge there has been no formal evaluation of these programs. Astin and Astin (1992) look at schools where these programs exist and find that these schools, net of other variables, are no more likely to produce students interested in scientific careers than schools that do not have these programs. But Astin and Astin admit that they had no data on the actual students who participated in the programs. We attempted to assess the success of the Mellon Minority Undergraduate Fellowship (MMUF) program. Although the limitations of our data set prevented us from doing a full evaluation, the results we obtained indicated that the MMUF as well as similar programs were highly effective in getting the individual participants to pursue an academic career. However, here, as in other parts of our research, there are questions about causal order. Since the MMUF program selects students who are doing very well academically and students also self-select themselves into the program, many of the participants in the program who go on to be college professors might have done so without participation in the program.

Plan of the Book

Our review of the literature in this chapter has highlighted some variables that others have found to be important influences on occupational choice and that we examined in our study. We have also discussed some of the hypotheses we held prior to conducting the research and briefly summarized some of our results. The balance of this book presents data, both quantitative and qualitative, that we collected in order to test our hypotheses and in many cases to examine hypotheses that emerged in the process of conducting the research. Our aim was to attain a clear understanding of why high-achieving minority students select academia as a career as opposed to other competing careers and how to increase the number of well-trained minority students who enter academia, thus enabling the system of higher education to have a more ethnically and racially diverse faculty.

In Chapter 2 we describe the design of our study, including the various phases of research we conducted. We emphasize the theoretical and policy-related concerns that dictated decisions made in the design of the study. We explain how we measured both our major independent variable (race/ethnicity) and our dependent variable (career choice).

Chapter 3 presents the basic descriptive findings of our major survey. It reveals what proportion of students in each ethnic group selected which careers as their final choice career as seniors, what their initial multiple career interests were as freshmen, and what their multiple career interests were as seniors. We also present data indicating the strength of commitment to various careers by showing which of two career choices the student is most likely to select as a final choice. These data demonstrate the relative weakness of academia as an occupation when compared to its major competition: business, law, medicine, even school teaching.

In Chapter 4 we begin to delineate what causes interest in an academic career. As most other studies of occupational choice have found, initial career interest as a freshman is one of the two most important determinants of career choice as a senior. We examine the variables that influence freshman interest in academia as a career. Our emphasis is on trying to explain why African Americans are less likely than whites to be interested in academia as freshmen.

Chapter 5 analyzes the importance of academic performance in the decision to become a college professor. Grades are shown to influence academic self-confidence, which in turn has a strong influence on selection of academia as a career. African Americans and Latinos receive lower grades than Asians and white students. This is true even when SAT scores are controlled. We discuss a series of theories aimed at explaining the ethnic differences in academic performance and present data from both our main survey and our pretest survey aimed at empirically testing some of these theories.

Chapter 6 concentrates on student values and students' images of academia as a career. Interest in the two major functions of academics—teaching and research—plays an important role in students' decision to pursue an academic career. The most important factors deterring students from an academic career we found to be the belief that it takes too long to get a Ph.D., a lack of confidence in ability to be a professor, and a desire not to be a student any longer. Surprisingly, we found that concern with the relatively low financial rewards of academia had little to do with a student's deciding against such a career.

In Chapter 7 we examine the influence of role models, faculty contact, and other in-school experiences. We analyze the effects of having same-gender, same-race role models on a series of dependent variables, including grades and interest in academia. We conclude that there is no empirical evidence to support the belief that same-sex, same-ethnicity role models are any more effective than white male role models. Faculty contact, however, is found to be an extremely important variable as an influence on students' selecting a career in academia.

In Chapter 8 we examine the influence of school characteristics. We find that for African American students (but not those in other ethnic groups), once grades are controlled, attending an elite school rather than a less selective school is a deterrent to selecting academia as a final-choice career. We also examine the belief that liberal arts colleges present an environment most conducive to minority students' selecting academia as a final-choice career. We find that, in contrast to expectations, the small liberal arts college is the least conducive environment for minorities, particularly African Americans. In addition, we find that liberal arts colleges are no longer more likely to produce future Ph.D.s than larger, selective schools, such as Ivy League schools. But in general, we find that school characteristics play a very small role in influencing selection of academia as a career.

In Chapter 9 we examine data from the census and the National Center for Educational Statistics (NCES) as well as data from our survey to analyze the pipeline of minorities and white students into academia. Our data show that the main reason why there is a shortage of minority faculty members is that not enough of them are earning Ph.D.s in the arts and sciences and deciding to work in academia. The data suggest that for

African Americans in particular the main reason behind the small flow through the pipeline is relatively low levels of academic achievement in all parts of the education system. Given these findings, we must reject the assertions made by some members of the academy that greater faculty racial and ethnic diversity could be obtained if educational institutions were more committed to pursuing this goal. In fact, we are led to the opposite conclusion: that unless more minority students select academia as their occupation and earn a Ph.D. it is impossible to increase the racial and ethnic diversity of higher education—with or without the use of racial preferences.

Chapter 10 puts forth a series of policy suggestions aimed at increasing the number of minority students who select academia as their first-choice career. If a substantially larger number of highly qualified minority Ph.D.s interested in careers in academia were available, racial and ethnic faculty diversity could be increased without the use of racial preferences in hiring. Our suggestions vary considerably in ease of implementation, although we try to concentrate on actions that can be reasonably taken by universities and colleges interested in getting more minority students to consider academia as a career.

2

The primary purpose of our research was to discover what factors would lead minority college graduates to select university professor as their first-choice career at the time of their graduating from college. We obtained data from 7,612 graduating seniors at 34 colleges and universities. The data included information on input variables, occupational choice, school characteristics, and school experience. The study was limited to "high-achieving" students; the sample included all African Americans and Latinos from the schools who were spring 1996 graduates with arts and sciences majors and who met our sampling criteria. From each school other than the historically black colleges and universities (HBCUs) we also took samples of Asians and whites.[1]

Based on past research (see Chapter 1), we knew that there was a strong correlation between the academic qualifications of students and the likelihood that they would want to be a university professor. A review of the occupational choices of college freshmen of a random sample of students at four-year colleges[2] reveals that only 1 or 2 percent of students select college professor as their first-choice occupation.[3] Of the students in our sample, however, in their freshman year 32 percent were interested in college professor as a career.[4]

Clearly a random sample of college graduates (especially since we were to focus on minority students) would not yield enough students wanting to be professors, unless that sample size were in the hundreds of thousands. We believe that the best way to study the factors leading students to select a career in academia is to study a sample of what might be called high-achieving college graduates. Since we were interested in the career choices of minority students, we had to study high-achieving minority college graduates. In addition, given the purpose of the study imposed by the sponsors of the research, we had to focus on those students who would become professors specifically in an arts and sciences discipline.

In order to obtain our sample we decided to study graduates of schools where we would be likely to find a relatively large number of high-achieving minority students who would be arts and sciences majors. In part because the Ivy League schools attract relatively large numbers of highly qualified minority students and in part because this research was initiated by and partially funded by the Council of Ivy Group Presidents, we decided to include all eight Ivy League schools in the sample. For theoretical reasons we wanted also to include high-achieving minority students from other types of schools.[5]

Theoretical Considerations

A number of theoretical considerations governed the choice of institutions of higher education to be included in the study. The central one is the hypothesis that many aspects of student behavior, particularly (from the point of view of our research) the choice of an eventual career, might be affected by variations in the academic environment. We hypothesized that three institutional variables might be most important: (1) high selectivity versus lesser selectivity; (2) predominantly white versus predominantly black student body; and, cutting across these two variables, (3) research orientation versus teaching orientation.

The expectation that the degree of selectivity of an institution of higher education will have an effect on undergraduate career aspiration is based primarily on the theory of relative deprivation. This theory, applied to career choice among college graduates, was developed and empirically explored thoroughly by James Davis (1966).[6] In order to test this hypothesis we had to look at some schools less selective than the Ivy League. We decided to include a sample of large state universities and HBCUs.

Selectivity is of course relative. Although compared with all four-year colleges in the United States (about 2,700) almost all of the schools in our sample are above average in selectivity (most colleges in the United States will admit virtually anyone who applies and is willing to pay the tuition).[7] Our design did, however, introduce some important variation in selectivity: all of the nine state universities and four HBCUs in our study are (with one exception) less selective than each of the eight Ivy League schools.

We did not, however, want to limit our sample of highly selective schools to the Ivy League. The Ivy League schools (with perhaps one exception) are heavily research oriented. Despite frequent proclamations by administrators about the importance of teaching (and their real concern with the importance of teaching), research is their number one priority; these schools are organized to maximize the reputation of the faculty, which is based almost exclusively on the quality of research. In almost all cases faculty members are hired and promoted primarily on the basis of their research productivity.[8] Tenure decisions are based almost exclusively on research production; only occasionally, where a candidate's research qualifications are "on the border," will teaching be a significant factor in such decisions.[9]

To represent highly selective schools where teaching is at least as—and usually more—important than research we decided to include thirteen selective liberal arts colleges. The inclusion of these schools enabled us to compare elite research-oriented schools with elite teaching-oriented schools. The inclusion of the state universities and the HBCUs (treated as a group of relatively less selective schools) allowed us to look at the effect of selectivity by comparing them with the Ivy League and the liberal arts colleges (treated as a group of relatively highly selective, or "elite," schools). Comparing the state universities with the HBCUs allowed us to assess the influence of the racial composition of schools. Although the HBCUs as a group are less selective than the state universities, both groups of schools (with the exception of one or two state universities) admit a substantial proportion of applicants. There are no highly selective HBCUs.

Claude Steele (1997) has suggested that some African American students, who believe they are stigmatized as less academically competent by white faculty and white students, may preempt negative judgments by not trying to succeed in the first place.[10] Whether the performance of African American undergraduates is best explained by Steele's theory or by the theory that these students benefit from the greater degree of social comfort they experience in schools where most of the students are also African American (and that they suffer from the racism they are hypothesized to experience in predominantly white schools) was not the focus of our study. Rather, our research was designed to determine whether African American students (holding constant SAT scores) are more likely to select academia as a career if they attend HBCUs or predominantly white schools.[11]

Another reason for including HBCUs in the sample has to do with the presumed significance of role models. As pointed out in Chapter 1 it is commonly assumed that the availability of role models and mentors of the same race or ethnicity is likely to encourage African American students to consider or embark on academic careers. If indeed same-race role models are important, there is a far greater likelihood that African American students in predominantly black institutions will be exposed to African American faculty who may serve as role models or mentors.[12]

Given the high selectivity of the Ivy League and the selective liberal arts colleges included in our sample, we may assume that all students admitted at those institutions have the ability to become college professors. This might not be true of every student admitted to these schools, since the institutions use a diverse set of criteria in admission.[13] But since some of the brightest minority students in the country graduate from these schools, almost all of them have the ability to become academics if they want to.

For the two sets of schools in our sample that are less selective (large public universities and HBCUs) the range of student ability and student performance is substantially greater than at the highly selective ones. The student body at state universities is frequently thought of as being highly heterogeneous in scholastic preparation, while at the elite schools the students are relatively homogeneous in scholastic preparation. A small portion of the students attending state universities and HBCUs have academic qualifications similar to those of the students attending the selective institutions in our sample. Some of these students may have been admitted to a more selective school but chose not to attend, either for financial reasons or personal reasons, such as the desire to be close to home (Ely 1998). But the great majority of students at these schools have academic credentials that are substantially lower than those of students admitted to our selective schools, and some of them have such low academic credentials that it is questionable as to whether they are able to do the work necessary to graduate. Indeed these less selective schools generally have considerably higher dropout rates than do the selective schools; and poor academic performance is one, if not the most important, reason for dropping out. William Bowen and Derek Bok (1998) report that about 85 percent of the students in their sample of selective schools graduated within six years of admission. The typical graduation rate within six years of admission for students at state universities is less than 50 percent; for African Americans and Latinos it is about 25 percent (NCES 1995, Table 303).

The dropout rate among the minority students at some of our state universities is substantially higher than that among the white students. This is in part due to the fact that some of these institutions practice a different kind of affirmative action than do the selective schools. The selective schools admit the academically most accomplished minority students in the country, even though the academically most accomplished African American and Latino students have lower academic qualifications (particularly on the SAT) than the most academically accomplished Asian and white students. The use of racial preferences by elite schools does not mean that they admit unqualified minority group students. Virtually all of the minority students admitted to elite schools under race preference admissions systems are qualified to do the work at these schools; they just are not as qualified as Asians and whites who are admitted—and many Asians and whites who are rejected. Given the diverse set of criteria used in admissions by selective schools, this would probably also be true for legacies, recruited athletes, and concert violinists.[14]

Some state universities have racial preference admission plans that cause them to admit African American and Latino students who have very low levels of academic preparation—so low that without racial preferences the majority of them would not be admitted into any college except those that admit all applicants.

We hypothesize that minority students who are the best academically prepared and who have experienced the greatest academic success will be more likely to become professors. Elite schools were "oversampled" because many of this type of minority student attend such schools.[15]

Cutting across the variables of degree of selectivity and racial composition of institutions, which may influence the extent to which able students develop generally high career aspirations, is the variable of research or teaching orientation. This variable, we hypothesize, may determine whether undergraduates who have generally high career aspirations develop a specific interest in academic careers.

The extent to which faculty are oriented to research rather than teaching undergraduates may affect the quality of the relationships between faculty and students, and thus the likelihood that students will find a career in academia attractive. Where faculty are oriented primarily to research, it may be less likely that they will devote much time to developing close relationships with undergraduate students. It is commonly supposed that such close relationships, in which faculty members become mentors and/or role models to the students, influence students positively in the direction of choosing to become professors themselves. Indeed, it has been shown in some previous research that such close relationships are important for the selection of careers in the arts and sciences (Baird 1976). We would expect, then, that faculty who tend to be more committed to teaching undergraduates than to research will be more likely to become the mentors or role models who "recruit" undergraduates into academia or are instrumental in maintaining the commitment of freshmen who enter college already interested in academia (see Chapter 7).

The inclusion in the sample of a set of small liberal arts colleges enables us to test this hypothesis. Although faculty at these colleges are now more involved in research than in the past (McCaughey 1994), they continue to place a strong emphasis on the importance of teaching. Earlier studies, particularly the work of Robert Knapp and Hubert Goodrich (1952), indicated that some of these colleges played a major role as the baccalaureate origins of eventual Ph.D.s, especially Ph.D.s in the natural sciences. Accordingly, we expected to find that they would continue to play a disproportionate role in producing undergraduates who are positively disposed toward an academic career.

The theoretical questions we were interested in examining led us to include four types of school in our sample:[16]

1. Ivy League institutions: predominantly white faculty and students, research oriented, relatively large, generally highly selective. All the Ivy League schools were included in our study: Brown, Columbia, Cornell, Dartmouth, Harvard, the University of Pennsylvania, Princeton, and Yale.
2. Liberal arts colleges: predominantly white faculty and students, teaching oriented, relatively small, generally highly selective. Thirteen liberal arts colleges were included in the study:[17] Amherst, Bowdoin, Carleton, Colgate, Hamilton, Middlebury, Oberlin, Pomona, Swarthmore, Tufts, Vassar, Wesleyan, and Williams.[18]
3. State universities: predominantly white faculty and students, research oriented, very large, generally less selective. We studied nine large state universities: Ohio State University, Rutgers University, SUNY at Stony Brook, the University of California at Los Angeles, the University of North Carolina at Chapel Hill, the Univer-

sity of Texas at Austin, the University of Virginia, the University of Washington at Seattle, and the University of Wisconsin at Madison. Texas and UCLA were selected in part because they were known to have relatively large numbers of Latinos among their graduates. Virginia and North Carolina were selected in part because we believed that they would have a relatively large number of African Americans among their graduates.

4. Historically black institutions. The historically black institutions included in the study vary in both size and research orientation. What they have in common, of course, is that the undergraduates are overwhelmingly African American and a large proportion of the faculty are as well. The faculty members with whom the undergraduates interact are therefore more likely than not to be of the same race as they are. The four historically black institutions we selected were: Florida A&M University, Howard University, North Carolina A&T University, and Xavier University of Louisiana.[19]

The GPA Cutoff at the Less Selective Schools

In designing our study we decided to ask the registrars at the state universities and the HBCUs to include only arts and sciences majors scheduled to graduate in the spring of 1996 who had GPAs of 2.8 (or about a B−) or higher.[20] The reasons for this were straightforward. We conceptualized the study as one of high-achieving minority college graduates. We knew that a good portion of the students attending the less selective schools were not in this category as a result of the substantial heterogeneity of their student bodies. We thought that students who obtained GPAs of less than 2.8 at the state universities and HBCUs would be extremely unlikely to select academia—or, for that matter, the major occupations that compete with academia, such as medicine and law—as their final career choice. (The validity of this assumption is clearly demonstrated in the analysis presented in Chapter 5.) We reasoned that it would be an unnecessary use of scarce project resources to survey students who were not high-achieving and who had little probability of being interested in becoming academics.

There was one potential drawback of this design: it introduced a problem in making comparisons between the less selective and the more selective schools. Having at least small samples of students with less than

2.8 GPAs would have made across-school comparisons easier and would have enabled us to test some of our hypotheses about students with low GPAs not being interested in academia.[21]

As it turned out, this problem was relatively easy to deal with. Our study can be viewed as being one of students at different types of institutions *after controlling for GPA*. As pointed out in Chapter 8 (where we analyze between-school differences), virtually all of the students (over 90 percent) at the selective institutions earned GPAs of 2.8 or higher. Therefore, by comparing students at the selective institutions with those at the less selective institutions, we were essentially comparing only students who had GPAs of 2.8 or higher. In almost all of the analyses in which we make school comparisons we omitted the students at the selective schools with GPAs below 2.75 (the cutoff point in our questionnaire) so that school differences would not be a result of uncontrolled GPA differences.

The Elite Nature of the Sample

The sample that we obtained using the procedures briefly outlined above resulted in an achieved sample of very high-achieving students. In fact, compared with American college students as a group, our sample is a highly elite subsample.

The SAT scores of the students in the study show clearly that our sample indeed represents an elite group. We cannot give the exact mean SAT scores of our sample, since we asked respondents to check off scores within categories rather than note exact scores.[22] In Table 2.1 we show the distribution of both verbal and quantitative SAT scores for the 83 percent of our sample who reported test scores,[23] comparing the distribution with that for all students nationally who took the SAT. Of the students in our sample who took the test, 60 percent scored 600 or higher on the verbal SAT, whereas only 7 percent of all students taking the test scored over 600 on this part of the test. And 73 percent of our sample scored 600 or higher on the quantitative SAT, whereas only 19 percent of all students did as well as this.

Not only is our sample as a whole an elite group compared with the nation, but the same is true for each ethnic group looked at separately. For example, among African Americans nationally, in 1992 about 1 percent scored 600 or higher on the verbal portion of the test (and nation-

46

Table 2.1 Distribution of SAT scores in the sample and the nation, by ethnicity (percent)

Ethnicity	Verbal		Math	
	Nation	Sample	Nation	Sample
All ethnicities				
700 or above	1	18	5	34
600–699	6	42	14	39
500–599	18	32	25	21
400–499	33	8	28	5
Below 400	42	1	28	1
Total %	100%	101%	100%	100%
Total N[a]	1,008,944	24,647	1,008,944	24,774
White				
700 or above	1	18	4	34
600–699	7	44	15	41
500–599	21	31	28	20
400–499	37	6	30	4
Below 400	34	—	22	1
Total %	100%	99%	99%	100%
Total N	680,806	18,157	680,806	18,242
African American				
700 or above	—	10	—	10
600–699	1	31	3	28
500–599	7	39	11	40
400–499	22	18	26	18
Below 400	70	3	59	4
Total %	100%	100%	99%	100%
Total N	99,126	1,458	99,126	1,470
Asian				
700 or above	2	20	13	50
600–699	9	41	21	33
500–599	17	28	26	13
400–499	26	9	22	3
Below 400	46	2	18	—
Total %	100%	100%	100%	99%
Total N	78,387	3,797	78,387	3,808
Latino				
700 or above	—	12	1	16
600–699	3	34	7	42
500–599	10	39	18	31
400–499	27	14	30	9
Below 400	60	2	44	2
Total %	100%	101%	100%	100%
Total N	69,193	1,235	69,193	1,254

Notes: Sample based on weighted data. National scores provided by the Educational Testing Service for 1992, the year in which most of the students in our sample took the test. Dashes indicate less than 0.6 percent.

a. Excludes those of "other" or unknown ethnicity.

wide among African Americans only 0.1 percent, or about 200 students, scored 700 or higher on the verbal portion of the SAT), whereas among our sample of African Americans, 41 percent scored 600 or higher.

It should be kept in mind not only that the students in our sample are academically talented but also that more than half of them are attending highly selective schools. The rest are among the best students at less selective institutions. We estimate that of the approximately 2,700 four-year colleges and universities in the United States, about 4 percent, or 100 institutions, are highly selective;[24] 21 of our schools (the 8 Ivy League institutions and the 13 liberal arts colleges) are among them. At least one of the state universities in our sample would also be among the 100 very selective institutions. Aside from these schools, the others admit a high proportion of students who want to attend despite the fact that the applicants have relatively low SAT scores. The graduating seniors from this large majority of less selective schools have substantially lower SAT scores than do the graduates of the selective ones.

At most of the less selective schools, significant numbers, if not the majority, of students do not major in the arts and sciences. Instead, they major in fields such as business, education, nursing, and physical education. In order for students attending the state universities or HBCUs to be in our sample, they had to have a major in the arts and sciences and a GPA of 2.8 or above.

An examination of the SAT scores of the minority students attending our elite schools suggests that the 100 elite schools in the country are admitting virtually all of the academically best-prepared minority students. This means that in the overwhelming majority of schools in the country, including the state universities and HBCUs in our sample, there were very few minority students who met our criteria of being an arts and sciences major and having a GPA of 2.8 or above.

It bears repeating that the students we studied represent an elite of very high-achieving college students, not a representative sample of all students. Such a group tends to be interested in only a limited number of occupations and makes choices accordingly (Bok 1993).

Collecting the Data

As described in Chapter 1, we began our study with a review of the existing literature on occupational choice, particularly with regard to the choices of minority students. We were helped in designing our questionnaires by the prior work of James Davis (1965), Leonard Baird (1973), and the many studies by Alexander Astin and collaborators (for example, Astin and Astin 1992).[25]

Qualitative Data

The next step was to conduct focus groups and individual in-depth interviews with minority and white college students. We conducted a total of twenty-seven focus groups at schools representing each of our four school types. Wherever possible, a moderator of the same ethnicity as the students led each focus group. We also conducted thirty interviews with individual minority undergraduates at Stony Brook and Columbia College. All of these were transcribed and analyzed.[26] The focus groups and the interviews gave us substantial insight into what variables might influence minority students in making career choices and their attitudes toward working as academics. Quotes from these interviews are used throughout this book.

Generalizations cannot be made on the basis of this type of data. The samples are unsystematic, and the groups have their own internal dynamics, which influence what participants say. But although we cannot use this type of qualitative data in making generalizations, it is extremely useful in gaining insight into the substantive issues being addressed. In general, the conclusions drawn from the focus groups were supported by the empirical data we collected from our survey. However, in certain areas the two sets of data led to different conclusions. The most significant difference had to do with the extent to which parents influenced career choice and pressured minority group students to select careers such as medicine and law over academia. Participants in the focus groups and the interviews repeatedly mentioned the existence of parental pressure, but the quantitative data seemed not to support this point: students' responses to the survey question on how important an influence their parents had been on career choice was not correlated with selection of academia as a career. In cases where qualitative and quantitative data lead to differing conclusions it is not always correct to assume that the quantitative data are more accurate than the qualitative data. There are many problems in doing surveys, not the least of which is normative responding—respondents answering questions the way they think they should rather than the way they really feel. Normative responding may have been at work in the survey responses, with students downplaying the importance of parents in making their career decision.

Pretest Survey

After completing our analysis of the qualitative data we conducted a pre-test survey among the minority and white graduates of three schools, each representing one of the types of school to be included in the final survey. We sent a mail questionnaire to all graduating African Americans and Latinos and samples of Asians and whites at Haverford College, Stanford University, and the University of Maryland at College Park.[27] A total of 840 questionnaires were returned from graduates of these three colleges.

The purpose of the pretest was primarily to see which of a large number of variables was correlated with the dependent variable, interest in academia. We knew that the pretest questionnaire was too long to obtain the kind of high response rate required for the final mail survey, so we used an analysis of the pretest data to decide which questions to eliminate from the survey and which questions to modify. Although most of the analyses presented in this book are based on the final survey, at times we use data from the pretest that were not available on the final survey.[28] Given the relatively small number of minorities in the pretest sample, all results from these data have to be considered with caution and as suggestions for further research rather than as firm conclusions.

After the analysis of the pretest was completed we began drafting the survey to be used as the final mail questionnaire. As part of this process we conducted individual pretests with more than one hundred Stony Brook students. We had each student fill out the questionnaire; then, with the filled-out questionnaire in hand, we interviewed the student about the answers that he or she gave. This enabled us to find out which questions were unclear and which questions students were misinterpreting. This was of great help in our developing what we believe to be a clear questionnaire. An example of the type of information we gained from this pretesting process is what we learned about role models. We hoped to find out if students had had a role model of a particular ethnicity and gender (see the discussion of role models in Chapter 1 and the analysis of the data in Chapter 7). It became clear to us during the pretest survey that the term "role model" meant different things to different students. We decided that these meanings might be important in determining the influence that "role models" had on students. We therefore developed a question in the final survey in which we asked students to indicate the meaning(s) they gave to the term "role model." As explained in Chapter 7, these data were useful in our analysis.

For details on how the main survey was administered, see Appendix C.

Phone Follow-Up with Nonrespondents

At the end of the period allowed for students to return the survey after the third mailing, we tried to contact nonrespondents by telephone, using a modified version of the mail survey. A commercial research company, with professional interviewers, carried out the phone interviews.

Sample Selection

Excluded from the sample at all institutions were all seniors not majoring in the arts and sciences and all seniors who were not American citizens; also, as stated earlier, at the less selective institutions (the large public universities and the HBCUs) students with a GPA below 2.8 were excluded. The sample was drawn from the population of seniors who might reasonably be expected to graduate in the spring of 1996, and it included all African American and all Latino students who were not excluded by the above-mentioned restrictions and samples of Asian and white students.[29] At the elite schools we did *not* use a 2.8 GPA cutoff, but included in the sample all African Americans and Latinos, and samples of Asians and whites who were expected to graduate in the spring of 1996.

Although we asked the registrars to exclude from the samples all students who were not U.S. citizens, some appear to have excluded only those defined as foreign students and included resident aliens. A number of students indicated on their questionnaires that they were not U.S. citizens; presumably they were resident aliens. We decided to include them in our study, since for our purposes the career plans of these permanent resident aliens, who will remain in this country, are just as significant as those of U.S. citizens.

For more details on how the samples were drawn at each type of school, see Appendix C.

Sample Characteristics

Two characteristics of the sample surprised us, and one especially.

First, we were unprepared for the very small number of African American seniors in the arts and sciences with GPAs of 2.8 or above at the large public universities. The state university with the highest number of African Americans who met our sampling criteria had 88 such African American seniors. The other state universities had lower numbers of African Americans who met our sampling criteria, all the way down to a huge university in the Midwest that had only 8 African Americans who were majoring in the arts and sciences, who had a GPA of 2.8 or higher at the end of the junior year, and who were expected to graduate in the spring of 1996. The number of Latino students at the state universities who met our criteria ranged from 234 to 9. Large numbers of Latino students with GPAs of 2.8 or above were found only at UCLA and the University of Texas at Austin. Significant sources for a minority pipeline into academia do not seem to exist at the large public universities. We discuss this problem at length in Chapter 9. As pointed out in that chapter, only 28 percent of African Americans who were arts and sciences graduates at the nine state universities in our sample had a GPA of 2.8 or higher. Thus, in most of these schools, the total number of African Americans in our sample ranges from small to very small indeed.

We can think of three reasons why we found so few African Americans at state universities who met our sampling criteria. First, and probably most important, African Americans majoring in the arts and sciences get lower grades than whites. We just mentioned that only 28 percent of African Americans who majored in the arts and sciences at our state universities received GPAs of 2.8 or higher. The figure for white students at the same schools is 65 percent. Second, we know that the elite private universities and colleges vigorously recruit the academically best-prepared African American high school students, attracting them with the prestige of their name and with generous financial aid.[30] Thus, there are relatively few African American students with high academic qualifications who end up attending relatively less selective schools. And third, a significant portion of African American students who enroll at state universities drop out or transfer prior to graduation.

Less surprising to us was the very small number of African American undergraduates at the small liberal arts colleges, and the even smaller number of Latinos. The range for African Americans among the liberal arts colleges was 46 to 4; for Latino students the range was 32 to 9. We assume that to many minority students, the idea of spending four years in a relatively isolated community, far from any urban concentration of minority populations, may seem rather uncomfortable. We were surprised at the relatively small number of minority students at some of the Ivy League institutions, given their high prestige and their use of affirmative action policies. At Ivy League schools the range for African Americans was 75 to 19 and for Latinos 64 to 22.[31]

The second thing that surprised us from the sample was that it is not true that Asian American undergraduates predominantly major in natural science fields. Indeed, in most of the schools we surveyed, Asian Americans are more likely to major in one or another of the humanities or social sciences. True, if we compare Asians not among themselves but with other ethnic groups, we find that higher proportions of Asians major in the natural sciences than proportions of the other groups; relatively small proportions of other ethnic groups major in the natural sciences, except for premedical students, who are likely to major in biology.

Response Rates

Because we were apprehensive about obtaining high response rates from undergraduates, we employed a mail survey (with two follow-up mailings) and a phone survey (in all but three schools—two schools declined to give us the phone numbers of students, and at one the numbers were incorrectly transcribed by the registrar). Response rates varied, to be sure, not just among categories of institutions but also among institutions within each category; but even without the telephone survey, the response rate to the mail survey was 63 percent; with the phone survey, the overall response rate was 76 percent.[32] Our original goal was to obtain a response rate of 75 percent.[33] The actual size of the achieved sample for each ethnic group and each school type is shown in Tables 2.2 and 2.3. By ethnicity, the response rate for African Americans was 75 percent; for Latinos 73 percent; for Asians 79 percent; and for whites 73 percent. By type of school, the response rate was 86 percent for the small liberal arts

Table 2.2 Distribution of sample by ethnicity, unweighted and weighted

	Total	Whites	African Americans	Asians	Latinos
Unweighted	7,509	3,051	1,518	1,777	1,163
Weighted	29,399	21,572	2,053	4,158	1,616

Table 2.3 Distribution of sample by type of school, unweighted and weighted

	Total	Liberal arts colleges	Ivy League schools	State universities	HBCUs
Unweighted	7,509	1,700	1,915	3,368	526
Weighted	29,399	6,168	8,116	14,322	793

colleges, 75 percent for the Ivy League schools, and 67 percent for the HBCUs and state universities.

Sampling Bias

Even though our relatively high response rate somewhat reduces the problem of potential sampling bias, the question remains whether those who failed to respond were in important respects different from those who did.[34] The fact that we carried out first a mail survey and then a phone survey of nonrespondents we believe provides us with an unusual opportunity to find out whether those who did and did not respond to the mail survey were in specifiable ways self-selected—that is, whether particular background characteristics or particular positive or negative attitudes toward the questions asked were correlated with response. We conceptualized the students whom we surveyed by phone as a sample of nonrespondents to the mail survey who can be compared with those who did respond. Detailed comparisons between data obtained from the mail survey with those obtained from the phone survey are presented in Appendix C.

Weighting the Data

Because we oversampled African Americans and Latinos, had a stratified sample of Asians, and undersampled white students, in order to describe and analyze the population of graduating seniors who met our sampling criteria at the thirty-four schools in our study, it was necessary to weight the data.[35] Surveys at about half of the schools in the sample were obtained in the fall of 1995 and the other half in the spring of 1996. Because we slightly changed sampling procedures from the fall data collection to the spring, and because of some problems with missing data, the weighting formula was necessarily complex. In essence, we wanted to weight the data up to the population size of the schools included in the study. In order to do this we constructed a large multivariate table in which we entered both the number of students in each cell in the population and the number of students in each cell in the achieved sample. The latter were then given weights to equal the population. Because the population is made up primarily of white students, the weighted population looks similar to the population of white students. However, since in virtually every part of the analysis we broke down the students into four ethnic groups, and sometimes into ethnic subgroups, we were able to make accurate comparisons of students in the four major ethnic groups included in this study.[36]

We followed one other basic principle in constructing the weights. For each cell in the weighting table we had two sets of numbers for the sample: the number of mail respondents and the number of telephone respondents. We used data from the mail survey to describe the portion of the population in a given cell represented by the respondents to the mail survey, and we used data from the telephone survey to represent that portion of the population in a given cell that did not respond to the mail survey. Assuming that the interviews obtained by telephone represent a roughly random sample of nonrespondents to the mail survey, we believe that this procedure eliminated a good deal of any response bias, which may have resulted from self-selection among students returning the mail survey.

An example should make our reasoning clearer. Suppose that on the question "Overall, how satisfied have you been with your undergraduate education at this college?" there was selection bias among the 63 percent of the students who returned the mail questionnaire, so that these students were more likely to say they were satisfied than the 37 percent of the sample who did not return the questionnaire. In the telephone sample, we would interview a random sample of the 37 percent of nonrespondents and find out that these students were indeed less likely to be satisfied. In the weighting, 63 percent of the students would be classified by the answers given by respondents to the mail survey and 37 percent of the students would be classified by the answers given by respondents to the telephone survey. To the extent that the achieved sample in the telephone survey is a random sample of nonrespondents to the mail survey, response bias on this question has been eliminated.

Since all of our analyses in this book are based on weighted data, we do not report number of cases in the tables, because the actual number of cases upon which the analysis is based is always substantially smaller than the weighted N.[37] However, since the tests of significance are based on the actual number of cases, the reader can be assured that relationships reported as being statistically significant are not based on a very small number of cases.

Classifying the Students by Race or Ethnicity

As sociologists studying race and ethnic relations have long pointed out, race is as much a social construction as a biological fact. In our study, race and ethnicity are determined by the students' self-identification on a question that begins "Do you consider your racial/ethnic background to be:" and then allows them to mark as many categories as apply.[38] For purposes of analysis, however, we found it necessary to use a coding scheme that places each student in only one of the following categories: African American, Asian, Latino, or white.

From the very beginning of the study we were aware that grouping together as "Asians" or "Latinos" students who came from very different cultural backgrounds represented a serious problem. Cubans and Chicanos come from very different cultures, and just because their parents or grandparents (or sometimes the students themselves) speak the same language is not necessarily a good reason to lump them together. The same can be said about Chinese and Indians or any of the subgroups in the two large ethnic groups of "Asians" and "Latinos." There are two reasons why we had to do this. First, most universities lump the people from these varying cultures together for the purposes of determining the extent to which the groups are underrepresented among either the student body or the faculty. Second, it simply would have been impossible without substantially increasing the costs of this research to get enough cases of the four large ethnic groups to allow for a finer breakdown. Because we are aware of the problems involved in using just four groups in identifying ethnicity, in several key places in the book we do disaggregate these groups to the extent that the size of the sample allows us to. Also, as discussed later, one of the most interesting findings of this study is that students from different ethnic or racial backgrounds tend to be similar in how they go about selecting careers. This is not to downplay the many ethnic differences that we did uncover. But generally, for our purposes, the ethnic groups were more alike than they were different.

Almost all of the students in our sample (91 percent) checked off only one of the four major ethnic groups used in this study. Latinos were the most likely to check two or more ethnic groups. Among those who identified as African Americans, 4 percent also identified as Latinos, 2 percent as Asians, and 8 percent as whites. Fully 23 percent of those identifying as Latinos also identified as white.[39] This may explain why in some parts of our analysis Latinos appear to be the most similar to whites. The fact that the proportion of each ethnic group also identifying as more than one major ethnic group tends to be small (with the exception of the quarter of Latinos who also identify as white) suggests that our method of coding ethnicity probably does not distort the substantive results of the study.

The coding scheme we used is as follows: If students said they were either "African American/black" or "Caribbean/black," they were classified as African American, even if they checked off any of the other racial categories.[40] We give "African American" priority in our coding scheme because people of mixed ethnic origin, if one of those ethnicities is black, usually identify as African American and are treated by others as African American. Among all those not classified as African American, students who indicated any one of the Latino groups (Cuban, Mexican American/Chicano, Puerto Rican, Other Latino) are classified as Latino, even if they checked off any of the other ethnic categories. Thus, a student checking off Cuban and white or Asian is classified as Latino. Among all those not classified as either African American or Latino, students checking off any of the Asian groups listed (Chinese, Indian, Japanese, Korean, Pacific Islander, Pakistani, Vietnamese, Other Asian) are classified as Asian, even if they also checked white.[41]

Among the 35 students not classified as either African American, Latino, or Asian who indicated that they are Native American/Alaskan Native, those who also indicated that they are white (22 students) are classified as white.[42] All students not classified as African American, Latino, or Asian who indicated that they are white are classified as white. Using this procedure, the sample provides, prior to weighting, data on 1,518 African Americans (20 percent), 1,165 Latinos (16 percent), 1,778 Asians (24 percent), and 3,053 whites (41 percent).[43] In 98 cases the student either failed to answer the ethnicity question or indicated a single category, Native American/Alaskan Native (13 students). These are treated as missing data in analyses involving ethnicity. In Table 2.4 we show the racial/ethnic distribution (both weighted and unweighted) of the sample within each of the four types of school studied.

Table 2.4 Distribution of sample by ethnicity and type of school, unweighted and weighted (percent)

Ethnicity	Total		Liberal arts colleges		Ivy League schools		State universities		HBCUs	
	Unweighted	Weighted	Unweighted	Weighted	Unweighted	Weighted	Unweighted	Weighted	Unweighted	Weighted
White	41	73	49	80	31	70	48	77	—	1
African American	20	7	15	6	21	7	10	5	99	97
Asian	24	14	22	10	31	18	24	15	1	2
Latino	16	6	13	5	17	6	18	6	—	1
Total %	101%	100%	99%	101%	100%	101%	100%	101%	101%	101%
Total N	7,509	29,399	1,700	6,188	1,915	8,116	3,368	14,322	526	793

Note: Dashes indicate less than 0.6 percent.

Measuring the Dependent Variable

The primary dependent variable for this study is career choice, specifically the choice of academia as a career. All other studies of occupational choice that we are familiar with ask the students, either as freshmen or as seniors, to indicate which from among a list of occupations is their occupational choice. This methodology is based on an inaccurate conception of how occupational choices are made. We believe (and our data back us up) that when students are freshmen a substantial majority do not have a clear single occupational choice. Some may, particularly students who want to go into medicine, engineering, or business. But students who are arts and sciences majors may be interested in a range of careers. The strength of this interest may vary considerably. Some have no idea about what career they are interested in when they enter college as freshmen; others are interested in several different careers.

Because we do not believe that most arts and sciences students have only one career that they are interested in, we allowed our students to indicate interest in as many of the twenty careers listed on the survey.[44] If a student had really made up his or her mind as to what career to pursue, of course the student could indicate interest in only one of the twenty. Indeed, some of them did just that. But most indicated that as freshmen they were interested in three or four careers.

The multiple-choice method of measuring the dependent variable makes more sense for measuring career interest as freshmen than forcing students to select a single occupation.[45] It also makes sense for measuring career interest as seniors. Our qualitative work suggested that there were many arts and sciences majors who had not made a clear career choice even in their senior year. Many of them still remained interested in several possible careers, and some still had no idea of what career they wanted to pursue. As a result, we again allowed our respondents to indicate interest as seniors in as many of the twenty careers included in the survey. At that point, however, we also asked the students which of the several careers that they were interested in as seniors they thought they would be most likely to pursue. Thus, we asked students to select from among all those careers they had indicated interest in as seniors the one career that they thought they were most likely to pursue.[46] In many parts of our analysis we use the answer given to this last question as the dependent variable. Using a multiple-choice approach to measuring the dependent variable in both the freshman and the senior year results in more students expressing an interest in particular careers than surveys that use a single-choice approach.

Determining Causality

In this book we aim to establish the "causes" of interest in academia (and other major competing careers). In survey data such as ours, there are substantial problems in determining whether two variables are simply correlated or one is a cause of the other.

Generally, in sociology one variable is considered a cause of another if the relationship meets three criteria.[47] First, the independent and dependent variables must be correlated. Thus, for example, faculty contact must be correlated with selection of academia as a career for faculty contact to be a cause of that career choice.

Second, the independent must precede the dependent variable in time. In research such as that reported here, in which all the data were collected at one point in time rather than longitudinally, it is frequently very difficult to establish causal order or time order. There is, for example, a strong relationship between the amount of contact students have with faculty and their interest in becoming professors. Can we then conclude that faculty contact is a *cause* of interest in academia? The answer is no— not without making some assumptions that we have no empirical way of checking. It is possible that coming into contact with faculty members and adopting one or more of them as role models or mentors might cause students to become interested in academia. It is also possible that those students who are initially interested in academia will seek out contact with faculty members. In that case the interest in academia precedes the faculty contact. The criterion of time order would thus be violated, and the relationship could not be considered to demonstrate causality.

The third criterion of causality is that there must be no antecedent third variable (a variable preceding the independent variable in time or logic) that, when controlled (held constant), will "wash out" or eliminate the relationship between the independent and dependent variable. In our data set in most cases there are no significant problems in meeting the first and third of these criteria for causality. In those cases, however, where determining the time order between the independent variable and some third variable is difficult or impossible, it is difficult to conclude that causality is at work. Take the case, discussed earlier, of students who participate in the Mellon Minority Undergraduate Fellowship (MMUF) program. These students are both self-selected (they must decide to apply for admission to the program) and socially selected (once they apply, the program must decide whether to accept them or not). It is possible that the variables influencing either self-selection or social selection (or both) might include high SAT scores and socioeconomic status. These variables might be the reasons why the participants in this program or others like it are more likely to become academics. And as we pointed out, these students might have become academics even if they had never participated in the program. In this sense, then, participation in the MMUF program would be a spurious cause of deciding to become an academic. The only way in which it could conclusively be shown whether such participation has a causal effect is to conduct an experiment in which students are randomly assigned to participate in the program. Randomization would rule out the outcome's being a result of either self-selection or social selection.

The problem of attributing causality arises at many places in the analysis. We have two ways of handling this type of problem, neither of them fully satisfactory. First, when looking at interest in academia as a dependent variable and faculty contact as an independent variable, we control for a stated freshman interest in academia.[48] If faculty contact still has an influence when freshman interest in academia is controlled, we assume that faculty contact is at least in part a cause of a student's choice of academia as the most likely career. We know that this is an assumption that some social scientists will not be comfortable with; they would prefer to say that the two variables are correlated without making any causal inferences.

This leads us to the second way in which we handle the problem of causal direction or time order. In many cases it seems logical to conceptualize the causal direction between two variables as being bidirectional rather than unidirectional. Thus, for example, interest in academia causes a student to seek out faculty contact and this contact in turn reinforces the student's interest in the career of university professor and makes the student more likely to actually select it as a final-choice career. Or in the case of programs like the MMUF, students who already have an interest in academia may be more likely to apply to such a program and participate in it; participation might then serve to solidify and maintain the initial interest in academia. In other words, the causal relationship runs in both directions. Much of our causal analysis here requires this assumption.

3

ETHNIC DIFFERENCES IN

OCCUPATIONAL CHOICES

The primary purpose of our study is to find out how to increase the number of minority students who are interested in academia as a career. To do this, we must understand the determinants of the career choice these students consider most likely when they are seniors in college.[1] While we cannot claim to know whether their most likely choice will be their actual choice, their most likely choice, together with various indicators of commitment to it, is the best predictor of what the students will do after they graduate.[2] We begin this chapter by looking at the careers selected by the four ethnic groups as the ones they are most likely to end up in. Next we consider their career choices as freshmen (reported retroactively) and as seniors. In subsequent chapters we analyze the possible reasons for these choices.

After the students indicated all the careers they had in mind on entering college and at the time of graduation (of the twenty listed in the survey), they were asked to pick the one occupation they were most likely to go into. Table 3.1 shows the proportion of each ethnic group that selected a particular career as the most likely final choice.[3] Seniors were allowed to select any number of occupations listed on the questionnaire that they had in mind as a career "now," even if they had not completely made up their mind. Then, of those selected as careers they had in mind, they were asked to pick the one that they thought they were most likely to end up in.

Of the twenty different career choices presented in the survey, we combined two we considered as indicating an interest in academia: "Researcher (in a university)" and "University/college professor."[4]

A key issue for our purposes is the extent to which each of the three groups of students interested in academia—those interested in research only, professor only, and both—selected academia as the one occupation

62

Table 3.1 Percentage of students indicating they are most likely to enter a particular occupation, by ethnicity

Occupation	Whites	African Americans	Asians	Latinos
Physician	12	**15**	**33**	13
Business	12	13	12	12
University professor	11	9	8	12
Lawyer	9	**16**	7	13
Teacher	8	8	5	8
Social services	6	7	3	6
Government	5	4	3	5
Fine/performing arts	5	4	3	5
Other research	4	3	2	2
Allied health[a]	3	2	**6**	3
Communications[a]	3	**2**	3	**2**
Journalism[a]	3	**1**	1	1
Psychologist[a]	2	3	2	3
Environment[a]	2	2	1	1
Computer analyst[a]	1	1	1	1
Architecture[a]	1	1	1	1
Engineering	1	1	1	1
Library[a]	1	**1**	1	**1**
University administrator	—	—	—	—
Other[b]	7	7	**4**	6
Undecided[b]	6	**3**	5	4

Notes: Significantly different from whites, chi-square $p < .05$ indicated by boldface.
Percentages may not total to 100 due to rounding errors.
Dashes indicate less than 0.6 percent.
a. Occupation not asked on telephone survey.
b. Not ranked.

they are most likely to pursue. Of those who said researcher only as seniors, 15 percent selected this as their most likely eventual occupation; of those who said professor only, 29 percent; of those who said both, 12 percent selected researcher in a university and 29 percent university professor. Thus, combining these two choices in our definition of students who are interested in academia, fully 41 percent picked academia as the one occupation they were most likely to pursue, indicating a stronger commitment on the part of those who selected both than of those who selected researcher only or professor only.

As the data in Table 3.1 make clear the small differences among the minority ethnic groups in the proportion wanting to be college professors are not significantly different from the proportion of white students. Eleven percent of whites, 9 percent of African Americans, 8 percent of Asians, and 12 percent of Latinos select college professor as their first choice. This is one of our most important findings. Contrary to our presupposition that high-achieving minority students would be less interested than similar white students in becoming academics, it turns out that *there are no meaningful differences in the proportion of all four ethnic groups who select academia as their final-choice occupation.* This means that increasing the number of minorities in the pool of Ph.D.s from which professors in the arts and sciences can be hired requires two things. First, although the proportion of each ethnic group that is interested in entering academia is the same, the absolute number of high-achieving African American and Latino students in the arts and sciences is relatively small and must be increased. Also, the proportion of high-achieving minorities who select academia as a first-choice career must be raised to a level above that currently found among high-achieving white students. The former is the more difficult to achieve, since it depends on social structural variables over which universities have little control. The latter aim is easier to achieve, as may be seen from the policy suggestions we outline in the last chapter of this book.

To make it easier to compare the final career selections of the four ethnic groups, in Table 3.2 we show the top five occupations for each group. These are the five most frequently chosen by all of the ethnic groups.[5] Besides university or college professor, the five choices include physician, business, lawyer, and teacher (of elementary or secondary school). These last four can be considered the major occupations "competing" with academia for high-achieving students.

As can be seen in the bottom line of Table 3.2, more than 50 percent of the students in each ethnic group are interested in one of the top five occupations, and among African Americans, Latinos, and Asians this number is closer to 60 percent. Thus, talent would be highly concentrated in just a few occupations.[6] The remaining students who did not select a top five occupation are widely distributed among the fourteen other occupations and the "other" category.

Occupational Choice(s) as Freshmen

It is important from the point of view of policy recommendations to understand to what extent students' occupational choices are already made

Table 3.2 Top five most likely occupational choices of each ethnic group

Rank	Whites	African Americans	Asians	Latinos
First	Business (12%)	Lawyer (16%)	Physician (33%)	Lawyer (13%)
Second	Physician (11%)	Physician (15%)	Business (11%)	Physician (13%)
Third	**Professor (11%)**	Business (13%)	**Professor (8%)**	Business (12%)
Fourth	Lawyer (9%)	**Professor (9%)**	Lawyer (7%)	**Professor (12%)**
Fifth	Teacher (8%)	Teacher (8%)	Allied health (6%)	Teacher (8%)
Total percent selecting top 5 occupations as first choice	51%	61%	65%	58%

by the time they enter college and to what extent the type of college they attend and the kinds of experiences they have in college influence their career decisions. Past research on occupational choice suggests that a student's choice of career when entering college is one of the strongest influences on the choice made at graduation (J. Davis 1964; Astin and Panos 1969; Astin and Astin 1992). These earlier studies have no clear message for us with regard to the effects of attending college. In any event, most of the earlier research involved a different student population from the one we surveyed, and we are interested in discovering the effects of attending different types of colleges and having different in-college experiences on students from different racial or ethnic backgrounds.

As described in Chapter 2, we asked graduating seniors to indicate all the careers they were interested in when they entered college. The utility of these data depends on the extent to which retrospective memory of occupational interests as freshmen are valid. There are three factors that give us reason to believe that these retroactive data are at least roughly accurate. First, James Davis (1966) reports a study in which Alexander Astin was able to check the validity of retrospective educational aspirations. Astin found a very high correlation between actual freshmen aspirations and later retrospective reports of these aspirations. Davis concludes that "memory of career plans should be as accurate as that of educational aspirations" (p. 18). Another reason to believe that our retrospective data are relatively accurate is that we find virtually identical results when we correlate our data on initial (retrospective) career aspirations with that on senior aspirations as researchers such as Astin, who have conducted longitudinal studies and collected data on freshman career interests during the freshman year, have found. Finally, our questionnaire gave the students the opportunity to list as many careers as they recalled being interested in as freshmen rather than forcing them to list just one. Students thus were more likely to report careers they were actually interested in as freshmen than if they had been forced to list only one choice. Thus, although perhaps the exact numbers we report for freshman career aspirations may not be precisely accurate, we believe they are accurate enough to utilize our data as a simulated longitudinal study.

We find that 25 percent of the seniors indicated only one choice as freshmen; 38 percent, two or three choices; and 34 percent, four or more choices. In addition, 3 percent of the respondents either declared themselves undecided or failed to fill out the question.

In Table 3.3, we show the percentage of students selecting each occu-

Table 3.3 Percentage of students selecting occupation as a career they had in mind when they entered college, by ethnicity

Occupation	Whites	African Americans	Asians	Latinos
University professor	34	**22**	32	30
Physician	25	27	**50**	**30**
Lawyer	25	**32**	21	**30**
Teacher	23	**20**	18	22
Government	22	**18**	15	**18**
Social services	22	20	14	23
Journalism[a]	22	**14**	15	**15**
Business	21	**24**	22	22
Communications[a]	20	**16**	14	**16**
Psychologist[a]	18	16	12	20
Fine/performing arts	17	**11**	11	12
Allied health[a]	16	19	25	17
Other research	16	**12**	15	**12**
Environment[a]	15	**3**	8	**9**
Engineering	10	8	6	11
Architecture[a]	9	**6**	10	8
Computer analyst[a]	6	7	8	5
Library[a]	4	**2**	2	4
University administrator	2	**4**	2	2
Other	10	**8**	5	8
Undecided	7	**4**	5	6

Notes: Percentages sum to greater than 100.
Significantly different from whites, chi-square $p < .05$ indicated by boldface.
a. Occupation not asked on telephone survey.

pation as freshmen, broken down by ethnicity. Somewhat surprisingly, college professor is the most frequently mentioned occupation by high-achieving white students recalling their occupational interests as freshmen: 34 percent of whites said that when they entered college, college professor was one of the occupations they were interested in. Only 22 percent of African Americans, however, mentioned college professor as an occupation they were interested in as freshmen, though it is their fourth most frequent choice.[7] As for the other two groups, 32 percent of Asians and 30 percent of Latinos expressed a freshman interest in academia as a career.

We present the top five choices of each ethnic group as freshmen in Table 3.4.

Table 3.4 Top five occupational interests of freshmen, by ethnicity

Rank	Whites	African Americans	Asians	Latinos
First	**Professor (34%)**	Lawyer (32%)	Physician (50%)	**Professor (30%)**
Second	Physician (25%)	Physician (27%)	**Professor (32%)**	Lawyer (30%)
Third	Lawyer (25%)	Business (24%)	Allied health (25%)	Physician (30%)
Fourth	Teacher (23%)	**Professor (22%)**	Business (22%)	Government (26%)
Fifth	Journalism (22%)	Teacher (20%)	Lawyer (21%)	Social service (23%)

Career Choice(s) as Graduating Seniors

Since even graduating seniors may not have made up their minds as to precisely which career they intend to pursue, our questionnaire offered students the opportunity to indicate as many careers as they had an interest in. For some, the choices probably include careers that students have a strong interest in and have given much thought to and others in which they are more casually interested.

In Table 3.5 we show the proportion of students who marked each of the careers or groups of careers as one they were considering. Given the fact that only around 10 percent of the total sample selected professor as the occupation they are most likely to end up in (Table 3.1), it is somewhat surprising to find that, for seniors, among all ethnic groups except

Table 3.5 Percentage of students selecting a career they have in mind as seniors, by ethnicity

Occupation	Whites	African Americans	Asians	Latinos
University professor	34	**30**	32	31
Business	23	23	24	24
Teacher	23	23	**17**	23
Government	19	19	**13**	21
Social services	19	21	**15**	20
Lawyer	18	**26**	16	**24**
Communications[a]	17	15	**14**	16
Other research	17	**13**	15	13
Journalism[a]	17	**12**	**11**	14
Physician	16	17	**40**	16
Fine/performing arts	12	**9**	**8**	10
Allied health[a]	11	12	**21**	12
Environment[a]	11	**3**	**5**	**6**
Psychologist[a]	9	**11**	7	**12**
Library[a]	6	**2**	**2**	5
Architecture[a]	4	3	4	5
Computer analyst[a]	4	4	5	4
University administrator	4	**6**	4	5
Engineering	2	2	3	1
Other	13	**11**	**8**	11
Undecided	3	**2**	2	**2**

Note: Significantly different from whites, chi-square $p < .05$ indicated by boldface.
a. Occupation not asked on telephone survey.

Asians, professor remains the single most frequently selected occupation by a substantial margin.[8] Even if the proportion of students indicating an interest in college teaching is slightly elevated by the students' knowledge of the researchers' interest in this occupation, it is clear that in every ethnic group a substantial portion of this elite population of students is interested in the occupation of college or university professor at the time of graduation.

Students who indicate university professor as one of the occupations they have in mind and who then do not select it as the one occupation they are most likely to go into represent a pool from which graduate students in the arts and sciences might be drawn at a later date, if things don't work out in these individuals' first-choice occupation. By "not working out" we mean anything from their not being admitted into the postgraduate school they wanted (or *any* postgraduate school, in the case of a first-choice occupation such as medicine, for example) to entering another career and not finding it satisfying.

In order to highlight the data in Table 3.5 we present in Table 3.6 the top five choices for each ethnic group. All of these groups, with the exception of Asians, mention the occupation of professor most frequently.

The reason why physician is not among the top five (except for Asians, for whom it does come first) is probably a result of the fact that in order to get into medical school (and perhaps also to enter some of the allied health occupations) undergraduates have to take prerequisite courses.[9] It is of course possible for students who have not taken these "pre-med" prerequisites to do so after they graduate,[10] but students who do so are those who decide that they want to be physicians only after they have graduated.[11] Since there are no prerequisites or even standardized tests to take for an occupation in communications or government, for example, it is much easier for a student to express a realistic interest in that occupation than it is in the occupation of physician. Even the occupation of lawyer does not have any undergraduate prerequisites. Many students interested in law major in political science; but the law schools do not require such a major and claim not to have a preference for it. Thus, a student majoring in art history, for example, can decide to become a lawyer.[12]

When we compare the proportion of students who select university professor as the one career they are most likely to pursue (Table 3.1) with the proportion expressing an interest in the career at the time of graduation (Table 3.5), we can see that the majority of students "interested" in

Table 3.6 Top five occupational choices of seniors, by ethnicity

Rank	Whites	African Americans	Asians	Latinos
First	**Professor (34%)**	**Professor (30%)**	Physician (40%)	**Professor (37%)**
Second	Teacher (23%)	Lawyer (26%)	**Professor (32%)**	Lawyer (24%)
Third	Business (23%)	Teacher (23%)	Business (24%)	Business (24%)
Fourth	Government (19%)	Business (23%)	Allied health (21%)	Teacher (23%)
Fifth	Social service (19%)	Social service (21%)	Teacher (17%)	Government (21%)

the occupation of professor often select another as the one they are most likely to pursue. There is no way of measuring the extent of commitment or rank order of preference for individuals of the careers listed in Tables 3.3 and 3.5.[13] The only way to gauge commitment is to see what percentage of students indicating interest in a particular career as graduating seniors also select that career as the one they think they will actually end up in. In the next section of this chapter we present data that show how students interested in specific pairs of occupations make their final selection. These data indicate that interest in the occupation of professor is relatively weak and that students who are interested in this occupation and any of the other major competing occupations are more likely to select the competing occupation when they make their choice of the one they are most likely to pursue.

Level of Commitment

Two factors indicate the extent of students' commitment to the occupation named as the one they are most likely to pursue. One is whether they intend to begin the graduate education necessary for their future career within the year after graduation or if they plan to take some time off before continuing their education. Three of the five most popular occupations require graduate degrees: college professor, physician, and lawyer. A career in business can be embarked upon directly from college; those who wish to obtain a Master of Business Administration (MBA) can, and indeed are often encouraged to, pursue it at a later date, sometimes at the expense of the employer. The same can be said of elementary and secondary school teaching, provided one takes the necessary education courses and teacher training preparation while one is an undergraduate.[14] But at least for the three occupations requiring a postgraduate degree before work is possible, those who say they will go directly on to pursue that degree are likely to be more committed.[15] Table 3.7 shows the proportion of respondents who intend to begin their graduate education within the year after graduation, for each of the five major occupations (and allied health), broken down by the ethnicity of the students.[16]

The data in Table 3.7 indicate that for all occupations combined all three minority groups are significantly more likely than whites to say that they will go directly on to the postgraduate training necessary for their chosen career. Students who select medicine and law are more likely to say they will go directly on than those selecting other occupations. Of all students whose final career choice is university professor, 58 percent say that they will go directly on; African Americans are more likely to give this response than whites. But as we point out in Chapter 8, this is not a race effect but rather a school effect. African American graduates of HBCUs are much more likely than African Americans who attend predominantly white schools to say they will go directly on. African Americans at predominantly white schools who select university professor as their most likely occupation are no more likely than their white fellow students to say that they will go directly on to graduate school.[17]

The second variable that may be used as a measure of commitment to career is the number of other occupations that students are considering at the time of graduation. If students' final choice is university professor and that is the *only* career they are considering at the time of graduation, they should be more likely actually to enter a Ph.D. program in the arts and sciences and pursue a career as a university professor than if they also list, for example, four other occupations that they are interested in. In Table 3.8, for each of the five major occupations (and allied health), broken down by ethnic group, we show the proportion indicating that this occupation is their only choice at time of graduation. The data indicate some small differences among the four ethnic groups; however, for the occupation that is our primary concern, university professor, there are no meaningful differences.

If both going directly on to graduate school and having the selected occupation as the only choice are indicators of commitment, they should

Table 3.7 Percentage of students planning to continue their graduate education within a year of graduation, by ethnicity (for all occupations, top five, and allied health)

Occupation	Whites	African Americans	Asians	Latinos
All occupations	36	**57**	**46**	**45**
Business	12	**30**	10	11
Lawyer	64	71	54	73
Physician	67	73	68	67
University professor	58	**71**	58	57
Teacher	39	**61**	32	**62**
Allied health	51	47	63	44

Note: Significantly different from whites, chi-square $p < .05$ indicated by boldface.

Table 3.8 Percentage of students selecting occupation as only choice, by ethnicity (for all occupations, top five, and allied health)

Occupation	Whites	African Americans	Asians	Latinos
All occupations	28	**36**	32	**34**
Business	38	40	**26**	32
Lawyer	24	**35**	22	**37**
Physician	48	50	43	58
University professor	20	23	18	24
Teacher	26	32	26	31
Allied health	37	40	51	43

Note: Significantly different from whites, chi-square $p < .05$ indicated in boldface.

be correlated. Indeed they are. Among those who select only one occupation, 51 percent say they intend to go right on to graduate school; among those who express interest in two occupations, 42 percent say they will go directly on; and among those who express interest in three or more occupations, only 30 percent say they will go directly on.

The data in Tables 3.7 and 3.8 suggest that minority group students appear to be at least equally committed to an interest in a career in academia as their white classmates. It suggests that mentioning an interest in academia is not a casual act for minority respondents; their level of real interest in the occupation is at least as great as that of white respondents.

The Strength of Competing Occupations

Our analysis of "strength" shows which of several (ultimately two) attractive occupations a student is likely to select as the one occupation that he or she will most likely end up in. As our data show, it is not easy for students to decide on an occupation. Even in their senior year, many do not really know which occupation they want to go into, and the majority have a strong interest in several occupations. Of course ultimately each student does have to make a choice. Our analysis of strength of commitment shows which of two potentially attractive occupations a student is likely to select as the one he or she will most likely pursue. We relied on their best guess just before graduation as to which of the several occupations that they were interested in they would ultimately choose. Our analysis shows that academia, although a very frequently expressed occupational interest, is ultimately a very weak occupation in its power to attract students with multiple occupational interests, especially when compared to its major competitors (medicine, business, and law).

Likelihood of Pursuing Senior Interests

Before making any pairwise comparisons, we look at an even simpler indicator of occupational strength. Table 3.9 shows for each ethnic group the proportion of those who as seniors expressed an interest in a particular occupation and then selected that occupation as the one they were most likely to go into.

The data for white students give us a clear picture of the relative strength of each of the ten most frequently chosen occupations.[18] Fully 70 percent of students who in their senior year are interested in the occupation physician identify that occupation as the one they will most likely enter. The attractiveness of medicine as a career is so strong that a good many of the remaining 30 percent who are interested in it as seniors but did *not* select it as their most likely eventual occupation may simply fear that they do not have a good chance of getting into medical school.

After medicine, there are two other occupations that have substantial strength: business, with 54 percent of white students expressing interest in it as seniors selecting it as the most likely one; and law, with 49 percent. Allied health and the fine and performing arts are the next strongest, followed by elementary and secondary school teaching; only after

Table 3.9 Percentage of students selecting occupation as most likely among those interested in the same occupation as seniors, by ethnicity

Occupation	Whites	African Americans	Asians	Latinos
Physician	70	**84**	**83**	**79**
Business	54	58	47	52
Lawyer	49	**62**	45	54
Allied health	43	38	38	44
Fine/performing arts	41	41	38	49
Teacher	35	35	27	36
University professor	31	31	26	34
Social services	29	32	**19**	27
Government	26	**19**	25	25
Other research	21	20	13	16

Note: Significantly different from whites, chi-square $p < .05$ indicated by boldface.

these do we find university professor, with 31 percent. University professor ranks seventh out of the ten; the only occupations with less strength are social services, government, and researcher outside of a university. These results are similar for all of the ethnic groups. It is interesting that the profession of schoolteacher (by very small margins) is stronger than that of university professor in every ethnic group.[19]

Pairwise Comparison

In the senior year, students usually feel quite a bit of pressure to make a career decision. This does not mean that all students actually do make a career decision at this time. Some defer the decision in various ways: they travel, or they take what they define as a temporary job. We know from our study of graduate students (Barber and Cole 1996a) that some students who eventually decide to pursue a career in the arts and sciences and enter a Ph.D. program make this decision only after working in other jobs. Nonetheless, those students who say as seniors that they want to be university professors are surely much more likely to follow through than those who do not.

Table 3.10 reveals the relative strength of competing occupations. The students represented in this table expressed an interest in both the column and the row occupation as seniors and then as seniors actually chose one of these two occupations as the one they were most likely to end up in.[20] The percentage tells us what proportion selected the column occupation.[21]

A review of the "physician" column shows that that profession is stronger than all the other nine most frequently selected occupations. That is, among all the students who as seniors expressed interest in both physician and university professor and then picked one of these two occupations as the one they were most likely to enter, 82 percent picked physician and 18 percent picked professor. An examination of the "university professor" column reveals that that choice is weaker than medicine, business, law, elementary or secondary school teacher, government, fine or performing arts, and allied health. It is stronger than only two occupations: social services and researcher outside of a university.

As just mentioned, Table 3.10 shows that medicine is the strongest occupational choice. The closest in strength to medicine is law, which in a direct comparison with medicine gets 40 percent of the students (medicine gets 60 percent). Law is stronger than the other eight occupations. Business is the third most powerful. After that comes a group of occupa-

Table 3.10 Percentage of students selecting column occupation as most likely among those interested in pairs of occupations as seniors (all students)

Occupation	Physician	Business	University professor	Lawyer	Teacher	Social services	Government	Fine arts	Allied health	Other research
Physician	—	32	18	40	10	14	9	38	26	15
Business	68	—	28	53	23	32	33	29	43	34
University professor	82	72	—	71	53	43	52	57	78	36
Lawyer	60	47	29	—	44	21	30	47	38	35
Teacher	90	77	47	56	—	40	44	55	66	30
Social services	86	68	57	79	60	—	51	60	55	31
Government	91	67	48	70	56	49	—	76	45	38
Fine/performing arts	62	71	43	53	45	40	24	—	62	30
Allied health	74	57	22	62	34	45	55	38	—	30
Other research	85	66	64	65	70	69	62	70	70	—

tions, each of which loses out to four of the others and wins in a comparison with another four. These are teaching, government, fine and performing arts, and allied health. Only then comes university professor, which loses in a direct comparison to seven of the nine other most frequently chosen occupations, including not only medicine, business, and law, but also teaching, government, fine and performing arts, and allied health. This table demonstrates conclusively that although academia is the occupation most frequently considered by seniors, it is also one of the weakest occupations in the end. When students have to make the final choice between academia and one or more other occupations, they usually select the other occupation as the one they will most likely end up in.

The weakness of academia when paired with elementary and secondary school teaching we found surprising; perhaps students emphasize the importance of teaching, and see research and other perceived aspects of the job of university professor as negative (this notion is considered in Chapter 6 and elsewhere).[22]

Table 3.11 shows, for each ethnic group, the strength of academia when matched in the senior year with each of the other nine most often chosen occupations.[23] Among whites, as in the entire sample of students (Table 3.10), academia is stronger than only two other occupations: social services and research outside of the university. The results for the three minority groups are similar.

Table 3.11 Percentage of students selecting academia as most likely among those interested in academia and other occupations as seniors, by ethnicity

Occupation	Whites	African Americans	Asians	Latinos
Physician	20	16	14	**4**
Business	31	24	20	28
Lawyer	29	32	26	28
Teacher	48	43	45	43
Social services	54	64	72	61
Government	48	63	36	41
Fine/performing arts	41	—	54	—
Allied health	21	—	25	—
Other research	61	67	78	68

Note: Significantly different from whites, chi-square $p < .05$ indicated by boldface.
Dashes indicate not enough cases to compute a percentage.

University professor is at least as strong among the three minority groups as it is among whites. Members of minority groups in our sample are certainly not less likely than whites to prefer an academic career when compared with specific other careers that compete with academia. If the number and proportion of members of minority groups in the academic pipeline are small, it is not because members of these groups are disproportionately less interested in academia.

Conclusions

This chapter summarized some of the most important results of the study. First, college professor is frequently indicated as an occupation students are interested in, despite the still difficult academic job market. As pointed out in Chapter 1, however, the level of demand for highly qualified minority professors is almost certainly substantially greater than the level of demand for highly qualified white professors. (Of course, it is possible that some minority group students might not be aware of this fact.) As freshmen, more students are interested in professor as an occupation than any of the other occupations. As seniors, they remain more interested in this than in any other occupation. In fact, one third of the seniors designated university professor as one of the occupations they were considering. When asked to say which is the one occupation they will most likely pursue, ten percent selected professor. Only physician and business were selected more often.

Second, we found little difference in the occupational preferences of the four ethnic groups we studied: approximately 10 percent of each group selected professor as their most likely occupation. The fact that African Americans and Latinos are not less likely than whites to be interested in college teaching means that the shortage of African Americans and Latinos in the arts and sciences pipeline cannot be explained by the reluctance of high-achieving African American and Latino college students to be interested in this occupation.

Third, there are no meaningful differences among the ethnic groups as regards the two indicators of commitment to the career of professor. On one measure (whether or not students who select academia as their final-choice career intend to enter a Ph.D. program within one year of graduation), African Americans are significantly more likely to say they will go on within the next year than any other ethnic group. This finding resulted primarily from the fact that many African Americans in our sample attended HBCUs, which are very successful in getting their students to continue their education without interruption. (In Chapter 8 we further explore the influence of HBCUs on students.)

Finally, in analyzing the relative strength of occupations, we find that medicine has far and away the strongest pull.[24] Virtually all students who are interested in that occupation select it as their most likely final choice. Medicine is even more popular with all three ethnic groups than it is with whites. The next two strongest occupations are business and law. Fine and performing arts, allied health, and even teaching are stronger than academia. Using paired comparisons to determine strength, we find that the only occupations among the ten most frequently chosen ones that are weaker than university professor are social services and researcher outside of the university. Again, we find only minor differences in the strength of occupations among the four ethnic groups. University professor is a relatively weak occupation for all of them, and no more so for minorities than for whites. In fact, for African Americans and Latinos, university professor may be slightly stronger than it is among Asians or whites.

In general, the data presented in this chapter suggest that large portions of high-achieving minority students are interested in academia when they enter college, and that most retain that interest through college; but when asked to make a "final" occupational choice, the majority of those with an interest in academia choose to go into some other occupation.

4

INFLUENCES ON INITIAL

OCCUPATIONAL CHOICE

Since initial occupational choice is an important influence on students' "final" choice of career as seniors, in this chapter we examine the freshman occupational interests of the four ethnic groups and try to explain the reasons for the difference between African Americans and whites in the selection of academia as a freshman career interest.[1]

Ethnic Differences in Initial Career Choice

One of the most important determinants of the decision to enter academia (or any other career) is generally the student's initial career choice when he or she enters college.[2] Although some students of course become interested in academia as a result of their experiences in college or the type of college they attend, in our sample fully 70 percent of all those who chose professor as the one occupation they are most likely to go into indicated that they were already interested in that occupation when they entered college. For African Americans, however, this figure is only 57 percent; for Latinos, 61 percent; for Asians, 71 percent; and for whites, 71 percent.[3]

Table 3.4 showed the relationship between initial interest in the career of professor and ethnicity. The only statistically and substantively meaningful difference is that between African Americans and whites: 34 percent of white freshmen as compared with 22 percent of African American freshmen initially expressed an interest in academia as a career. In order to understand the reasons for this racial difference, we must find a third variable or set of variables that when held constant (controlled) will reduce the difference between African Americans and whites to insignificance.

Table 4.1 presents the proportion of respondents expressing an interest in academia as freshmen (broken down by ethnicity) in relation to

Table 4.1 Percentage of students selecting professor as freshmen by selected predictor variables, by ethnicity

Predictor variable	Whites	African Americans	Asians	Latinos
A. School type				
Liberal arts	35*	27	29	25
Ivy League	39	21	35	36
State universities	30	20	30	29
HBCUs	—	22	—	—
B. SES				
Low	35	20	33	26*
Low-medium	30	23	30	39
Medium-high	32	26	38	35
High	36	24	29	28
C. At least one parent was (is) a college professor				
Yes	41*	26*	39*	26
No	27	18	28	26
D. Parents' influence on occupational choice				
Not important	32	18	29	23
Somewhat important	30	20	33	26
Important	30	19	29	28
E. Gender				
Male	34	27*	31	33
Female	33	20	32	28
F. Verbal SAT				
< 500	17*	13*	17*	14*
500–599	26	22	29	27
600–699	36	26	33	38
700 or higher	53	37	43	38
G. Math SAT				
< 500	23*	16*	17*	24
500–599	29	20	27	27
600–699	32	29	30	31
700 or higher	42	31	36	38
H. Combined SAT				
< 1200	23*	16*	21*	21*
1200–1299	27	27	27	31
1300–1399	32	28	35	39
1400 or higher	48	34	37	36

Table 4.1 (continued)

Predictor variable	Whites	African Americans	Asians	Latinos
I. Number of occupational choices as freshman				
One	7*	**3***	4*	6*
Two or three	30	**23**	31	24
Four or more	57	52	60	60
J. Limited financial rewards in academia				
No	37*	**28***	32	**30**
Yes	30	**17**	31	31
L. Major (mutually exclusive)				
Physical sciences	48*	**26***	39*	45*
Mathematics/computer sciences	42	**22**	28	22
Biological sciences	43	**28**	37	40
Humanities	40	**28**	33	34
Social sciences	23	19	27	25
Other	14	15	8	**5**

Notes: Numbers in boldface indicate significantly different from whites at $p < .05$.
Data for K (political orientation) not shown.
*Independent variable significant for this ethnic group at $p < .05$.

a series of variables that we thought might influence freshman career choice. For any one of these eleven variables to be a full or partial explanation of the correlation between race and initial interest in academia, the difference between whites and African Americans in each category of the variable would have to be not statistically significant. This would be indicated by the figure for African Americans not appearing in bold print—meaning that for that particular category of the third variable there was no statistically significant difference between whites and African Americans. Ideally we would like to see no significant difference between the two races for all the categories of the third variable.[4] (Since there are no statistically significant differences between whites on the one hand and Asians and Latinos on the other in freshman interest in academia, the data on these two ethnic groups are shown in Table 4.1 merely for descriptive interest.)

School Type

A significant portion of our sample of African Americans (about a third) attended HBCUs.[5] We wondered whether type of school attended might explain some or all of the difference in level of interest in a career as professor between African Americans and whites. As the data on school type in Table 4.1 indicate, African Americans at all types of schools are less interested in academia as freshman than are whites. In fact, the proportion of African American students at HBCUs who said they were interested in academia as freshmen is 22 percent, the same percentage as for all African Americans.

In general, type of school has very little influence on freshman interest in academia. Given the long-standing belief that small liberal arts colleges are particularly likely to both attract and graduate students who are interested in academia, it was of some interest to note that it is only among African Americans that we find liberal arts students slightly more interested in academia as freshman.

Socioeconomic Status (SES)

Initially we hypothesized that minority members might be less interested in academia as a career than white students because they were more likely to come from lower SES families and that as a result children of these families might be more interested in earning the higher material rewards offered by occupations such as business, medicine, and law.[6]

We had four measures of the students' SES: their mother's educational level, their father's educational level, their self-assessment of what class their parents were in, and their reports of their parents' income.[7] The data show that in general white students are more likely to come from higher SES backgrounds than minority students. Both Asians and whites are considerably more likely than African Americans and Latinos to come from families whose total family income is $100,000 or above; the obverse is true for families whose total income is less than $20,000, though only small portions of minority students reported coming from families with income under $20,000. We may conclude that whites come from the highest SES families, with Asians slightly behind, and that most African Americans and Latinos come from lower-middle to middle-class families; only a small proportion have grown up in poverty.

Using the four measures of SES we had obtained, we created an index of socioeconomic status. Using the dichotomies described in the note to

84

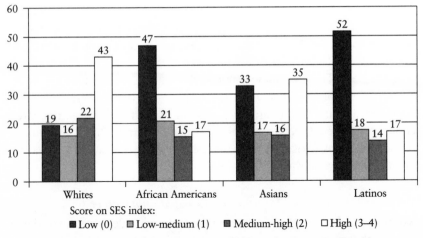

Note: Distribution for African Americans, Asians, and Latinos differs from whites at $p < .05$.

Figure 4.1   Distribution of SES index, by ethnicity

Table B4.1 in Appendix B, we gave each student one point for each high-status characteristic of his or her family. This yielded an SES index with scores ranging from 0 to 4. We combined categories 3 and 4 to create a four-category index. In Figure 4.1 we show the relationship between score on the SES index and ethnicity.

Although ethnicity is correlated with SES, it turns out that socioeconomic status has no meaningful influence on freshman interest in academia (see Table 4.1). The only ethnic group for which there is a significant correlation between SES and interest in academia is Latinos—and for this group the correlation is nonlinear. The data in the SES section of Table 4.1 also show that we cannot explain the freshman difference in interest in academia between African Americans and whites by differences in SES. In all of the SES categories, African Americans are less likely than whites to be interested as freshmen in an academic career, and in two of the four categories this difference is statistically significant.

Effect of Parents' Being Professors

It is generally believed that the selection of occupations by children may be influenced by the occupation of their parents. Students whose parents were academics are likely to be more familiar with the career and may well be inclined to follow in their parents' footsteps. Among our respondents, 16 percent of both African Americans and Latinos, 20 percent of Asians, and 23 percent of whites told us that one or both of their parents work or have worked as a college professor. As can clearly be seen from Panel C of Table 4.1, this factor has the expected effect on all groups except Latinos.[8] Thus, we may conclude that having a parent who is or has been a college professor is one influence on initial freshman interest in academia; but this variable does not explain the difference in initial career choice of academia between African Americans and whites. In both parental categories African Americans are less likely than whites to want to be professors when they enter college.

Parental Influence on Occupational Choice

Minority students in the focus-group interviews made us aware of the influence that parents try to exert over their career decisions. Indeed, as most of the students participating in the focus groups perceived their parents' aspirations for them, it appears that the parents tend to prefer that their children enter what they (the parents) consider to be secure, practical, lucrative occupations, and these do not include academia. The students did not specify whether parental efforts to influence their career decisions occur early or late in their college years, and we cannot relate parental influence directly to initial career choice. Indeed, what quantitative data we do have (see Table 4.1, Panel D) suggest that for none of the ethnic groups do parents have any influence on interest in academia as a career. It is possible that parental influence has more effect on decisions made during college than on initial decisions. But the evidence gleaned from the focus groups suggests that the parents of minority students interested in careers in academia "beat on them" all through college, urging them to go into a career with greater material rewards and one they perceive as more prestigious and secure. The following examples of statements from the focus groups make this clear (Barber and Cole 1996b).

An African American woman at an Ivy League school told us how academia was not within her parents' "line of focus":

> I see being a professor as something that has a level of prestige, but where we're from, the people who are considered prestigious are doctors and lawyers and people who are in those types of professions, you know, engineers. So doing something that's not that, even though it might actually be prestigious, is not really within their [her parents'] line of focus. (p. 40)

Another African American woman reported how her parents would prefer her to go into an occupation in which she would earn more money:

> My parents are the type of parents who allow me to do whatever I want to do and are totally supportive. But then on the other hand, they're always, like, "Why do you want to be a professor? Professors don't make any money. You're about to graduate from an Ivy League school, you can go into jobs like your sisters and make more money and not have to worry." (p. 40)

And still another African American woman at an Ivy school reported that her parents had similar attitudes:

> I think money is the big issue, because I think our parents' generation is having a real hard time figuring out why we would choose a life of poverty when we have the option of being very wealthy or in the upper class, when they didn't have the option. For this reason, I couldn't go into any "ologies," no sociology, no psychology, my dad stated that from the beginning. The only "ology" I could go into was biology. (p. 40)

A Latina at an Ivy League school illustrated the narrow range of occupations that her parents thought were acceptable:

> My mom, I don't think she's ever really let go of the idea of my being a doctor. Every so often I'll get a press clipping, "Latino doctors needed in the community." And my mom is, like, "You still have time to take an extra bio course." I'm, like, "Mom, I'm way past that point." That's the things they see as important: doctor, lawyer, engineer. You have an idea of what success is, it's really limited to a number of fields. (p. 41)

This Latina declared that she was going ahead with her plans to become a historian even though her parents were quite upset:

> My father wanted me actually, and my mother also, to be a doctor or something to that effect, an engineer, that I can make lots of money and so on. They've always said how much they've struggled and so on, and they want me, since I have all these opportunities, not to also struggle, so they want me to be financially secure. So at first, I went for psychology, to be a child psychologist and so on,

but I wasn't truly happy. What really made me happy was history, so I switched over there. Even though they're very disappointed in me now, I'm just going ahead with it. (p. 42)

An Asian American male at an Ivy League school gave us some insight into why such a high proportion of Asians, particularly at Ivy League schools, make medicine their first choice:

My decision to become a physician is mainly based on the influence of my family, and I'd have to say the Korean community in Ohio, because it is really close-knit. For some strange reason, a lot of the Korean families in the Midwest seem to be physician-led families. Every Korean family I know in Ohio has a physician in it. I guess that's kind of a strong influence. I'd have to say my family also, like over the past five generations, my family have had a physician. And my brother and I are the only two children in our family, and my brother is not choosing to become a physician, so I kind of just . . . I guess I do have some individual interest in the field, my whole family does not determine my lifestyle. I'd have to say the family is the strongest influence in my career choice. (p. 42)

A young man at a historically black college reported being in conflict with his parents over what career he should pursue:

I came to college to get away from home. I don't know if they're happy I'm here or not. I know they hate that I'm not going to law school and have no interest in being in the law field. I know that my experience with them has always been that their support is very conditional, based on whether or not you are doing what they would have you do with your life. (p. 52)

A Latina at a liberal arts college who is thinking of being a sociology professor described the reaction of her mother:

I don't think my mom is so happy with the fact that I'm a sociology major. "What are you going to be, a social worker? You make no money." She tells me the poor have to go into a field where you can make money or find a job. She thinks that I should have studied something where I can make money. I guess she feels if I've made it this far, I might as well go for it all, go into something that would leave me a lot more than sociology. She thinks I'm just going to be a social worker. I think she would look at a professor as someone who has money, so I think that would be OK. (p. 53)

At a large state university a Latino student described very well the situation of first-generation college goers:

I've noticed that if you are first generation here, every parent wants you to be a doctor. If not a doctor, it's a lawyer. Then once you grow up and find your own life, that goes out the window. You have to choose yourself. So when you were saying did my parents influence my career choice, no way. My parents wanted me to be a doctor just like every other person whose parents were immigrants and came from another country. They want you to have a better life than they did. They want you to shoot for the top. They want you to be the richest person in the world, and being a doctor is being a really big thing, and lawyers too. Growing up, they tried to influence me towards being a doctor; they try to influence you toward the moon and to go to the stars. So you'll always land somewhere. Because if you're not a doctor, you are going to aim high anyway. But they're not going to push you to be a teacher, because it's pretty pathetic. (pp. 53–4)

But other minority students who are interested in academia reported receiving support from their families. An African American woman at an Ivy League college said:

My parents were trying to get out of the ghetto, so they went to college and postgraduate school so they would have money. So they went for the money, they want me to go for the happiness. In that way, my parents have been a tremendous encouragement, especially for me to pursue my music, which they know is most important to me. (p. 40)

An Asian American man at an Ivy school said:

I think my parents would be impressed if I were to be a college professor because I think they just regard college professors as being prestigious and respectable. (p. 45)

White students in the focus groups, unlike students from the other ethnic groups, seem to have experienced little or no pressure from parents to choose or not choose a particular career. Nor do they appear to have felt constrained to follow or not follow in their parents' footsteps. The only exception was a young woman from an Ivy League school whose father reacted negatively to her desire to "help people" (not as a physician):

> He can't understand why I would want to do that. You know, "You've gone to an Ivy League school, you're a chemistry major. Use that to make some money." (p. 43)

Finally, we should note that the students' reports of the degree to which their parents had influenced their career choice does not in any way help to explain the difference between African Americans and whites shown in Panel D of Table 4.1. African Americans were significantly less likely to be interested in academia as freshmen in all three categories of parental influence.

Gender

Although gender was generally not significantly correlated with interest in academia, it was among African Americans: in this racial group 27 percent of males and 20 percent of females expressed a freshman interest in academia as a career. Since a substantial majority of the African American students in our sample were women, we wanted to be sure that gender was not the reason for the observed racial difference in interest in academia. The data in Panel E of Table 4.1 clearly show that African American men and women are both significantly less likely than their white counterparts to express a freshman interest in academia.

Academic Preparation as Measured by SAT Scores

The strongest influence on whether students select the career of college professor as freshmen is their scores on the SAT tests: the higher the score, the more likely the students are to indicate that they are interested in being a college or university professor. For example, looking at Panel F of Table 4.1 one sees that among white students with a verbal SAT score of 700 or higher fully 53 percent expressed an interest in academia as freshmen.

In fact, the data in Table 4.1 show that respondents' verbal SAT score influenced the freshman interest in academia of all four ethnic groups. From the highest-scoring to the lowest-scoring group, verbal SAT makes for a 36 percentage point difference in freshman interest in academia among whites, a 24 point difference among African Americans, a 26 point difference among Asians, and a 24 point difference among Latinos. When we compute mean verbal SAT scores for students expressing an interest in the various occupations, we find a mean of 644 for those expressing an interest in academia as freshmen.[9] All other occupations, including physician, have lower means (622 for physician). Among students with the highest ability as measured by the verbal SAT—that is, those scoring 700 or higher—there is a significant gap between whites and the three minorities. Whereas fully 53 percent of whites in the high-scoring group expressed an initial interest in academia, 37 percent of African Americans, 43 percent of Asians, and 38 percent of Latinos expressed a similar interest.

With regard to African Americans in particular, Panel F of Table 4.1 shows that in every category African Americans are less likely to want to be professors than whites. This difference is statistically significant in the top two categories. Thus, differences between African Americans and whites in verbal SAT scores cannot explain the difference in freshman interest in academia.

Scores on the math SAT and scores on the combined SAT (as seen in Panel H of Table 4.1) also have strong influences on the likelihood of students expressing interest in academia as freshmen. Math SAT scores are not as strong an influence as verbal SAT scores. The mean math SAT score for those expressing a freshman career interest in becoming professors is 667, surpassed by small margins by those interested in becoming physicians (675), researchers outside of the university (682), engineers (681), and computer analysts (681). As for the combined SAT score, students with a freshman interest in academia have the second highest mean score, 1310; those wanting to be researchers outside of the university have a combined mean of 1319, and those wanting to be physicians have a combined mean of 1296.

The mail survey did not have a question on high school GPA; the pretest did. Although the number of cases for minority groups was small on the pretest we found an association between high school GPA and freshman interest in academia for all four ethnic groups (data not shown). This association was not as pronounced as that found for SAT scores. The pretest also had a series of items describing the high school from which the student had graduated, such as whether the school was public, private, or religious, whether it was integrated, whether almost all students who graduated went on to college, and whether a test was required for admission. None of these items was meaningfully correlated with initial career choice of college professor. We were specifically interested in African Americans and Latinos who attended predominantly (80 percent or more) white schools. Attending a predominantly white school made African Americans less likely to want to be a college professor but had no influence on Latinos. For a possible explanation of this anomalous result see our discussion of the work of Claude Steele in Chapters 5 and 8 and of James Davis in Chapter 8.

Differences between African Americans and whites in their scores on the math SAT explain some of the freshman difference in interest in academia as a career. Recall that the overall difference between the two ethnic groups in the proportion interested in academia as a career as freshmen is 12 (Table 3.3). In each of the categories of math SAT (going from the lowest to the highest) we find a 7 point difference, a 9 point difference, a 3 point difference, and an 11 point difference. Thus, in four of the categories of the control variable of math SAT scores the difference is somewhat reduced. But in two of the categories the relationship remains statistically significant. Later we consider the fact that the lower scores of African Americans on the math SAT is an important reason why they are less likely to be interested in academia as freshmen.

The combined SAT score, like the math SAT score, reduces the difference between African Americans and whites in freshman interest in academia in some of the categories. Going from the lowest to the highest, the difference is 7 points, 0 points, 4 points, and 14 points. In all of the SAT variables we find the greatest difference between African Americans and whites in the highest SAT category.

Before leaving the variable of SAT let us consider why whites in the highest SAT category in each of the three SAT variables have higher proportions interested in academia as freshmen than the other ethnic groups. This may be explained simply by the total number of occupational choices each group made as freshmen. Whites made more choices than any of the ethnic minorities. Making many choices of freshman occupational interest is, not surprisingly, strongly correlated with freshman interest in academia (see Panel I of Table 4.1). When we look only at those with the highest SAT scores and control for number of occupations selected as freshman interests, the regression coefficients for ethnicity become statistically insignificant (data not shown).

Number of Occupational Choices as Freshmen

As just mentioned, African Americans make fewer occupational choices as freshmen than do whites.[10] Only 24 percent of whites but 36 percent of African Americans make a single choice as freshmen. And 38 percent of whites versus only 24 percent of African Americans make four or more choices.[11] The fact that African Americans make fewer freshman choices than whites explains some of the difference in their likelihood of mentioning academia as a freshman career interest. Among those who make only one occupational choice there is a 4 point difference between the two ethnic groups in the proportion expressing interest in an academic career as freshmen; among those making two or three choices there is a 7 point difference; and among those making four or more choices there is a 5 point difference. The differences remain statistically significant in two of the categories; but since they are all lower than the original 12 point difference we can assume that the number of choices made as freshmen is one of the explanations for the African American–white difference we are trying to explain. The number of occupational choices made as a freshman may be viewed as an indicator of the scope of a student's interests; thus, these data suggest that African Americans may have a somewhat more limited scope of interests.[12] It appears that among high-achieving students, whites have a somewhat broader scope of interests when they matriculate than do African Americans.

Limited Financial Rewards in Academia

Prior to collecting our data we had hypothesized that students who were more interested in the financial rewards attached to an occupation might be less likely to be interested in an academic career.[13] We also thought that minorities might be more likely to be interested in financial rewards. African Americans and Asians in our sample are indeed slightly more interested in financial rewards than are whites.[14] Latinos are very slightly more interested in financial rewards than whites, but this difference is not statistically significant (data not shown). The only measure we have of the students' interest in financial rewards is a question they answered in their senior year. They were asked to say whether "other jobs offer greater financial rewards" made a career as a professor unappealing. If we are willing to make the assumption that those students who answered yes to this question were more interested in financial rewards and probably were also more interested in such rewards as freshmen, we can see whether this variable influenced freshman choice.

Panel J of Table 4.1 shows that for both whites and African Americans, concern with financial rewards has a significant effect on freshman interest in academia. Concern with financial rewards has no effect on Asians or Latinos. However, this variable does not explain the difference between African Americans and whites because in both categories of this variable there is a statistically significant difference in the likelihood of each of the two racial groups being interested in academia as freshmen.

Political Identification

One question in the mail survey asked the students to describe their political beliefs (see Appendix A, Mail Questionnaire, Q36). We do not feel comfortable making the assumption that a student's political beliefs as a senior are the same as they were when that student entered college. College has been found to have the effect of making students more liberal (Pascarella and Terenzini 1991). The college experience may influence a student's political beliefs, which in turn might influence his or her interest in academia. In general, academics have political views to the left of the general public. This is particularly true at the more selective colleges and universities (Ladd and Lipset 1975; Hamilton and Hargens 1993).[15] We found that for all ethnic groups except Asians there was a statistically significant relationship between political views and freshman interest in academia, with those on the left being more interested than those who described themselves as conservative (data not shown). We do not know if this relationship is causal. But we can say that controlling for political views does not reduce the difference in interest in academia between African Americans and whites as freshmen.

Major Field of Study

We thought it possible that the subjects students were interested in and selected as their major might be correlated with interest in academia. In this case, although the question was asked in the senior year, we feel a bit more confident in assuming that there was a significant correlation between senior major and subject interest as a freshman than we do in assuming a similarity over time in political beliefs. The data show that field of major was significantly related to freshman interest in academia for all four ethnic groups. Perhaps the most interesting finding here is that those students who major in the social sciences are in general less likely to be interested in academia as freshmen. This may be because many social science majors (those who major in political science or economics, for example) may be interested in law or business. Students who major in mathematics and computer sciences we found to be less interested in academia than those majoring in the physical sciences. This is not surprising, given the excellent job market for mathematicians and computer specialists in the new economy.[16]

Major subject, although correlated with freshman interest in academia, does not help explain the difference on this variable between African Americans and whites, since the former are significantly less likely than whites to be interested in academia as freshmen for every major except social sciences and "other" (see Table 4.1).

Interest in Research and Ethnicity

The list of occupations on our mail questionnaire included both "researcher (in a university)" and "university/college professor." For purposes of analyzing interest in an academic career, we combined the two choices. But when we separate them we find that African Americans are less likely than the other ethnic groups to be interested in being a researcher (in a university). The data are displayed in Figure 4.2.

This figure shows the three types of students whom we classified as being interested in academia as freshmen: those who indicated they were interested only in research in a university and did not indicate an interest in being a professor; those who indicated an interest only in professor but not in research in a university); and those who indicated an interest in

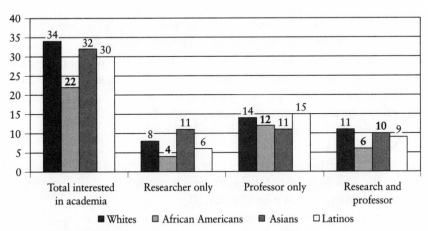

Significantly different from whites, chi-square $p < .05$ indicated by boldface.
Note: The proportion of research/professor among whites does not add up to the three separate groups due to rounding error.

Figure 4.2 Interest in academia as freshmen, by ethnicity

both. When we add the three groups together, we get the total who were classified as being interested in academia. The first panel in Figure 4.2 displays the total interested in either researcher and/or professor and presents the same data as Table 3.4. Of the "researcher only" group, only 4 percent of African Americans and 8 percent of whites made this selection, for a 4 point difference. Of those who selected both, only 6 percent of African Americans and 11 percent of whites are in this group, for a 5 point difference. Adding these differences results in the finding that African Americans are 9 percent less likely to be interested in the "researcher (in a university)" choice than are whites. The overall difference between the two ethnic groups is 12 points. By contrast, if we look at those who said that they wanted to be only professors, we find 12 percent of African Americans and 14 percent of whites, a trivial difference of 2 points.[17] Thus, by combining the two occupations—professor and researcher in a university—to identify interest in academia, we obscured the two different aspects of an academic career that are more and less attractive to students from different ethnic backgrounds.

Although the data in Figure 4.2 effectively illuminate the different foci of interest in academia between African American and white students, they raise the question of why African Americans are less interested in research. Both African Americans and Latinos are also significantly less likely than Asians and whites to be interested in a research job outside of the university. One possible reason is that the type of secondary education African Americans receive does not put as much emphasis on research as the secondary education received by whites. In other words, African Americans may have less interest in any career involving research because they have had less exposure to research in high school than have whites. The lack of interest in research among African Americans probably relates to the concept of effective scope. It is possible that African Americans live in an environment in which they simply are less exposed to research and are less likely to know what it is. This would not be so for teaching, since students of all races are exposed to teaching from kindergarten through high school. (This finding is relevant for policy considerations, and we return to it in Chapter 10.)

There is another possible reason why African Americans may be less likely than white students to be interested in research. Research in the natural sciences and in some of the social sciences requires a certain level of quantitative skills. African Americans have lower scores on the math SAT than do whites. In a logistic regression analysis (not shown) we find that an important reason why both African Americans and Latinos are less interested in research as freshmen is their lower level of quantitative ability as measured by the quantitative section of the SAT.[18] When math SAT scores were controlled there were no statistically significant differences in freshman interest in research at a university among the four ethnic groups.

Conclusions

Initial career choice is one of the strongest influences on final career choice. Among all students, fully 70 percent of those who select university professor as their most likely occupation already indicated an interest in this occupation as freshmen. It is therefore important to understand the variables that influence initial career choice for each of the ethnic groups. There is indeed an important difference related to ethnicity in the likelihood of this freshman choice: African Americans are 12 percent less likely to make it than are whites. We devoted a substantial amount of this chapter to understanding this difference.

First, looking at variables that influence freshman interest in academia as a career, we saw that type of college attended had no meaningful correlation with freshman choice. We had hypothesized that SES might influence the students' interest in a career in academia. African Americans and Latinos do come from lower SES families than Asians and whites, but SES has no meaningful relationship to freshman interest in academia. As expected, having a parent who was a college professor increases the likelihood that the child will be interested in academia when he or she enters college. This was not true, however, for Latinos.

We had expected that parents would try to influence minority group members to go into careers other than academia because parents of minority group students might not be as familiar with the career of academia as parents of white students and because minority group parents might want their children to earn more money than they perceive can be made in an academic career. Although we found a good deal of qualitative support for this hypothesis in our focus groups, the survey data show that the extent to which parents influence the career choice of students was not correlated with interest in academia as freshmen. In Chapter 6 we study how the degree of parental influence on "final" career choice influenced the selection of academia as compared with the four competing occupations, and in doing so we discover that parental influence does have a significant effect. Thus the quantitative data supports what came out in the focus groups.

SAT scores, or the level of academic preparation and ability, is the single most important determinant of freshman interest in academia. The higher students' SAT scores the more likely they are to be interested in academia as freshmen. The verbal score is more important than the math score.

Another variable that had a strong influence on interest in academia as a freshman career was the number of career choices that the student made as a freshman. The more choices the student made, the more likely academia was to be among those choices. We interpret the number of choices made as an indirect indicator of the scope of the student's interests.

Concern over the financial rewards attached to academia had an influence on the freshman career choices of whites and African Americans but not the other two ethnic groups. Finally, students who majored in the social sciences or in math and computer sciences were less likely to be interested in academia as freshmen than students majoring in the natural sciences or humanities.

In examining possible reasons for ethnic differences in choice of career, we found two basic reasons why African Americans are less likely than white students to be interested in an academic career as freshmen. The first is that African Americans are less likely to be interested in research in a university, one of the two occupations (along with professor) that we lumped together as indicating an interest in a career in academia. The reason why African Americans are less interested in research is their

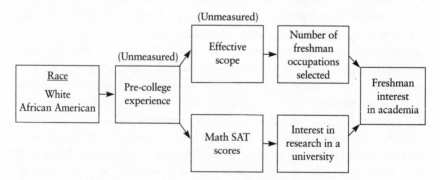

Figure 4.3 Causal model explaining why as freshmen African Americans are less interested than whites in a career in academia

lower level of quantitative preparation as indicated by lower scores on the math SAT. We also speculated that perhaps African Americans had not been as exposed to research in high school as white students.

The second reason why African Americans are less likely than whites to be interested in an academic career as freshmen is that they make fewer career choices as freshmen, which we believe indicates that they have a narrower scope of interests. The reasons for this are undoubtedly some aspect of environmental differences between these two ethnic groups—environmental differences not directly measured by any of the data we collected.

The causal model explaining why as freshmen African Americans are less interested than whites in a career in academia is displayed in Figure 4.3.

5

THE INFLUENCE OF

ACADEMIC PERFORMANCE

Past researchers have found academic performance to have a strong influence on the career choices made by college students. James Davis (1966) found that students with high college grades were more likely than those with low grades to maintain a commitment to "high performance" careers and to be recruited into such careers. Other studies of the career choices of college students have also found college grades to be an important variable (see Chapter 1). In this chapter we examine the influence of college grades on the selection of academia as a career by high-achieving minority students.[1] We also consider the determinants of grades and examine the reasons why African Americans and Latinos get lower grades than whites and Asians even when a measure of academic preparation, SAT scores, is controlled.

Chapters 5 through 8 examine what we have determined to be the most important factors influencing the career choices of high-achieving minority students, particularly their decision as to whether or not to select academia as their most likely career, using the same methodological procedure. We created a large multinomial regression model, containing thirty-three independent variables, aimed at predicting what type of students would select academia as opposed to the other major competing occupations (medicine, law, business, and teaching). Theory and past research suggested that all thirty-three of the variables would have an influence on the decision to become an academic. Our model and the regression coefficients for each of the four ethnic groups are presented in Table B5.1 in Appendix B. An explanation of multinomial logistic regression and its use in this book are presented in Appendix C.

The procedure followed in Chapters 5 through 8 is as follows: first, we examine the effect of a variable, such as GPA, on either the selection of all five competing occupations (where the independent variable is relevant for the occupations other than academia, as it is with GPA) or just for academia alone (where the independent variable would not be relevant for selection of occupations other than academia).[2] If we find that the variable has a statistically significant and substantively meaningful influence on the decision to become an academic, we examine that relationship with all the other variables in the multinomial regression model controlled. This allows us to see whether the relationship between the particular independent variable being examined (here GPA) and selection of academia as most likely occupation is no longer statistically significant when all of the other variables are controlled. If the initial variable of interest, as is the case with GPA, is no longer significant when all the other variables in the model are controlled there are two possible explanations. First, if the reason why the initially significant relationship becomes insignificant is that variables antecedent in time to GPA (such as SAT scores) are causing it to become insignificant, the original causal relationship is spurious. If, however, the reason why the initial significant relationship becomes insignificant is that variables have come into play in the intervening time between the variable being examined (here GPA) and the student's selection of academia, the initial independent variable remains causal, and we have succeeded in specifying the mechanisms through which the variable influences selection of academia. As we shall see later in this chapter, this latter scenario is the case for GPA.

Grades and Occupational Choice

Figure 5.1 shows the association between GPA and selecting academia as a most likely career. Clearly, grades have a strong influence on the selection of academia as a final-choice career. Students with high grades are significantly more likely to select academia than students with lower grades.[3]

As can be seen in Figure 5.1, African Americans are the ethnic group most strongly influenced by academic performance. In fact, African Americans with GPAs of A or A− are three times more likely to want to become college professors than those with GPAs of B or less.[4] The relationship is important but somewhat weaker for the other three ethnic groups, particularly Latinos.

Given the strong effect that grades have on the selection of the career of academia, it is important to compare the grade distribution for the four different ethnic groups. The data presented in Figure 5.2 show that

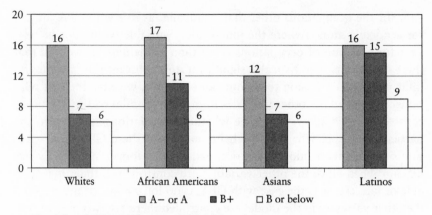

Note: Effect of GPA is significant ($p < .05$) for all four ethnic groups.

Figure 5.1 Percentage of students selecting college professor as most likely, by college GPA and by ethnicity

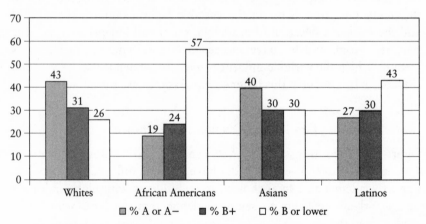

Note: For African Americans and Latinos, distribution significantly different from whites at $p < .05$.

Figure 5.2 Grades, by ethnicity

African Americans by a wide margin get the lowest grades.[5] Latinos get somewhat better grades than African Americans, but both groups have grades substantially lower than those received by whites and Asians. (Whites receive the highest grades, with Asians slightly behind; there is no statistically significant difference between the grade distribution of Asians and whites.) These data have important policy implications. If African Americans and Latinos achieved the same grades as Asians and whites, higher proportions would select both academia and medicine as first-choice careers.

In order to see how the number and proportion of African Americans and Latinos selecting professor as their career would increase if both groups had the same grade distribution as whites we adjusted the figures for the two groups using the grade distribution of whites. In the sample only 19 percent of African American students had GPAs of A or A−; of these, 17 percent selected academia as their most likely career. This yielded a total of 65 African Americans with GPAs of A or A− who said that college professor was their most likely occupation. However, suppose that African Americans had the same GPA distribution as whites. This would mean that 43 percent of African Americans (as opposed to 19 percent) would have GPAs of A or A−. If we make the assumption that the proportion of African Americans with GPAs of A or A− who selected college professor as their most likely career would remain the same (that is, 17 percent), we would have 159 African Americans who had GPAs of A or A− wanting to become college professors. These data are presented in Table 5.1.

If African Americans had the same GPA distribution as white students

Table 5.1 Number of African American and Latino students aspiring to be college professors assuming they had the same grade distribution as white students

Grade	African Americans		Latinos	
	Unadjusted	Adjusted	Unadjusted	Adjusted
A or A−	65	159	65	112
B+	52	70	70	75
B or lower	69	32	58	38
Number wanting to be professor	186	261	193	225
Total N	1,974	2,053	1,540	1,623
Total percent wanting to be professor	9.4%	12.7%	12.5%	13.9%
Percent increase	40%		17%	

Notes: "Unadjusted" refers to the number of students selecting academia as their most likely occupation. "Adjusted" refers to the estimated number of students who would select academia as their most likely career if they had the same grade distribution as whites.

there would be a 40 percent increase in the proportion selecting college professor as their most likely occupation. Since GPA was not as highly correlated with selection of academia as a final-choice occupation for Latinos, if this group had the same GPA distribution as whites there would be a 17 percent increase in the proportion selecting academia as their most likely career.

The data in Table 5.1 contain another interesting finding. Although African Americans with grades of B or lower are only one third as likely as those with grades of A or A— to select college professor as their most likely career (as shown in Figure 5.1), since more than half of African Americans even in our sample had GPAs of B or below, the absolute number of African Americans wanting to be professors is highest among those with the lowest grades.

If some of the African Americans (and to a lesser extent Latinos) in our sample who attended elite schools and ended up receiving relatively low grades had gone to somewhat less selective colleges, they might have obtained higher grades.[6] (We discuss this possibility in Chapter 8.) One of the reasons why African Americans at the elite schools in our sample have grades in the lowest category is that they were competing with white and Asian students who had better academic preparation, as indicated by the fact that on average the African American students' combined SAT scores are approximately 200 points lower. Thus, a significant portion of the African Americans in our sample who receive GPAs of B or lower and who want to be college professors might actually have the skills to become successful academics. As a rough attempt to determine the degree of academic preparation of African American and Latino students in the lowest GPA category who selected academia as their first-choice career, we examined their SAT scores. More than 50 percent of the African American students in this category had SAT scores in our lowest category, less than 1200; but more than 50 percent of Latino students in this category fell into our highest SAT category, 1300 or more. These Latinos in the highest SAT category who end up in the lowest GPA category we consider to be underperforming, a phenomenon analyzed extensively later in this chapter. This suggests why GPA has a relatively weak influence on the decision of Latinos to select academia as their first-choice career. Latinos who have high levels of academic preparation as indicated by their SAT scores decide to become college professors even though they do not get the highest grades. But many of the African Americans in our sample in the lowest GPA category may not have the skills that are necessary to be a successful academic.

Since high levels of academic achievement at the college level are correlated with high levels of achievement at the graduate level, even if African Americans who do not do well in college should apply to a Ph.D. program and be admitted, they are not likely to do as well in graduate school as their peers with higher college GPAs. This means that they will probably be more likely to drop out of Ph.D. programs, where rates of attrition are generally high (Bowen and Rudenstine 1992). If they do not drop out their length of time to degree is likely to be at the long end (ten years or more), and should they succeed in obtaining a Ph.D. in the arts and sciences they might not have the top-level research skills needed to obtain a job in research universities and many selective colleges. Data presented in Chapter 3 suggest that although high-achieving African American college graduates are just as likely as whites and Asians to select academia as a first-choice career in their senior year, data in Chapter 9 show that smaller proportions of African Americans and Latinos actually complete Ph.D.s than whites and Asians. (The same argument made here about African Americans applies to Latinos, but to a lesser extent, as their GPA distribution is somewhat higher than that of African Americans.)

Our point is that in addition to how many Ph.D.s are awarded to underrepresented minorities such as African Americans and Latinos educators must be concerned with the extent to which these Ph.D.s have the research skills necessary to do well in the highly competitive world of research universities and selective colleges. Many academics believe that just as the standards for the college degree have been substantially watered down over the last forty years, the standards for Ph.D. degrees have also been substantially watered down. In order to get a Ph.D. in sociology prior to the late 1960s, for example, it was necessary to pass examinations in both French and German. In the late 1960s many graduate schools lowered their language requirements and students were required to pass an examination in only one language, which they could select. Nowadays most Ph.D. programs in sociology require no foreign language skills at all.

Some might argue that although it is true that standards in some areas, such as knowledge of foreign languages, have declined, standards in other areas, such as statistics and quantitative methods, have gone up. While it is true that in order to get articles published in leading journals sociologists must be familiar with quantitative methods much more complex than those learned by earlier students, the actual level of methodology and statistics required for the degree in most programs is rudimentary; and in some programs it would not be unusual for students who have barely learned these low-level methods (e.g., statistics usually required for undergraduate majors) to be awarded the Ph.D. degree. Today we have a phenomenon in some academic disciplines that could be called the "terminal Ph.D." These are students who get a Ph.D. but have no chance to get a full-time academic job. Some of them go into industry; many of them work as low-paid adjuncts. Some departments grant such Ph.D.s because they need graduate students in order to justify the existence of their graduate program and the low teaching loads that go along with having such a program.

To our knowledge there is no systematic research on whether or not and to what extent the quality of skills held by Ph.D. recipients have actually changed since the 1950s. This is an interesting and important question, but one well beyond the scope of this book.[7] But whether or not there has been a decline in standards for Ph.D.s, a substantial majority of Ph.D.s end up doing little or no research (J. R. Cole and S. Cole 1973; S. Cole 1992, Chapter 9). If we are to increase faculty racial diversity in our research universities and selective colleges, we must not only increase the numbers of minorities earning Ph.D.s in the arts and sciences; we must also increase the number of minority Ph.D.s who actually have active and successful research programs.

As we pointed out in Chapter 3, substantial portions of these high-achieving students in each of the four ethnic groups are interested in academia as a possible career when they enter college, but by the time they graduate only about 10 percent select academia as their most likely career choice. This means the factors that influence persistence with freshman-year interests are extremely important. We found grades to be correlated with persistence for all four ethnic groups; but for reasons not readily apparent GPA had a somewhat stronger influence on the persistence of white students than on the three minority groups (data not shown). GPA had a strong influence on recruitment into academia for all four ethnic groups. Although the total number of recruits is not great in each of the ethnic groups, students with A or A− GPAs were at least three times as likely to be recruited into academia than students with GPAs of B or less (data not shown).[8] All the data presented thus far in this chapter underscore the great significance of raising the academic performance of African Americans and Latinos as a means of getting more of them to select academia as a first-choice career.

106

How Grades Influence the Selection of Career

In order to study the question of how grades influence the selection of academia as a career and its four main competitors (medicine, law, business, and teaching), we used multinomial logistic regression, a technique used to study a dependent variable with several categories that cannot be ranked. This is true in the present case, where we are simultaneously looking at how GPA and other variables influence the selection of six categories of occupations: professor, doctor, lawyer, businessperson, teacher, and "other" (all the other occupations included in the study combined). The technique also enables you to control for many more variables than do simpler tabular techniques where it is difficult to control for more than two variables. In the following analysis we have converted the results of our multinomial logistic regressions into proportions for easier interpretation. The actual regression models are presented in Table B5.1 of Appendix B.

In Figure 5.3 we show separately for each ethnic group the predicted probability of students in that group selecting each of the five leading occupations by GPA.[9] The predicted probabilities displayed in Figure 5.3 are based on the assumption that GPA has a linear effect on selecting the different occupations as final choices. In fact, the effects of GPA are not exactly linear; but for the purpose of illustrating the importance of GPA on students' decisions, making the assumption of linearity is legitimate.

First let us consider the influence of GPA on our occupation of major concern, academia. For white students, GPA is strongly related to the selection of academia as a career (Figure 5.3A). In the lowest GPA group (B− or less) fewer than 5 percent of white students select academia as their first-choice career, and for students with these grades it is the least popular career choice among the top five competing occupations. For whites in the highest GPA group (A) about 20 percent select academia as their most likely occupation, and it is the most popular choice. When we look at the actual data instead of the predicted probabilities based on the assumption of linearity we see that the proportion of whites selecting academia as a first-choice career remains relatively low through GPAs of 3.3 and then sharply increases for students with GPAs of 3.7 through 4.0, with a particularly large jump for students in the highest GPA category. These data emphasize one of our main conclusions: the commonsense finding that students who do very well in college are much more likely to

A. Whites

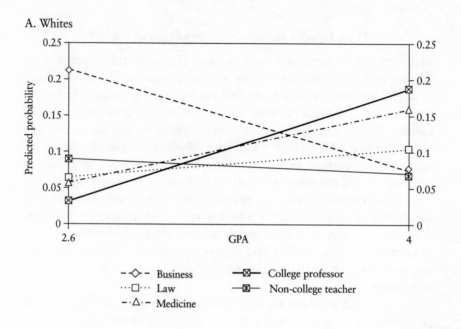

B. African Americans

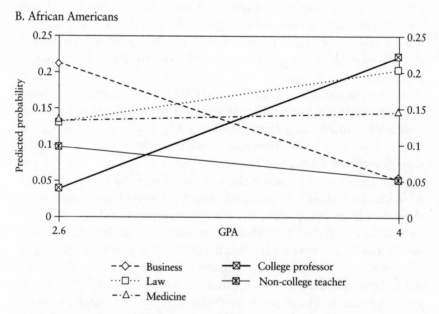

Figure 5.3 Predicted probability of students wanting to be top five occupations, by GPA. A: Whites. B: African Americans. C: Asians. D: Latinos.

C. Asians

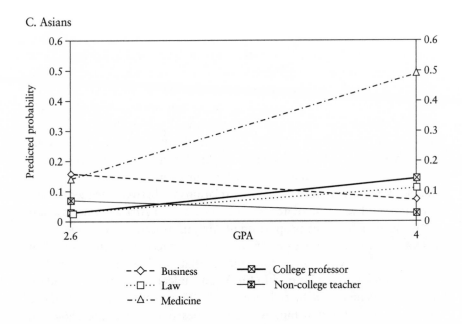

D. Latinos

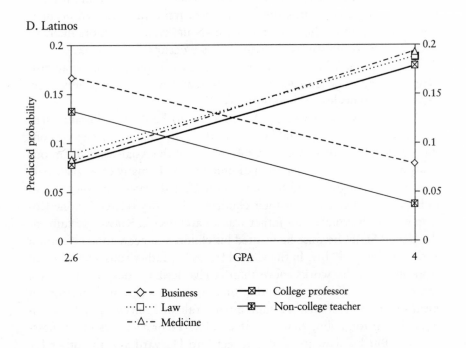

want to become college professors than students who do not do very well.

For African Americans (Figure 5.3B) the relationship between GPA and desire to become a college professor is also strong, almost identical to that observed for white students. In the lowest GPA category only about 4 percent of African Americans select academia as their most likely occupation and among the top five occupations it is the least likely to be selected by a significant margin. However, at the top of the GPA scale more than 20 percent of African Americans select academia as their first-choice career and it is the most likely occupation. No other evidence in this book indicates more clearly the relationship between academic performance and selection of academia as a career for African Americans. If we want to increase the proportion of African Americans who select academia as their first-choice career we must be concerned with raising that group's level of academic performance to that of whites and Asians.

If we look at the relationship for Asian students between GPA and selecting academia as a first-choice career (Figure 5.3C) we also find a strong positive relationship. Academia goes from being the choice of about 2 percent in the lowest GPA group to about 13 percent in the highest GPA group, where it is the second most frequently selected occupation. Asians with the highest grades are about seven times more likely to select college professor as their first-choice occupation than those with the lowest grades. Physician is the preferred occupation for Asian students at every grade level accept the lowest, and even there it is only a few percentage points lower than business.

The reasons why so many Asians want to be doctors became very clear in the focus groups and in some of the individual interviews we conducted (see the quotes in Chapter 4). Many of the Asian students in our study are immigrants or children of immigrants. In many cases their parents sacrificed a good deal to come to the United States, and they did so in hopes of a better life for their children. The story related by one Korean student is typical. Her father was an architect in Korea. He came to the United States because he wanted his children to get a good education and "get ahead" in life. In the United States her father runs a small retail store in which he works more than twelve hours a day, seven days a week. His view of getting ahead in life, however, is extremely narrow: it means going to Harvard (or, failing that, Yale or Princeton) and becoming a doctor (or, failing that, a dentist, a lawyer, or a successful businessperson). But his daughter failed to get into Harvard and the other Ivy

League schools; instead, she was in an honors program at a state university. This fact alone was enough for her parents to begin to think of her as a failure and a disappointment to them. The fact that she wanted to be a sociology professor rather than a doctor was even more upsetting. Throughout college they put pressure on her to change her major to pre-med, a field in which she had no interest. Parental pressure was so great that in her junior year she started to take pre-med courses. When we interviewed her she was highly ambivalent about what occupation to pursue. She had no interest at all in medicine or the allied health professions; but she didn't want to disappoint her parents, who did not hesitate to remind her constantly of how much they had sacrificed for her benefit. Given the narrow definition of success that many Asian parents have, it is not surprising that a high portion of Asian students enter college as pre-med students and that a large majority of those who do well enough to get into medical school end up pursuing medicine as a profession.

Although the parents of African American students were for the most part not immigrants, many of them have worked very hard to rise from poverty into the middle class. They also tend to have a relatively narrow definition of "getting ahead," though this attitude is not as pronounced among African American parents as it is among Asian. In order to fulfill their parents' expectations, African American children have to be doctors, lawyers, or successful businesspeople—not professors. As we shall see in Chapter 6, the stronger an influence parents have on career selection, the less likely African American and Asian students are to select academia as their most likely choice.[10]

For Latinos in the lowest GPA category about 8 percent select academia as their first-choice career; virtually the same percentage select law and medicine (Figure 5.3D). As GPA increases the proportion selecting all three of these occupations (professor, lawyer, doctor) rises at the same rate; at the highest GPA level slightly less than 20 percent select each of these occupations.

Now let us briefly consider the relationship between grades and the selection of the major occupations competing with academia. As shown in Figure 5.3, there is a strong association between grades and the choice of physician as a final-choice occupation for all the groups except African Americans. This relationship is not surprising, as it is difficult to be accepted into medical school unless one has a relatively high GPA. Students know this, and if their GPA is not high they are likely to select an occupation other than physician. When we ran the multinomial regression model with all thirty-two independent variables (other than GPA) controlled, we found that GPA also had a significant influence on the selection of medicine as a first-choice career by African American students.[11] When all thirty-two variables are controlled African Americans with high grades are about two and a half times as likely as those with low grades to want to be physicians. This means that one or more variables in our regression model are "hiding" the effect of GPA on African American students' selection of medicine as a first-choice career. Since occupations other than academia are not the primary focus of this book, we leave the identification of these variables for future research.[12]

Figure 5.3 also shows that for every ethnic group there is a relatively strong *negative* relationship between GPA and selecting business as a most likely career. Figure 5.3C might suggest that the relationship is weaker for Asians; but this is in fact not the case. Asians with low GPAs are more than three times as likely to select business as their most likely career than Asians with high GPAs. The line looks flatter than it does for the other ethnic groups because in absolute terms there are fewer Asians at the low GPA point who want to be businesspeople than is true for the other three ethnic groups. Once again, the low numbers are explained by the overwhelming interest of Asians in medicine. The reason for the negative association between GPA and selecting business as a first-choice career may be that business can be entered without going to graduate school, so those interested in other occupations that require high grades (such as academia and medicine) are likely to switch into business as a second-choice career if they do not do well in school. Or perhaps those students initially interested in business as a career know that grades are not as important for their career success as they are for those interested in careers such as academia and medicine, so they do not try as hard in school. The negative association between GPA and the selection of business as a career remains significant for all four ethnic groups (although for white students the association becomes very weak) when all thirty-two variables in the model are controlled (data not shown).

Figure 5.3 also shows that GPA has a significant effect on the selection of law as a most likely career for all ethnic groups except African Americans. When all thirty-two variables are controlled, we see that for both African American and white students there is no significant independent relationship between selecting law as a first-choice career and GPA. The failure of GPA to have an influence on the selection of law did not surprise us. On the surface the lack of relationship may seem strange given the tremendous competition to get into the handful of elite law schools. It is as hard to get into elite law schools as it is to get into elite colleges. However, if we consider the entire range of law schools in the United States the lack of correlation becomes more understandable. Many law schools have relatively low admission standards and accept a good portion of students willing to pay the tuition. One white student at a state university told us that he had taken the exam to get a job with the county police and had also applied to a local law school. He was unable to obtain the job as a police officer but was admitted to the law school.[13]

In Figure 5.3 we also observe a negative association between GPA and the selection of teacher as most likely career, although the negative association is not meaningful for white students. Hardly any Asians at any GPA level wanted to be teachers, but those with low GPAs were four times more likely to select this career than those with high GPAs. Among African Americans and Latinos Figure 5.3 shows a clear decline in the proportion selecting teaching as their first-choice career as GPA goes up. Perhaps students who did not do as well academically as they had expected selected teaching as a second- or third-choice career (much as we hypothesize for the choice of business).

Explaining the Influence of GPA

As pointed out earlier, when we control for all of the variables in the full multinomial regression model GPA becomes statistically insignificant (see Table B5.1). There are two possible reasons why this could be so. First, if the variables in the model that are antecedent in time to GPA are causing GPA to become insignificant, then the effect of GPA would be spurious and our analysis above erroneous.[14] Alternatively, variables interceding in time between GPA and career selection may be in play. This explanation, unlike the first, is welcome because it gives us useful information; it tells us the mechanisms through which GPA has its effect. Here is a simple example to help explain how intervening control variable(s) add to our understanding. Suppose we find that women professors publish fewer articles than men professors. We want to know why. The only way to conclusively find out why is to have data on some third variable (or several additional variables) that intervene between gender and publications in time and that, when controlled, will "wash out" the effect of gender on publications (that is, in the case of multinomial regression, make the original independent variable statistically insignificant). Suppose we hypothesize that the reason why women publish less is that they have family responsibilities that reduce the amount of time and energy available for publication. In this case we would control for family status, comparing the publication rates of men and women who were unmarried, married with no children, married with one child, married with two children, and married with three or more children. If our hypothesis is correct, when the family status variable is controlled gender would become statistically insignificant: there would be no difference in publications between men and women.[15]

In order to determine the reasons why GPA becomes insignificant when the full model is controlled, we broke up the full model into parts, and then step by step entered sets of variables in the model into the equation to see what the results would be. The results of this analysis are presented in Table 5.2. The first row of Table 5.2, "Base," shows the percentage differences we find in Figure 5.3. Thus Figure 5.3B shows that for African Americans there is an 18 point percentage difference between the proportion of students with the lowest grades and those with the highest grades who want to become professors. This percentage difference is one simple way to measure the influence of GPA on wanting to become a professor.[16]

Table 5.2 Strength of influence of GPA on decision to become a professor with other variables controlled, by ethnicity

Model type	Whites	African Americans	Asians	Latinos
Base	17	18	12	13
Spurious	15	17	14	14
Self-confidence	12	8	6	5
Academic activities	6	2	1	−2
Full model	3	2	2	−2

Note: Figures show the percentage difference between those with the highest and those with the lowest GPA wanting to be professors. The base model contains only GPA. The spurious model contains school type, combined SAT, SES, freshman aspirations, college major, and GPA. The self-confidence model contains all variables in the spurious model plus academic self-confidence. The academic activities model contains all of the variables in the preceding model plus whether or not the student participated in a professor program/summer research program/own research project, if the student had an academic role model and faculty contact. The full model contains all variables listed in Appendix B, Table B5.1.

In Table 5.2 we can see what happens to the percentage difference (the strength of GPA) as we control for different sets of variables included in the full regression model. First, we begin by controlling for those variables in the model that might be considered antecedent in time to GPA. These factors, which are listed in the note to Table 5.2, include such clearly antecedent variables as SAT scores and SES. Comparing the percentage differences in the row labeled "Spurious" with those labeled "Base" we can see that there are no meaningful differences. In fact for Asians and Latinos the percentage difference actually goes up very slightly. This means that GPA has not become insignificant as a result of controlling for the antecedent variables in the model, so the causal effect of GPA is not spurious.

In the next step we introduce only one additional variable that intervenes in time between GPA and occupational choice: academic self-confidence. This variable is discussed at some length in the next section of this chapter. Here we are only interested in its effect on the relationship between GPA and the selection of college professor as the most likely occupational choice. Since the percentage differences when self-confidence is controlled (in addition to all of the antecedent variables) are substantially lower than the base, we can conclude that self-confidence is an important reason why GPA influences the selection of college professor as the most likely occupation. In other words, a causal chain is at work. Getting good grades increases academic self-confidence, and academic self-confidence leads students to select academia as their first-choice career. Thus, when self-confidence is controlled we can substantially reduce the effect of GPA. Academic self-confidence here is like family status in the example we gave earlier. It is a primary reason why GPA has its effect. In the next row of Table 5.2, "Academic activities," we introduce variables that were both influenced by GPA and in turn had an influence on the choice of professor. For example, as indicated in the note to Table 5.2, one of the variables in this category is having conducted one's own research project. Generally only students with relatively high GPAs conduct their own research projects, and (as explained in Chapter 6) conducting one's own research project has a significant independent effect on wanting to become a college professor. When variables such as these are controlled, the percentage difference for GPA is reduced even further, becoming slightly negative for Latinos. To be consistent with our later analyses, in the last row of Table 5.2, "Full model," we show the percentage difference when the full model is controlled. Adding in the variables not already controlled for has little effect on the influence of GPA, since the variables not previously controlled for were not correlated with GPA. Thus this "stepwise" procedure of entering parts of the full model separately has allowed us to identify which variables were responsible for making GPA insignificant in the full model. The most important of these variables was academic self-confidence, and it is to a discussion of the influence of this variable that we now turn.

As is the case throughout this book, given that all the data were collected at one point in time, in the students' senior year, establishing causality is difficult. Academic self-confidence is a variable that probably works in two directions. Students who enter college with academic self-confidence probably get higher grades in college independently of both their high school GPA and their level of academic preparation as measured by the SAT score. And of course getting high grades in college is the most important determinant of academic self-confidence. In this case we believe, but have no way of proving, that the influence of GPA on academic self-confidence is substantially stronger than the influence of initial academic self-confidence on GPA.

Academic Self-Confidence

We have found that having self-confidence in one's academic ability is an important influence on the decision to become a college professor. Not surprisingly we found that the strongest influence on academic self-confidence was college GPA. Students with the highest GPAs were substantially more self-confident than those with lower GPAs (data not shown). We employed two measures of academic self-confidence by asking students two questions. The first was: "In general, comparing yourself with *all* people your age, how would you rate your academic ability?" There followed five choices: among the highest 10 percent; above average; average; below average; and among the lowest 10 percent. The second question was worded similarly, but instead of asking the students to compare themselves with all others in their age cohort it asked them to compare themselves with "seniors at this college" or their classmates.[17] In analyzing the data we combined the categories "average" with "below average" and "among the lowest 10 percent," since not many students in this generally elite sample placed themselves in the bottom categories.

Figure 5.4 shows the relationship between both types of academic self-confidence and the probability of selecting academia as a most likely career for each ethnic group. Both types of self-confidence are strongly related to the selection of academia. Those who defined themselves as being in the top 10 percent academically were substantially more likely to select academia as a career than those who had lower levels of academic self-confidence.

Because academic self-confidence has such a strong influence on the selection of academia as a career it is important to see the ethnic distribution on these variables. This is shown in Figure 5.5. On both measures of self-confidence white students are most likely to think of themselves as being in the top 10 percent and the least likely to think of themselves as

A. Classmate self-confidence

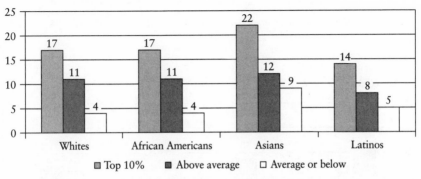

Note: Academic self-confidence is significant at $p < .05$ for all four ethnic groups.

B. Age cohort self-confidence

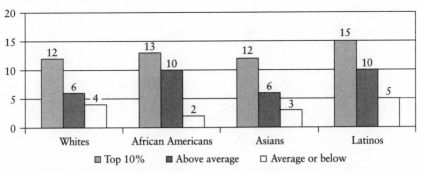

Note: Academic self-confidence is significant at $p < .05$ for all four ethnic groups.

Figure 5.4 Percentage of students selecting college professor as most likely career, by two types of academic self-confidence and by ethnicity. A: Classmate self-confidence. B: Age cohort self-confidence.

A. Classmates

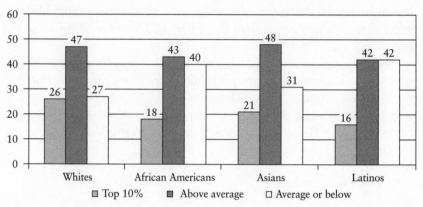

Note: Distribution for African Americans, Asians, and Latinos differs from whites $p < .05$.

B. Age cohort

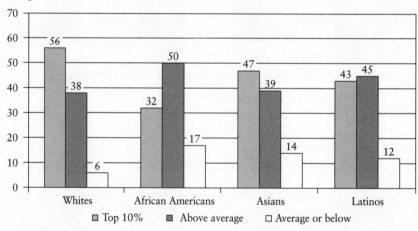

Note: Distribution for African Americans, Asians, and Latinos differs from whites $p < .05$.

Figure 5.5 Two measures of academic self-confidence, by ethnicity. A: Classmates. B: Age cohort.

being average or below. Next came Asians, followed by Latinos, with African Americans having the lowest levels of academic self-confidence. The reader should note that this is the exact order of the four ethnic groups in the distribution of their grades shown in Figure 5.1.[18] Just as we did with GPA, we wanted to see what proportion of African American and Latino students would select college professor as most likely career if they had the same level of academic self-confidence as white students. Using the same technique of standardization as we did for grades (Table 5.1) we came up with the figures shown in Table 5.3. Adjusting for cohort self-confidence would increase the proportion of African Americans wanting to be college professor by 124 percent; and for Latinos, 87 percent. Adjusting for classmate self-confidence has a smaller but still important effect. For African Americans it would increase the proportion selecting college professor by 20 percent and for Latinos by 38 percent. Clearly, the relatively low levels of academic self-confidence of African

Table 5.3 Unadjusted and adjusted number of African American and Latino students aspiring to college teaching, by age cohort academic self-confidence

Self-confidence	African Americans		Latinos	
	Unadjusted	Adjusted	Unadjusted	Adjusted
Cohort self-confidence:				
Average or below	4	3	5	5
Above average	53	77	42	62
Top 10%	47	153	59	132
Number wanting to				
be professor	104	233	106	198
Total N	1,073	1,149	934	1,000
Total percent wanting to				
be professor	9.7%	20.3%	11.3%	19.8%
Percent increase	124%		87%	
Classmate self-confidence:				
Average or below	34	24	30	40
Above average	93	107	79	93
Top 10%	57	89	53	91
Number wanting to be				
professor	184	220	162	224
Total N	1,967	2,053	1,554	1,623
Total percent wanting to				
be professor	9.4%	10.7%	10.4%	13.8%
Percent increase	20%		38%	

Notes: "Unadjusted" refers to the weighted number of students aspiring to college teaching; "adjusted" refers to the estimated weighted number of students who would aspire to college teaching if they had the same self-confidence distribution as whites.

Americans and Latinos are keeping down the proportions wanting to be college professors.

There is a much greater difference between African Americans and Asians on the one hand and whites on the other on cohort self-confidence than on classmate self-confidence. This is why adjusting for the former has much more of an effect than adjusting for the latter. We believe that the reason for the differences in the two types of self-confidence have to do with comparative reference groups. When a student thinks of his or her classmates these are people he or she knows. Perhaps these other people in their class that they are considering are of the same ethnicity as they are. A national cohort, however, is a group one does not know, and estimation of relative academic ability in this case could be heavily influenced by scores on standardized tests such as the SAT. This interpretation is supported by examining the correlation between SAT scores and the two types of self-confidence. The correlation between combined SAT scores and cohort self-confidence is as follows: for African Americans, $r = .35$; for Latinos, $r = .40$; for Asians, $r = .49$; and for whites, $r = .48$. But if we look at the correlations between SAT scores and classmate self-confidence we find the following results: for African Americans, $r = .05$ (not statistically significant); for Latinos, $r = .18$; for Asians, $r = .24$; and for whites, $r = .25$. Thus, for every ethnic group SAT scores are much more highly correlated with cohort self-confidence than with classmate self-confidence.

Figure 5.6 shows the effect of classmate self-confidence on the selection of college teaching as the most likely occupation. It is very clear that among students with low levels of academic self-confidence virtually no one wants to become a college professor. Among those with high levels of academic self-confidence the proportion wanting to be college professors varies from 14 percent for Asians to 21 percent for Latinos. These data are drawn from a multinomial regression that showed the effect of self-confidence on selection of each of the other four leading occupations. Since the results are so similar to those for GPA, we need not report them or discuss them in detail here. For all four ethnic groups, when self-confidence was low, college professor was the least popular of the five leading occupations; when it was high, college professor was the most popular of the leading occupations, except for Asians. For Asians, again, medicine was the most popular occupation at every level of self-confidence. For African Americans at the highest level of self-confidence law tied with academia as the most popular choice.

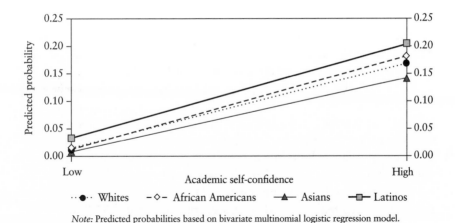

Note: Predicted probabilities based on bivariate multinomial logistic regression model.

Figure 5.6   Predicted probability of selecting college professor as most likely career, by academic self-confidence and by ethnicity

To make sure that academic self-confidence when compared with classmates was not spurious, we ran a regression in which we controlled for all the antecedent variables (see note to Figure 5.3) plus GPA. With all these variables controlled, self-confidence continued to have a strong independent effect on selection of academia as a first-choice occupation. In fact, when all of the variables in the regression model were controlled, the effect of academic self-confidence was reduced in size but still significant among the three minorities, but not whites. This means that there are some variables intervening between self-confidence and selection of academia that could explain how self-confidence works. In general, they are the variables we call "academic activities" in Table 5.2; exactly which ones they are is not important here. What is important is how powerful a variable academic self-confidence is when it comes to the selection of college professor as a first-choice career. This is well illustrated in Figure 5.6 and by the fact that academic self-confidence is the most important variable through which GPA has its influence on the choice of college professor as most likely occupation.

The Problem of Underperformance

Since grades have an important influence on wanting to be a professor, we should examine in more detail the influences on GPA. The correlation we are particularly interested in is that between SAT scores and GPA. To-day there is a movement for colleges and universities to stop requiring standardized tests like the SAT as a requirement for admission.[19] Al-though some critics of the SAT have substantive reasons for wanting to do away with the test (claiming, for example, that it causes teachers to teach to the test; see, for example, Sacks 1999), the primary reason be-hind this movement is the fact that African Americans (and Latinos to a somewhat lesser extent) have SAT scores that are much lower than those of whites.[20] This came up in Chapter 2 when we looked at the distribu-tion of the SAT scores in 1992 of all students who took the exam in that year broken down by ethnicity. These data show that if a highly selective college wants to maintain a diverse student body and if SAT scores are one important criterion for admission, of necessity the school must admit African Americans and Latinos with lower SAT scores than those of re-jected white and Asian students. It is this practice of racial preferences that has led to debate and litigation over affirmative action and racial preferences in admission.[21]

Before looking at the influences on grades (particularly SAT scores), we should note some of the difficulties in studying them. A 1994 study conducted by the Educational Testing Service (ETS) (Ramist et al. 1994) reveals some of the pitfalls of relying on freshman GPAs (the standard practice) in determining the reliability of the SAT (that is, how well it pre-dicts grades).[22] That study shows that freshman grades are significantly influenced by the type and difficulty of the courses selected by students. Practically all colleges in the United States give students a good deal of latitude in the selection of courses. Students who select quantitative and science courses tend to get lower grades than students who select courses that do not require quantitative skills or are in the humanities and the so-cial sciences. Leonard Ramist, Charles Lewis, and Laura McCamley-Jenkins (1994) argue convincingly that a specific college course grade (af-ter sufficient controls for difficulty, restriction of range, and validity have been made) is a more meaningful dependent variable than GPA.[23] They found a correlation of approximately $r = .70$ between SAT scores and grades in particular courses. For the social sciences this is a very high cor-relation and indicates that SAT scores are a good predictor of academic performance.

Ramist and his colleagues found also that African American students, even though they took easier courses than whites, received lower grades, and that their grades, when properly measured, represented a significant underperformance from what one would expect from both SAT scores and high school performance (Ramist, Lewis, and McCamley-Jenkins 1994). According to this source, the courses in which African Americans are the most likely to underperform are, for the most part, science and laboratory courses. (As we indicated in Chapter 4, African American students are less likely than students in the other ethnic groups to enter college with an interest in doing research because of their lower levels of quantitative skills.) By "underperformance" here we mean that African American students get lower grades than what would be predicted on the basis of their SAT scores and high school GPAs. To put it another way: if we consider a group of African American students and a group of white students all of whom have the same SAT scores and the same high school GPAs, the African Americans will on average get significantly lower college grades than the whites.

The phenomenon of underperformance of African Americans (and to a lesser extent Latinos) has been noted and studied for many years. Robert Klitgaard (1985) points out that studies of underperformance arose from the belief that tests like the SAT might be biased against racial or ethnic groups such as African Americans. If this were true, then African Americans should do better in college than white students with the same SATs. However, in every study done on the topic, just the opposite was found: African Americans with the same SAT scores as white students get lower grades in college. To our knowledge there are no methodologically sophisticated researchers today who believe that any meaningful part of the difference in SAT scores between African Americans and whites can be explained by bias in the tests (for one of the latest researchers to reach this conclusion see Jencks 1998). Klitgaard (1985) reaches a stunning conclusion:

> For students having test scores one standard deviation above the mean—that is, moving out toward the right tail [these are exactly the type of students in our study]—the overprediction of blacks' grades compared to whites' is about half a standard deviation. For colleges whose average students are in this range, this overprediction corresponds to about 240 points on the combined SAT verbal plus math, holding high-school grades constant. *In other words, to have unbiased prediction for blacks compared to whites, you would have to subtract about 240 points from the blacks' test scores.* (p. 164, italics added)[24]

In part because SAT scores overpredict the grades of African Americans, some educational researchers have believed for years that SAT scores are a better predictor of the performance of whites in college than the performance of African Americans. In fact, in our data the correlation between GPA and combined SAT scores is $r = .26$ for whites, $r = .29$ for Asians, $r = .19$ for Latinos, and only $r = .11$ for African Americans. We should point out that we have done none of the things which Ramist and his colleagues (1994) emphasize must be done to make a correlation between SAT scores and GPA accurate; that is, we have not taken into account the difficulty of courses taken, nor have we corrected for restriction of range or validity. Restriction of range is a particularly important problem in our study because our sample is limited to high-achieving students and therefore we have very few students with SAT scores below 1100. Although our data also show a lower correlation between SAT and GPA for African Americans than for other ethnic groups, we do not think that this means that the SAT scores would not be good predictors of African American academic performance *in particular colleges*.

Let us consider why the correlation coefficient between SAT scores and GPA for African Americans is so low in our sample. We believe that this is in part a consequence of affirmative action. The best-prepared African Americans, those with the highest SAT scores, are most likely to attend elite schools, especially the Ivy League (see Chapters 2 and 8). Because of affirmative action, these African Americans (those with the highest scores on the SAT) are admitted to schools where, on average, white students' scores are substantially higher, exceeding those of African Americans by about 200 points or more (Herrnstein and Murray 1994).[25] Not surprisingly, in this kind of competitive situation, African Americans get relatively low grades (see Chapter 8 for a detailed analysis). It is a fact that in virtually all selective schools (colleges, law schools, medical schools, etc.) where racial preferences in admission is practiced, the majority of African American students end up in the lower quarter of their class (Klitgaard 1985). African Americans with lower SAT scores go to less elite schools, where they generally get about the same grades as African Americans in highly selective schools. Thus, partly due to affirmative action, there is little difference in the GPAs of African Americans who score high on the SAT and those who score lower—hence the low correlation.[26]

If we consider African Americans who scored 1300 or higher on the combined SAT and compare them with those who scored less than 1200, we will find a difference of only 11 percentage points in the proportion earning A− or higher averages. Making the same comparison for whites, we find a 24 point percentage difference. If we make the same comparison within each type of school included in the study we find a 9 point difference for the liberal arts colleges,[27] an 18 point difference for the Ivy League, a 27 point difference for the state universities, and a 29 point difference for the HBCUs. These data strongly support our hypothesis that the reason for the relatively low correlation between GPA and SAT scores for African Americans is in part affirmative action. As Ramist and his colleagues (1994) show, when one does adequate nonbiased correlations, one finds that SAT scores are just as good an indicator of African American school performance as they are of white school performance.

Let us now examine the extent of underperformance among the students in our sample.[28] The data are presented in Table 5.4. The data show the grade distributions for each ethnic group, controlling for combined SAT scores. We have broken down African Americans into those who attend predominantly white elite schools, those who attend predominantly white state universities, and those who attend HBCUs. When we examined the data for African Americans prior to dividing them into three different groups, we found what everyone else studying this topic has found: within each SAT category African Americans got lower grades than whites. Dividing the African Americans in the way we have enables us to gain some insight into the reasons for their underperformance, which have up to now not been well understood.

When we compared the extent of underperformance of African Americans at all the predominantly white schools in our sample and HBCUs it became clear that African Americans do not underperform at HBCUs. Looking at African Americans with SAT scores of 1300 or higher who attend all the predominantly white schools in our sample we see that 27 percent received GPAs of A or A− compared with 51 percent of the white students (data not shown). Of African Americans with SAT scores of 1300 or higher attending all the predominantly white schools, 48 percent had GPAs of B or less compared with only 19 percent of white students (data not shown). Similar levels of underperformance were found at lower SAT levels.

Table 5.4 demonstrates that African Americans at predominantly white schools, Latinos, and Asians (to a much lesser extent) underperform white students with the same SAT scores.[29] Asians in fact do not significantly underperform whites. In a full regression model, including all

Table 5.4   GPA, by SAT, by type of school, by ethnicity (GPA 2.8 or higher) (percent)

| Combined SAT scores | Whites | African Americans | | | Asians | Latinos |
		Elite	State	HBCUs		
1300+						
A or A−	52	24	43	55	50	36
B+	30	36	17	12	31	33
B or less	17	40	39	33	19	31
Total	99	100	99	100	100	100
1200–1299						
A or A−	33	14	23	38	26	23
B+	34	29	27	16	32	35
B or less	33	56	50	46	42	42
Total	100	99	99	100	100	100
Less than 1200						
A or A−	28	6	16	26	20	20
B+	39	24	24	31	31	29
B or less	33	69	60	42	49	51
Total	100	99	100	99	100	100

the variables that we found to influence grades, the coefficients for African Americans and Latinos remain significant with all the variables controlled; but the coefficient for Asians is almost zero and therefore, of course, not significant (data not shown). Thus, although we present data for Asians in Table 5.4 (and 5.5), we will not discuss them.

When we first put together the data for Table 5.4 we simply divided African Americans into those attending predominantly white schools and those attending HBCUs. Since it was clear that the African American students attending predominantly white schools underperformed and those attending HBCUs did not, it would have been easy to jump to the conclusion that there was something about the atmosphere on the predominantly white campuses that was not present at HBCUs and that caused the underperformance—perhaps some forms of subtle or not-so-subtle institutional racism. However, it then occurred to us that before we could make this conclusion we had to examine differences among the predominantly white schools in our sample. Some of them—the elite schools— were highly selective, and African Americans attending these schools were at a competitive disadvantage with the white and Asian students.

At the state universities the white and Asian students were more nearly similar to the African American students in their level of academic preparation. Thus, African American students would not be at as much of a competitive disadvantage at the state schools. This observation led to two hypotheses as to why African American students might be underperforming in the predominantly white schools. One was the difficulties (including decline in academic self-confidence) that students at a competitive disadvantage might encounter (discussed at length in Chapter 8). The other was related to the racial composition of the student body.

The data presented in Table 5.5 allow us to determine the extent to which the underperformance was a result of both of these school characteristics. Comparing the proportion of African American with the proportion of white students at the elite schools who reported GPAs of A or A− at all three SAT levels (see Table 5.5), we can see that the extent of underperformance of African Americans at these schools is strong. Is the reason for this that these elite schools are predominantly white or because African American students there are at a competitive disadvantage? Looking at the data for the levels of underperformance of African Americans attending predominantly white state universities, we can see that these students still underperform white students but that the level of underperformance is about half of what it is at the elite schools. The difference in degrees of underperformance between African Americans at elite schools and at state universities may be a result of being at a competitive disadvantage.[30] Now compare African American students at the state universities with those at the HBCUs. The underperformance of the African American students at the state universities compared with the lack of such underperformance at the HBCUs is probably a result of factors that are present on predominantly white campuses that are not present at predominantly black schools.

Table 5.5 Percentage difference with GPA of A or A− compared with whites

Combined SAT scores	African Americans			Asians	Latinos
	Elite	State	HBCUs		
1300+	−28	−9	3	−2	−16
1200–1299	−19	−10	5	−7	−10
Less than 1200	−22	−12	−2	−8	−8

Researchers who have studied underperformance have all found that the extent of underperformance is greatest in the higher SAT categories. This is certainly true for African Americans at predominantly white elite schools and Latinos, as can be seen clearly in Table 5.5.[31]

Explanations of Academic Underperformance

Although many efforts have been made to explain why minority groups achieve lower grades than their SAT scores predict, thus far, to our knowledge, none of these explanations has been empirically confirmed. Frederick Vars and William Bowen (1998), after showing the extent of underperformance in selective schools included in the College and Beyond data set,[32] suggest that this phenomenon can only be explained in two ways. First, there might be some variables affecting African Americans and whites differently before they take the SAT that do not affect SAT scores but do affect GPA. Vars and Bowen have some evidence suggesting that this type of explanation is highly unlikely to explain more than a very small part of the underperformance differential.[33] Based on what we have learned in conducting this study, we agree with them. If underperformance is not a result of the first type of explanation then it must be a result of the second: what happens to African American students after they enter college. Vars and Bowen do not give any specific examples or present any data on what these conditions might be.

The data presented in Tables 5.4 and 5.5, however, provide convincing evidence that the underperformance phenomenon is a result of problems that African Americans encounter at predominantly white schools. Some of these problems result from being at a competitive disadvantage as a result of affirmative action; others simply have to do with the racial composition of the schools.

Because we thought it was possible that some of the difference in grades between African Americans at predominantly white schools and those at HBCUs were due to different school grading policies, we ran a regression in which we looked only at whites and African Americans, and divided the African Americans into those who were at predominantly white schools and those who were at HBCUs. We controlled for SAT scores; all thirty-four institutions in the sample (using dummy variables), to make sure that the difference is not a result of different grading policies at the different schools; and field of major. We found that the OLS regression coefficient for African Americans at predominantly white schools was −.205, indicating that on average in this elite sample with truncated range on GPA the average African American students at predominantly white schools (with SAT scores the same as the white students) had a GPA about two tenths of a point below that of the average white student. The coefficient for African Americans at HBCUs was a positive .109, meaning that African Americans attending HBCUs (with SAT scores, institutional grading patterns, and field of major controlled) received GPAs one tenth of a point higher than all the white students in the sample. It is of course possible that the school effect might be a result of uncontrolled selectivity, just as Dale and Krueger (1999) found that the Bowen and Bok (1998) "selectivity" of school effect was an artifact of uncontrolled selectivity. However, it is difficult to think of possible ways in which African Americans who choose to go to an HBCU would have characteristics differing from African Americans who choose to attend a predominantly white school that would make them less likely to underperform.

Another theory to explain the academic underperformance of African Americans has been proposed by Claude Steele, a social psychologist at Stanford University. In his paper "A Threat in the Air: How Stereotypes Shape Intellectual Identity and Performance" (1997), Steele expounds his theory and then presents the results of some laboratory experiments that appear to provide strong support for it.[34] Since Steele's theory is so important, we present a brief summary here, and in Chapter 8 we look at how this theory might explain some of the results of our research.

Steele writes that in the United States a negative stereotype exists, portraying African Americans as being less intelligent than whites. He then argues that fear of invoking or confirming this negative stereotype causes African American students to experience an unusual amount of anxiety when taking standardized tests. The elevated level of test anxiety in turn causes lower levels of performance. Of crucial significance is Steele's contention that the fear of invoking the negative stereotype influences primarily those students who are identified with the "domain" for which academic performance is significant. In the case of African American students, those who have disidentified with school (that is, do not care about it and do not measure their self-esteem in terms of their academic performance) are not as subject to this fear of invoking negative stereotypes as are African American students who do identify with the domain of school and do gauge their self-worth by how well they do in school. Since students with high SAT scores (those who have been relatively successful in school) are more likely to identify with the domain of school than those with lower SAT scores, this could explain the higher levels of underperformance at high SAT levels that many researchers (including ourselves) have found.

Steele also stresses that while the fear of stereotyping may be generally felt, it is especially likely to be activated in particular situations. (In Chapter 8 we suggest that affirmative action may create conditions conducive to activating the negative stereotype.) At the same time, certain interventions (Steele calls them "wise" interventions) can deactivate this fear and thus improve the performance of stereotyped groups. Steele supports his theory by a series of experiments in which he removes the threat of stereotyping and finds that when this is done, underperformance vanishes.[35] It is important to realize that even after they are desensitized from the fear of stereotyping African Americans do not perform as well as whites in general, but only as well as whites who have the same SAT scores. Thus, Steele's theory is useful, not in explaining the large SAT gap between African Americans and whites, but in explaining underperformance holding SAT constant.

There is a further important question. Presumably test anxiety (including that caused by stereotype threat) was present when the minority students studied by Steele, by Vars and Bowen, and by us took the SAT exam—which is used in all cases as a control for level of preparation. Thus, the African American SAT scores should have been lowered by test anxiety to a level below their real scholastic preparation levels. Therefore, if one could remove the stereotype threat as a source of test anxiety, the stereotyped groups might be expected to do even better than the nonstereotyped groups within SAT categories.[36]

Of course SAT scores are not the only determinant of GPA. The model that Vars and Bowen (1998) ran included gender (because women usually get higher grades) and whether or not the student was an athlete (because athletes usually get lower grades). We looked at the correlation between GPA and a large number of variables for each ethnic group. But when we ran a regression model with all of these variables included, it reduced the level of underperformance of African Americans and Latinos by only a very small amount. For example, controlling for nineteen additional variables other than SAT, the level of underperformance for African Americans was only reduced by 4 percent. However, as we pointed out earlier, the level of underperformance for Asians, which was relatively small to begin with, was reduced to zero when we controlled for these additional nineteen variables. (See Table B5.3.)

Additional Hypotheses to Explain Performance Differences

Because it is not possible to explain away the academic performance differences between African American and Latino students on the one hand and white and Asian students on the other, let us consider some hypotheses in addition to Steele's that may explain them. In each case, where possible, we use whatever data are available from our main survey or pretest in order to test the validity of the hypothesis. Since our surveys were not designed to answer this type of question, we frequently use crude indicators and do not expect to show large effects. Yet any confirming or disconfirming evidence may be useful to future researchers.

Hypothesis: College professors discriminate against African American students. It is certainly possible that college professors, either because they have been consciously or subconsciously influenced by negative racial stereotypes or because they are actually prejudiced, may give minority group students lower grades for the same-quality work as whites. Some African American faculty have told us that they believe that such behavior is widespread—not only among white professors, but also among African American professors. They attribute this not only to stereotyping and prejudice but also to the probability that white students are more likely than African American students to complain about a "bad" grade (a B+ in our elite schools). According to this hypothesis, professors presumably are simply trying to forestall complaining by those students who they suspect will do so.

We believe that there are two reasons why this hypothesis is unlikely to explain much of the underperformance gap. One is a technical reason: in many college courses (particularly the large ones), professors do not know the students to whom they are assigning grades. Indeed, in some large courses, grades are based on multiple-choice tests that are machine graded, and the final grades are determined simply by adding up these grades. In such large courses, professors rarely know anything about the students except their ID numbers. Even in small classes blind grading procedures are sometimes utilized. The second reason has to do with the political attitudes of faculty. Many surveys (Ladd and Lipset 1975; Ham-

131

ilton and Hargens 1993) have shown that college professors as a group are far to the left of the general population (this is especially true in the social sciences and humanities). It is unlikely that professors with such political attitudes would have a "taste" for discrimination (Becker 1957). Even if some professors do discriminate against minority students, there are probably at least as many who discriminate in their favor—thus canceling the effect of professorial attitudes on grade distribution.

We tested the discrimination hypothesis using data both from the pretest and the main survey.[37] On the pretest, one item asked students whether they felt they had been harassed by faculty because of their racial or ethnic background. Presumably, if students felt they were being discriminated against in grading, they would be more likely to respond "yes" to this question. When we controlled for this item in a regression equation showing underperformance, we saw no meaningful change in the level of underperformance of African Americans and Latinos (data not shown). One item on the main survey asked students whether they agreed or disagreed with the following statement: "Some faculty members at this college have made my undergraduate experience more difficult because of my racial/ethnic background" (see Appendix A, Mail Questionnaire, Q16). Again, if students believed they have been discriminated against in grades, they would have been more likely to agree with this statement. Adding this item to the regression model has no effect on the extent of underperformance of minority students (data not shown).

In short, the effects of these indicators of perceived discrimination are minuscule, and we may conclude that the existing data do not offer any support for the hypothesis of discrimination by faculty. Of course, it remains possible (but we believe unlikely) that minority students are discriminated against in grading and are not aware of it.

Hypothesis: Differences in academic preparation are inadequately measured by SAT scores and high school GPAs. As we pointed out earlier, differences in academic preparation should not be correlated with SAT scores but should be correlated with grades. It would not be surprising if, for example, we were to find that minority students who attended predominantly white high schools do better academically than those who attended predominantly minority high schools. But the presumably better quality education they received at the predominantly white high schools should also influence SAT scores, and unless such a variable influenced college GPA considerably more than SAT scores where minority students attend high school could not be a cause of underperformance. Also, there may be some aspects of family background, such as emphasis placed in the home on schooling and discussion of ideas, that may not be highly correlated with SAT but might effect grades in college.

The only way to test this hypothesis is to control for high school characteristics and other measures of family background and see if the coefficients for African Americans and Latinos are reduced in the regression on GPA. For such a test, the only available data was from our pretest. The results were discouraging. Attending a high school that is more than 80 percent white had no statistically significant effect on college GPAs of African American and Latino students. Attending a predominantly minority high school has negative, but not statistically significant, effect for African Americans. Since we assume that predominantly white high schools are more likely to be in affluent areas and to be better schools, this finding is somewhat puzzling. One speculative conclusion is that those minority group members who attend primarily white schools may be burdened by the fear of negative stereotyping hypothesized by Steele, and this may have a negative influence on their ability to learn in high school. More research is clearly needed on this point.

We also found that attending private (nonreligious) high schools or a high school in which most of the graduates go to college has no effect on the college grades of minorities. This is further evidence that attending "good" high schools does not seem to have a positive payoff in college GPA for minority students. We also found that attending a private religious school had a small but statistically significant *negative* effect on GPA for African Americans and Latinos and a very small but significant positive effect for Asians (data not shown). Attending a high school that requires an admission exam had no statistically significant effect on the GPA of any of the minority groups.

Let us now consider the results of our analysis of the effects of family background variables (see Appendix A, "Pretest Questionnaire"). Twenty-four questions on the pretest measure aspects of the students' family background and how well they got along with their parents. When we ran an equation predicting GPA that included all twenty-four items (data not shown) whether or not a given item is statistically significant,[38] the result reduced the amount of underperformance for African Americans by about a third.[39] Although the results based on these pretest data must be treated very cautiously, it does seem that aspects of family background that are not accounted for by the traditional measures of SES may have a small influence on the underperformance of African American students.[40] Meredith Phillips and her colleagues (1998) have found that measures of family background reduce the black-white test gap. Further research is required on this topic.

Hypothesis: Underperformance results from the fact that studying hard and competing violate subcultural values of Latinos and African Americans. Acceptance of the value of academic success and therefore caring about grades are treated in certain subcultures as selling out to the white establishment. This is a cultural version of Claude Steele's "disidentification" hypothesis discussed earlier. We hypothesize that African Americans and Latinos may reject academic success because they adhere to subcultural norms supporting disidentification and in some ways punishing identification.

The effects of the subculture described above may occur in high school (Fordham 1996), but many African American and Latino students who attend relatively selective colleges grow up in predominantly white neighborhoods are not exposed to an ethnically based student subculture prior to entering college. As several qualitative accounts of the experience of minorities in college have suggested, (see, for example, Institute for the Study of Social Change 1991, which deals with Berkeley), when these students enter college, they are welcomed by existing students in their ethnic group. The older students then socialize the new students into a more or less militant subculture whose attitudes toward the norms of "racist" white society include disidentification from the domain of school. As described in the study about Berkeley just cited, many phenotypically white Latino students find it especially difficult to accept the demand that they become part of the appropriate ethnic group on campus.

There are several reasons why we believe that this hypothesis is not likely to explain much of the underperformance gap. Many high-achieving African American students, such as those we have in our sample, have very high career aspirations. More than half want to be doctors, lawyers, or academics. They know that in order to pursue these career goals they must get relatively high grades. In addition, qualitative data from our focus groups suggest that some African Americans feel that their academic performance reflects not only on their own ability but also on that of their ethnic group. If they underperform, then, it is not because they have rejected the domains of education and achievement but, more likely, as Steele suggests, because they so strongly identify with them.

We used our pretest data to test the hypothesis that subcultural values can explain underperformance. These data provide three rough measures of the extent to which students may be involved in the ethnic subculture on campus. They were asked whether they "participated in campus protest/demonstrations," whether they "attended a racial/cultural awareness event or workshop," and whether they "participated in a racial/ethnic student organization." Adding up the number of positive responses to these three items, we created what we call a racial/ethnic participation index, with scores from 0 to 3. According to the subcultural values hypothesis, students who receive a high score on this index should have higher levels of underperformance. For all three minorities the cultural values index when controlled dropped the level of underperformance, although the size of the drop was smallest for African Americans (data not shown). Thus, both Asians and Latinos who score 3 on the index have a significantly higher level of underperformance than those who score 0 on the index. African Americans who score 3 on the index also have a greater level of underperformance than those who score 0, but the difference is not so large as to be statistically significant.[41] Thus we may conclude that our pretest data (contrary to our expectations) give some support to the cultural values hypothesis as an explanation of the underperformance of minority group students. Two of the three variables included in the racial/ethnic participation index (participation in a racial/ethnic student organization and participation in a campus demonstration) were included on the main survey, so we used a truncated racial/ethnic participation index on our main survey data to test this hypothesis. We found that the numbers went in a direction consistent with the subcultural values hypothesis, although the results are not statistically significant for any of the minority groups.[42] As with our other tests, this one uses relatively crude indicators of subcultural values and thus we must be cautious about accepting these results.[43] Nonetheless, this hypothesis deserves more research.

Hypothesis: Minority students are in different social networks from whites, and this may account for differences in grades. It is hypothesized that in general the networks of white students consist of better students than those of African American and Latino students. Therefore, when students turn to peer groups for academic support, white students may get more and better academic support than African Americans and Latinos. Students in white networks may, for example, be better informed about an individual faculty member's grading characteristics and may be more likely to avoid courses taught by professors who give relatively low grades.

Some data from the pretest may be used as a very rough surrogate measure of network participation. Respondents were asked if they have a close friend on campus who is African American, Asian American, white, or Latino. According to the hypothesis, perhaps African Americans and Latinos who have as a close friend a white or an Asian student will have better contacts with students who are more academically competent than those who do not have such close friends. However, when these variables are added to the model the coefficients for friends are negative and the underperformance of minority groups increases very slightly (data not shown). These data offer no evidence in support of the network theory. But given the inadequacy of our network measure, this theory is definitely worth further pursuit.

Hypothesis: African American and Latino students assume that, because of affirmative action programs, they do not need as high grades as whites in order to get into law, medical, or graduate school. Given this assumption, they are less likely to work hard to achieve high grades.

It seems to us not at all likely that this hypothesis can explain much regarding the underperformance phenomenon. Even if some African American and Latino students may be aware that they will benefit from affirmative action programs at the postgraduate level, they are likely to know also that in order to be admitted at all they must have good grades. At most schools practicing race sensitive admissions, minority students admitted under these programs are good students, but they do not have as high qualifications as white students. Thus, for example, even though there is tremendous self-selection in influencing who applies to American medical schools, slightly more than half the African Americans applying to American medical schools are rejected by all the schools to which they apply (Association of American Medical Colleges 1991).[44] The difficulty of getting into medical school and the best law schools, business schools, and arts and science Ph.D. programs, even with race sensitive admissions policies in effect, is widely known. It is therefore unlikely that African Americans will not study hard because of affirmative action.

We can test this hypothesis by using data from the pretest. A three-part question asked whether "it would be harder or easier for members of an underrepresented racial/ethnic minority (a) to get into a Ph.D. program in the arts and sciences, (b) to get a job as a professor, (c) to have a successful career as a professor." Again we constructed an index by counting how many times the student said "easier." We believed that students who more often said "easier" were more aware that they might be the beneficiaries of affirmative action. Controlling for whether or not students think that their ethnicity will make it easier for them to get into graduate school should reduce the coefficient for African Americans and Latinos. But our calculation indicated that a belief that affirmative action makes it easier to pursue a career in academia had no influence on underperformance (data not shown). We may conclude that there are no data in our study to support this "affirmative action" hypothesis.

In summarizing all the analyses we have done on the various possible explanations of the underperformance phenomenon, we may conclude that there is some good evidence supporting Claude Steele's theory that fear of stereotyping is an important factor.[45] There is also some evidence that aspects of family background not correlated with simple measures of SES might help explain some of the grade gap between minorities and whites, and that subcultural values may also do so. The other theories we tested did not yield any positive results. In some cases the theory may simply be wrong; in others our data may be inadequate. The latter is especially likely for the network theory.

Conclusions

Students with higher grades are more likely to want to become college professors and physicians. Students with lower grades are more likely to want to become businesspeople and teachers. Grades have little influence on the choice of law. In general students with higher grades are also more likely to persist with a freshman interest in academia and to be recruited to an interest in academia during the course of college. Our data show that if African Americans and Latinos had the same grade distribution of white students, there would be a meaningful increase in the proportion selecting academia as a first-choice career.

Grades have a strong influence on academic self-confidence, which is one of the reasons why GPA influences occupational choice. But academic self-confidence has an effect independent of GPA on wanting to become a professor. If African Americans and Latinos had the same levels of academic self-confidence as white students there would be a large increase in the proportion wanting to be college professors.

African Americans and Latinos underperform white students. Even when SAT scores (used here as a measure of academic preparation) are controlled, these groups get lower grades. African Americans who attend HBCUs, however, do not underperform significantly; and African Americans who attend elite schools are much more likely to underperform than African Americans who attend nonelite schools. This suggests that the cause of underperformance is the type of experiences that African American students have at predominantly white institutions that they do not have at HBCUs (some of these experiences may be a result of affirmative action policies practiced by the predominantly white schools). Underperformance is greatest for African Americans and Latinos who have the highest SAT scores. This evidence supports Claude Steele's theory that fear of invoking negative racial stereotyping increases test anxiety and thus performance for those minority students who care most about school. It is not unreasonable to make the assumption that those who do well in school (receive relatively high SAT scores) care more about school than those who do not do as well in school.

We examined five hypotheses aimed at explaining underperformance of minority groups. In our data (from both our pretest survey and our main survey) we found no evidence to support the hypothesis that professors discriminate against African American and Latino students in their grading. We did find that some variables measuring academic preparation and family background (not taken into account by our index of SES) serve to reduce the level of underperformance of African Americans and Latinos. We also found some evidence to support the hypothesis that underperformance results from the fact that studying hard and competing for good grades violates subcultural values of minority group students. We found no evidence that differential social networks of minority students explains underperformance, nor did we find any evidence for the hypothesis that because of knowledge of affirmative action programs African American and Latino students do not make as much of an effort as white students to do well in school.

Although our data suggest findings that are far from conclusive, they should be looked upon as guideposts for future research.

6

ATTITUDES TOWARD ACADEMIA

The results of our survey show that approximately one third of freshmen and one third of seniors express an interest in a career as a university professor. There are no significant differences in interest in this occupation between minority and white students.[1] Our data also show that students with an interest in becoming university professors tend also to be interested in other occupations. In fact, it is not at all unusual for graduating seniors to apply simultaneously to graduate school and a professional school (such as law school) and not make a career choice until they find out which schools they have been admitted to (Barber and Cole 1996a). However, when it comes to making a final decision as to whether to go to graduate school with the goal of entering academia or to pursue another occupation, a majority of students with a stated interest in being a university professor select some other occupation (see Chapter 3). This chapter continues our exploration of why this occurs by examining students' perception of university professor as an occupation.

Based on our qualitative research (as well as personal experience) we selected a series of ten aspects of life as a university professor that might be appealing to students and ten that might be unappealing (see Appendix A, Mail Questionnaire, Q7 and Q8). What is there about being an academic that resonates positively or negatively in terms of the students' values, and how do these responses differ by ethnicity?

In general, for all ethnic groups, the most appealing features of academia involve the two primary tasks performed by academics: teaching and research. The students also find appealing the life of an intellectual. As for possibly unappealing features, as the possibility of relatively low pay and prestige is not the most important factor deterring students from entering an academic career. However, as explained later, for African American and white students financial concerns about the amount of money they could earn as professors did have an independent negative effect on their decision to select academia as a final-choice career. Financial concerns did not have any effect on Asian or Latino students. Perceived difficulties in getting a job or attaining tenure had no influence on the decision to become a professor. The unappealing factors, which differ somewhat for each ethnic group, include the perception that it takes too long to get a Ph.D.; the feeling on the respondents' part that they are unwilling to be students any longer; and the idea that the career of professor emphasizes research rather than teaching.

What Makes a Career as College Professor Appealing

All students who completed our survey, including those who had never expressed any interest in an academic career, were asked to indicate which of ten aspects of academia might make the career of college professor appealing to them. In Table 6.1 we show the responses given to each of these items by each ethnic group.[2]

Table 6.1 Percentage of students indicating which of ten aspects would make the career of university professor appealing, by ethnicity

Factor	Whites	African Americans	Asians	Latinos
The opportunity to teach undergraduates	63	**56**	63	63
To live and work in the world of ideas	69	**56**	66	65
Academic knowledge can be used to improve public policy	49	**54**	46	**59**
The opportunity to mentor minority students	28	**84**	**47**	**67**
Academia is relatively liberal and tolerant	44	37	37	41
Professors are under less pressure than doctors or lawyers	24	23	24	25
Living in an academic community would be attractive	58	**33**	52	52
I got really involved in the subject of my major	56	56	53	**60**
I would get a lot of satisfaction from doing research	42	37	40	47
Professors have a lot of time off	44	**38**	35	38

Note: Significantly different from whites at $p < .05$ indicated by boldface.

Teaching and Research

Perhaps the most important point about the findings related to the appealing characteristics of academia, from a policy point of view, at least, is that every ethnic group is substantially more likely to see the opportunity to teach undergraduates as an appealing aspect of the career than the chance to do research. Thus, although research is crucial for a professor's career advancement (at least in research universities), what attracts many academically high-achieving students to the occupation of professor appears to be the teaching, not research. Data from the focus groups give us insight into the students' attitudes toward both teaching and research.

An African American woman at an Ivy League school indicated that it was teaching that attracted her to the profession:

> As far as being a professor, it was like coming here and realizing that professors have this key, this tool, that they can sort of expand the horizons of all their students. I want to have that power. I want to write, as well, but my primary goal for getting a Ph.D. is to be able to teach and to make something click with my students. (Barber and Cole 1996b, p. 26)

A Latino at an Ivy League school indicated how important teaching was to him:

> It's great that I know so much, but it would be even greater if I could pass that knowledge on to someone else. Furthermore, just interacting with students, you yourself are learning more every day, just by what they are saying. Think about that. But you're also helping them learn. It's like back and forth, it's a learning process. (p. 11)

An Asian American woman at an Ivy school said that if she did become a professor, she would want to do it only for the sake of teaching:

> If I did it, it would be because I would want to teach. When I see a professor in my department who really, really loves what he's doing, it shows. It's like, "Wow! I'd like to be like that." It's the imparting of enthusiasm to future generations. (p. 13)

141

A student at a historically black university said:

> I think it would be exciting to be a college professor because each
> semester you get new students. And you can only get out of the
> classroom what you put into it. If you're doing your best and put-
> ting your all into each class, then you will get your all out of the
> class. So I think it can be exciting. (p. 14)

The focus groups also yield some vivid evidence of the students' attitudes toward doing research. An Ivy League Latino had been turned on
to the excitement of research by prior experience at another school:

> I've had a lot of research experience, and I think you have to do
> research before you can say you want to go to graduate school.
> I've worked in labs at Penn State, where I had to do 7 days a week
> testing, getting into the lab at 7 A.M., and I loved it. There's this
> sense that you're doing the stupid preparation for the project, get-
> ting stupid stimuli together, the stupid stimuli won't do what you
> wanted, the computer program won't work, the subjects don't
> show up . . . Then you come to the point that everybody says intu-
> itively should be the most boring part, the data analysis. But you
> plug it into the computer and you're like "Yes!" Nobody knows
> what a point value .0001 means. What it means is that you're not
> an idiot. You actually came up with something that works. It's not
> lonely work, it's important. (p. 12)

A young woman at a historically black college saw her future in research
and publishing:

> I'm a real research-based type of person, and I'll probably be doing
> a lot of research like most of the big-name professors do at the
> large research universities. I love writing and I love reading and I
> like political things and that's what kind of fuelled me to go into
> English and pursue a career as a professor of English. (p. 18)

Mentoring Minorities and "Doing Good"

Prior to the survey we had expected that minorities might be attracted to
academia by the opportunity this career offered to mentor minority students or to do work that might be useful in solving some of the problems faced by minority groups in society. As the data in Table 6.1 show,
minority students were significantly more likely than whites to see the

opportunity to mentor minority students as a positive aspect of being a university professor. There were relatively small differences, however, among the four ethnic groups in the extent to which they saw a career in academia as offering an opportunity to develop knowledge that might be socially useful. In the focus groups we did find minority students who saw both mentoring and ability to bring about change in the larger society as appealing aspects of becoming a university professor. A woman in molecular biology at a state university explained that she was going to graduate school in order to become a role model for other African American college students:

> I'm not here to win a Nobel Prize. That's not why I came to graduate school, so I could just be like Ms. God in Molecular Biology. I mean, I came here eventually to be a professor and help. Take this back to my community, and make other people see that this graduate school thing is a viable option for everybody. So, I mean, I have a different agenda in being here. (Barber and Cole, 1996a, p. 12)

Similarly, for a Latina at an Ivy League college getting a Ph.D. was a way to help her people by being an effective role model:

> In terms of Latino, there should be more of them in higher education. If we really want to become more institutionalized, more of an active role in college or government, whatever it be, we can't just say, like a lot of people do, "This country is not helping me." The thing is that maybe you're not actually in the system, and the reason why is we don't have the proper degree. Now you got to get a Ph.D. and have a little more of an edge than the other person. I just think people should go to higher education because it's an example. I think the best gift you can give to another person is to be a good example. (p. 11)

Our quantitative data show only a small difference in the importance attributed by minority students and whites to the ability to influence public policy (see Table 6.1). Yet in the focus groups we found that the ability to influence public policy may be particularly important to some minority graduate students. Some of these students told us that doing something to help their community was an important motivating factor in their decision to go to graduate school. An African American man, a graduate student in history at an Ivy League school, wanted to write his dissertation on issues of race and identity because treatment of this topic would be socially useful. It was through his undergraduate experience that he reached this point:

I went to Middlebury College in Vermont, and I was very active in student government and took courses in black history and political science, sociology, and as I began to consider possible career choices, I saw the activities of professors being both very much involved in bringing about change through their writing, educating other people, and I saw that was something I would like to do. (p. 13)

A Latina graduate student at an Ivy League university saw her graduate study as leading directly to something she defined as useful for Latino children:

I decided to go to graduate school in education and linguistics because I wanted to do something where there is work and I'm also interested in second language acquisition. I'm primarily interested in the underrepresented population in the United States, in terms of learning English as a second language and how they are marginalized in the school and society because of language problems. I'm trying to make a difference there. (p. 13)

Another Latina graduate student at an Ivy League university explained why she planned to go back to Puerto Rico after receiving her doctoral degree:

A lot of people are leaving the island for the United States. I feel that I have to go back because somebody has to. Besides the fact that I loved it there. They need people with Ph.D.s. They don't have a whole lot of people with Ph.D.s at the university that I was at for computer science. So that would be a great thing. (pp. 13–14)

Autonomy

We had hypothesized that the autonomy of academia would be an appealing aspect of the career. Yet relatively small portions of the students indicated that they found "Professors are under less stress than doctors or lawyers" or "Professors have a lot of time off" to be appealing aspects of the career. Perhaps, not having really participated in the world of work, the students have not come to appreciate autonomy as an aspect of their profession, or perhaps at their age this is just not important to them. Their answers may suggest a lack of knowledge of what it is actually like to work in different occupations, and this may be relevant for policy purposes.

In the focus groups a few students saw autonomy and flexible working hours as appealing aspects of the profession. Typical of these students was a woman in an HBCU:

> I wouldn't trade the academic setting for going to work from 9 to 5. I would not do that if you paid me a million dollars because I don't like that environment. As a college professor you have a lot of time. I know professors who take their whole summers, go to another country to study a topic, and just do whatever it is that [is] their life love or their academic love, and they dedicate most of their time to it. I think that's beautiful, because now I have all these other classes I have to fulfill, when I wish I had the time to actually figure out the things that I don't have time to figure out in my major, because I'm so busy doing this other stuff. (Barber and Cole 1996b, p. 17)

What Makes a Career as College Professor Unappealing

All students who completed our survey, including those who had never expressed any interest in an academic career, were asked to indicate which of ten aspects of academia might make the career of college professor unappealing to them. In Table 6.2 we show the responses given to each of these items by each ethnic group.

As can be seen from Table 6.2, the one aspect of academia that the students were most likely to say was unappealing is that there is too much emphasis on research and publications rather than teaching. This was the most frequently mentioned unappealing item for all four ethnic groups. In addition, almost half of the students indicated that "other jobs offer greater financial rewards" was an unappealing aspect of academia. Each of the minority groups was significantly more likely to mention this as an unappealing factor than were white students. Only a small minority of students, however, thought that academia had less prestige than other jobs. Finally, while past studies of the decision to go to graduate school have shown that debt and financial factors were strong considerations

Table 6.2 Percentage of students indicating which of ten aspects would make the career of university professor unappealing, by ethnicity

Factor	Whites	African Americans	Asians	Latinos
Other jobs offer greater financial rewards	42	**51**	**49**	**46**
Academia is very competitive	36	**20**	40	33
I don't think I have the ability	19	**11**	**28**	17
Getting a Ph.D. takes too long	36	28	33	33
It is hard getting a job in academia	46	**33**	**55**	47
There is too much emphasis on research and publications rather than teaching	58	**53**	60	60
It is very hard to get tenure	33	**40**	**46**	**38**
I don't want to be a student any more	30	**22**	**23**	**22**
Other jobs have more prestige	11	**17**	14	13
I am in too much debt to consider a Ph.D.	19	**23**	21	**29**

Note: Significantly different from whites at *p* < .05 indicated by boldface.

(J. Davis 1964), our study indicated that concern with debt was only a minor factor deterring students from considering a career in academia.

As mentioned earlier, we found an overemphasis on research as opposed to teaching to be the most unappealing aspect of the career of college professor for all four ethnic groups. Again, to help us gain insight into the attitudes of the students toward both research and teaching, we turned to the qualitative data from the focus groups. Students revealed a variety of negative, or at least ambivalent, attitudes toward research. For example, an Asian American at an Ivy League school saw the necessity to publish as an unattractive aspect of the career:

> My impression is that if you go into academia, you're going to be stuck in the professor life, and after going for four years for your Ph.D. [note the lack of knowledge of how long it really takes to complete a Ph.D. degree] you're going to have to publish and publish and publish. I mean, just for myself, I like to think about law. (Barber and Cole 1996b, p. 12)

An Asian student whose father is a professor said that he wanted to teach but didn't want so much "other pressure":

> My father is a college professor, so I have some insight into what college professors actually do. In general, I'd like to be a professor

some day but, again, I don't want to be under too much pressure. That's the bottom line. I'd love to teach but I don't want all that other pressure that has nothing to do with teaching. (p. 12)

An African American woman at a black university decided against academia because she was not particularly interested in research: "I considered being a professor, like in my sophomore year, and I still haven't ruled it out. I just am not sure that it is the path I want to take, because I'm not particularly fond of research" (p. 18). A Latina at a liberal arts college decided not to become a professor because she didn't like doing research:

I thought for a long time about doing research and becoming a college professor; but I decided not to, because I really don't like research. I just saw the life style of people that are doing research. It really takes forever, and you have to be in the lab all the time, and it's very competitive. That's not the type of life that I want to have. I decided that's not for me. It's really isolated from people, too, so that's something I didn't like either. It's just getting to know people that were doing it that made me decide I didn't want to do it. (pp. 19–20)

There were also some students who found research attractive but were not interested in the teaching aspect of the job. We did not include teaching among the unappealing items on the questionnaire; but since many students explicitly found teaching appealing and research unappealing, we should report what some students in the focus groups said in a negative vein about teaching. Some of those interviewed specifically stated that teaching would not appeal to them. For example, a Latino at an Ivy League school described his image of teaching as follows:

Teaching the same kind of course year after year, the things you have to deal with, the students wanting extensions, the students who are just taking the course to fulfill a major or just to fulfill a requirement and they're not really interested in it. You get frustrated and you get like, "Why am I here if some of the students don't want to be in these classes?" (p. 11)

A Latina at a state university saw teaching as "boring": "Being a professor is boring. I've seen professors with the same notes for 10 years—teach the same thing year after year. It gets dull, routine—I hate routine"

(p. 21). Another Latina at a state university recognized that she was temperamentally not suited to be a college teacher:

> I have absolutely no patience for certain levels of stupidity. It's like, if a student started yelling at me, or doing something really obnoxious, my temper would not take it. So there is no way that I could be a teacher at any level. In the field of law I want to go into, I'll be much more isolated. It will just be me and my paper work. I won't have to deal with anybody else, and their ignorance, their stupidity will not get in my way. I can do my work and not have to worry about anyone. (p. 23)

(Note this student's unrealistic perception of her chosen field of law.)

Another Latina at an Ivy League school was worried that, like some of her professors, she would become a perfunctory teacher in order to concentrate on research:

> I feel like there are a lot of professors at this school that are teaching simply because they need to do their research and this is the facility to do it at, and they don't necessarily like teaching. I've looked at it from the sense that if I do go to grad school, most likely I'll do research, and would I like to be teaching? Because if I wouldn't I don't want to be in that position, because some of them really seem like they're miserable, and it's miserable for the students to sit in a classroom with a professor who doesn't want to teach. (p. 12)

Finally, a Latina at an Ivy school dismissed both research and teaching as boring: "To me it seems like a very boring job, because professors have to research on their own, and you have to do class preparation on your own, and you have to present it in class. I just don't see the thrill in doing that" (p. 11).

Although only a small percentage of students in the survey reported worry about lack of ability as a reason not to go into academia, this concern did emerge in some of the focus groups. For example, a white man at an Ivy League school was worried that he would never be able to measure up to his professors:

> There's a problem about going into academia and that is that you're always in school. Like my advisor, he's still in school now. He's junior faculty; he's been here for two years. In order to get

tenured, he has to publish a book, and he's going to be graded on it. I like to think that I've attained a certain level of knowledge, but then I compare myself to my advisor and see that amazing gulf that has got to be crossed at some point. I want to go into academia, but it's really scary. Am I going to know that much in five years? And geez, I won't ever leave the library. (p. 14)

An Asian man at a state university also expressed this type of insecurity:

To become an economics professor, you have to know everything, inside and out. In order to become a professor, you have to be the best in that area. To be an actual professor teaching psychology requires a more basic understanding than if you are a clinical psychologist, more of a grasp of what students may raise up. If you become a clinical psychologist, you're not really tested. You're the one asking questions. As a teacher it's the other way around. Students will ask you questions and you really can't show your weakness. I feel like professors can lose face if students stump them. That might aggravate them a lot. They're always being tested, day in and day out. (p. 22)

Perceptions of Academia as Causes of Career Choice

Tables 6.1 and 6.2 show the reactions of our sample to a list of items we thought might be appealing or unappealing about a career in academia; but they tell us nothing about whether or not a respondent's view of this aspect of academia had any influence on that person's selecting this career over others. To find this out we must compare the students who said that a particular aspect was appealing or unappealing with those who did not find that aspect appealing or unappealing and see if there is any difference in the proportion selecting academia as their most likely career.[3]

In Table 6.3 we present the result of ten different logistic regression analyses in which we computed the probability of students selecting professor as their final-choice occupation who found a particular aspect of academia appealing or unappealing (while controlling for freshman interest in academia). Subtracting the predicted probability for those who did not find the item appealing or unappealing from the predicted probability of those who did results in a measure of how strong an influence each aspect was on selecting academia as a career.

Eight of the ten appealing items listed in Table 6.3 have a statistically

Table 6.3 Predicted probability of wanting to be a college professor by appealing aspects of academia, by ethnicity

Appealing aspect	Whites			African Americans			Asians			Latinos		
	Yes	No	Difference	Yes	No	Difference	Yes	No	Difference	Yes	No	Difference
To teach undergraduates	10	4	**6**	11	3	**8**	8	4	**4**	13	6	**7**
For world of ideas	10	3	**7**	10	4	**6**	7	4	**3**	12	8	**4**
To improve public policy	9	7	2	8	6	2	7	6	1	10	11	−1
To mentor minorities	11	7	**4**	8	6	2	5	7	−2	10	11	−1
For liberal/tolerant atmosphere	10	6	**4**	9	7	2	9	5	**4**	11	10	1
For reduced pressures	7	8	−1	8	7	1	6	6	0	9	11	−2
For academic community	10	5	**5**	10	6	**4**	8	5	3	12	8	**4**
Due to interest in major	12	4	**8**	10	4	**6**	8	4	**4**	14	6	**8**
For research satisfaction	14	4	**10**	13	4	**9**	10	3	**7**	16	6	**10**
For time off	6	10	**−4**	7	8	−1	6	6	0	6	13	**−7**

Note: Items that are statistically significant at $p < .05$ are in bold. Probabilities predicted from a logistic regression model controlling for freshman interest in academia.

significant effect on the selection of professor as a first-choice career among white students, although one—the "time off" item—goes in the opposite direction from expectation. Those who say that having a lot of time off is an appealing aspect of academia are less likely than those who did not check this item off to want to be academics. The two items not statistically significant are the "improve public policy" aspect and the "reduced pressure" aspect. If we determine which aspects are the most important influences on choice of academia as a career by looking at the size of the difference between those who mentioned the item and those who did not, we would conclude that for white students the three most important items are research satisfaction, interest in major, and living in the world of ideas. For African American students the most important aspects are research satisfaction, teaching undergraduates, and (tied for third) interest in major and living in the world of ideas. For Asians the most important aspects are research satisfaction, interest in major and teaching undergraduates (tied for second), and academia's liberal/tolerant atmosphere and the world of ideas. For Latinos the most important aspects are research satisfaction, interest in major, and teaching undergraduates. All four ethnic groups reported that satisfaction from doing research is the aspect of academia that most appeals to them. In addition, it is interesting to note that although many minority students mentioned the opportunity to mentor minority undergraduates as an appealing aspect of academia, this factor had no causal effect on any of the minorities (having in fact a slight, though statistically insignificant, negative effect on Asians and Latinos), but it did have a causal effect on white students.[4] The opportunity to improve public policy did not have a causal effect on any of the ethnic groups.

If we look at the unappealing aspects for whites (see Table 6.4) we see that three of the items—the competitiveness of academia, the difficulty getting a job, and the difficulty of obtaining tenure—had causal effects in the opposite direction from that predicted. In all three cases students who said that these items were unappealing aspects of academia were *more* likely to want to be college professors than those who did not check these items off as unappealing. In these cases, for these respondents, wanting to be an academic probably preceded attitudes toward academia. Even though those students who wanted to enter academia were aware of these negative aspects of the occupation, they still selected it as their first choice. We might consider these questions to be level-of-information questions; that is, those who wanted to be academics were more

Table 6.4 Predicted probability of wanting to be a college professor by unappealing aspects of academia, by ethnicity

	Whites			African Americans			Asians			Latinos		
Unappealing aspect	Yes	No	Difference	Yes	No	Difference	Yes	No	Difference	Yes	No	Difference
Limited financial rewards	6	10	**-4**	6	9	**-3**	6	7	-1	10	10	0
Competition	10	7	**3**	10	7	3	7	5	2	10	11	-1
Lack ability	5	9	**-4**	6	8	-2	4	7	-3	9	10	-1
Takes too long	4	11	**-7**	4	9	**-5**	5	7	-2	5	14	**-9**
Hard getting jobs	11	6	**5**	9	7	2	8	4	**4**	12	9	3
Emphasis on research, not teaching	7	10	**-3**	6	9	-3	5	8	**-3**	6	17	**-11**
Hard to get tenure	11	7	**4**	7	8	-1	8	5	3	11	10	1
Don't want to be a student	3	10	**-7**	2	9	**-7**	4	7	-3	5	12	**-7**
Other jobs have more prestige	6	8	**-2**	4	8	-4	3	7	-4	10	10	0
Too much debt	7	8	-1	6	8	-2	6	6	0	10	10	0

Note: Items that are statistically significant at $p < .05$ are in bold. Probabilities predicted from a logistic regression model controlling for freshman interest in academia.

aware of some of the difficulties attached to the career than those who were not interested in such a career.

In general all of the unappealing items had weaker effects on career choice than the appealing items. Which ones had a stronger or weaker effect differed from one ethnic group to the other. For whites the two most important unappealing items were tied: "takes too long" and "don't want to be a student." For African Americans the most important item was "don't want to be a student." For Asians there was no meaningful variation in the influence of the unappealing items; all had a minor effect. Latinos were the only group for which "emphasis on research, not teaching" was a strongly unappealing item. More research is required to understand why this item had such a negative impact on Latinos, relatively small causal impact on white students and Asians, and did not have a significant causal impact on African Americans. (Also unappealing for Latinos was that it "takes too long" to get a Ph.D.) Considering all four groups and all the unappealing items, "takes too long" was the single most unappealing.

There were a few differences between the groups. First, although concern about financial factors has a small but significant negative influence on both whites and African Americans, it has no influence on Asians or Latinos. Second, concern that there is too much emphasis on research and not enough on teaching has a particularly negative effect on Latinos. In fact, although many students mention "too much research" as an unappealing aspect of academia, this variable does not greatly differentiate those who want to be professors from those who do not, except for Latinos. Third, "too much debt" plays no significant role for any of the four ethnic groups. Finally, the supposed low prestige of academia also has no significant effect on any of the ethnic groups.

The view that professors have low prestige is in fact a misperception. A large number of studies conducted in the United States have shown that among the major occupations university professor and physician have the highest prestige—more than lawyers or businesspeople. Cross-national studies have shown that university professor is among the highest-prestige occupations in all countries where studies of occupational prestige have been conducted. The fact that the parents of some minority students and some of the students themselves perceive university professor as having lower prestige than the major competing occupations may simply indicate their lower level of knowledge about this occupation than its major competitors.

Controlling for Other Variables

Since interest in research and in teaching were the two most important reasons given for why a career in academia would be appealing, we wanted to make sure that these variables had independent effects and were not spurious. In a multinomial regression in which all thirty-three variables were controlled, both interest in research and interest in teaching continued to be statistically significant causes of selecting college professor as a final-choice career for all four ethnic groups.

The other variable we were interested in was concern with financial rewards. In Figure 6.1 (pages 156–157) we show the effects of concern with financial rewards on the selection of all five leading occupations separately for each ethnic group. As indicated earlier, concern with the perceived limited financial rewards of the academic profession had an influence on the decision of both African American and white students as to whether or not they should become academics. Concern with financial rewards has a strong influence on the selection by all four ethnic groups of teaching as a final-choice career.

In all four ethnic groups students who are concerned with the limited financial rewards attached to academia are more likely to want to go into business and law. There is no significant relationship between concern with financial rewards and selection of medicine for all four ethnic groups. Given that medicine is still probably the highest-paid or next-highest-paid occupation, this seems surprising. Medical students may be hesitant to express their concern with the financial rewards attached to the profession for fear that it may hurt their chances of admission. However, the circumstances in which we asked the question—specifically in relation to academia—probably would have minimized any attempt by these students to hide their "real" motivation for pursuing a career in medicine. We believe that although medical students clearly are attracted by the high level of financial rewards attached to their job, this is not the most important reason for their pursuing this career—after all, if one wanted to make a lot of money, it would be better to pursue a job in investment banking or some similar business field. What we think is so attractive about medicine is not the absolute amount of money physicians earn, but the fact that admission to medical school (any medical school) virtually guarantees an upper-middle-class lifestyle. One rarely flunks out of medical school (graduation rates are close to 95 percent), so once a student receives an admission letter to any medical school, that student is guaranteed a place in the upper middle class.[5]

When the full model is controlled the concern with financial rewards continues to have a strong independent effect for African Americans insofar as it influences their choice of academia as a final-choice career; but it no longer has an influence on the selection by white students of academia as a final-choice career. In part this was a result of antecedent variables, such as GPA. However, with the antecedent variables controlled concern with finances has a substantive meaningful impact on the selection by white students of academia. This means that its influence on career choice by white students is explained by some of the variables in the model intervening between financial concern and occupational choice.[6]

More Data from the Focus Groups

When we began this research we thought that concern about earnings—the fact that on average for these high-achieving students it would be easier to earn more money (in some cases substantially more) in medicine, law, and business than it would be in academia—would be a deterrent, especially for minorities, to selecting academia as a career. As pointed out earlier, concern about financial matters did have statistically significant (but relatively small) effects on whites and African Americans and no statistically significant effect on Asians and Latinos. Data from the focus groups provide insight into the attitudes of the students toward monetary rewards as an influence on occupational choice.

The matter of how much money can be made in different occupations was generally not a salient concern in focus groups with African American students at Ivy League schools. Their parents may be concerned about it, but they seem not to be. As this young man said:

> I tend to think that salary wouldn't be the determining factor in me not becoming an academic. I think it's more like, when I think about academia, I think about a very closed environment, you know, these people who are too intellectually high brow to really see what's going on in the urban cities. (Barber and Cole 1996b, p. 45)

The issue of earnings also was played down among Ivy League Latino undergraduates. One man told how his older brother was making a lot of

155

A. Whites

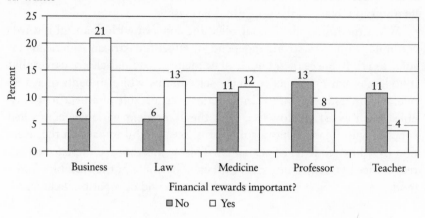

B. African Americans

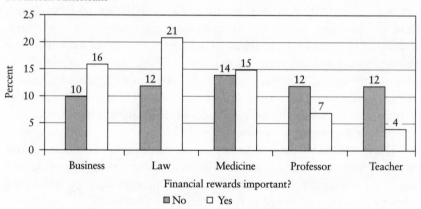

Figure 6.1   Effect of concern over financial rewards on selection of each of the five top occupations, by ethnicity. A: Whites. B: African Americans. C: Asians. D: Latinos.

C. Asians

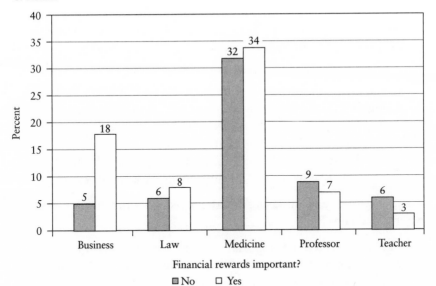

Financial rewards important?

◼ No   □ Yes

D. Latinos

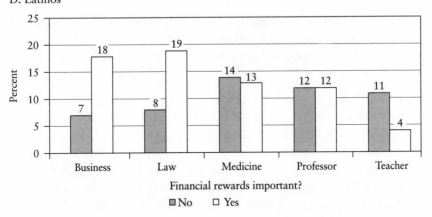

Financial rewards important?

◼ No   □ Yes

money, but he didn't care: "He's making money, bringing it in, and he's worked at it and he's getting more and more and he's happy with it. Whereas for myself I don't really care about money, I just want to be happy" (p. 45). A Latina emphasized the importance of psychological rewards over monetary ones:

All the career choices that I've ever liked I know they're very low paying, but I can't switch over to another career, be a doctor, be a lawyer, because I don't like medicine or law. I like the interaction between people. It's psychological rewards that I enjoy from work. I know that it's going to be one of the lowest paying jobs, but I can deal with that because I will be enjoying my work. (pp. 45–46).

Another Ivy League Latina clearly articulated the difference between her parents and herself:

I think money's more important for our parents. My mother always points out, "Your father and I have worked really hard in our lives, and we don't want you to work as hard as we did, so be a doctor, be a lawyer." So for them, they see it as an insurance, almost as a success for them, that their child doesn't have to work as hard as they did. So it's more important for them than I think for us. (p. 46)

An African American male at a historically black university indicated that lack of money was not a concern, and he was one of the few students both in the focus groups and in the survey to indicate that having time off is an attractive aspect of the career:

Money has never been a major issue, so I know professors don't make much, though some do if they do research, if they become deans, or if they work at certain universities. But I just want to be a professor because deep down, I'm a family person, and I know I would have my summers off and my vacations off, and being a good father is important to me because I never had one when I grew up. So being a professor, I'd be able to be a father. (p. 17)

Some students in the focus groups did express concern with the low pay of academics and a desire to be successful. A man at a historically black university said, "I did think about being a college professor, but I know it's not for me. I don't want to be poor, and I have to support the life style that I might want to live in the future" (p. 18). Another man at the same school talked about how he wanted to be a role model for black males by being very successful, with the clear implication that success means a lot of money:

> I never really considered being a college professor or anything of that nature. What I have thought about is I would rather be an example of what you can do, especially to Black males and what they can do if they go to college, choose a career that they are good at, and how to be successful at it. I plan to be very successful. (p. 18)

We found views similar to those from our survey in the interviews we conducted with graduate students. We found there that too much competition both among students and faculty is seen as one of the more negative aspects of graduate school, and apparently some undergraduates who are interested in an academic career also become aware of this high level of competition. A Latino graduate student at an Ivy League university complained about competition in his department and related it to funding:

> My department is really cut-throat—it's very competitive. That was because for a long time they have taken in about sixty first-year students, and after one year they fund only half of them. It was very hard to have any sense of community, since people are being so competitive. (Barber and Cole 1996a, p. 21)

A Latina at an Ivy university relates an experience of intense competition among students working in a specific area: "I'm not a twentieth or nineteenth century person. Among those people, there's real competition—the students are stealing each other's ideas, back-stabbing, and it's really bad" (p. 21). One African American woman at an Ivy League school was in a department that she felt was so competitive that it caused even the few minority students to compete with each other:

> In this department, competition unfortunately develops between the few people of color. Competition is not necessarily my mentality. I could put my energies in other places, but sometimes there are people who feel they have to compete. I think that's sad because I think we should be supportive of each other. Why can't we at least among the people of color support each other and help each other out? (p. 21)

The focus-group interviews contain much information on the perception of minority group students about whether and how they would be advantaged or disadvantaged in academia. Many students see their minority status as both an advantage and a disadvantage. For example, an African American male undergraduate at a state university said that his ethnicity "will be an advantage because we are underrepresented in academia, but it will be a disadvantage because I don't think I will be making as much as my white counterparts" (Barber and Cole 1996b, p. 57). An African American woman undergraduate at the same school also saw her ethnicity as both an advantage and a disadvantage:

Everyone is stressing that you're part of an underrepresented group, so that's an advantage, that you can represent that group. But that's a disadvantage, because now you're carrying the weight of being there and eventually becoming one of the burnt out professors, because there's not many of you and you have to carry that weight. (p. 57)

A woman at a small black college clearly felt that being a member of a minority was an advantage: "A career in science, for me, is a big advantage, because there are opportunities out there for minorities. I mean, the list just goes on. So, yeah—I would say it's an advantage being a minority, and a woman" (p. 57). A Latina undergraduate at a state university acknowledged that coming from a minority group was an advantage, but she didn't like affirmative action programs, as she felt she could compete with anyone:

As a minority, I don't want to be pointed out for a job because I am Hispanic. I like being put on things fairly, because I can hold my own with anyone, regardless of race, regardless of sex. I feel that it makes us look bad that they're making these laws that we have to be hired on the basis of our race. (p. 58)

In the focus groups some members of minority groups, particularly African Americans and Latinos, indicated that one reason why they wouldn't be interested in an academic career is that they were interested in doing work that would help their people or improve social conditions for their people. Some thought that they could accomplish this with an academic career, but others saw the world of academia as too remote— the proverbial ivory tower. In the pretest we found items aimed at measuring a desire to help the group not to be correlated with decision to become an academic. Nonetheless, the focus groups suggest that some students do think this way. For example, an African American woman at a liberal arts college said, "I'm not interested in profit. I'm more interested in making a difference. Particularly, in terms of injustices. I would like to work some time volunteering, trying to change things" (p. 15). Another African American in the same focus group said:

> I think professors are somewhat isolated. I'm in urban politics, urban redevelopment. I think that professors do some of the studies that provide a framework for some of the things that are going wrong in urban development, but I think that they are too isolated from what I want to do. I want more of a connection with what's really going on down in the street, in the community, and me articulating the needs of the people. (p. 10)

But another African American woman at a liberal arts college thought that she could make a difference by becoming a professor:

> Yeah, definitely I'm open to it. I think there definitely needs to be some kind of change in the educational system. It's a possibility that I could get involved in that. There's a lot that could be done, that needs to be done. Like sympathizing with minorities and people of color is still not the central concern. I mean, the professors now are from a generation which—that's not one of their focuses. Society is changing, so there should be more representatives of people of color as educators. (p. 16)

An African American male undergraduate at a state university thought he could make more of a difference by teaching at a lower level:

> I did think about being a professor, being that I want to go into teaching, but the level of difference that I want to make, I want to start out with more of a mass who hasn't already acclimated to society. I want to start off with children or pre-teens where I could make a difference. The only benefit I think in being a college professor is the constant learning, which is something that I like, but I could read books for that. (p. 16)

Conclusions

Looking at our respondents' attitudes toward academia and how they influence career choice can provide information useful in developing policies aimed at increasing minority interest in an academic career. The most important data in this chapter are presented in Tables 6.3 and 6.4, where we show how attitudes toward each of the appealing and unappealing factors influenced selection of academia as a final-choice career. In general, the most important appealing aspects of academia appear to be those connected with the two main functions of the job: research and teaching. Students in all four ethnic groups who said that teaching undergraduates and having the opportunity to do research were appealing aspects of the academic career were more likely to select this career as their first choice than those who did not mention these factors.

Three of the unappealing items—difficulty in getting a job, difficulty in attaining tenure, and excessive competition— were correlated with the dependent variable in the "wrong" direction; that is, those who mentioned these items as unappealing were more likely rather than less likely to want to be professors. All of these are realistic difficulties connected with the current situation in academia. We interpreted these attitudes as indicating a greater level of knowledge about some of the problems of academia on the part of those who were interested in pursuing it as a career.

Of the other negative items, the time it takes to obtain a degree, reluctance to remain a student, and, for Latinos, the belief that there is too much emphasis on publication over research were the most important deterrents to entering academia as a career.

For all four ethnic groups the belief that they would get satisfaction from doing research was the single most important appealing item that influenced selection of academia as a career. Interest in teaching undergraduates and an interest in their major were two other appealing aspects that had statistically significant effects for all four ethnic groups. The unappealing aspects were less important influences on career choice than were the appealing aspects. No unappealing aspect had a statistically significant effect for all four ethnic groups, and the unappealing items that were statistically significant varied for the four ethnic groups.

7

ROLE MODELS, INTERACTION WITH

FACULTY, AND CAREER ASPIRATIONS

WITH MELISSA BOLYARD

In this chapter we focus our attention on how experiences students have within college might influence their interest in becoming a college professor. We concentrate on the students' interaction with faculty, which past research (see Chapter 1) has shown to be an important influence on the decision to become a professor. First, we look at whether the students have role models among the faculty and if so, whether this increases the probability of their selecting college professor as their most likely career choice. We also consider whether the race and gender of the role model have any influence on the students' career interest in academia and a few other dependent variables—a type of data that we believe has not been collected before now. Second, we examine the impact of faculty contact on the decision to become a professor. We also show how several other within-college experiences influence career decision making by our sample of high-achieving minority students.

For many years academic researchers, governmental officials, and the lay public have assumed that the number and type of role models available to a student will have an important influence on that student's performance in school and selection of a career. These assumptions became highly visible in the 1978 Supreme Court case of Regents of the University of California v. Allan Bakke (438 U.S. 265, 1978).

Bakke was a white male student who had applied for admission to the medical school of the University of California at Davis. Under its existing affirmative action program the medical school had a certain number of places "set aside" for African American and other minority applicants to guarantee that there was diversity in the type of physicians being trained. It turned out that Bakke, who was denied admission, had higher paper qualifications—MCAT scores and college GPA—than most of the

163

African American students who were admitted under the affirmative action program. The court concluded that it was illegal to engage in "reverse discrimination" against Bakke. Quota systems were illegal, said the court; but it was legitimate to take race into account as one of many factors influencing admissions decisions in a specific case. This latter opinion, expressed by only one of the nine Supreme Court justices, Justice Powell, has since been used by institutions of higher education to claim that their use of racial preferences in admissions is legal.

In the *New York Review of Books* Ronald Dworkin made the argument that was actually made before the Supreme Court: that affirmative action would provide black students with physician "role models." As Dworkin put it: "Affirmative action . . . tries to provide 'role models' for future black doctors, not because it is desirable for a black boy or girl to find adult models only among blacks, but because our history has made them so conscious of their race that the success of whites, for now, is likely to mean little or nothing for them" (quoted in J. R. Cole 1979, p. 265).[1]

Jonathan Cole (1979) analyzed the assumptions made about role models in the Bakke case. Many of those same assumptions, without the benefit of supporting evidence, have worked their way into common belief to such an extent that they virtually hold the position of facts rather than of propositions to be empirically verified. As labor economist Ronald G. Ehrenberg (1995) pointed out in an introduction to a collection of papers on role models in education, "Beliefs often drive public policy even before they are confirmed as facts" (p. 482).

Cole points out that it has been assumed that the presence of same-gender and same-race role models is a necessity in the occupational socialization of students into many occupations, that "a critical element in the effective socialization into the professions and the selection of specific occupations is the presence of persons of the same race or gender who will act as role models for potential students. It is further assumed that not only is it necessary to have role models, but that women depend on other women for role models. Minorities depend on other minority group members for role models, and so on." He continues:

> The argument proceeds that without a sufficient critical number of minority doctors who can act as role models for minority youth, it will be very difficult, if not impossible, to increase both the absolute and relative number of minority doctors in American society.

Consequently, affirmative action that admits minorities to medical school programs under a special admissions policy serves the important, indeed compelling, state interest of producing role models who will in due course significantly influence the numbers of young minority group members who want to become physicians . . . There are two empirical social-science assumptions here. First, it is assumed that role models are important factors in recruitment and learning processes for minority (and female) students. Second, it is assumed that the role model effect on students involves race or gender matching—that is, black students are more influenced in career decisions by black role models than by white role models; female students are more influenced in career decisions by female instructors than by male instructors. (J. R. Cole 1979, pp. 265–266)

After reviewing the sparse existing literature on the effects of role models, Cole concludes: "The real point is that for all practical purposes the role model argument like so many of the other empirical issues in *Bakke* remains entirely at the conjectural level and should have been treated as such . . . In sum, the facts that are assumed to exist simply don't" (p. 269).

Even though it was published many years ago, the review of the literature on sex differences published by Eleanor Maccoby and Carol Nagy Jacklin (1975) remains the most thorough such analysis. They find that even for young children the literature they reviewed did not indicate that children are more likely to model themselves on others of their own sex: "On the whole it simply cannot be said that young children spontaneously imitate people of their own sex more than people of the opposite sex. This is true of imitations of parents as well as of models who are unfamiliar to the child" (pp. 287–288).

At about the same time as the publication of Cole's book on women in science (1979), a comprehensive review of the literature on role models was published by Jeanne J. Speizer (1981). Speizer reviewed studies on role models in high school and college as well as in graduate school. She also examined the work done on single-gender colleges, much of which claimed that such schools have a beneficial effect on the achievement of women, in part because they provide women with more role models than do co-ed schools. (Speizer dealt almost exclusively with studies of same-gender role models, as virtually no studies existed at the time of the influence of same-race or same-ethnicity role models.) She also reviewed studies on mentors and sponsors. Speizer found that most of the relatively few studies that claimed to show an influence of role models have severe methodological problems, which bring their conclusions into doubt.

In her conclusion, Speizer wrote: "Role models, mentors, and sponsors are concepts which still need to be defined and studied. Despite their almost universal acceptance, *there is very little supportive evidence for their validity.* Until methodologically sound studies are conducted on large, randomly selected populations, these concepts should be considered as suggestive rather than proven" (Speizer 1981, p. 712).

Our more recent search of the large literature on role models found virtually no studies of the type that Speizer called for over twenty years ago. Most papers on role models simply assume the importance of same-gender and same-race/ethnicity role models on a large variety of dependent variables. An example is Janice C. Bizzari's "Women: Role Models, Mentors, and Careers" (1995), in which she states, "According to recent studies, evidence suggests, potential can be denied or lost for women in certain male-dominated careers for lack of women mentors or role models in the field" (p. 145). The studies she cites are either qualitative or nonsystematic.

There are a few exceptions, in which the concept of role model is looked at systematically using relatively large data sets. All of these studies have been done by economists, and most appear in an issue of *Industrial and Labor Relations Review* edited by Ehrenberg (1995). One study that did not appear in the Ehrenberg volume is that reported by Mark O. Evans (1992). Evans conducted a study of the influence of same-gender and same-race role models on how much students learned in high school economics classes. Evans used data from the Joint Council on Economic Education's National Assessment of Economic Education Survey conducted in the spring of 1987. From that survey he had information on 2,440 students who took a high school economics course, including the results of a test of economic knowledge, which Evans used as his dependent variable. From his careful study, Evans concluded that there is no evidence of same-gender role model effects but that black students do slightly better on the test when they have black teachers, particularly when their mothers do not have a college degree. The effect, although statistically significant, is relatively small. It should be noted that Evans (like the studies reported later from the Ehrenberg volume) considered the race and gender of the teacher, but did not determine whether the students looked upon the teacher as a role model.

Ronald Ehrenberg, Daniel Goldhaber, and Dominic Brewer (1995) reanalyzed the data collected in the 1960s by James Coleman (see Chapter 1) to see if matching the teacher's and student's race had any effect on the amount that students learned. Their main conclusion was that African American teachers did not help African American students and under some conditions had a negative effect on how much white students learned. Donna Rothstein (1995), a student of Ehrenberg's, used the "High School and Beyond" data set (a longitudinal study conducted by the National Center for Educational Statistics) to investigate the effect of attending a women's college on labor market and educational outcomes. She found that when appropriate input variables were controlled, single-gender schools conferred no advantage on young women. But she also found that among those who attended women's colleges the percentage of female faculty had a small positive effect on postcollege wages.

Now let us summarize the papers presented in the Ehrenberg symposium, "Role Models in Education," sponsored by the Cornell School of Industrial and Labor Relations–Cornell Institute for Labor Market Policies and held at Cornell University in April 1994. The revised papers were published the following year in an issue of *Industrial and Labor Relations Review*. As we pointed out earlier, none of the studies in the Ehrenberg collection, although all based on large systematic data sets, determined whether the students considered their teachers to be role models. Despite this fact, the papers in the Ehrenberg collection do offer some interesting and suggestive findings.[2]

Harvey Rosen and Brandice Canes (1995) studied how the number of female faculty in science and engineering fields might influence the number of women entering the fields. They correctly point out that a cross-sectional analysis would not answer this question because the same factors that make a particular field attractive to women professors might make it attractive to women students. Instead, Rosen and Canes chose to look at change over time in the number of women professors. They found no evidence that this variable had any effect on the number of women who majored in the sciences.

Sara Solnick (1995) studied female students at women's colleges and at coeducational institutions and found that the women at the all-women schools are more likely to shift from "traditionally female" majors to either neutral or traditionally male majors. She found no evidence to support her second hypothesis: that women who begin in traditionally male majors would be more likely to persist in those majors if they attend a women's college. Solnick's research does not specify the mechanisms through which the women's colleges have their influence. Indeed her results could easily be due to the self-selection of particular types of students into women's colleges.

Donna Rothstein (1995) examined how the percentage of female faculty at a college or university might influence the likelihood of women's attaining an advanced degree and later earnings. She found that the proportion of women had no direct effect on earnings but that it had a small indirect effect on earnings through the proportion of women who go on to attain an advanced degree. Again, in order to understand fully these findings we would have to know more about how the students attending colleges having a high proportion of women as faculty might differ from those who attend colleges with a lower proportion of women as faculty.

In a study conducted by Rothstein and Ehrenberg (1994) the authors found that "attendance at a HBCU substantially enhanced the probability that a black college student would receive a bachelor's degree within seven years after starting college; however, on average, it had no apparent effects on the student's early career labor market success (as measured by 1979 earnings) or the student's probability of enrolling in graduate school" (Ehrenberg 1995, p. 484). Jill Constantine (1995) asked the same question but uses earnings data from a later period in the career history of the students she studied. She found that attending an HBCU does have a significant influence on later earnings. The reasons for the difference in findings between the two studies are unclear. However, Ehrenberg (1995) points out that the 1986 wave of the NLS-72 data, which Constantine utilized in her study, was a subsample of the original sample and oversamples college graduates who earn more money than nongraduates. This may account for the difference between her findings and those of Rothstein and Ehrenberg.

Finally, Ehrenberg, Goldhaber, and Brewer (1995) used data from the National Educational Longitudinal Study of 1988 to determine whether the race or gender of the teacher has an influence on how much students learned. They found that the gender and race of the teacher have no significant influence on how much the student learns but that they do influence how the teacher evaluates the student. Thus white female teachers were more likely than were white male teachers to evaluate their white female students highly. They noted that their data provide no evidence that black students will learn more when they have black, rather than white, teachers. They add that there are two interpretations that can be given to their data:

> At face value, our findings may be interpreted in either of two conflicting ways. On the one hand, if it is argued that what is crucial is how much students learn in classrooms, one might conclude that teachers' race, gender, and ethnicity per se do not matter. On the other hand, if it is argued that teachers' subjective evaluations of students mirror the encouragement they provide these students and the "track" on which they place the students or to which they encourage them to aspire, our results suggest that in some cases teachers' (race, gender, and ethnicity) do matter. (Ehrenberg, Goldhaber, and Brewer 1995, p. 560)

Our general conclusion remains the same as when J. R. Cole published his book on women in science: so far, there is no systematic evidence that same-gender or same-race/ethnicity role models have significant influence on a range of dependent variables that they are assumed to influence, including occupational choice, learning, and career success.

Role Models and Occupational Choice of High-Achieving Minority Students

We designed our study to provide the type of systematic empirical evidence that Speizer called for in her review. Every student was asked to respond to the following: "Indicate which of the following you have ever taken a class with and/or has served as an important role model to you." The students were then given a list in which instructors were identified by both their gender and their race or ethnicity (for example, African American male instructor, African American female instructor, Asian male instructor, Asian female instructor, etc.). Thus, there were eight different types of instructor who the students could indicate had served as an important role model.[3]

Most of the students in our sample told us that they had at least one type of instructor who had served as an important role model for them. In fact, only 21 percent of white, African American, and Latino students reported that they did not have any role model among their teachers while they were in college. But 37 percent of Asian students reported that they did not have a role model among their teachers.[4] Later in this chapter we show that Asians did not differ significantly from the other ethnic groups in their extent of faculty contact. Thus, although Asians have contact with faculty members they may not develop the type of relationship that leads a student to think of a faculty member as a role model.

Figure 7.1 shows the percentage of students in each ethnic group at each type of school who reported having at least one role model. Eighty-five percent of students attending an HBCU reported having at least one role model. This is the highest percentage in the figure and corresponds with other data (which we report later) indicating that the level of faculty contact at HBCUs is higher than at any of the other types of school. Size of school did not always have the effect we had expected. African American students, for example, were more likely to have a role model at the large state universities than they were at either the liberal arts colleges or the Ivy League schools. At each type of school Asians were significantly less likely than white students to report having a role model. The consistency of this finding across schools suggests that the problems faced by Asian students are similar at all types of school.

A majority of our students (about 70 percent) reported having a same-gender role model (data not shown).[5] There were no meaningful

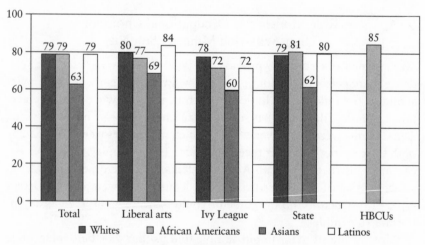

Note: For African Americans and Latinos school type significant at $p < .05$.

Figure 7.1 Percentage of students with at least one role model, by ethnicity and by school type

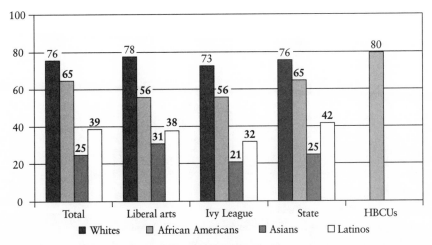

Figure 7.2 Percentage of students with same-race role model, by ethnicity and by school type

differences among the school types or the ethnic groups, with two exceptions. In all schools Asians were 10 to 15 percent less likely to report having a same-gender role model; and at Ivy League schools African Americans were about 10 percent less likely to report having a same-gender role model.

Not surprisingly, fewer students report having a same-race or same-ethnicity role model. (By this we mean a role model of the same race or ethnicity as the student regardless of gender.) We would have expected this because of the overall scarcity of minority faculty at predominantly white schools. These data are illustrated in Figure 7.2. There were statistically significant differences in the likelihood of having a same-race role model for all minority groups compared with whites at all three predominantly white schools. However, a majority of African American students reported having a same-race role model at all three predominantly white schools. At HBCUs 80 percent of African Americans reported having a same-race role model.

Finally, we looked at the extent to which the students reported having both a same-gender *and* a same-race role model. These data are presented in Figure 7.3. About two thirds of African Americans at HBCUs and two thirds of white students at predominantly white schools re-

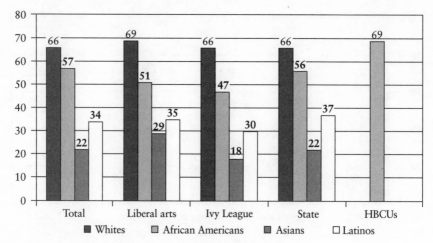

Significantly different from whites at *p* < .05 indicated by boldface.
Note: School type significant at *p* < .05.

Figure 7.3 Percentage of students with same-gender and same-race role model, by ethnicity and by school type

ported having a same-gender, same-race role model. All minorities were significantly less likely than white students to have such a role model at the predominantly white campuses. Given how few minority faculty are employed at most predominantly white schools, it is somewhat surprising to find that about half of African Americans report having a same-gender–same-race role model at these schools. But only about a third of Latino students and a fifth of Asian students had such a role model at predominantly white schools. The data, particularly on African Americans, suggest that students probably seek out faculty members who are like them and that a relatively small number of faculty can serve as role models for a relatively large number of students.

Now we come to the key question on role models. A majority of students have role models, and some have same-gender and same-race role models. Does having role models and do the gender and race or ethnicity of the role model influence students' choice of career? Before we proceed, we should note the limits of our analysis. We have excellent data on the extent to which the students in our survey had same-gender and same-race role models among faculty members. We have no data on what role models the students might have had who are not faculty members. Thus, our analysis is limited to the influence that college faculty members have as role models. Our data can tell us nothing about the potential influence of other types of role model, including precollege teachers and nonteachers. Our primary dependent variable is whether the student selects a career as an academic. We also analyze the influence of faculty role models on the students' performance in school as measured by GPA, the likelihood that a student who intends to take an advanced degree will go directly on or take time off before beginning postgraduate study, the extent to which the student has academic self-confidence, and the student's level of satisfaction with the schooling that he or she has received. These are all important dependent variables, but they do not cover all of the possible ways in which role models might influence students. For example, we know nothing about the extent to which role models might influence future career success as measured in terms of earnings or other indicators. The relatively small influence that role models have on the dependent variables that we report, however, suggests that in general the importance of role models may be substantially overestimated by society at large. In short, although we have just pointed out the limitations of our data, we believe that these data are important. After all, the wisdom of having same-gender and same-race role models as faculty members has been one of the primary justifications by universities for the use of racial preferences in hiring faculty members.

In studying the influence of role models on interest in an academic career we controlled for only one variable: interest in being a professor as a freshman. The purpose of doing this is to strengthen the probability that the direction of causality goes from having a role model to selection of academia as a career, rather than the other way around. The results, broken down by ethnicity and gender, are presented in Table 7.1.

The probabilities reported in Table 7.1 were generated the same way as prior data reported in this book were generated. For each group (for example, white females) we ran a logistic regression equation in which the dependent variable was whether or not the student selected professor as most likely career, and the two independent variables were whether or not the student reported having a role model and whether or not the student was interested in academia as a freshman. We then used the regression coefficients to estimate the probabilities reported in Table 7.1. To put it more simply, the number 8 for white females who reported having a role model, for example, is the proportion saying that academia was their first-choice career once freshman interest in academia was controlled.

Table 7.1 Predicted probability of wanting to be a college professor, by ethnicity, by gender, by type of role model

Type of role model	Whites		African Americans		Asians		Latinos	
	Females	Males	Females	Males	Females	Males	Females	Males
Any role model								
Yes	8	**8**	**9**	13	**9**	7	11	**15**
No	4	**4**	**2**	6	**3**	4	8	**2**
Same sex								
Yes	8	9	11	15[a]	9	8	11	15
No	10	8	6	0	10	7	14	17
Same race/ethnicity								
Yes	8	9	10	15	10	6	12	15
No	6	8	8	5	9	9	12	15
Same sex and race/ethnicity								
Yes	8	9	11	**16**	11	5	11	15
No	9	8	7	**4**	8	9	12	15

Notes: All models control for freshman interest in college professor; any role model variable runs on all cases; the three role model type variables run only on cases with at least one role model. Numbers in bold indicate significant role model effect, $p < .05$.

a. Tests of significance could not be computed because there was no variability in the outcome among cases who identified no same-sex role model.

The first section of Table 7.1 shows the influence on selecting professor as a most likely career by whether or not the student reported having any role model regardless of the gender or race of the role model. The results are not what we expected to find. For four of the eight racial/gender groups, whether or not the student has a role model at all—regardless of the gender or ethnicity of that role model—has no statistically significant influence on the student's choice of academia as a career.[6] But what is perhaps even more important than the fact that role models have no influence on the selection of academia for half of the groups we examine is the relatively weak effect of the variable even where it is statistically significant. Look back at Figure 5.3, the graph showing the effect of GPA on choice of professor as a career. GPA makes a real difference. For example, almost no African Americans in the lowest GPA category want to be professors, whereas more than 20 percent of those in the highest category want to be professors. In Table 7.1, even where the influence of having a role model is statistically significant, the proportion of students with a role model who want to be a professor is not much more than the overall proportion for that ethnic group: 9 percent for whites, 10 percent for African Americans, 8 percent for Asians, and 11 percent for Latinos.[7] These data call into serious question the importance of faculty role models on students' deciding to become professors.

Before examining the balance of Table 7.1, we should note how the data on same-gender role models, same-race role models, and same-gender–same-race role models was computed. First, we selected only those students who reported having at least one role model. Then, to see if for example the gender of the role model had any additional influence over simply having a role model, we followed the same procedure outlined earlier. Thus the second section of Table 7.1 shows that, for white females who reported having at least one role model, if the role model was of the same gender the predicted proportion selecting academia as a first-choice career was 8 percent; and if the role model was not of the same gender the predicted proportion selecting academia as a first-choice career was 10 percent (with freshman interest in academia controlled). The data in the "same sex" portion of Table 7.1 show that for all eight groups we studied the gender of the role model had no significant influence on selecting professor as most likely career.[8] We may conclude therefore that the gender of a role model has no influence on whether or not students select academia as a most likely career.[9]

The data in the next section of Table 7.1, on the influence of having a same-race role model, show that for none of the eight groups we analyzed did the race of the role model make any difference. Apparently African American male students are no more influenced to select academia as a career by having an African American role model than by having a white role model. These data cast serious doubt on the validity of one of the arguments used to support racial preferences in the hiring of college and university faculty.[10] There are of course many reasons other than providing effective role models for creating a diverse faculty. Thus we cannot conclude from our data that the practice of using racial preferences in hiring is not justified. We can say only that such hiring practices cannot be justified on the basis of the same-race role model argument.

When we examine the influence of same-gender–same-race models we do find one small, but statistically significant, relationship: that for African American males. But even here the size of the relationship is relatively small. African American males who have a same-gender–same-race role model are only 3 percentage points more likely to want to become a college professor than those who have a role model of any variety.

Latino students as a group illustrate most clearly the lack of importance of the gender and race of the role model on the choice of the academic profession. For this group whether or not they have a role model makes more difference in the selection of academia as a career than for any other group. However, the gender and race of the role model have no influence at all on the effectiveness of the role model in influencing the student to select academia as a most likely career.

Since the exact meaning of the term "role model" is not clear and students might define the concept in different ways, we asked the students to indicate which from among a list of characteristics applied to their concept of the term "role model."[11] The answers given by the students who reported having at least one role model are presented in Table 7.2. Our interest here is not so much in what characteristics students think role models possess, but whether defining role models in a particular way influences selection of academia as a most likely career. In brief, it did. For all eight groups we examined (except Asians) if a student defined a role model as "someone whom I would like my professional life to be like," having a role model had a statistically significant effect on likelihood of selecting professor as the most likely career (data not shown). The same was true for those who thought of role models as "someone who has mentored me." In five of the eight groups we examined, having a role model defined in this way had a statistically significant effect on selecting

Table 7.2 Of students selecting a role model, percentage identifying
characteristic as important, by ethnicity

Characteristic	Whites	African Americans	Asians	Latinos
To model my entire life after	10	11	12	9
Would like my personal life to be like	12	**10**	13	**10**
Would like my professional life to be like	42	**47**	47	43
Possesses traits that I admire	89	**86**	88	90
Is a very good teacher	76	**64**	76	**70**
Is very knowledgeable	78	76	79	**82**
Really cares about helping others	67	**73**	77	71
Has mentored me	38	**46**	41	41

Note: Significantly different from whites at $p < .05$ indicated by boldface.

academia as a career (data not shown).[12] With a few exceptions for students who defined role models in other ways, having a role model had no significant influence on selecting academia as an occupation (data not shown). Thus, defining a role model as someone whose professional life the student would like to emulate or as "someone who has mentored me" has a significant influence on interest in academia. Defining a role model in other ways generally does not affect a student's interest in academia.

Next we consider the influence of having professors as role models on other dependent variables.[13] In general whether or not a student had a professor as a role model had no meaningful influence on the selection of other occupations competing with academia such as law, medicine, and business. Having a professor as a role model also did not influence whether a student said that he or she would go directly on to graduate school.

Having a professor as a role model did have a very small positive effect on GPA; the effect was significant for African American males, Asian males, and white males and females. The only group for which having a professor as a role model increased academic self-confidence was African American males. For all other groups, having a role model had no effect on self-confidence. The one dependent variable where having a professor as a role model did have a positive effect was in students' level of satisfaction with the education they were getting at their college. The only two groups for which this coefficient was not significant were African American males and white females. Our general conclusion is that not only does having a role model have only a minor influence on students' wanting to be a professor; but it also has little or no influence on the other dependent variables we examined.

Faculty Contact

The results of research often run counter to conventional wisdom or common sense, but in the case of the importance of students' interaction with faculty or, as we shall call it, faculty contact, research generally confirms conventional wisdom: faculty contact does indeed play a major part in influencing the decision to become an academic.

Before beginning our analysis of faculty contact, recall that there is a problem with establishing causal order. Faculty contact may cause students to become interested in becoming a university professor; but it is also possible, indeed likely, that students who are interested in academia as a career will seek out contact with faculty members. We believe that the causal connection between these variables operates in both directions. We should also point out that in our analysis of faculty contact we control for freshman interest in academia. If faculty contact were a spurious cause of interest in academia it should have no effect when freshman interest and other antecedent variables are controlled.

Having faculty as role models is one way in which students might be influenced by faculty. Our questionnaire contained several other indicators of the extent to which the students had contact and were influenced by faculty members. On the mail questionnaire we asked how important faculty members (either the student's official faculty advisor or other faculty members) had been as an influence on the student's career plans;[14] whether or not the student had served as a research assistant to a faculty member; whether the student had served as a teaching assistant to a professor or graduate student; whether a faculty member had urged the student to become a college professor; whether in most classes the instructor had been able to identify the student by name; and whether the student perceived that faculty members were generally available outside of class.

In Table 7.3 we show the responses given by students of different ethnicity at the four different types of school to these faculty contact questions. The data here confirm some of our prior convictions and disconfirm others. We had expected faculty-student interaction to be greatest at the teaching-oriented liberal arts colleges and HBCUs, somewhat less at

Table 7.3 Faculty contact index items, by ethnicity and by school type (percent)

Item	Whites	African Americans	Asians	Latinos
Faculty had important influence on career decision				
Liberal arts colleges	22	24	18	20
Ivy League institutions	14	13	12	18
State universities	19	**27**	**13**	23
HBCUs		38		
Research assistant				
Liberal arts colleges	29	28	34	28
Ivy League institutions	30	32	**53**	36
State universities	26	27	**36**	**32**
HBCUs		28		
Teaching assistant				
Liberal arts colleges	25	19	30	26
Ivy League institutions	10	**6**	**17**	8
State universities	7	7	7	6
HBCUs		8		
Faculty urged student to become academic				
Liberal arts colleges	18	**28**	16	20
Ivy League institutions	19	25	17	24
State universities	14	**28**	**10**	**24**
HBCUs		45		
Instructors know my name				
Liberal arts colleges	92	91	**84**	88
Ivy League institutions	38	41	**26**	34
State universities	38	44	**23**	**31**
HBCUs		89		
Instructors available outside class				
Liberal arts colleges	99	98	97	97
Ivy League institutions	90	88	86	92
State universities	93	**86**	**84**	**82**
HBCUs		91		

Notes: Significantly different from whites at $p < .05$, chi-square indicated by boldface. School is significant ($p < .05$) for African Americans and whites on faculty influenced, for Asians on research assistant ($p < .05$), for all four groups on teaching assistant ($p < .05$), for Asians on faculty urged ($p < .05$), for all four groups on "instructors know my name" and on "instructors available outside class."

the research oriented Ivy League, and even less at the large state universities, which frequently have very large classes with sections run by graduate student teaching assistants. We used the questionnaire items included in Table 7.3 to construct a "faculty contact" index. For each of the first five items on that table a student received one point if he or she gave a response indicating faculty contact. (The last item in Table 7.3 was not included in the index because there was virtually no variance in the responses given to this question.) By computing means on this index we were able to obtain the scores for type of school and ethnic groups within type of school; these are presented in Table 7.4. The data in this table confirmed our hypothesis that there would be the highest level of faculty contact in the HBCUs and the liberal arts colleges. But somewhat surprisingly the level of faculty contact in the state universities was not much below that in the Ivy League.

In general within school type there is not much difference in the level

Table 7.4   Descriptive statistics for faculty contact index, by school type and by ethnicity

	Mean	Standard deviation
Liberal arts colleges	1.85	0.04
Whites	*1.84*	0.05
African Americans	*1.92*	0.10
Asians	*1.85*	0.07
Latinos	*1.87*	0.09
Ivy League schools	1.14	0.04
Whites	1.08	0.06
African Americans	1.18	0.07
Asians	**1.31**	0.06
Latinos	1.08	0.06
State universities	1.03	0.03
Whites	1.04	0.03
African Americans	**1.35**	0.08
Asians	**0.89**	0.04
Latinos	1.04	0.03
HBCUs	1.96	0.06

Notes: Numbers in bold represent minority group difference from whites for each school type; numbers in italics represent school type difference from Ivy League schools for each ethnic group, $p < .05$. School type for non–Ivy League differs from Ivy League, $p < .05$.

of faculty contact among the four racial groups. There were a few exceptions. In the Ivy League Asians scored the highest on the faculty contact index. This is somewhat paradoxical given the fact that Asian students are the least likely to have role models at all types of school. One plausible explanation for the high level of Asian faculty contact in the Ivy League is the very high proportion (about 50 percent) of Asians in Ivy League schools who want to be physicians. We believe that many students who want to get into medical school try to do research projects with faculty members in order to enhance their acceptance chances.[15] But perhaps the most important point to be taken from Table 7.4 is that neither African Americans nor Latinos have lower levels of faculty contact than whites at any of the three predominantly white schools.

Looking back at the results in Table 7.3, note that at all three predominantly white schools both African Americans and Latinos were more likely than white students to have been urged by faculty to consider a career in academia. We should also point out that although African American students are more likely than white students to be urged to consider academia as a career at the three predominantly white schools, they are even more likely to be pushed in that direction at the HBCUs. Almost 20 percent more African American students attending HBCUs report having been urged by professors to consider academia as a career than African Americans who attend predominantly white schools.

As mentioned earlier, there was not much variance on the question of whether instructors were available outside of classroom. The overwhelming majority of students at both Ivy League schools and state universities report that their instructors are available, counteracting the assumed image of professors at research universities who never interact with undergraduates. In general, we conclude that there are not large or systematic differences in the level of faculty contact between white students and minority students at the three predominantly white types of school.

In order to demonstrate the influence of faculty contact on the decision to become a professor, we once again used a multinomial logistic regression equation in which the dependent variable was selection of academia as most likely career. The results in Figure 7.4 show the influence of faculty contact with all the other variables in the model controlled. Since all the antecedent variables are controlled, the influence of faculty contact cannot be spurious. What we see in Figure 7.4 is that for whites, Asians, and Latinos faculty contact has a strong independent effect—

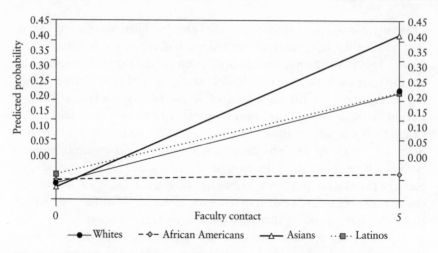

Figure 7.4   Independent effects of faculty contact on wanting to be a college professor, by ethnicity

with the strongest for Asians. However, for African Americans faculty contact has a relatively weak effect.

Research Projects

In Chapter 6 we saw that interest in doing research was the strongest causal influence of all appealing items on the decision to become a professor. It is also true that, with the exception of Asians, having carried out an independent research project while in college had a strong influence on a student's selection of college professor as the most likely career (see Figure 7.5). The reason why this variable is probably not correlated with interest in academia for Asians is that many Asians who want to go to medical school do independent research with the idea that this will help them get into medical school.

When we used all thirty-three variables in the multinomial regression model (see Table B5.1) we found that the only group for which working on an independent research project continued to have a significant effect (independent of variables such as faculty contact, GPA, and the like) were African Americans. African Americans who had done a research project on their own were twice as likely as those who had not done such a research project to want to be an academic. This once again highlights the importance of getting African American students, in particular, inter-

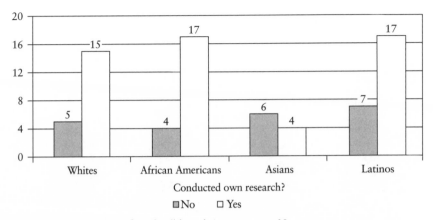

Note: Own research significant for all four ethnic groups at $p < .05$.

Figure 7.5 Percentage of students interested in college professor, by own research and by ethnicity

ested in doing research. As mentioned in Chapter 4, one of the reasons why African Americans enter college with a significantly lower interest in academia than other ethnic groups is that they are less interested in research. We point out in Chapter 4 that this could be a result of lack of exposure or low quantitative preparation as indicated by relatively low scores on the quantitative portion of the SAT.

Influence of Graduate Students

In one part of the questionnaire we asked the students how much influence various people had on their career choice (Appendix A, Mail Questionnaire, Q6). One group mentioned in the list was graduate students. In Figure 7.6 we show how responses given to this question influence the likelihood of selecting college professor as a first-choice career for students in each of the different ethnic groups. Clearly, the more important graduate students were in influencing career decisions, the greater the likelihood that the student would select college teaching as a first-choice career. There are two interrelated reasons for this. First, some graduate students acted as instructors in courses, sections, or laboratories, and contact with these graduate students had the same effect as contact with faculty members. Second, graduate students have already for the most part made a commitment to academia as a career. Graduate students who

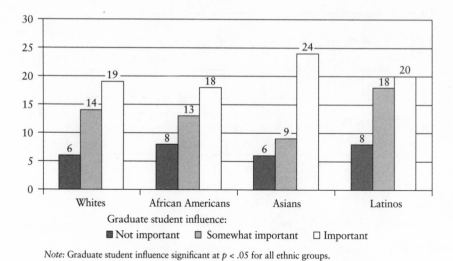

Note: Graduate student influence significant at $p < .05$ for all ethnic groups.

Figure 7.6   Percentage of students selecting professor as most likely occupation, by graduate student influence and by ethnicity

influenced students may have been serving as role models and thus influenced the career choice of the students. When all thirty-three variables in our multinomial regression model were controlled, having graduate students as an influence on career choice remained a significant factor in selecting college professor as most likely career.

Influence of Parents

Although parental influence is not specifically part of students' college experience, it does affect students throughout their years at college. We pointed out in Chapter 1 that parental influence had no effect on freshman interest in academia; but when it comes to final career choice, the results are different. As may be seen in Figure 7.7 parental influence has quite a strong influence on Asian students. Among Asian students, those who say that their parents did not exert an important influence on their career choice were three times more likely to select college professor as a final-choice career than those who say that their parents did exert an important influence on career choice. The results were meaningful but less strong for African American students and not meaningful for Latino and white students. When we controlled for all thirty-three variables in the

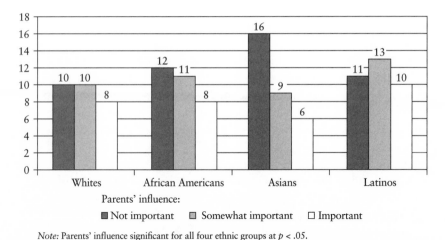

Note: Parents' influence significant for all four ethnic groups at $p < .05$.

Figure 7.7 Percentage of students interested in college professor, by parents' influence and by ethnicity

multinomial regression, the results for Asians were still very strong, although not quite so strong as in the two-variable relationship: Asians whose parents did not exert an important influence on career choice were twice as likely to select college professor as a final-choice career as Asians whose parents did exert an important influence. For African Americans, the strength of the relationship in the full model actually became somewhat stronger: for African Americans, as for Asians, when parents had a strong influence on career choice the students were half as likely to select professor as a career than when parents did not exert a strong influence on career choice.

Conclusions

Whether or not students have role models has a small influence on their decision to become a college professor. For four of the eight groups of students we studied, the effect of role models on choice of academia as a career was not statistically significant. The gender and ethnicity of the role model does not make any significant difference. Thus, students who have same-gender and same-race role models are not more likely to want to become a professor than students who have different-gender and different-race role models. There was one exception: African American males who had same-gender–same-race role models were more likely to be interested in academia than those who did not have such role models. But even for African American males the difference between having any role model and a same-gender–same-race role model was very small. We conclude that having faculty role models is a very weak influence on selecting college professor as an occupation, and the gender and race or ethnicity of the role models have no meaningful influence on this career decision.

We also analyzed the influence of role models on other dependent variables and found that having faculty role models had a slightly negative influence on the decision to enter business or medicine as careers. Role models had no influence on the decision to enter law or teaching. Role models also had no influence on the decision of those who would pursue careers requiring postgraduate training regarding whether they would go directly on or wait a while to continue their education. Having role models generally had a positive effect on grades and on satisfaction with the education the student had received.

Although having role models had only a weak effect on the decision to become a college professor, contact with faculty in general had a much stronger influence. Indeed, faculty contact is one of the key variables influencing the decision to become a college professor. We also found that students who are influenced by graduate students in their career choice are more likely to be interested in academia.

We did not examine the gender or ethnicity of the professors with whom the students had contact. Perhaps contact with faculty of the same gender or race may influence students even if they do not define these faculty members as role models. More research is needed on this question.

8

THE INFLUENCE OF SCHOOL

CHARACTERISTICS

In this chapter we analyze the extent to which the characteristics of the schools attended by our sample of high-achieving minority students influence the students' decision on whether or not to pursue a career in academia. We examine three basic hypotheses.

First, we thought that relatively small liberal arts colleges, with their emphasis on teaching, might tend to recruit more students into academia than larger colleges that are equally selective (that is, the Ivy League). When we began this study we had every reason to suspect that this hypothesis would be confirmed. We predicted that the liberal arts colleges would have higher levels of faculty-student contact, which is crucial in the decision to become an academic. Also, for many years researchers have believed that there is something about the atmosphere or culture of liberal arts colleges that pushes students into academia. Many studies have shown that liberal arts colleges, at least in the past, produced the highest proportion of graduates who earn Ph.D. degrees (for the discussion of the literature see Chapter 1).

Second, it has long been assumed that African American students have a more difficult time adjusting to predominantly white colleges than to HBCUs, where almost the entire student body and large portions of the faculty are African American. By comparing students in our two less selective types of school, HBCUs (almost all African American) and state universities (predominantly white)[1] we can see whether students at HBCUs are more likely than those at state universities to select academia as a career.

Third, we wondered whether less selective colleges (in our sample, the state universities and the HBCUs) would be more likely to recruit into academia than the selective colleges (the Ivy League and the liberal arts colleges). This would essentially be a test of the theory put forth by James

Davis (1966) in his "Campus as a Frog Pond" article. But in today's climate this comparison can also be seen as involving the "fit" hypothesis proposed by African American scholars (Sowell 1993; S. Steele 1994) to argue that affirmative action or the use of racial preferences in admission is actually harmful to the students it is supposed to help. To our knowledge very little data have been collected on the fit hypothesis. William Bowen and Derek Bok (1998) claim that their data, which use very different dependent variables from ours, do not support the fit hypothesis and that the benefits of racial preferences in admissions outweigh any harm they may cause. The data presented in this chapter provide another test of the fit hypothesis.

In the final part of this chapter we discuss the influence of school characteristics other than school type and of the possibility of doing a study using the school as the unit of analysis. We are particularly interested in learning the extent to which the level of interest of minority students in an academic career varies within the four school types in our study.

Liberal Arts Colleges and the Production of Minority Academics

As discussed at length in Chapter 1, a sizable body of research claims to show that small, highly selective liberal arts colleges are the most likely to produce Ph.D.s in general and scientists in particular. The most important reason why this is thought to be so is that these colleges are small enough to foster high levels of student-faculty contact, a crucial variable in the student's decision to persist with or adopt an interest in an academic career (see Chapter 7). Also, these schools are more teaching oriented than schools of equal or higher selectivity that emphasize research (as is the case, for example, with the Ivy League schools). Robert McCaughey (1994), in his study of selective liberal arts colleges, points out that many of these schools are putting greater emphasis now than they did in the past on the research output of their faculty. However, teaching and interacting with students remains the primary focus of these colleges. Before we began this study, we had hypothesized that the liberal arts colleges in our sample would be more likely to graduate students who would select academia as their first-choice career among both minorities and the majority white student body.[2]

The proportion of students with GPAs of 2.8 or above selecting each of the five top occupations as their first choice, including university pro-

Table 8.1 Percentage of students selecting five top occupations, by ethnicity and by school type (only students with GPA of 2.8 or higher)

	University professor	Physician	Law	Business	Teaching
Whites					
Liberal arts	11	9	7	**12**	8
Ivy League	11	14	9	19	5
State	10	11	10	9	10
African Americans					
Liberal arts	8	**8**	19	**11**	10
Ivy League	8	21	20	16	3
State	12	15	17	8	10
HBCU	12	14	16	11	10
Asians					
Liberal arts	7	**26**	9	14	5
Ivy League	9	47	6	12	2
State	8	27	8	10	6
Latinos					
Liberal arts	12	**12**	10	**18**	7
Ivy League	15	19	18	15	2
State	12	11	13	8	11

Note: Numbers in bold represent school type significant for this ethnic group and occupational choice at $p < .05$.

fessor, arranged by ethnicity and school type, is shown in Table 8.1.[3] If we examine only students who select academia as their first-choice career we find that 11 percent of the graduates of liberal arts colleges, 10 percent of the graduates of Ivy League schools, 10 percent of the high-GPA graduates of state universities, and 11 percent of the high-GPA graduates of HBCUs select academia as the one career they are most likely to pursue (data not shown). There are no substantive differences in the proportions of graduates wanting to become academics among the four school types.

The same conclusion does not apply to the African American students in our sample. Here we find that the proportion of graduates of the nonelite schools (the state universities and the HBCUs) who want to be college professors is 50 percent greater than the proportion of African American graduates of the elite schools (the Ivy League and the selective liberal arts colleges). Among students with GPAs of 2.8 or higher 8 percent of African Americans at the elite colleges and 12 percent of African Americans at the nonelite colleges selected academia as a first-choice career. This difference is not statistically significant, and one might be tempted to dismiss it as "only" four percentage points. However, given the concentration of talented African American students at the elite schools, if 12 percent as opposed to 8 percent became college professors there would be great many more African American college professors. A rough computation shows that this would mean an addition of 40 highly qualified students aspiring to be professors in the arts and sciences from this ethnic group *every year;* over just a ten-year period there would be an addition of 400 more highly qualified African Americans wanting to be college professors. Of this number, 250 would come from the Ivy League schools, the rest from the liberal arts colleges. It is of course unlikely that all those who aspire to be college professors as college seniors will actually earn Ph.D.s and end up in the academy. However, an increase from 8 percent to 12 percent in the proportion hoping to earn Ph.D.s would make an important difference.

When we look at each of the ethnic groups separately (see Table 8.1) we find that for all four ethnic groups the proportion wanting to become college professors at the liberal arts schools is either the same or slightly less than at the other three types of school. To check whether the proportion of students at the different types of school who wanted to be college professors was an artifact of input variables we conducted a series of logistic regression analyses, one for each ethnic group. The dependent variable was whether the student selected academia as the first-choice occupation. Type of school was a nominal variable, with the liberal arts colleges being the omitted category. Initial interest in academia as freshmen and combined SAT scores were controlled. In none of the equations was type of school statistically significant (data not shown). This reinforces our conclusion that liberal arts colleges are no more likely than the other three types to produce students interested in academia. Our original hypothesis on this subject was not supported by the data.

Given the fact that our data showed that among similar types of students the liberal arts colleges were no more likely than the Ivy League to produce students selecting academia as their first-choice career, we wondered whether it was still true that liberal arts colleges produced the highest proportion of Ph.D.s among their graduates. In 1989 Carol Fuller conducted a comprehensive study for the Ford Foundation on the Ph.D. productivity of different types of school, using the Carnegie classification and differentiating between public or private institution.[4] She found that, in general, private universities and colleges have the highest rate of Ph.D. productivity. In fact the highest rate (4.67 percent of graduates) is found at private Research I universities. The second highest rate is found at private Liberal Arts I colleges (3.46 percent). Private Research II universities have a rate of 2.48 percent. The highest group among the public schools was Research I universities, with a rate of 1.98. These data are interesting because they show that even in the 1970s and early 1980s private research universities were producing higher rates of Ph.D.s from among their graduates than were the liberal arts colleges.

Fuller also examined the Ph.D. productivity of institutions classified by selectivity, using average SAT or ACT scores of the undergraduates to measure selectivity. She found a strong and linear relationship between the selectivity of an institution and its rate of Ph.D. production. She found a huge gap in productivity between the most selective institutions and the next category. For the most selective institutions (those receiving an ACT score of 27 or higher—SAT scores were converted into ACT scores) Ph.D. productivity was 5.90 percent. In the next highest selectivity category Ph.D. productivity fell to 2.52 percent. In the lowest selectivity category Ph.D. productivity was 0.50 percent. This very strong relationship between selectivity and Ph.D. productivity suggests that input factors play a strong role in influencing the Ph.D. productivity of the various undergraduate institutions.

We used the data from our own study to see what proportion of students from each ethnic group who graduated between 1982 and 1986 from each of our four types of school had actually earned a Ph.D. in the arts and sciences between the years 1991 and 1995. We found that overall and for each of the four ethnic groups a higher percentage of Ivy League graduates received Ph.D.s than liberal arts school graduates: approximately 12 percent of Ivy League graduates, 9 percent of liberal arts college graduates, 9 percent of high-GPA graduates of state universities, and 6 percent of high-GPA graduates of HBCUs earned Ph.D.s in the years 1991 through 1995. Assuming that the past studies, which showed that the liberal arts colleges were the most likely to produce future Ph.D.s, were valid, we can only assume that the academic and cultural environment at the Ivy League schools has changed (perhaps beginning in the 1960s) and that both the type of students attending these schools and the environment at these schools make them more conducive today than in the past to the production of future scholars.

Table 8.1 contains some other data that are at least tangentially relevant to our interest in the factors influencing recruitment of minority students to a career in academia. Of all the careers that compete for talent with academia, that of physician is probably the most important, because in order to become a physician, like an academic, one must have relatively high levels of academic achievement in college. As pointed out in Chapter 5, there is a negative correlation between interest in business and teaching and GPA, and the strength of the correlation with GPA for law varies substantially from one ethnic group to another. But GPA is strongly related both to the selection of academia and the selection of medicine as a most likely career. In order to get more high-achieving minority students to select academia as their first-choice career, it probably will be necessary to reduce the number of such students who select physician as their first-choice career.[5]

In general there are higher proportions of minority students who select physician as a final-choice career than academia (Table 3.2), although the differences are relatively small. The graduates of Ivy League schools in particular are substantially more likely than those of any other type of school to select medicine as their first-choice career. In fact, fully 21 percent of Ivy League graduates want to become doctors. This is substantially higher than the 11 percent of liberal arts college graduates, 14 percent of high-GPA state university graduates and 12 percent of high-GPA HBCU graduates who select medicine as their first-choice career (data not shown). Note that in Table 8.1 every ethnic group graduating from Ivy League schools is more interested in medicine than their compatriots at other school types.[6]

Why are Ivy League graduates more interested in medicine than graduates of other types of school? There were several factors we thought could account for the greater interest in medicine. First, Ivy League institutions have particularly large Asian and relatively large African American and Latino populations. We know that minorities (particularly Asians) are more interested in medicine than are white students. Also, perhaps those students who want to be doctors would be more likely to self-select Ivy League schools because they believe that they would have the best chance of getting into a good medical school by completing their undergraduate work at an Ivy League school. A third possible reason might be that Ivy League students in general have higher socioeconomic status than students attending the other types of school and there might be a correlation between SES and interest in medicine. Also, Ivy League students might have higher SAT scores (and presumably higher MCAT

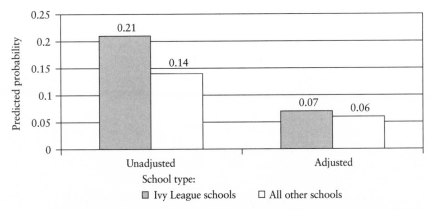

Figure 8.1   Percentage of students at Ivy League selecting physician as most likely career and those at all other schools, with and without controls (only students with GPA of 2.8 or higher)

scores), receive higher grades (perhaps as a result of grade inflation), and have higher levels of academic self-confidence.[7] In Figure 8.1 we show the proportions of students who want be physicians from Ivy League schools and all other schools unadjusted and then adjusted for the control variables. All of the variables mentioned above that we thought might help explain the Ivy League students' greater interest in medicine, with the exception of SAT scores, are in fact statistically significant influences on the selection of medicine as a career. As the adjusted bars show, these control variables together explain why Ivy League students are more interested in medicine than students from the other types of school.

Any increase in the proportion of Ivy League graduates deciding to become professors will probably be at the expense of those deciding to be doctors. Therefore, administrators of Ivy League schools, or other similar schools having high proportions of minorities wanting to be doctors, may find our analysis useful as they consider whether and how to attempt to convince future doctors to become future academicians.

Liberal Arts Colleges and African Americans

In the course of our research it became clear to us that of the four school types we studied the liberal arts colleges presented the most difficult environment for African American students. Although the survey showed no difference in the proportion of African American student graduates of liberal arts colleges and Ivy League schools who select academia as their first-choice occupation, we did find other evidence that the environment of the liberal arts schools was more difficult for African Americans to deal with than the environment of the other predominantly white types of school. In most of the analyses that follow, the differences between how well African Americans perform at the liberal arts colleges and how well they do at the Ivy League schools are not very large, but they are consistent in indicating that African Americans have more difficulty at the former than at the latter.

First, when we examined the Ph.D. output of schools in our sample we found that by a small margin, the liberal arts colleges had the lowest proportion of African American graduates earning Ph.D. degrees. (We studied what proportion of arts and sciences graduates during the years 1982 through 1986 received a Ph.D. degree from 1991 through 1995.) Among the African American graduates of liberal arts colleges 4.97 percent received a Ph.D. compared with 6.12 percent of Ivy League graduates, 6.48 percent of high-GPA graduates of the state universities, and 6.43 percent of the high-GPA graduates of the HBCUs.

Second, looking at the "unadjusted" data of Figure 8.2 we can see that African Americans are less likely to receive grades of A or A− at the liberal arts schools than they are at the Ivy League schools, and much less likely than they are at the state universities or HBCUs.[8] It might be ar-

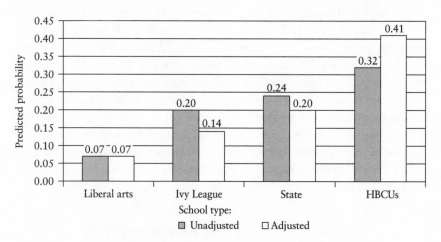

Figure 8.2 Percentage of African Americans with A or A− by school type, with and without controls (only students with GPA of 2.8 or higher)

gued that perhaps the difference between the liberal arts schools and the other types of schools in the proportion of African Americans getting A or A− is a result of African Americans at the Ivy League having higher SAT scores than African Americans at the liberal arts colleges or differences between the types of school in the distribution of grades, which would effect all racial groups. In order to see if this is the case we conducted analyses of the GPAs of African Americans using school type, SAT scores, dummy variables for individual schools, and field of major as adjusted data. The "adjusted" data in Figure 8.2 represent the percent receiving GPAs of A or A− when all of the above variables are controlled.[9] The fact that the adjusted and unadjusted proportions receiving A or A− at the different types of school are virtually identical means that the difference by school cannot be explained by any of the variables we controlled for in computing the adjusted data.

Third, African Americans are more likely to underperform at liberal arts colleges. Later, when we present data on GPA by ethnicity with SAT scores controlled, we find that among the top SAT group (1300+) only 12 percent of African Americans attending liberal arts colleges had GPAs of A or A−. This compares with 28 percent of African American students at Ivy League schools, 44 percent at state universities, and 55 percent at HBCUs, all with similarly high GPAs. And when we compare the GPAs of the top SAT group (1300+) of African Americans to white students within school type we also see a greater difference at the liberal arts schools than at any other type of school (see Table 8.2, p. 202).

Fourth, African American students at liberal arts colleges have lower levels of self-confidence compared with their cohort than do African Americans at any of the other types of school. As explained in Chapter 5, minority students have lower levels of academic self-confidence than white students both when compared with classmates and when compared with their age cohort. At both the Ivy League schools and the state universities the differences in self-confidence between African Americans and whites can be explained by the lower GPAs and SAT scores of the African Americans (see Table B8.3). In fact, at Ivy League schools, when both GPA and SAT scores are controlled, African Americans actually have significantly *higher* levels of academic self-confidence when compared to classmates than do white students.

In all the analyses we conducted of academic self-confidence (with one exception) the differences in both types of self-confidence could be explained by the lower GPAs and SAT scores of the minority students.

The one exception was cohort self-confidence at the liberal arts colleges. Here, when both grades and SAT scores were controlled, all three minority groups continued to have lower levels of academic self-confidence than whites (see Table B8.3). Something at liberal arts colleges lowers the level of academic self-confidence for all three minority groups.

Fifth, at every type of school African Americans are less satisfied than white students with the quality of education they have received (see Figure 8.3). However, the difference in level of satisfaction between African Americans and whites is greatest at the liberal arts colleges (24 points). At the Ivy League schools the difference is 14 points, and at the state universities the difference is 4 points.[10] African Americans are most satisfied with their school experience at HBCUs.

Grades have a strong influence on level of satisfaction; but at liberal arts colleges even African Americans who receive GPAs of A or A− have relatively low levels of satisfaction. If we look only at students with GPAs of A or A− the difference between African American and white students in level of satisfaction is 23 points at the liberal arts colleges and 6 points at the Ivy League schools; at state universities in this GPA category African Americans are actually 3 points more likely than whites to be very satisfied with the level of education they have received. African Americans with GPAs of A or A− who attend HBCUs are equally satisfied as those at Ivy League schools, slightly more satisfied than those at state

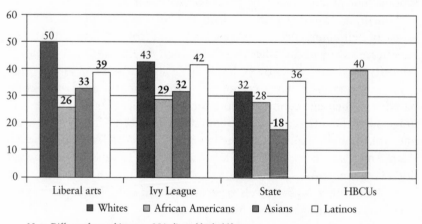

Note: Different from whites $p < .05$ indicated by boldface.

Figure 8.3   Percentage of students very satisfied with undergraduate education, by school type and by ethnicity

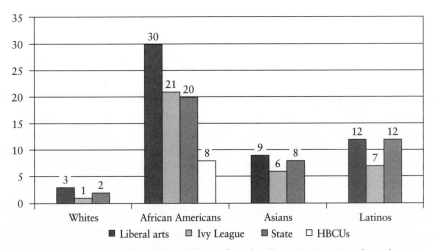

Note: The fact that school type is statistically significant for African Americans is not due to the inclusion of the HBCUs. Even when students attending these schools were left out of the analysis, there was a statistically significant difference between the liberal arts schools and the other predominantly white schools.

Figure 8.4　Percentage of students who say they experienced difficulty in school because of their ethnic background, by ethnicity and by school type

schools, and substantially more satisfied than those at liberal arts colleges (data not shown).

Sixth, the questionnaire contained one item in which we asked the students whether some faculty members at the college they attended had made their undergraduate experience more difficult because of their "racial/ethnic background."[11] Answers to this question were correlated with race. At predominantly white schools we find that among African Americans 23 percent agreed, among Latinos 10 percent agreed, among Asians 7 percent agreed, and among whites only 2 percent agreed. But with the data broken down by type of school, as Figure 8.4 shows, African American students attending liberal arts colleges were more likely to agree with the statement "Some faculty members at this college have made my undergraduate experience more difficult because of my racial/ethnic background" than were African Americans at any of the other types of school.[12]

Seventh, and finally, as discussed in detail later, African American students are less likely to persist with a freshman interest in academia if they attend either the liberal arts colleges or the Ivy League than if they attend a state university or an HBCU.[13] But there is a very large difference between the liberal arts colleges and the Ivy League schools in persistence with interest in the career of physician. At the liberal arts colleges only 30 percent of African American students who expressed a freshman interest in being a physician actually selected this occupation as the one they would most likely enter. At the Ivy League schools this figure is 62 percent.[14] Thus African Americans are twice as likely to persist in their plans to be a physician at the Ivy League schools than they are at the liberal arts colleges.[15] All of these data support the conclusion that African American students have a particularly difficult time at small liberal arts colleges.

Our findings on the liberal arts colleges suggest a paradox. These colleges are places where teaching is highly valued, faculty generally has close relations with students, and the curriculum generally emphasizes a nonoccupational orientation. All these characteristics presumably would attract students, including minority students, to academia. But there is another side of the ledger. Minority student communities are small in absolute number on these campuses. Indeed, the small class size and the inability to be anonymous or "hide" may hurt the academic self-confidence and aspiration to academic careers of some minority students. The very smallness of these colleges may create a situation in which well-prepared minority students are forced to interact and compete with even better prepared white students. This also happens at the Ivy League schools, but their larger size may make the comparisons between different students less visible and less consequential. Also, the fact that there are many more minority students at Ivy League schools may permit a greater level of peer social support at these schools and probably makes it easier to cope with the various kinds of assaults on academic self-confidence.[16] When minority students are in very small numbers they are essentially "tokens" (Kanter 1977) and experience the difficulties that tokens face.

HBCUs and the Production of African American Academics

There is substantial disagreement in the literature over whether African American students do better when they attend predominantly black colleges (HBCUs) or predominantly white colleges. Some argue that African Americans find predominantly white colleges less accepting and more difficult to adjust to (Allen, Epps, and Haniff 1991). We believe that there is indirect evidence for the validity of this conclusion in our findings that African American students do not underperform at HBCUs but do underperform at all three types of predominantly white schools (see Chapter 5).

In our study, the most relevant comparison for African American students at HBCUs is African American students at state universities. The data in Column 1 of Table 8.1 show that African Americans at HBCUs are more likely to select college professor as their most likely career than African Americans at the elite schools, but no more likely to make this selection than African Americans at the predominantly white state universities.

Before we can conclude that HBCUs are no more likely than state universities to produce students selecting academia as their most likely career, however, we should make sure that there are no input differences that might lead to the prediction that the state universities should produce more students who want to be academics. For example, if the state universities had more students entering college with an interest in academia and higher SAT scores, they should produce more students wanting to be professors. In order to make sure that this was not the case we computed a logistic regression model in which selecting college professor as a first-choice occupation was the dependent variable and both initial freshman choice and SAT scores were controlled. In this model we found no differences between the two types of school in the proportion of African American students who selected college professor as their first choice (data not shown).

In another part of this study we find that among high-GPA students the proportion of graduates at the state universities and HBCUs who actually earned a Ph.D. in the years 1991 through 1995 was almost identical. We can therefore conclude that, as far as becoming academics goes, African American students do no better and no worse at predominantly black schools than at predominantly white schools.

There is, however, one important difference between African Americans attending HBCUs and those attending the three predominantly white schools. One indicator of commitment to a career in academia is a plan to enroll in graduate school within a year after graduating from college. Of all those who said that academia was their first-choice occupation only 58 percent said that they had plans to enroll in graduate school within a year of graduation. Among African Americans, type of school played a significant role in this decision. Among African Americans who selected college professor as their first-choice occupation and graduated from a liberal arts college 59 percent said that they would go directly on;

among those who graduated from Ivy League schools 53 percent gave this response; among those who graduated from state universities 59 percent said they would go directly on; but among HBCU graduates fully 88 percent said that they would go directly on to graduate school.[17] Not only were African American students who selected academia as their first-choice occupation more likely to go directly on if they attended an HBCU, students selecting other occupations were also more likely to say they would go directly on with their graduate education if they attended an HBCU.

Why were African Americans who attend HBCUs more likely to indicate that they planned to go directly on with their education than African Americans at the other types of school? We found that the single most important factor was what we call "occupational orientation." Some students view a college education primarily as a means to enter an occupation. Others view a college education not primarily as a necessary step to enter an occupation, but as a way of obtaining a broad liberal arts education. We designed an occupational orientation index to measure how focused each student was on an occupational goal. The index contained three items. A student received one point for each of the following: saying "I spend less time than average socializing"; indicating an interest in only one occupation as a freshman; indicating an interest in only one occupation as a senior. The higher the students' score on this index the more likely they were to say that they would go directly on with their education. Among those who received a low score on the index 43 percent said that they would go directly on, among those with a medium score 64 percent, and among those with a high score 78 percent said that they would go directly on.[18]

The Frog Pond Hypothesis and the Fit Hypothesis

In Chapter 1 we mentioned James A. Davis's paper "The Campus as a Frog Pond" (1966). Davis noted that the distribution of grades in schools of varying quality is the same. Then, using relative deprivation theory, he hypothesized that, controlling for ability, the less selective the school a student attends, the more likely the student would be to persist with high-achievement career aspirations. The mechanism for this is quite simple. Controlling for ability, the less selective the school, the higher the student's grades will be. Students compare themselves with others at the same school rather than with their national cohort. Thus, students who

200

attend highly selective schools and thereby get lower grades will develop lower levels of academic self-confidence and thus be less likely to persist with a high-achievement career aspiration.[19] Davis presented evidence to support his hypothesis. One of our goals was to see if the theory proposed by Davis would pertain to our study of the career choices of high-achieving minority students.

It is certainly not true today that the distribution of grades in various types of school is the same. In the schools in our sample only a small minority of students at the elite schools receive GPAs of B− or less (see Table B8.4). At the state universities about 40 percent receive GPAs of B− or less and at the HBCUs 59 percent receive GPAs of B− or less.[20]

Actually for the relative deprivation theory to be correct it is not necessary that the grade distribution at the various schools be the same. As Davis has pointed out (personal communication), as long as the students' reference groups are others on their campus rather than the national cohort, differences in grade distributions from one type of college to another should not matter; and the data presented in Chapter 5 suggest that comparisons with classmates are more important than comparisons with age cohort. Consider students at an elite school who receive a GPA of B−. These students are in the lower quarter of their class. When they compare themselves with classmates who have done better academically they are likely to conclude that academically they are average or below average (put in terms of our measure of self-confidence). With such relatively low levels of self-confidence, these students might be less likely to pursue high-achieving occupations such as academia. If the same students had attended less selective schools they probably would have received higher GPAs since there would have been less academic competition at these schools, and they may have concluded that academically they were average or above average. Even if they had received the same GPA at a nonelite school, a GPA of B− has very different consequences for a student attending a school where almost everyone has a higher GPA than it does for a student attending a school where this is the average or above average GPA.

In Table 8.2 we show GPA distribution by SAT score, by school type, and by ethnicity. Because there were not enough African Americans and Latinos in the highest SAT category we combined SAT scores into 1300 or higher, 1200–1299, and less than 1200. This last category contains the great majority of students in the nation.

The data show that, especially for African Americans but also for La-

Table 8.2 GPA distribution, by SAT score, by school type, by ethnicity (only students with GPA of 2.8 or higher) (percent)

SAT score	Whites			African Americans				Asians			Latinos		
	Liberal arts	Ivy	State	Liberal arts	Ivy	State	HBCUs	Liberal arts	Ivy	State	Liberal arts	Ivy	State
1300+													
A or A−	48	55	54	12	28	44	55	38	55	48	31	32	46
B+	30	29	31	38	35	17	12	32	29	34	40	35	26
B or less	22	16	15	50	38	39	32	30	16	19	29	34	28
Total	100	100	100	100	101	100	99	100	100	101	100	101	100
1200–1299													
A or A−	29	23	39	10	17	23	38	23	46	22	18	18	34
B+	35	36	32	21	35	27	16	42	23	32	34	31	40
B or less	36	41	28	69	48	50	46	36	31	46	48	51	26
Total	100	100	99	100	100	100	100	101	100	100	100	100	100
Less than 1200													
A or A−	14	21	31	3	10	17	26	27	0	20	8	18	24
B+	40	37	39	27	20	24	31	23	67	30	28	38	28
B or less	45	42	30	70	69	60	42	50	33	50	64	45	48
Total	99	100	100	100	99	101	99	100	100	100	100	101	100

Note: For whites, elite schools differ from nonelite schools at $p < .05$ for all three SAT categories. For Latinos, elite schools differ from nonelite schools at $p < .05$ for the two lowest SAT categories. For African Americans, elite schools differ from nonelite schools at $p < .05$ for less than 1200 SAT. For Asians, elite schools differ from nonelite schools at $p < .05$ for all three SAT categories.

tinos, there is an inverse correlation between grades and school selectivity, controlling for SAT scores. The African American students in the highest SAT category (1300 or higher) best illustrate this. Among this group, only 12 percent of those attending selective liberal arts colleges received GPAs of A or A−; among those with the same SAT scores attending the Ivy League, 28 percent received GPAs of A− or above.[21] Among those attending the state universities, however, fully 44 percent received such GPAs; and, of HBCU students, 55 percent did. The relationship is substantially weaker for Latinos and nonexistent among Asians and whites. Thus, although it is no longer true that grade distributions are roughly the same in all types of school, the observation that Davis made that when ability is controlled grades will vary inversely with school selectivity is true for African Americans (and partially true for Latinos), though it appears not to be true for Asians and whites.

We should also point out that these data are relevant for the "fit" hypothesis sometimes put forth by opponents of affirmative action. According to this hypothesis (Sowell 1993; S. Steele 1994), as a result of affirmative action the best African American students are placed into schools in which their white classmates have significantly better academic preparation. Thus, African American students end up getting lower grades, developing lower levels of academic self-confidence, and lowering their occupational aspirations. This would not occur if African Americans were admitted to schools where their academic qualifications were as good as or better than those of their white classmates.[22]

In Figure 8.5 we graphically display the logic of the fit hypothesis. The figure shows African American students grouped roughly by their SAT scores and colleges arranged in order of their selectivity as determined by mean SAT scores. Using these data, suppose, for example, a college with a mean SAT score of 1400 wants to have a diverse student body and ensure that between 5 and 10 percent of its freshmen class will be African American.[23] It is impossible for these schools to admit African American students who have the same SAT scores as the white and Asian students whom they admit. It is impossible because there are none. (There are in fact a few African American students who receive SAT scores of 1400 or more, but as the data in Table 2.2 make clear there are very few. Only one tenth of one percent of African American students score 700 or higher on the verbal SAT. Only 1 percent of African Americans score 600 or higher on the verbal SAT.) Suppose that administrators at one of these most selective schools wants to admit African Americans so that their

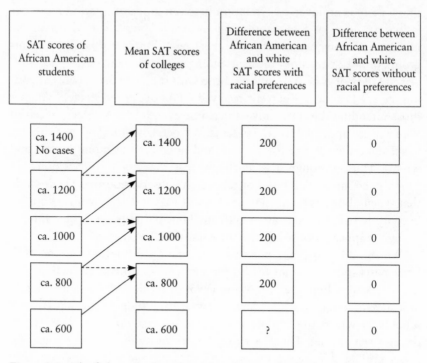

Figure 8.5   The fit hypothesis and racial preferences in admissions

student body will be ethnically diverse. There is only one thing they can do: set up an admissions program of racial preferences and admit African American students with SAT scores of between 1100 and 1200, which would be about 200 points lower than the scores of the white and Asian students admitted. In fact the SAT scores of the admitted African Americans will be substantially below a good portion of white and Asian students who are rejected.[24]

Now an SAT score of 1200 is nothing to sneeze at. Only about 10 percent of all students taking the exam in 1992 scored higher than 1200. (All SAT scores referred to in this book refer to scores before the "renormalization," which took place in the mid-1990s, shortly after this study was completed.) Students with SAT scores of 1200 generally have a good level of academic preparation and are most definitely capable of doing high-level college work. The only problem is that African American students with scores of 1200 who are admitted to schools with a mean

SAT score of approximately 1400 are going to be competing with white and Asian students whose mean SAT score is on average 200 points higher. We know what the consequences of this are. In elite schools most African Americans end up in the bottom quarter of their class, compare themselves negatively with their classmates, and develop lower levels of academic self-confidence. As we soon point out, these developments have an effect on these students' career choice.

Now let us consider the schools in the second rank: those whose mean SAT scores of students admitted are 1200. They too would like to have an ethnically diverse student body and admit between 5 and 10 percent African Americans into their freshman class. In their case there are African American students who have the same SAT scores as the whites and Asians whom they admit. There is only one problem: virtually all of these students have been admitted and many given generous scholarships by the most elite institutions in the first rank. So if the schools in the second-rank category also want to be racially diverse, they too must adopt an admissions policy of racial preferences; they must admit African American students who have average SAT scores of between 900 and 1000. Thus the African American students at both the top schools and the second level of school will have SAT scores 200 points lower than their white and Asian classmates. The same is true for those schools having mean SAT scores of 1000 or 800. Schools with mean SAT scores of 600 or below do not have to practice racial preferences for two reasons: first, most of them have an open admissions policy, accepting any students who apply. Second, many African American students have SAT scores as high as 600. So it would not be necessary for these schools to use racial preferences in order for them to admit African American applicants.

Scholars including Thomas Sowell and Shelby Steele argue that the system of racial preferences is harmful to the very African American students it is supposed to help. This system results in a poor fit between the academic preparation of minorities and the schools they attend. Without a system of racial preferences African Americans with SAT scores of 1200 would go to schools where whites and Asians have similar scores, African Americans with SAT scores of 1000 would go to schools where whites and Asians have similar scores, and so on. The mismatch would be eliminated.

Who might be hurt by the elimination of this system of racial preferences? First, the most elite schools would be less racially diverse. It is important to remember, however, that out of the approximately 2,700 four-year colleges in the United States only between 50 and 100 are in the top rank. If these schools were willing to eliminate their admissions policy of racial preferences, the other schools below them would not need to have such policies either. Given how few minorities are admitted to this small number of top-ranked schools, the issue of racial preferences seems to be primarily symbolic rather than utilitarian. Second, a relatively small number of African American students would go to somewhat lower-prestige schools than they do under the current system of racial preferences. Assume that the students who would be most affected by the elimination of race sensitive admissions policies would be African Americans who attend the 100 most elite schools. A generous estimate of the number of African Americans at these schools is 4,000. In 1992 there were about 78,000 African Americans receiving BA degrees (National Center for Educational Statistics 1995). If we assume that today there are closer to 100,000 African Americans receiving BA's, this would mean that only 4 percent of African Americans getting college degrees would be negatively affected by the elimination of race sensitive admissions policies. The data we present would also suggest that these 4,000 students would end up in higher-prestige occupations than they do under the current system of racial preferences in admissions.

We have no data that can be used to assess what impact being less racially diverse would have on the most prestigious schools.[25] Economists have conducted many studies in which they try to assess the economic value of going to a selective school. Most of these studies show a small but significant positive effect on income of attending a prestigious school (Kane 1998).[26] These same studies, however, also show that GPA has a small statistically significant negative effect on outcomes such as earnings—an effect that is usually at least as large as the effect of attending a highly selective school.[27] Since admissions policies employing racial preferences result in African Americans receiving lower GPAs than they might if they attended somewhat less selective schools, it seems to us that abandoning racial preferences would have little or no effect on outcomes such as income or prestige of occupation entered.[28]

Now let us turn to some data that are relevant to both the frog pond theory and the fit hypothesis (both these theories use the same mechanisms to reach their conclusions). The primary question we want to ask is: Does the selectivity of the school minority students attend influence their likelihood of persisting in a freshman interest in academia? If we find that, for example, African American students who attend one of our two categories of elite school are just as likely or more likely to persist with an interest in academia than are those attending one of our two categories of nonelite school (state universities and HBCUs), this would constitute strong evidence against the frog pond and fit theories. If, however, students attending the less selective schools were more likely to persist with an interest in academia, this would constitute evidence in support of the frog pond and fit theories.

In Table 8.3 we break down the data on academia presented in Table 8.1 by whether or not the students were initially interested in academia as a possible career. The data in Table 8.3 show (as we have also shown previously) that in general only a small number of students select professor as their most likely choice who were not already interested in it

Table 8.3 Percentage of students selecting university professor as most likely career, by freshman interest in career, by ethnicity, by type of school (only students with GPA of 2.8 or higher)

	Freshman interest in academia	
Ethnicity	Yes	No
Whites		
Liberal arts colleges	24	5
Ivy League	24	2
State universities	20	6
African Americans		
Liberal arts colleges	16	3
Ivy League	14	5
State universities	31	6
HBCUs	31	5
Asians		
Liberal arts colleges	14	4
Ivy League	16	5
State universities	22	3
Latinos		
Liberal arts colleges	28	4
Ivy League	27	7
State universities	23	8

Note: School type is significant at $p < .05$ for African Americans interested in professor as freshman and for whites not interested in professor as freshman.

as a possible career as freshmen. But more important, as the data in Table 8.3 clearly indicate, there are school differences: *high-achieving African Americans are much more likely to persist with academic aspirations if they go to either a state university or an HBCU than if they go to either one of our elite groups of schools.* There is approximately a 15 percentage point gap in persistence between African American graduates of elite schools and African American graduates of nonelite schools, a statistically significant difference.[29] To put it another way, African American students are twice as likely to persist with an interest in academia if they attend nonelite schools than if they attend elite schools.

The theories of relative deprivation and the fit hypothesis employed by Davis and Sowell hypothesize that students at elite schools develop lower levels of academic self-confidence than students of similar ability at nonelite schools. In Chapter 5 we showed that African American students have the lowest levels of academic self-confidence on two different measures (see Table 5.3). Lower self-confidence was in general a result of lower levels of academic achievement as measured by GPA. If Davis's theory of relative deprivation is correct, when we hold constant academic self-confidence, the coefficient for elite schools should become statistically insignificant. Using only African American respondents we computed a logistic regression equation in which persisting with a freshman interest in college professor is the dependent variable (thus the sample was limited to only those who expressed a freshman interest in academia). As independent variables we entered the elite schools (grouped together) as a dummy variable, with the state schools and the HBCUs as a comparison group. The data presented in Table B8.5 indeed do show that when classmate academic self-confidence is controlled, the coefficient for the elite schools becomes statistically insignificant.[30] This means that when academic self-confidence is controlled, the effect of type of school on persistence is reduced. The Davis hypothesis and the fit hypothesis for African American students are confirmed.

In Chapter 5 we discussed the theory of Claude Steele as a possible explanation of underperformance. Steele emphasizes that the probability that the stereotype threat will be activated is situational. If he is correct, we might expect that those students who attend elite institutions would be the most subject to stereotype threat, for several reasons. First, students attending these schools have been high performers in the past—they received high SAT scores and high GPAs in high school. Thus, they have not had the kinds of experiences of academic failure that are likely to activate disidentification from the domain. However, the prestige and aura of the elite schools are so great that at least some students, regardless of their previous academic success, may not be quite sure that they really belong there. This happens to white students as well (witness the doubts expressed by some white students in our focus groups). A white male senior at a prestigious Ivy League school expressed clearly this sense of insecurity and his related doubt about becoming a college professor:

> Most of us come from more or less the top of our high school class. Then I got here and found myself smack in the middle of the barrel and that was a weird place to be. One of the reasons I'm not particularly thinking about becoming a professor is I think I wouldn't be that good at it. All my professors here are brilliant. And I see some friends who are brilliant going into academia. Why should I push one of them out of the way, or even try, because they're going to do it and do an excellent job. No student will ever catch them off guard; they'll always know their stuff. I don't feel comfortable saying that about myself. (Barber and Cole 1996b)

Second, the majority of African American and Latino students attending elite schools are doing so under affirmative action programs; and, as we have discussed above, a consequence of this is that they receive relatively low grades. Just as Claude Steele argues that an unintended consequence of remedial programs is to trigger a fear of stereotyping, we believe that an unintended consequence or side effect of affirmative action programs is also likely to do so. We raised this issue with Steele. He agreed that affirmative action programs at elite schools could contribute to activation of stereotype threat, but argued that the threat would be activated at those institutions even without affirmative action (personal communication). We don't disagree with this view, but we believe that the extent to which stereotype threat is activated is a variable and it is possible that affirmative action programs may exacerbate it. In other words, affirmative action programs may intensify the sense that African American students have that they are expected to underperform academically, and this concern may have negative effects on their performance.[31] Many minority students may be apprehensive that others will say or think that they would not be attending an elite institution or even receive as high grades as they do if it were not for affirmative action programs.[32]

209

Using Schools as the Unit of Analysis

We identified several significant dependent variables that can be used to characterize the schools in our study.[33] The first is the percentage of students from a particular ethnic group among the total of graduating students and the percentage in each ethnic group who selected college professor as their most likely career. The data are presented in Table B8.6. If we look at the schools with twenty or more graduating minority students, the range in the proportion selecting college professor for African Americans is from 2 percent to 19 percent; for Latinos, from 2 percent to 27 percent; for Asians, from 2 percent to 18 percent; and for whites, from 1 percent to 23 percent. This is a lot of variation.[34] The variance in the proportion wanting to be college professors may, of course, be in part a result of the proportion of incoming students who were interested in careers in academia as freshmen. In the second part of Table B8.6 we show the range of the students interested in academia as freshmen. To control for this variable, we computed a third variable, the percent selecting professor as their most likely choice divided by the percent selecting professor as freshmen, or "persisters." The higher this percentage the more likely a school is to produce college professors, given the type of students who enroll. As can be seen in Table B8.6, the range on this variable is even greater: for African Americans, for example, it ranges from 12 percent to 76 percent. A third variable is the percentage of students who were "recruited" to an interest in academia. These are students who did not indicate an interest in academia as freshmen, but ended up selecting college professor as their most likely career. Once again, in every type of school and for every ethnic group, there is a substantial range.

The most important conclusion from Table B8.6 is that the rates at which students from some types of schools and from particular schools go into academia are considerably higher than from others. For example, the overall percentage range for the Ivy League is different from the percentage range for the state universities; and within the Ivy League, the percentage of African American graduates who select college professor as their most likely career varies between 2 percent and 19 percent. Our quantitative data do not enable us to determine what it is about particular schools that influences their students to select academia as a first-choice career and what it is about other schools that influences their students to be not interested in academia as a first-choice career. Some follow-up qualitative studies of some of these schools would be desirable;

although the differences between these schools cannot be teased out of our data, in-depth qualitative analyses are likely to suggest the factors that are at work.

Conclusions

It has long been believed that selective liberal arts colleges are the type of school most likely to produce Ph.D.s, particularly in the sciences. The reason for this is thought to be the high level of faculty-student contact, a variable that is truly important in the decision to become an academic (see Chapter 7). Our survey data, however, show that the graduates of the thirteen liberal arts colleges in our sample were no more likely to select academia as a first-choice career than graduates of the other types of colleges.

Our survey data suggest that the liberal arts colleges present a difficult environment for African American students to do well in. African American students at the liberal arts schools are more likely than their counterparts at the Ivy League schools to get low grades, have relatively low degrees of academic self-confidence (a finding that in the case of cohort self-confidence cannot be explained by grades), are most likely to underperform (that is, earn GPAs lower than what would be predicted by their SAT scores), have low levels of satisfaction even when grades are controlled, and believe that some faculty members made their undergraduate experience more difficult because of their racial or ethnic background. We believe that the primary reason that African American students fare less well at liberal arts colleges is the small number of each ethnic group on these campuses, which makes them feel like tokens.

Our data also leads to the conclusion that HBCUs are neither more nor less likely than predominantly white schools to produce African American graduates who select academia as their first-choice career. African American graduates of HBCUs, however, are more likely than African American graduates of predominantly white schools to say that they will continue their graduate education within a year after graduating. This is explained primarily by the higher occupational orientation of students at HBCUs.

We also presented data that allowed a test of the relative deprivation theory put forth by James Davis in his "frog pond" paper and the "fit" hypothesis put forth by Thomas Sowell and others. We found that the theory is supported for African American students but not for students in other ethnic groups. African American students at the elite schools (the liberal arts colleges and the Ivy League) get lower grades than students with similar levels of academic preparation (as measured by SAT scores) than African American students at the nonelite schools (state universities and HBCUs). Lower grades lead to lower levels of academic self-confidence, which in turn influence the extent to which African American students will persist with a freshman interest in academia as a career. African American students at elite schools are significantly less likely to persist with an interest in academia than are their counterparts at the nonelite schools. The lower levels of academic self-confidence when compared with classmates may explain part of this persistence gap. In addition, affirmative action may contribute to the activation of fear of negative stereotyping, which Claude Steele suggests may explain the underperformance of African Americans.

When we used schools as the unit of analysis we found relatively large differences in the extent to which minority students at different schools within a school category were likely to be interested in academia. More research is needed to understand the reasons for these observed differences.

THE PIPELINE INTO ACADEMIA

WITH ELIZABETH ARIAS

As we pointed out in Chapter 3, the shortage of minority faculty cannot be explained by lack of interest in academia as a career among minority students. In fact, the three minority groups we studied had approximately the same interest in academia as white students. In this high-achieving sample, approximately 10 percent of each ethnic group selected university professor as their first-choice career in their senior year right before graduation.[1]

If interest in academia on the part of high-achieving college graduates cannot explain the small numbers of minority group members in the pipeline, then there must be other factors determining their underrepresentation. In this chapter we look at some of those factors.

We begin by examining some characteristics of our sample that suggest why relatively small numbers of minorities were becoming academics. In general, at all three types of predominantly white schools we found smaller numbers of minority students than we had anticipated. Before we asked the registrars at the thirty-four schools we had approached to select the sample according to the criteria we had decided to use (see Chapter 2), we knew (from sources such as *Peterson's Guide to Colleges*) that some state universities had relatively small proportions of minority students. Although we tried to select our state universities so that they would be roughly representative of the category, we specifically chose some, such as the University of North Carolina at Chapel Hill and the University of Virginia, because they seemed to have at least a significant minority of African Americans. We selected other state universities, such as the University of Texas at Austin and UCLA, because they had relatively large proportions of Latino students (mostly Chicano). Other state universities had small proportions of minority students, but because of their large size we thought that we would get samples of approximately 100 African Americans.

When we received the samples from the registrars, we were surprised at how few African Americans there were at the state universities who met our criteria: that is, students who were majoring in the arts and sciences with a GPA of 2.8 or more. One large state university had only 8 African Americans in its graduating class of 1995–96 who met our criteria. Another very large state university had only 29 African American students in its graduating class who met our criteria. On average among the nine state universities that were in our sample 6.1 percent of the arts and sciences graduates were African American, but only 1.7 percent had GPAs of 2.8 or higher. Thus, only 28 percent of African American arts and sciences graduates of our state universities had GPAs of 2.8 or over.[2] Thus, while we expected to have a sample size of approximately 900 African Americans from the nine state universities, we ended up with a sample size of 348.[3]

There was a similar scarcity of Latinos in our sample from the state universities. In fact, if we had not specifically selected two state universities (the University of Texas at Austin and UCLA) that we knew to have large numbers of Latino students, we probably would have had a Latino sample from the state universities that was even smaller than the African American sample. But the University of Texas at Austin alone had 277 Latino arts and sciences majors in their graduating class with GPAs of 2.8 or higher. In general at the state universities we examined, 6.8 percent of their arts and sciences graduates were Latino, and 41 percent of these had GPAs of 2.8 or higher. This gave us a sample of 570 Latino students from the state universities.

A higher proportion of Asians were arts and sciences majors at the state universities, 10.6 percent; 54 percent of the Asians received GPAs of 2.8 or higher. This gave us a total sample of 1,185 Asians at the state universities.

We were also somewhat surprised at the small numbers of African Americans and Latinos who were graduating from the selective liberal arts colleges. In order for us to get enough African American and Latino graduates from this type of school we had to include thirteen schools in this category in the sample. We selected schools we knew had the largest proportions of minorities in their graduating classes.[4] Although in general the Ivy League schools had significant numbers of minorities in their graduating classes, we were again surprised at how few African Americans and Latinos graduated from some of these schools despite the schools' ability to draw the best-qualified minority candidates and their strong affirmative action programs.[5] There was one Ivy League school in which only 2 percent of its graduating class were African Americans and another in which only 2 percent of its graduating class were Latino (see Table B8.7).

To sum up, we had many fewer African American and Latinos in our sample, especially at the state universities, than we had expected. The small numbers of both African American and Latino students who were arts and sciences majors and had GPAs of 2.8 or higher tell us why we find so few members of these ethnic groups earning Ph.D.s in the arts and sciences. The data from our nonrandom sample give us a good clue to the answer to the question why certain ethnic groups are underrepresented in college and university faculty. Now let us look at data more broadly based than just our sample.[6]

Educational Attainment of the Four Major Ethnic Groups, 1990

Table 9.1 presents data on the educational attainment of the four major ethnic groups, from three sources: the 1990 Census of the United States; the National Center for Educational Statistics (NCES) *Digest of Educational Statistics* for the years 1995 through 1998; and our own survey. Our aim is to make a rough prediction of how many Ph.D.s in the arts and sciences who will end up working in academia will be produced in each of the next ten years. Demographic conditions and levels of educational attainment may change over this period, so this analysis must be seen as providing only a rough estimate of the size of the Ph.D. cohorts that will be emerging. In fact between 1990 and 1998 (the latest year for which census data were available at the time this analysis was conducted) there were significant demographic changes. Following our analysis of 1990 data we will look at similar data for 1998.

Although in making decisions in our analysis of these data we have consistently tried to err on the side of overestimation, the increasing educational opportunities for minorities and the fact that more Latino students will be born in the United States and thus obtain more education (when compared with immigrants) might lead to an increase in the num-

215

Table 9.1 The academic pipeline for the four ethnic groups, 1990

	Whites	African Americans	Asians	Latinos
1. Estimated population size for single year cohort[a]				
Percent	76%	11%	3%	10%
	3,029,000	429,000	120,000	401,000
2. Percent high school graduates[b]	91%	77%	83%	56%
Number	2,756,000	330,000	100,000	225,000
3. Percent high school graduates never enrolling in college[b]	32%	40%	19%	40%
Number	882,000	132,000	19,000	90,000
4. Percent high school graduates dropping out of college[b]	26%	31%	19%	29%
Number	717,000	102,000	19,000	65,000
5. Percent high school graduates with terminal associate degree[b]	10%	9%	10%	10%
Number	276,000	31,000	10,000	23,000
6. Percent high school graduates with college degree[b]	32%	19%	51%	21%
Number	882,000	63,000	51,000	47,000
7. Percent of college graduates with arts and sciences major[c]	47%	47%	51%	53%
Number	415,000	30,000	25,000	25,000

8. Percent arts and sciences graduates with GPA of 2.8+[d]	65%	28%	54%	41%
Number	270,000	8,400	14,000	10,200
9. Percent arts and sciences graduates who select college professor as first-choice career as seniors[d]	10%	11%	8%	12%
Number	27,000	924	1,120	1,224
10. Number receiving Ph.D.s in 1991–92[e]	26,000	1,223	1,559	811
11. Percent Ph.D.s in arts and sciences[e]	52%	34%	61%	62%
Number	13,500	416	951	503
12. Percent Ph.D.s in arts and sciences working in academia[b]	45%	40%	39%	48%
Number	6,075	166	371	241

a. Census of the Population, 1990, Age cohort 25–29 years.
b. Census of the Population, 1990, Age cohort 35–39 years.
c. NCES, *Digest of Educational Statistics*, 1995, Table 257.
d. Survey of nine large state universities (see Chapter 2 for list).
e. NCES, *Digest of Educational Statistics*, 1995, Table 264.

ber of minority Ph.D.s produced in the arts and sciences. But we believe that more than small improvements are needed to solve the problem of underrepresentation of minority faculty.[7]

In Row 1 of Table 9.1 we show the size of a one-year cohort of people between the ages of 25 and 29. We selected this age group because these are the people who either are currently in Ph.D. programs or will enter them in the near future. To get a one-year estimate we simply took all the people in a five-year age group and divided it by five. Thus, on average we estimate that in 1990 for any given age between 25 and 29 there were 429,000 African Americans in the population.[8] This figure includes U.S. natives and nonnatives. For whites, African Americans, and Asians we considered only those who were non-Hispanic. The census has a separate category for Hispanics (the group we call Latino in this book).

In Rows 2 through 6 our analysis is based on data from the 1990 census on the age cohort 35–39. In other words, we estimate the numbers resulting in each category by applying the rates (or proportions) experienced by the 35–39 birth cohort to the 25–29 cohort. We believed it was necessary to use this older cohort because some people do not complete their education until later in life. In fact, looking at cohorts even older than the 35–39 cohort for some of the ethnic groups one finds slightly higher percentages of high school and college graduates than what is indicated in this table. Row 2 shows the proportion of each ethnic group that has graduated from high school.[9] This goes from a high of 91 percent for whites to a low of 56 percent for Latinos. The low number for Latinos is undoubtedly because there are many immigrants in this age cohort who came to this country with relatively low levels of education and did not obtain additional education once they were in the United States. If we look at only U.S.-born Latinos in the 35–39 age cohort we find that fully 92 percent of them have completed a high school education. But in 1990 only 44 percent of the 25–29-year-old Latino cohort are U.S.-born. Of U.S.-born Asians in 1990 98 percent in the 35–39-year-old cohort have completed a high school education. But in the 25–29-year-old cohort only 19 percent of Asians were born in the United States. These data suggest that as the second generation of these ethnic groups mature there will be substantially more people who will be eligible to decide to become university professors and the extent of their underrepresentation may decline. Astin (1982) studied data on the percentage of Latinos who had not completed high school at different ages and interpreted this as indicating high dropout rates, although he was aware that some of the people he was studying could be immigrants. Our data suggest that the problem is more likely one of immigrants arriving in the United States without a high school degree than unusually high school dropout rates among Latinos.

Row 3 of Table 9.1 shows the proportion and number of high school graduates who never enrolled in college. This was computed by subtracting the sum of all those with higher levels of education (including some college) from the total of high school graduates. African Americans and Latinos are somewhat less likely to continue their education after graduating from high school, whereas Asians are substantially more likely than whites to do so.

Row 4 of Table 9.1 shows us the proportion and number of students who began college and later dropped out. (These are the people whom the census reports as having "some college.") There has been a great deal of concern about the dropout rate of African Americans in particular; but our data show only a 5 point gap between African Americans and whites. This is not as large a gap as the data from particular schools indicate. These data (Harriet Zuckerman, personal communication) usually show about a 20 percentage point difference in African American and white dropout rates.[10] Looking only at dropout rates from particular schools may lead to the erroneous conclusion that higher dropout rates are a major cause of the difference in college completion rates between African Americans and whites. What our data suggest is that many African Americans who drop out of a particular school may return to college later in life and complete a degree, perhaps at another school. The census data offer some support for this interpretation, as the proportion of African Americans who are classified as college dropouts declines somewhat as age increases; yet the proportion of whites classified as college dropouts stays roughly the same (around 25) as age increases. The data in Row 4 show that the dropout rate of Latinos is between that for whites and African Americans and the dropout rate for Asians is substantially below that for whites.

Row 5 of Table 9.1 shows the proportion and number of high school graduates who receive a "terminal" associate degree.[11] These degrees are usually granted by two-year community colleges, both private and public. Taking the total proportion with an associate degree as their highest level of education, we used this percentage to compute the number of high school graduates with an associate degree; and computing the number and then taking this number as a percentage of high school graduates, we computed the percent in Row 5. In all four ethnic groups about 10 percent have an associate degree as their highest level of education.[12]

Row 6 of Table 9.1 presents what is perhaps the most important data in the table: the proportion and number of each ethnic group completing college. There are significant differences among the four ethnic groups. Thirty-two percent of whites in the 35–39 age group have completed a college degree. But this 32 percent yields a very large number of college graduates. Asians are the most likely to complete college (51 percent) and African Americans the least likely (19 percent). Latinos are similar to African Americans (21 percent). Although the number of Asians aged 25 to 29 is only about one quarter of the number of African Americans, because of the higher rates of high school and college completion 51,000 Asians in each year's age cohort have college degrees. Latinos, although almost as numerous in this age group as African Americans, have fewer who complete a college degree (47,000) primarily because their rate of high school completion is much lower than that of any other ethnic group.[13]

Rows 3 through 6 include all possible outcomes for high school graduates, so the percentages in these rows total 100 percent.[14] That is, the percentage of those who never enrolled in high school, those who enrolled and dropped out, those who received terminal associate degrees, and those who graduated from college equals the total number of high school graduates.

We are interested in learning how many students in the four ethnic groups will be receiving Ph.D.s in the arts and sciences. We assume that if a student does not major in the arts and sciences the chances of that student's getting a Ph.D. in an arts and sciences subject is very low. Thus, students majoring in business, engineering, or education are unlikely to get Ph.D.s in the arts and sciences, although they may receive a Ph.D. in the field of their college major.[15] Row 7 of Table 9.1 shows the proportion and number of college graduates majoring in the arts and sciences based on NCES statistics for degrees granted in the academic year 1992–93.[16] There is no difference between white students and African American students in the proportion majoring in an arts and sciences subject.[17] Asians and Latinos are slightly more likely than either whites or African Americans to major in an arts and sciences subject.

Row 8 of Table 9.1 displays our most controversial assumption. We assume that students who do not do well in school would be unlikely to want to become university professors. Consider a student who receives a

GPA of 2.0, the minimum required for graduation at some schools. What are the chances of such a student selecting university professor as his or her first-choice career goal? We assume that it is close to zero because, as shown in Chapter 5, academic performance and GPA in particular are strongly related to the decision to select university professor as a first-choice career (see Figure 5.3).

We do not assume that there are no students with GPAs of less than 2.8 who might select university professor as a first-choice career. But we do assume that if students with GPAs below 2.8 select university professor as a first-choice career most of them will find it difficult, if not impossible, to be admitted to graduate school. If they are admitted to graduate school, these students would be the most likely to drop out; and if by some chance they complete a Ph.D. in the arts and sciences they would be very unlikely to be the type of scholar that most research universities and selective colleges would be interested in hiring. They probably would end up taking jobs either outside of the academy or in junior colleges or perhaps some four-year colleges that have trouble recruiting faculty with high academic credentials.[18]

Thus, in the analysis presented in this chapter we use data we collected from our sample of nine state universities to estimate the proportions of each ethnic group having GPAs of 2.8 or above. We believe that these schools are most similar to the typical college or university in the country. Our nine state universities are among the better state universities and, as indicated by the average SAT scores of their graduating seniors, these schools are probably more selective than the typical college in the United States. Many of the state universities in our sample are "flagship" schools and undoubtedly have better students (and thus students more likely to want to be college professors) than other state universities or colleges in the same states. But it is not clear that the distribution of grades at these schools would be any different from the distribution of grades at the average four-year college.

The data we collected from the nine state universities in our sample show considerable variability among the four ethnic groups in the probability of receiving a GPA of 2.8 or higher. We found 65 percent of white students, only 28 percent of African American students, 54 percent of Asian students, and 41 percent of Latino students majoring in the arts and sciences and receiving GPAs of 2.8 or higher.

The relatively poor academic performance of African American students compared to white students has been documented in much prior research. Robert Klitgaard (1985) reported data indicating that African American students are usually at the bottom of their classes in law school. William Bowen and Derek Bok (1998) reported that African Americans generally have lower ranks in their class than white students. Nettles, Thoeny, and Gosman (1986) reported that in their sample of colleges African American students had GPAs that were significantly lower than those of white students.

The percentage reported in Row 8 of Table 9.1 is important for this analysis because we make the assumption that only among students who receive GPAs of 2.8 or higher will we find those who actually earn a Ph.D. in the arts and sciences and ultimately teach in a college or university. If our figure of 28 percent for African Americans is too low an estimate, we may be underestimating the number of African Americans who are likely to be interested in becoming university professors in the arts and sciences. But as explained later, data from the census support the general validity of our estimates.

Row 8 of Table 9.1 shows that there are approximately 270,000 white students, only 8,400 African American students, 14,000 Asian students, and 10,200 Latino students who are in a position to select university professor as the career they will enter. In Row 9 of Table 9.1 we use data from our survey on the proportion of state university students in each of the four ethnic groups with GPAs of 2.8 or higher who actually select university professor as their first-choice career. Here we estimate the number of students in each ethnic group who are likely to graduate as arts and sciences majors with GPAs of 2.8 or above and select university professor as their first-choice career. These figures clearly indicate why there are so few minorities in the Ph.D. pipeline. Although we estimate that there are 27,000 white college graduates each year who want to become college professors in an arts and sciences field, there are less than 1,000 African Americans and slightly more than 1,000 Asians and Latinos who make this choice.

Row 10 of Table 9.1 contains data from the NCES statistics for 1991–92 on the actual number of Ph.D. degrees granted to students in the four ethnic groups. This number includes Ph.D.s in *all* fields, many of which are not in the arts and sciences—for example, in fields such as engineering and education. We used the NCES data to compute the proportion of total Ph.D.s that were in arts and sciences fields.[19] Both the proportion of Ph.D.s granted in arts and sciences fields and the number of Ph.D.s is reported in Row 11 of Table 9.1. These data indicate that whereas in each year there are approximately 13,500 Ph.D.s granted to white students in arts and sciences fields, there are only 416 such degrees granted to African Americans, slightly fewer than 1,000 to Asians and slightly more than 500 to Latinos.[20]

Finally, we must consider the fact that not all Ph.D. recipients end up working in academia. The only data we have on the proportion of Ph.D.s working in academia is from the 1990 census, which has a variable indicating in what type of institution the individual was employed. We took all Ph.D.s in the 35–39 age cohort and determined whether they were likely to be arts and sciences or other Ph.D.s based on the occupation reported.[21] Then, using the data on place of employment, we estimated the proportion working in colleges and universities.[22] The resulting data indicate that of those people having Ph.D.s in the arts and sciences 45 percent of whites, 40 percent of African Americans, 39 percent of Asians, and 48 percent of Latinos worked in academia.[23] Row 12 of Table 9.1 shows the estimated number of new Ph.D.s in each year's cohort who will take jobs in an arts and sciences field in academia. The number for whites is 6,075, but the numbers for the minorities are shockingly low. For instance, whereas 7 percent of all students earning a BA degree in 1990 in the United States were African American, these figures indicate that only 2.4 percent (166) of all Ph.D.s in arts and sciences who will enter academia in the near future are African American.[24] The corresponding figures for whites are 83 percent versus 89 percent (6,075), for Latinos 5 percent versus 3.5 percent (241), and for Asians 5 percent versus 5.9 percent (371). Although these figures shed a positive light on the situation for Asians, the majority of Asian faculty are concentrated in the natural sciences.[25]

The numbers presented in Row 12 of Table 9.1 are so low that it leads us to wonder whether some of our estimates may be inaccurate. But even if we assume that some of our estimates of the parameters are too low, revising those estimates upward would still yield very low numbers of minority Ph.D.s entering employment in academia in arts and sciences fields in any given year. Suppose, for example, that our estimate of the proportion of African Americans receiving GPAs of 2.8 and higher is too low and that the actual number is closer to 50 percent rather than 28 percent. All this would do is roughly double the number in Row 9 and give us an estimate of approximately 2,000 African Americans who want to become a college professor in the arts and sciences upon graduation from college. Likewise, if the estimate of the proportion of African Americans who receive Ph.D.s in arts and sciences fields is too low, raising the estimate to the same proportion as given for whites would only slightly increase the number of African Americans in this category.

It is interesting to compare the numbers in Row 9 and Row 11 of Table 9.1. The reason why we do not use the figures in Row 12 in our comparison is that the decision as to whether a Ph.D. recipient will actually take a job in or outside of academia is probably not made until relatively late in the process of obtaining a Ph.D. and considerably after college graduates make their career choices. We assume that most students who intend to get Ph.D.s in the arts and sciences probably start out thinking they will work in academia, and that many change their minds as they encounter the realities of the academic job market and become familiar with the opportunities available for Ph.D.s outside of academia (which they may not be aware of in their senior year of college). This is, however, speculation; future research should address this question directly.

The number in Row 9 is a rough estimate of the number of students graduating each year who select university professor in the arts and sciences as their first-choice career. It should not be surprising that the actual number of Ph.D.s granted to students in the arts and sciences (Row 11) is considerably below those aspiring to this degree as college seniors. First, we know that the students in our state universities are probably better students than those in the general population and are therefore more likely to select academia as a first-choice career.[26] This means that our estimates in Row 9 are probably somewhat too high. We also know that some students who tell us that academia is their first-choice career will never enroll in Ph.D. programs, changing their minds about what career they want to enter before ever enrolling in graduate school. This is especially likely given the fact that only 58 percent of those who told us that academia was their first-choice career intended to enroll in a graduate program in the year following their graduation from college.

Still other students will enter graduate school and never complete the Ph.D. We know that there are high dropout rates from Ph.D. programs and that generally less than 50 percent of those enrolling end up completing a Ph.D. (Bowen and Rudenstine 1992). Sure enough, in general we find the numbers in Row 11 to be approximately half of those in Row 9, with the exception of Asian students.[27] Thus, for example, whereas we estimate that in any given year there will be 27,000 white students who graduate with the intention of earning a Ph.D. in the arts and sciences and obtaining a job in academia there are only about 13,500 Ph.D.s ac-

224

tually granted. For African Americans there are about 1,000 who intend to enter academia in the arts and sciences and slightly more than 400 students earning Ph.D.s in an arts and sciences subject. And for Latinos there are slightly more than 1,200 who say they want to become academics in their senior year and slightly more than 500 Ph.D.s granted. For Asians, however, there are slightly more than 1,100 students expressing an intention to earn a Ph.D. in the arts and sciences but only slightly less than 1,000 who earn such a degree. This may indicate that Asian students are more likely to persist with an aspiration to be an academic and actually complete a Ph.D. than are students in the other ethnic groups.[28] Actually our estimate of the numbers of Asians wanting to be academics may be too low. As we have pointed out throughout this book, a large portion of high-achieving Asians want to go to medical school and become physicians. About half of all Asians who apply to medical school are not accepted. It is quite possible that once these Asians are rejected from the medical schools they apply to they decide to pursue a Ph.D. in an arts and sciences subject.

What is clear from Table 9.1 (even if some of our assumptions have yielded underestimates) is that there are very few African American and Latinos earning their Ph.D.s in an arts and sciences subject. Let us assume that about 500 African Americans earn a Ph.D. in an arts and sciences subject and enter academia in any given year. This figure is about two and a half times larger than the number indicated in Row 12 of Table 9.1. Given the fact that there are approximately 3,700 institutions of higher education (including about 1,000 community colleges) in the United States and within each of these educational institutions in the neighborhood of forty different departments, it is clear that there are too few African Americans coming out of the education pipeline to supply the demand for African American professors. The situation is just as bad for Latinos. Although Asians are overrepresented in academia in general, they are underrepresented in departments in the humanities and the social sciences; unless more Asians in these fields can be convinced to enter academia, this underrepresentation is likely to persist.

We may assume that the situation for Latinos will improve as more second-generation Latinos enter the educational pipeline. The educational attainment of U.S.-born Latinos is far greater than the Latino population in general. We may also assume that, since the number of Asians attending highly selective colleges has increased so dramatically and could possibly rise even further in the years ahead, the shortage of

Asian Ph.D.s in the humanities and social sciences might be somewhat alleviated. The situation for African Americans is the most troubling.

Educational Attainment of the Four Major Ethnic Groups, 1998

We repeated the analysis presented in Table 9.1 using the Current Population Survey (CPS) for 1998 to bring our information more up to date and to provide comparisons.[29] The data are presented in Table 9.2 (pages 228–229). A comparison of the figures in Row 1 of the two tables demonstrates that substantial demographic changes have taken place between 1990 and 1998. The white population has declined significantly, probably because whites who were 25 to 29 in 1990 are the tail end of the baby boom, whereas whites who were 25 to 29 in 1998 are part of the baby bust.[30] In addition, the population for all three minority groups has increased significantly. For African Americans this may be a result of high fertility rates. For Asians and Latinos the increase is probably primarily due to a continuation of high rates of immigration.

Comparing the data in Row 2 of the two tables, we see that there have also been changes in the rate of high school graduation. The rate for whites has risen slightly, from 91 percent to 94 percent; but the rate for African Americans has risen quite substantially, from 77 percent to 88 percent. This indicates that during the period 1990 to 1998 African Americans have made significant progress in closing the gap in high school graduation between their ethnic group and whites. There have also been increases in the rates of high school graduation for both Asians and Latinos.

The increase in the proportion of African Americans graduating from high school is certainly an encouraging statistic. But from the point of view of this book, we should be concerned not only with how many students graduate from high school, but how well they do in high school. If the increase for African Americans between 1990 and 1998 is a result of more "social promotions" or of political factors, but is not accompanied by an increase in the proportion who do well in high school, the increase will have less of an impact on the pipeline into academia. The fact that the proportion graduating from college has remained the same in this time period and very significantly below the proportion of whites who graduate from college in both time periods is disconcerting. In a large study of American high school students Laurence Steinberg (1996) found that African Americans received the lowest grades in high school. This finding held up when social class was controlled.

The data in Row 3 of Table 9.2 shows that there has been a slight increase in the proportion of all three minorities who never enroll in college, but the data in Row 4 show that the college dropout rate has substantially declined for all four ethnic groups. There have been only minor changes in the percentage of students receiving a terminal associate degree except for Latinos, where the percentage has declined from 10 percent in 1990 to 6 percent in 1998. Unfortunately, there has been very little change in the proportion of high school graduates who earn college degrees. Between 1990 and 1998 the percentage of African American high school graduates earning college degrees actually declined, from 19 to 18. However, given the increase in the size of the African American population and the rapid rise in the proportion graduating from high school, the total number of African Americans who receive college degrees has increased substantially during this period.

The data in Row 6 of Table 9.2 indicate little change in the *percentage* of high school graduates among the three minority groups who graduated from college but an encouraging increase in the *number* of all three minority groups who graduate from college. And if we jump ahead to Row 9 we note increases in the number of minorities who we estimate want to be college professors when they graduate from college. For example, between 1990 and 1998 there was an approximately 30 percent increase in the number of African American college graduates who wanted to become college professors in the arts and sciences. This number could be higher were it not for our assumption that African Americans continue to receive relatively low grades in college.

The bottom line of Table 9.2, in which we estimate the number of new Ph.D.s who will end up working in academia, shows almost a doubling of the number of Asians between 1990 and 1998, but only small increases in the number of African Americans and Latinos.[31] We can only conclude that the increase in the numbers of these two ethnic groups who graduate from both high school and college is not being effectively translated into Ph.D. production. This is likely the result of relatively poor academic performance in college, relatively low proportions of seniors who follow through on an intention to become college professors, and high dropout rates from graduate school. In conclusion, the data from 1998 show that whereas there has been a significant increase in the number of Asians entering academia, the number of African Americans and Latinos

Table 9.2 The academic pipeline for the four ethnic groups, 1998

	Whites	African Americans	Asians	Latinos
1. Estimated population size for single year cohort[a]				
Percent	2,502,000	509,000	178,000	559,000
	67%	14%	4.7%	15%
2. Percent high school graduates[b]	94%[a]	88%[a]	90%	63%[a]
Number	2,352,000	448,000	160,000	352,000
3. Percent high school graduates never enrolling in college[b]	31%[a]	43%[a]	22%[a]	46%
Number	729,000	193,000	35,000	162,000
4. Percent high school graduates dropping out of college[b]	20%	25%	15%	22%
Number	470,000	112,000	24,000	77,000
5. Percent high school graduates with terminal associates degree[b]	10%	7%	9%	6%
Number	235,000	31,000	14,000	21,000
6. Percent high school graduates with college degree[b]	35%[a]	18%[a]	48%	23%
Number	823,000	81,000	77,000	81,000
7. Percent of college graduates with arts and sciences major[c]	47%	47%	51%	53%
Number	387,000	38,000	39,000	43,000

8. Percent arts and sciences graduates with GPA of 2.8+[d]	65%	28%	54%	41%
Number	251,000	106,000	21,000	18,000
9. Percent arts and sciences graduates who select college professor as first-choice career as seniors[d]	10%	11%	80%	12%
Number	25,000	1,170	1,700	211
10. Number receiving Ph.D.s in 1991–92[e]	28,000	1,667	2,690	984
11. Percent Ph.D.s in arts and sciences[e]	52%	34%	61%	62%
Number	14,560	567	1,641	610
12. Percent Ph.D.s in arts and sciences working in academia[b]	45%	40%	39%	48%
Number	6,552	227	640	293

a. Current Population Survey, March 1998 Supplement, age cohort 25–29 years.
b. Current Population Survey, March 1998 Supplement, age cohort 35–39 years.
c. NCES, *Digest of Educational Statistics*, 1995, Table 257.
d. Survey of nine large state universities (see Chapter 2 for list).
e. NCES, *Digest of Educational Statistics*, 1997, Table 272.

doing so is so small at the current time as to make it virtually impossible for institutions of higher education to achieve their goal of increasing faculty diversity by hiring more African American and Latino professors.

We must be particularly concerned with several of the numbers for African Americans in Table 9.1 and Table 9.2. The first is the proportion of African American high school graduates who end up receiving a college degree. Whereas 32 percent of white high school graduates end up graduating from college, the 1990 census data suggested that only 19 percent of African Americans between the ages of 35 and 39 do so. The data for 1998 do not show any improvement. This is in part due to the fact that African Americans are less likely to enter college (40 percent of African Americans who never enroll versus 32 percent of white students in 1990). It is not implausible that the greater reluctance of African Americans to enter college is tied to the level of their academic performance in high school. We also find that African Americans are somewhat more likely than whites to drop out of college. This is also probably related to level of academic performance.

Finally, among arts and sciences graduates only 28 percent of African Americans as opposed to 65 percent of white students earn a GPA of 2.8 or higher (Table 9.1). All these data lead to the same conclusion: If we want to increase the number of African American students in the Ph.D. pipeline, we must work to improve the academic performance of African Americans at every level of education. As we point out in the next chapter, on policy implications, there may not be that much that American universities and colleges can do to improve the performance of African Americans at the lower levels of the education system; but there are things that might be done to improve the performance of African Americans in college. If African Americans did as well as white students in college, we can assume that the number of African American Ph.D.s entering academia in any given year would more than double. Although this would not be nearly enough to fill demand, it would certainly help to alleviate the current serious shortage of African American Ph.D.s in the arts and sciences.

The Number of Minority Ph.D.s in Different Fields, 1995–96

Up until now we have been trying to estimate how many minority members will enter academia in an arts and sciences field without making any distinction among these fields. In this section we examine the distribution of Ph.D. degrees among the various fields by ethnicity. These data come from the NCES's 1998 *Digest of Educational Statistics*. In Table 9.3 we show the numbers and proportions of Ph.D.s granted to each of the four ethnic groups in a series of different fields.

The arts and sciences subjects listed in Table 9.3 are area/ethnic and cultural studies, biological and life sciences, communications, humanities, mathematics and computer sciences, physical sciences, psychology, and social sciences. The non–arts and sciences subjects are business, education, engineering, health professions and related sciences, and others. This table documents the very small number of Ph.D.s granted to African Americans and Latinos in virtually all arts and sciences subjects.

Only 19 Ph.D.s were granted to African Americans in mathematics and the computer sciences in 1995–96, for example, and only 56 Ph.D.s were granted to African Americans in all of the physical sciences. Even in the biological and life sciences, where African Americans earned 79 Ph.D.s in 1995–96, only about 5 percent of all Ph.D.s granted to African Americans were in this field. About 10 percent of all Ph.D.s granted to white students were in the biological and life sciences. These figures confirm the very pessimistic outlook for achieving adequate representation of African American faculty members in the natural sciences. Even the most popular fields—the humanities (148), psychology (159), and the social sciences (121)—show relatively small numbers of Ph.D.s granted to African Americans. Note, however, that 34 percent of African Americans who receive Ph.D.s earn them in the field of education. This percentage is down significantly from prior years, when approximately half of all Ph.D.s granted to African Americans were in the field of education.

The figures presented in Table 9.3 on African Americans represent strong evidence against those who claim that there are African American scholars to be hired if only the universities would make a strong enough effort.[32] These data lend strong support to the conclusion that the reason for the shortage of African American faculty members in our universities and colleges does not primarily lie in any lack of willingness on the part of these educational institutions to search out African American scholars, but is more likely a function of the very small number of such scholars coming through the educational pipeline.

The figures for Asians presented in Table 9.3 suggest that there are a reasonable number receiving Ph.D.s in the natural sciences (especially if we make the assumption that a majority of the nonresident aliens who

Table 9.3 Percentage and number of Ph.D. degrees granted in 1995–96 to members of the four ethnic groups, by discipline

Discipline	White		African American		Asian		Latino		Nonresident alien	
	%	No.	%	No.	%	No.	%	No.	%	No.
Area/ethnic and cultural studies	0.40	117	1.30	22	0.40	13	0.30	3	0.20	28
Biological/life sciences	10.22	2,838	4.82	79	17.54	464	10.11	101	11.25	1,284
Business	2.94	817	2.75	45	2.91	77	2.00	20	3.53	403
Communications	0.84	232	1.22	20	0.60	16	0.50	5	0.63	72
Education	18.48	5,128	34.47	564	5.93	157	21.82	218	4.89	558
Engineering	9.04	2,510	4.52	74	21.58	571	8.90	89	27.39	3,124
Humanites[a]	12.02	3,339	9.04	148	6.50	172	13.21	132	6.49	740
Health professions and related sciences	4.83	1,342	3.91	64	6.27	166	5.20	52	4.32	493
Mathematics and computer sciences	3.29	914	1.16	19	6.88	102	1.00	18	8.24	940
Physical sciences	8.81	2,446	3.42	56	14.70	389	6.81	68	14.04	1,601
Psychology	11.12	3,087	9.72	159	3.78	100	14.81	148	1.70	194
Social sciences[b]	8.90	2,471	7.40	121	6.16	163	9.50	95	7.85	895
Others (non–arts and sciences)	9.06	2,515	16.20	265	6.65	176	4.80	48	9.80	1,118
Total	100	27,756	100	1,636	100	2,646	99	999	100	11,405

Source: NCES, Digest of Educational Statistics, 1998, Table 271.
a. English language and literature, foreign languages and literature, liberal arts and sciences, general studies and humanities, philosophy and religion, visual and performing arts.
b. Includes history, multi/interdisciplinary studies.

are earning Ph.D.s come from Asian countries). But in the social sciences and humanities the number of Ph.D.s granted to Asians is only slightly higher than the number granted to African Americans. Of course, as pointed out earlier, Asians represent a significantly smaller proportion of the population—although at elite schools there are more Asian students than there are African American students. If our aim is to have Asian professors at the schools where Asians are students, if the majority of Asian Ph.D.s in the social sciences and humanities end up at the elite schools we may be able to make some progress toward reducing the underrepresentation of Asian faculty in these fields.

The data for Latinos presented in Table 9.3 are just as discouraging as those for African Americans. First, we begin with the fact that at least in 1995–96 there were fewer Latinos earning Ph.D.s than there were African Americans. The number of Latinos earning Ph.D.s in the natural sciences is only slightly higher than the number of African Americans earning Ph.D.s in these fields, but it is still way too low for us to have any hope of reducing the underrepresentation of Latino professors in these fields. In the social sciences and humanities the number of Ph.D.s earned by Latinos is slightly less than the number earned by African Americans—a number far too low to significantly reduce the underrepresentation of Latino faculty members in these fields.

Perhaps the only bright spot in Table 9.3 is the large number of Ph.D.s earned by nonresident aliens. These are heavily concentrated in engineering and in the natural sciences; but even in the humanities and the social sciences there are substantial numbers of Ph.D.s granted to this group. In fact, in the humanities there are two and a half times as many Ph.D.s granted to nonresident aliens as there are to African Americans and Latinos combined. In the social sciences there are four times as many Ph.D.s granted to nonresident aliens than there are to African Americans and Latinos combined. We do not know what the ethnic composition of these nonresident aliens is. But to the extent that some of them are black, Latino, or Asian and they stay in the United States and assume positions as professors, this group may help alleviate the underrepresentation of the ethnic minorities we have found in our study.

There is, however, a potential problem in using foreigners to solve the diversity problem. Consider blacks from Africa who receive Ph.D.s in this country and then teach here. Since these people are not from the African American subculture and may not even identify with African Americans, it is questionable whether they will serve all of the functions that diverse faculty are supposed to (see our discussion of the value of diversity in Chapter 1). Yet most universities are quite pleased to hire such Ph.D.s since they serve to increase the number of "black" professors employed. There is a similar problem with the use by universities of the category "Latino." As we have pointed out earlier, the people grouped in this category come from very different cultures and have different levels of educational attainment and problems. When universities hire people from Argentina and Chile, for example, and classify them as "Latino" they may not be providing Chicano students with faculty who will serve their interests.

Conclusions

The data provided in this chapter prompts us to reach the conclusion that the main reason why there are so few African Americans and Latinos earning Ph.D.s and thus why there is an undersupply of minority Ph.D.s to be hired as faculty at institutions of higher education is that these groups have generally lower levels of educational attainment than whites and Asians. There simply are not enough African Americans and Latinos who are graduating from college with a major in the arts and sciences and who do well enough in college to believe that academia is a viable career option for them. The very small numbers of African Americans and Latinos who were arts and sciences majors and had GPAs of 2.8 or higher at the nine state universities in our sample was the first sign of the shortage of these groups in the educational pipeline. Data from the 1990 and 1998 census and the NCES *Digest of Educational Statistics* led us to believe that the conclusion we had reached on the basis of the nine state universities in our sample was one that could be generalized to the entire population.

Our data suggest that there will be more Asians who become college professors in the arts and sciences in any given year than African Americans. Given that Asians represent a much smaller percentage of the population this might be seen as evidence that the shortage of Asian faculty members will be alleviated. The problem is that Asian students are not evenly distributed among the different types of school. Asians, because they do unusually well in high school, tend to be concentrated in the most selective educational institutions. There is a shortage of Asian faculty members in the social sciences and humanities at these schools. If the proportion of Asians enrolled in selective schools continues to increase and (as in our sample) slightly more than half of them major in the social sciences and humanities, there is a possibility that the shortage of Asians in these fields might be alleviated in the future. It would also be helpful if just some of the very high proportion of Asians who select medicine as their first choice could be persuaded to enter careers in academia instead of medicine. The underrepresentation of Asian faculty members in the social sciences and humanities at selective institutions is a real problem; but it is not of the level of seriousness of the general underrepresentation of African Americans and Latinos.

The data on U.S.-born Latinos indicates that their level of educational attainment is higher than that of African Americans. Therefore, as we have more second- and third-generation Latinos moving through the educational system, the shortage of Latinos may be somewhat alleviated.[33] The greatest problem lies in the underrepresentation of African Americans on the faculties of our schools of higher education. The data we have uncovered suggests that improving academic performance is the most important step to take in order to increase the number of African Americans in academia.

It may also be worthwhile to repeat here what we have said earlier. Some critics of institutions of higher education, particularly the selective institutions, have claimed that they could increase the diversity of their faculties if they simply made a greater effort to recruit existing African American Ph.D.s. The data presented in this chapter suggest that this is not a sound argument. The reason why institutions of higher education have difficulty in recruiting minority faculty members is that there simply are not enough minorities earning Ph.D.s in the arts and sciences.[34]

As long as the number of minority Ph.D.s in the labor pool remains so small, colleges and universities are playing what may be seen as a "zero-sum" game in their attempts to diversify. Thus, if university A hires an African American scholar who is currently employed at university B, university A will become somewhat more diverse and university B somewhat less diverse. Overall, the system of higher education retains the same level of diversity. The only way to end this zero-sum game is to increase substantially the number of minority Ph.D.s entering the academic labor pool. Racial preferences in hiring will do nothing to increase the level of systemwide faculty ethnic diversity.

10

POLICY RECOMMENDATIONS

Earlier chapters presented the results of our investigation of the reasons why minority members are underrepresented on the faculties of our institutions of higher education. In this final chapter we briefly review the relevant findings and lay out policy implications and recommendations that follow from our findings. All of our recommendations are aimed at achieving one goal: increasing the ethnic and racial diversity of academic faculties. Universities and colleges of course have many goals, only one of which may be to increase faculty diversity. It is therefore possible that some of the recommendations we make could clash with other goals deemed important to individual educational institutions. Each institution has to decide how committed it should be to achieving faculty diversity and whether particular recommendations fit in with its overall goals.

Academic Achievement of Minority Students

Perhaps our single most important finding is that presented in Chapter 9, on the educational attainment of minority group members. We found that African Americans and Latinos do not have high enough levels of educational attainment for large numbers of them to decide they want to pursue a career as university professor. There are two aspects of this problem. The first is the difference between whites and Asians on the one hand and African Americans and Latinos on the other in terms of the proportions and numbers of each group completing college. The second is a question of how well African Americans and Latinos perform, or how much they learn at each level of the educational system. Graduating from high school without gaining the necessary academic skills to complete college is not going to produce more minority professors. Similarly, graduating from college but having low levels of academic achievement will keep down the number of students who decide to become college professors. Our strongest conclusion is that if we want to have more African Americans and Latinos becoming college professors, society in general (including, but not limited to, institutions of higher education) must work to increase the level of educational attainment and achievement among these two groups.

The fact that African Americans and Latinos do not have as high a level of educational attainment as whites and Asians results from a large number of macro social problems, including changes in the economy and the persistence of racism in some areas of the society. These problems are very difficult to overcome. It would be easy for institutions of higher education to conclude that there is very little, if anything, they can do to overcome these problems. And perhaps it is true that such institutions can make only a small dent in these problems. Nonetheless, there are steps that colleges and universities can take to help increase the educational attainment of African Americans and Latinos at all levels. We assume that many universities and colleges are already involved with community groups in projects whose ultimate aim is the improvement of minority students' educational attainment. Because our research did not examine students' precollege experience, we make no recommendations on this important area of concern.

In 1997 Clifford Adelman, a senior research analyst with the U.S. Department of Education, published an article in the educational journal *Change* entitled: "Diversity: Walk the Walk and Drop the Talk." In this article Adelman made some policy suggestions that, if initiated, could serve to improve the educational attainment of minority high school students. We believe that Adelman's suggestions are sound and that programs like the ones he proposes may help improve the academic performance of minority group students. We urge university and college administrators who are interested in having their institutions help improve the education of minority students to review Adelman's recommendations, summarized as follows.

Adelman argues that just graduating from high school is not enough to prepare minority students to do college work and that if they do not acquire the basic skills necessary in high school, remedial courses in college are unlikely to be successful. He presents data indicating that students who participate in remedial college courses have only one chance in eight of completing a bachelor's degree by the age of 30. He also presents data indicating that although minority access to college has increased, there has not been a corresponding increase in completion rates. He concludes that "we will not improve completion rates until higher education makes a massive, creative effort (with courage, conviction, and real money) to improve the precollegiate academic resources of minority students" (p. 43).

Adelman is critical of existing outreach programs conducted by institutions of higher education:

> Only 32 percent of institutions of higher education even sponsored a precollegiate outreach program for disadvantaged students. The median number of participating faculty was six per college, the mean student/staff ratio was 46:1, and 42 percent of participating students attended only during the summer. One out of seven participating students entered after high school graduation, which means they didn't stay long . . . The average reported annual time in these programs was 250 hours. That number sounds decent—until we see how the time was used. Colleges were asked to indicate the three most important services carried out within their largest outreach programs. The top item on the list was "social skills development." Preparatory courses and remediation ranked fifth and sixth. Social skills development will not get you a degree. Academic preparation will increase the chances dramatically. (p. 44)

Increasing the Number of Minority Students Who Enter Academia

The recommendations we make throughout this chapter are all aimed at increasing the number of minority college graduates who will enter graduate school with the aim of attaining a Ph.D. in an arts and sciences subject. The actions we recommend will not directly lead to an individual school's increase in the ethnic or racial diversity of its own faculty. Rather, we hope that these actions will increase the size of the pool of minority Ph.D.s some years down the road. Thus, we recommend that schools, especially those with relatively large enrollments of high-achieving minority students, participate in a communal effort, which may not directly benefit them but will benefit other institutions of higher education. Because the "payoff" of our suggested programs is in the future and indirect, individual schools need to have a strong commitment to the general benefit to enact these programs.

We suggest that some organization, perhaps either the National Research Council or the American Council on Education, collect data each year on the number of minority graduates of each college and the number and proportion who enter different types of postgraduate programs, including Ph.D. programs. The publication of this information should serve to increase the prestige of undergraduate schools that are successful in graduating relatively large numbers of minority students and having them enter careers such as academia. Publication of such statistics might also serve to motivate those schools that are not doing so well in this particular area to increase their efforts.

Finding: We found little difference among the four ethnic groups we studied in their occupational preferences insofar as academia is concerned: approximately 10 percent of each ethnic group selected college professor as their most likely occupational choice. The low numbers of African Americans and Latinos who actually wind up in the pool of potential faculty, therefore, is caused not by a lack of interest, but by the relatively low absolute numbers of these ethnic groups in the undergraduate population, particularly the dearth of such undergraduates in arts and sciences programs who perform at a high level academically. A very high proportion of minority students who complete high school with high GPAs and receive high SAT scores attend the most selective ("elite") colleges and universities, particularly high-prestige private research universities, such as the Ivy League schools.

Recommendation: Although our proposal may be difficult and costly for the elite institutions (the Ivy League schools and the highly selective liberal arts colleges), in order to have a major impact on the overall diversity among faculty in higher education as a whole the elite schools, and particularly the Ivy League schools, should increase their effectiveness in interesting currently enrolled minority students in a career as professor in arts and sciences fields. They should try to raise the percentage of minority students with this career interest to a level substantially above that of white students. Small increases here can make large long-term differences in the availability of highly qualified minority faculty members.

239

Using the Admissions Process

Finding: Initial career interest is one of the key determinants of a graduate's most likely career choice. Fully 70 percent of all those in our survey who chose college professor as the one occupation they were most likely to go into indicated that they were already interested in that occupation when they entered college.

Recommendation: Schools that are not highly selective can do little through the admissions process to increase the number of minority students who enroll as freshmen with an initial interest in becoming college professors. Schools that are selective, however, can use the admissions process to increase the number of such students.

We advise selective colleges to add a question to their admission applications that ask prospective students to indicate what career(s) they think they might be interested in pursuing. The question should be a multiple-choice question that allows the students to indicate as many occupations as they are currently interested in. College admissions officers might then be more attentive to applicants' career plans. If they ultimately admitted more African American, Latino, and Asian freshmen with an interest in academia, the number of minority students pursuing graduate study in the arts and sciences would quite likely increase.

The admissions process at highly selective schools is already difficult and complex. Many interests and goals must be served. But if selective colleges and universities are to increase the number of minority students who go on to graduate study in the arts and sciences, they must give more attention to applicants' career interests in the admissions process, and admissions committees should give preference to minority applicants who are interested in academic careers.

Finding: We found that 21 percent of the graduates of the Ivy League schools selected medicine as their first-choice career. This figure is considerably higher than that of the selective liberal arts colleges or for high-achieving students at state universities and HBCUs. The primary reason why Ivy League students are more likely to want to become physicians than students at other types of school is that they enter college with this aspiration. Thus, students wanting to be physicians are self-selecting into the Ivy League. Medicine has for many years been the highest-prestige and highest-paying occupation in the United States. It is also one of the most important, and it serves the national interest for talented students to enter medicine as a career. It is inevitable that a significant portion of the graduates of elite private schools such as the Ivy League will want to become physicians. Nonetheless, we believe that administrators and faculty members at the Ivy League schools and other selective schools with a similar proportion of their graduates entering medicine should seriously address the question of whether it is in the interest of these schools and the functions they serve in society for such a large portion of their graduates to enter one occupation. Schools may legitimately decide that it is not part of their role to determine what occupations their graduates enter. But the premise of our research, after all, was that the sponsoring schools would try to adopt policies in order to increase the number of minority students who select careers as professors in an arts and sciences subject. Thus, to this extent the sponsoring schools have already decided that influencing the occupational choice of enrolled students is a legitimate goal.

One factor contributing to the high proportion of students at the Ivy League (and presumably other similar elite private schools) who enter with the goal of becoming physicians is that the proportion of African American and Asian students who want to be physicians is extremely high. In the case of Asians this proportion approaches 50 percent. We also found that among those students who reported an interest in both academia and medicine, the overwhelming majority selected the latter career as their first choice.

Recommendation: The Ivy League schools (and other schools with more than 15 percent of their graduates selecting medicine as their first-choice career) should pay particular attention to the freshman career interests of African American and Asian students who apply for admission. To the extent that it does not interfere with other goals of the admission process, these schools should try to give preference to African American and Asian applicants who are interested in academia over those who express an interest in medicine.

We cannot emphasize enough the importance of taking freshman career interests into account if schools are seriously interested in increasing the number of minority graduates who enter academia. Since relatively few students are recruited to a career interest in academia during college, it is imperative to increase the number of minority students who have this interest when they enter college. Also, since increasing the number of students who decide to enter academia means reducing the number who decide to enter medicine,[1] it would be good to give academia a head start in this race by manipulating the occupational interests of the students who are admitted.

Increasing Commitment after Admission

Although about a third of high-achieving minority students (somewhat less for African Americans) are interested in becoming professors when they enter college, commitment to this career is relatively weak. At the end of college, when students are making their choices as to what career to pursue, students who are interested in both academia and other major competing occupations (medicine, law, business, and teaching) are more likely to select an occupation other than academia (see Chapter 3). Our research turned up a large number of findings that point to ways that institutions of higher education can act to increase the likelihood that minority students with an initial career interest in academia will actually follow through with this interest and enter a graduate program in the arts and sciences.

All schools, both selective and less selective, should consider adopting some of the recommendations suggested below (or similar ones). How these suggestions are actually implemented will vary depending on specific conditions existing at individual schools.

Finding: The overwhelming majority of students we interviewed told us that career counselors or placement officials had very little influence on their choice of career. Most schools have advisors for students who are interested in becoming physicians, lawyers, and teachers; but few, if any, schools have advisors for students who are interested in becoming professors.

Recommendation: Every four-year college should appoint a staff member whose primary responsibility will be to serve as an advisor to students who are interested in careers as professors. This person would also be responsible for coordinating the programs we suggest that are aimed at increasing and maintaining interest in an academic career. We will refer to this individual as the "faculty advisor."

Finding: Existing programs sponsored by foundations and other institutions aimed at getting minority students interested in becoming college professors have been very successful. Our multinomial regression models show that these programs have an especially significant influence on African American and Latino students even when all other variables are controlled, including initial interest in academia, grades, and academic self-confidence.

Recommendation: Every institution of higher education interested in increasing the ethnic diversity of faculty should set up a program, with or without the support of external organizations, whose goal is to get minority students interested in entering academia. This program should be run by the faculty advisor. Although existing programs aimed at increasing minority commitment to academia, such as the Mellon Minority Undergraduate Fellowship (MMUF) program, have been very successful, they have generally been limited to a relatively small number of participants who have been self- and socially selected. We suggest that universities and colleges attempt to increase the size of these programs substantially, so as to include all minority group members who have an interest in academia. Whether these larger programs are effective may be determined by evaluation research.

The MMUF program, sponsored by the Andrew W. Mellon Foundation, is a significant source of funding for programs aimed at encouraging minority students to become academics. Yet to our knowledge no systematic evaluation of this program has ever been done. In the course of conducting the research for this book, at the request of Harriet Zuckerman, Vice President of the Mellon Foundation, we conducted a preliminary evaluation of the effectiveness of the MMUF program and found that it was highly effective—but no more so than other similar programs.[2] One way in which the MMUF program could increase its effectiveness is to stop putting as much money as it does into liberal arts colleges, places our research has clearly shown to be a hostile environment for African American students and where such students are less likely to persist with career interests in academia than they are in less selective institutions. The MMUF program should fund large programs at some of the less elite state institutions and HBCUs. At the same time, the programs it currently funds at large elite universities, like the Ivy League schools, are definitely worth continuing.

Students should be recruited into these programs at the beginning of their freshman year. Information on whether each freshman minority student has an interest in academia would preferably be obtained from the college application, which we have recommended contain a multiple-choice question on occupational interests. If such a question is not in-cluded on the application, colleges might use their in-house institutional research capacity to survey student career interests and attitudes at the beginning of the freshman year in order to identify students with an in-terest in academic careers and especially those with positive attitudes to-ward research, teaching, living in the world of ideas, and generally pursu-ing an academic lifestyle.

At highly selective schools all minority students who indicate a fresh-man interest in academia should be invited by letters and telephone calls to participate in the pre-academia advisory program. Less selective schools might consider inviting all students with a freshman interest in academia who have a combined SAT score of 1100 or higher or a high school GPA of A− or higher. (Students who enter college without ade-quate academic preparation, as indicated by SAT or ACT scores and high school GPA, are unlikely to do well enough in school to make college professor a viable occupational choice.) Using an indicator of academic preparation in determining who will be invited to participate in the pre-academia advisory program might be particularly important at HBCUs. At these schools, since virtually all the students are African American, it is possible that a pre-academia advisory program including all students who express a freshman interest in academia might be too large to be successfully administered. At schools that have large numbers of under-graduates majoring in fields such as business or education, as is the case in many state universities, it might be advisable to invite only students who intend to major in an arts and sciences subject to participate in the pre-academia advisory program.

At predominantly white schools the number of minority students ad-mitted in any given year is not too large and (according to our findings) only about a third of them are likely to express interest in an academic career, so it should be possible to conduct individual interviews between the students and the faculty advisor or assistants to the advisor, in order to invite freshmen to join the pre-academia advisory program. Senior mi-nority group students who have participated in the program or graduate students may be used as assistants and help in the socialization of the freshmen.

Finding: Most undergraduate students are unfamiliar with the de-tails of life as a professor, particularly the advantages of the academic life. In addition, parents of many minority students, particularly Asians and African Americans, have very little knowledge about what a career in academia entails and pressure their children to enter a career other than academia. This pressure is often successful.

Recommendation: Colleges should prepare a promotional brochure and a videotape in which the job of college professor is described in a favorable but realistic light. Advantages and disadvantages of the academic life should be realistically portrayed. Information on the relative pay of professors and those of major competing occupations should be presented. Advantages, such as autonomy, which neither students nor parents are likely to be aware of, may be stressed. The video might, for example, follow a minority student as he or she goes through graduate school, gets a Ph.D., lands a first job, and so on. These promotional materials should not just portray academia in a favorable light; they should also inform students about some negative aspects of other careers that they may not be aware of. The burnout rate among doctors, for example, is exceptionally high; doctors are more likely to be addicted to drugs than people in any other occupation. Working over a hundred hours a week as a law associate in a large firm—a position only a tiny fraction of lawyers attain—is not fun. The proportion of associates who make partner is even more daunting.

To some extent these promotional materials are propaganda, in that they are intended to change students' views about different occupations; but they should at the same time be completely honest about the difficulties of life in academia.

These materials would not only be useful as tools to maintain the commitment of students who are relatively unfamiliar with academia; they could also be used by students interested in academia to convince their parents that the job is a respectable one, with reasonably good prospects for a decent income. Videos and brochures would be expensive to produce and probably would require the cooperation of a group of institutions. But they would be extremely useful in increasing the proportion of minority students who persist with a freshman interest in academia.

Increasing Faculty-Student Contact

Finding: Having a considerable amount of contact with faculty is a major correlate of choosing college professor as the most likely career. This correlation holds for all ethnic groups, at all types of schools.

The amounts of contact reported by students are similar for the three types of predominantly white schools, but the amount is much higher at the HBCUs. Indeed, the strongest predictor of interest in academia is an index of contact with faculty, along with initial interest in academia and GPA.

Pre-academia advisory programs should have as one of their goals to inform the participants about the details and advantages of a career in academia. They should also focus on increasing the amount of contact that students interested in academia have with faculty members. Faculty members who participate should actively encourage minority students to consider pursuing an academic career.

Recommendation: Pre-academia advisory programs should have two components. One would have the goal of informing students about the benefits and advantages of a career in academia and increasing their level of faculty contact. (The second component, discussed below, is aimed at improving the academic performance of students with an interest in academia.) Faculty contact could be fostered through a series of regularly scheduled meetings attended by students, advisors, and guest speakers. Groups should be kept relatively small so as to allow the student participants to interact with the faculty advisors and guest speakers. Having minority faculty participate as guest speakers would be desirable, but our research has suggested that white faculty members can be effective role models for minority students and a majority of the speakers could be recruited from among white faculty. Talks could focus on the biography of the speaker and why he or she chose to become an academic. Speakers could be encouraged to talk both about their research and their teaching philosophy, how much time they spend on teaching and how much on research, how faculty get tenure and what it means, the state of the job market for minority Ph.D.s, the pay professors receive, opportunities for earning extra income, the interest of most schools in increasing the diversity of their faculty, and so forth.

These sessions ideally will lead to the formation of informal contacts between the student participants and the faculty speakers. Students should be encouraged to visit the faculty members in their office, where the students can discuss their courses and their interests. Some faculty members might be willing to invite some of the student participants to lunch or to a get-together at the home of the faculty member. The more contact that can be generated between the student participants and the faculty members, the greater the likelihood that the student will decide to pursue a Ph.D. with the aim of becoming a college professor.

Finding: Having a professor as a role model makes a small but significant difference in the decision to become a college professor (even when contact with faculty is controlled). For students in all ethnic groups, it makes no difference whether the role model is of the same gender, the same race, or the same gender and race. From our questionnaire we learned that being a role model has many different meanings for students, but a common idea was that such a person served as a mentor or was someone who "really cares."

The finding that matching gender and race of role models has no influence on students' career decisions has no bearing on the overall importance of faculty diversification. It does mean, however, that existing faculty, whatever their race or gender, can have quite an effect on students' career decisions. Our research has shown that graduate students can also have an effect on students. Respondents who reported being influenced by graduate students in making their career choice were more likely to select academia as a career than those who did not report being influenced by graduate students.

Recommendation: Any programs that increase the contact between undergraduates interested in academia and graduate students will be useful in getting undergraduates to maintain their interest in academia and ultimately select it as a career.

The faculty advisor should therefore make a concerted effort to involve existing graduate students (both minority members and non-minority members) in the undergraduate advisory program. Graduate students could be invited to speak to the undergraduates about why they decided to pursue graduate study and what it is like to be in graduate school. Graduate students should be invited to any informal functions sponsored by the advisory program. Graduate students should be encouraged to befriend and mentor undergraduates who are interested in academia. In addition, graduate students, along with senior minority undergraduates, could be used as assistants in the advisory program.

Some schools, particularly large state universities, already have graduate students intimately involved in undergraduate education. This is beneficial both to the graduate students, who learn how to teach through their participation, and to the undergraduates, who benefit from contact with graduate students. Schools that currently do not involve graduate students in undergraduate education in a significant way should try to increase their involvement. We are not suggesting that graduate students be used to take the place of faculty members as instructors, but that they be used in addition to faculty members as teaching assistants, discussion section leaders, and in other capacities in which they would interact with undergraduates. Liberal arts colleges that have few or no graduate programs might try to involve graduate students from nearby universities in their undergraduate education program.

It would also be a good idea to invite alumni of the college (particularly minority members) who have earned Ph.D.s and are working in academia to serve as guest speakers at meetings of the advisory program. Giving students the chance to see others who were formerly in their position and who now have successful careers in academia will increase their confidence that they too can have a successful academic career.

In addition, our research (as well as that of others) has found that peers also influence students' career decisions. Students who attend colleges where many freshman are interested in academia as a career are more likely to select that career themselves than students who attend colleges where relatively few freshmen are interested in academia as a career.

Having a program such as the advisory program we propose should serve to put students into contact with others with a similar interest in academia as a career, increasing the interaction among the participants and making it more likely that students in the program will develop friends among students who want to be academics. This should serve to reinforce their own interest.

Improving the Academic Performance of Minority Group Students

Finding: We found a strong correlation between how well minority group students do in college and their decision to select college professor as a career. Students who earn high GPAs are much more likely than students who have lower GPAs to select academia as their first-choice career (see Chapter 5).

We also found that African American students and to a lesser extent Latinos underperform academically. That is, compared with white students with the same SAT scores, the minority students earn lower GPAs.

Recommendation: One of the primary aims of the advisory program we have proposed (or any other program aimed at increasing the number of African Americans and Latinos who select academia as their first-choice career) should be to improve the academic performance of the minority student participants. The goal should be to eliminate the underperformance and, going beyond that, to have the minority students perform at an even higher level than their SAT scores would predict. Since the reasons for minority students' underperformance are not fully understood, this will not be an easy task. But we know enough to suggest several strategies that might be effective.

Finding: African American students who attend less selective schools are more likely than those who attend selective schools to persist with a freshman interest in academia. Our findings support the relative deprivation theory put forth by James Davis in his paper "The Campus as a Frog Pond" (1966). They also support the fit hypothesis, an argument sometimes made by opponents of affirmative action.

Recommendation: Instead of recommending that minority students go to the most prestigious school they can get into, high school guidance counselors should recommend that each student go to a school where he or she is likely to do well academically. An HBCU may be such a school. Guidance counselors, in short, should try to reduce some of the lack of fit between the level of academic preparation of minority students and the schools where they enroll.

Finding: Social psychologist Claude Steele has suggested that one reason why bright African American students underperform is their fear of activating a generally negative stereotype about the intellectual ability of African Americans. Steele has shown in experiments that if this fear can be reduced, the performance level of African Americans is increased. Paradoxically, highly visible affirmative action programs that include special minority-targeted financial aid may send a positive message that elite colleges and universities care strongly about having a diverse student body, but their very visibility may also enhance "stereotype vulnerability." One condition that can contribute to the fear of activation of this negative stereotype is the possible belief on the part of minority students that they were admitted to a selective school because of affirmative action programs and that they "don't really belong" in these schools.

Recommendation: If colleges and universities continue to practice race-sensitive admissions they should try to reduce to a minimum any negative psychological effects that affirmative action programs may have. We suggest that scholarships that are earmarked for minorities not be labeled as such, but rather awarded in the same way as non–affirmative action scholarships are awarded. The idea is to increase the minority students' belief that they have been admitted to the college because of their high academic qualifications and ability, rather than because of the need of the college to maintain ethnic diversity among the student body.

In addition, as part of the advisory program minority student participants should be given "pep talks" in which it is emphasized that they have been admitted because of their outstanding scholastic performance and that the college has high expectations that they will do as well in college as they have done in the past. The students should also be informed about the importance of doing well in college in order to be admitted to, and receive funding from, the best graduate schools. The participants should be advised to make their academic work their top priority and to avoid letting extracurricular activities interfere with their academic work.

Also as part of the advisory program individual interviews should be scheduled with every student participant four to six weeks after the beginning of each semester. The faculty advisor and assistants (upperclassmen and graduate students can help freshmen and sophomores) should discuss with each student how he or she is doing in each course. If the student is having difficulty in any course, tutoring should be arranged. This tutoring could be conducted by upperclassmen who have taken the particular course the student is having difficulty with. Some of these tutors could be work-study students; others might be volunteers. By providing students with close monitoring and offering them tutoring in courses with which they are having difficulty, they should become convinced that the college really cares about how well they are doing. This should increase their identification with the college and reduce any feelings of alienation that these minority students might experience on predominantly white campuses. Ultimately, at all schools, including HBCUs, the advisory program ideally would raise the GPAs of the students who participate.

Finding: Research by Leonard Ramist, Charles Lewis, and Laura McCamley-Jenkins (1994) has suggested that the courses in which African American students are the most likely to underperform are science courses and laboratory courses.

Recommendation: The tutoring program suggested earlier should concentrate on science courses. It might be a good idea to arrange for tutoring and group study sessions for science courses right from the beginning rather than waiting until students realize that they are having difficulty.

Many colleges and universities are dissatisfied with the quality of their current academic advising system. If the advisory program we suggest is instituted and carried out, it should improve the general academic counseling that minority students will receive. In addition, since those students who are interested in academia as freshman are generally the students who have the best academic preparation (see Chapter 4), the program we have suggested has a good chance of succeeding. Trying to improve the GPAs of students who do not have good high school academic preparation would be more difficult.

Finally, it is worth repeating our finding here that if African Americans and Latinos had the same grades as white students and Asians, they would be significantly more likely to select academia as a final-choice career. To the extent that the tutoring and advisory programs that we have suggested work to improve the GPAs of the participants, their interest in academia as a career will increase.

Finding: Our research found some tentative support for the hypothesis that one reason for the underperformance of minority students is the existence of ethnic subcultures that devalue academic performance and even brand students who try to do well in school as in some sense traitors to their own ethnic group.

Recommendation: We believe that to the extent that the above "subcultural values" theory has any validity, the advisory program we have suggested may act as a counter to anti-achievement values. By interacting with other minority students who are interested in academic achievement and with faculty members, faculty advisors, graduate students, senior members of the advisory program, and alumni—all of whom emphasize the value of scholarly work and achievement— minority students may avoid or deflect any anti-achievement subcultural values.

Exposing Minority Group Students to Teaching Experience

Finding: Our research has indicated that students are drawn to an academic career for two primary reasons: their interest in doing research and, almost as important, their interest in teaching. Students generally find the possibility of teaching undergraduates to be an appealing aspect of academia, and African American and Latino students (as also white students) are attracted to the possibility of mentoring minority students. By contrast, some students are turned off by what they perceive as the excessive emphasis in academia on research and publication. Only those students who are most committed to a career as college or university professor have a strong interest in both research and teaching.

Recommendation: The tutoring offered through our suggested advisory program will be of value not only to the student receiving the tutoring but also to the student providing the tutoring. Students interested in academia like the idea of teaching, and a positive experience as a tutor can serve to increase the commitment of the tutor to his or her interest in pursuing an academic career.

It would also be desirable to have programs that give students a structured opportunity to participate in teaching and mentoring activities. Participants in the suggested advisory program should be offered the opportunity to act as teachers and mentors to minority high school students both during the school year and during the summer. The student-teachers might meet periodically to discuss teaching problems they encounter. Course credit might be given for participation in such a program.

Finally, in addition to students becoming introduced to teaching, they may also be attracted to an interest in academia by involvement in research. This idea is discussed in the following section.

Exposing Minority Group Students to Research

Finding: An important determinant of whether a student selects academia as a final-choice career is whether or not the student believes that he or she would get satisfaction from doing research. In our study, African American "persisters" (students who expressed an interest in academia as freshmen and then as seniors selected academia as their first-choice career) differed from "defectors" (students who expressed an

252

interest in academia as freshmen and then as seniors selected some other career as their first choice) in the probability of their saying they would get a lot of satisfaction from doing research by 26 points, Latinos by 32 points, and Asians by 30 points. (Among white students the difference was 37 points.) We also found that doing a research project on one's own made a student more likely to select academia as a first-choice career. Finally, participation in a summer research training program also made students more likely to select academia as a first-choice career.

Recommendation: The more heavily undergraduates can be involved in research, the greater the likelihood that they will select college teaching as a career. Programs therefore should be instituted that offer students the opportunity to do research. Members of our recommended advisory program should be encouraged to participate in such programs.

Some selective colleges require all students to conduct an individual research project in their junior and senior years. These schools are particularly successful in recruiting minority members into the profession of academia. Schools that do not have mandatory programs like this, should set up voluntary programs in conjunction with their academic departments. Each department should be encouraged to offer students the opportunity to conduct individual research projects. Many departments will be found to have such programs in place already; if so, students with an interest in academia should be encouraged to participate in them. The faculty advisor could work in collaboration with representatives of the various departments to match minority students with professors in their major who would take an active role in supervising the research. In some cases the students could do research in conjunction with larger projects being conducted by faculty members. Students would receive academic credit for engaging in independent research; and as part of the course requirement they would be obligated to write a paper reporting the results of their research.

Some colleges might want to make participation in such a research program a prerequisite for graduation with honors rather than awarding honors strictly on the basis of GPA. The more incentives that can be built into such research programs for both minority group students and their faculty supervisors, the more successful the program is likely to be.

Research programs such as these not only will serve to increase the commitment of students interested in an academic career to that occupation, but may also serve as a mechanism to recruit students who enter college without an interest in such a career. Our findings suggest that interest in, and experience with, research is one of the main factors causing students to switch their career interests from other fields to academia.

Besides research conducted during the academic year, schools should consider setting up special summer research training programs that minority members with an interest in college teaching could be encouraged to enroll in. These programs could take different forms. For example, one possibility is to have all participating students work on one research project under the direction of a single faculty member. Or students might be assigned to work with faculty or advanced graduate students on ongoing research projects. If students could be paid for participating in such programs it would increase both their incentive to participate and the rate of participation.

Problems of Minority Group Students at Schools with Few Minority Students

Finding: Our research suggests that selective liberal arts colleges do not provide African Americans with an environment that is conducive to pursuing high-achievement careers. Given the high expectation about the effectiveness of liberal arts colleges in attracting minority students to academia, based in large part on these schools' emphasis on good teaching and high levels of faculty-student contact, these results are disappointing. The very small number of African American students at these schools appears to foster an academic environment in which these students do not feel comfortable. African Americans in particular have lower levels of academic self-esteem at the selective liberal arts colleges, receive grades that fall even further below those predicted by their SAT scores than at all other types of schools, have lower levels of satisfaction than other ethnic groups at these schools, and are more likely to believe they have been discriminated against. All of these factors combined dampen their interest in academia as a career.

Recommendation: Liberal arts colleges should look more closely at the unique problems that minority group members experience on their campuses. More research should be conducted by these colleges in order for them to better understand the problems that high-achieving minority group students face when they are part of a very small group in a relatively small college.

Our research has suggested that the problems faced by minority group students at liberal arts colleges may be ameliorated when the size of the minority student population is relatively large. This suggests the importance of increasing the size of the minority student population, especially at the larger liberal arts colleges. Given the competition for high-achieving minority students among selective colleges, this will be a difficult goal to accomplish without admitting students who do not have the academic qualifications to succeed at the liberal arts colleges. Admitting minority students without adequate preparation, however, would only exacerbate the problem. Ultimately the success of all selective schools in increasing the size of the group of qualified minority students admitted will depend on increasing the pool of such students.

Developing Stronger Commitment to Academia among Minority Students

Finding: Only 58 percent of students interested in becoming college professors say that they will go to graduate school within the year following their graduation from college. Not going directly on may reduce the chances that students will actually follow through with an intention to become a professor. Students at HBCUs are much more likely to go directly on, primarily because they have more of an occupational orientation than students at other colleges.

Recommendation: The intensive advisory program we are suggesting, along with research apprenticeships and teaching experience, will serve to increase the occupational orientation of the students who participate in these programs. Thus one consequence of conducting successful programs such as those we propose would be a higher percentage of students going directly on to graduate school.

Increasing Interest among Minority Students in Specific Areas

Finding: The proportion of students wanting to become academics is highest in the physical sciences and the humanities; is lower in mathematics, computer science, and the biological sciences; and is lowest in the social sciences.

Recommendation: Administrators should tell chairs of departments with low rates of majors who select academia as a career that it would be desirable to increase the proportion of their majors, particularly minority students, who elect to enter academia as a career. The low rate of interest in academia among students in the biological sciences is mostly due to the fact that the best students in these fields are more likely to be interested in a career in medicine. Students in mathematics and computer science may have good job opportunities in business. Students in the social sciences are more likely to be interested in law and business than in academia. Still, it would seem possible to make some changes in the majors—particularly in the social sciences—that might serve to increase the interest of students in an academic career. At selective schools, making research projects a graduation requirement might serve this purpose. At less selective schools, establishing honors programs within departments in which independent study, research projects, and more intellectually challenging courses were offered might also serve to make students majoring in these subjects, including minority students, more inclined to pursue an academic career.

Problems Faced by Asian Students

Finding: Asian students are the least disposed to become college professors, regardless of what type of school they attend. Even Asians in the natural sciences are not much interested in academia; overwhelmingly, they want to become physicians. Indeed, Asians in the natural sciences are less interested in becoming professors than those in the social sciences when other relevant variables are controlled. At Ivy League schools, there is no evidence of underperformance by Asian students compared to white students; but at state universities and liberal arts colleges, Asians show some degree of underperformance. At all types of institutions, when grades and SATs are controlled, Asian students have less academic self-confidence than white students; and even when they receive good grades, they are least satisfied with their college experience. Asian students are more likely than other students to mention "lack of ability" as a reason for not wanting to be a college professor. They are less likely than others to report having role models among the faculty. And at state universities Asian students show lower levels of faculty contact than other students. The survey data we have collected cannot explain Asian students' relatively low levels of academic self-confidence, but our information does suggest that satisfaction for Asian students is strongly influenced by the amount of time spent socializing, contact with faculty, and GPA.

Recommendation: College officials with a concern for student affairs might give more attention to the extent to which Asian students display low levels of academic self-confidence and to what degree they are satisfied or, as often is the case, dissatisfied with their college experience. Both academic self-confidence and satisfaction with college influence the decision to become a professor. Schools with significant Asian student populations should do more research on why Asians show relatively low levels of satisfaction and academic self-confidence and why in general they seem to be the ethnic group least integrated into the campus community. The special problems of Asian students should be seen to. Steps taken to address this group's special problems should help to increase the number of Asian students who decide to enter academia as a career.

Dealing with Problems in Academia

Finding: We found that there are some perceived aspects of the career of college professor which act as a disincentive for students to select this career. Perhaps the most important negative aspect of an academic career is the length of time that it takes to earn a Ph.D. degree. Many students also perceive that there is too much emphasis on publication and not enough emphasis on teaching. Some students also believe that academic life is characterized by too much competition. Although our quantitative data did not show that concern about getting a job was a disincentive for those interested in academia, qualitative research suggested that, particularly for Asian students, the difficult academic job market is a disincentive.

Recommendation: Although we are very much aware that this suggestion sounds naïve and is very difficult to do much about, we cannot fail to mention that it would be easier to get more minority students into academia if the profession could be made more attractive. It is widely believed that "time to degree" for the Ph.D. in the arts and sciences is substantially too long (Bowen and Rudenstine 1992). Reducing the time to degree so that a Ph.D. could be earned in five years instead of eight or more would make the profession more attractive to all students, including minority students. Although there is much talk in academia about "paper counting," or reducing the emphasis on quantity of publication and increasing the emphasis both on quality of publication and teaching as criteria for promotion and tenure, this remains an elusive goal. To the extent that this goal could be achieved, academia would become a more attractive profession. The fact that so many fields in academia are characterized by excessive competition and a corresponding lack of emphasis on the pursuit of knowledge as a communal enterprise is troubling to many current academics as well as prospective future academics, including minority students.

The tight job market in academia makes it difficult for teachers of undergraduates to urge them to spend the great amount of energy and time required to earn a Ph.D. The job market is in fact better for African Americans and Latinos as a result of existing affirmative action programs. Asian students see the difficulty of getting a job as a serious impediment to their finding academia appealing, even though some universities and colleges include Asians in their affirmative action programs. If students knew that once they earned a Ph.D. they would have a good chance of getting an academic job, the profession would, again, be more attractive to all students, not just minority students.

Although all of the goals just mentioned are difficult to achieve, any progress toward solving the basic problems of the academic profession would make this profession more attractive to minority students, and the greater the number of those interested in making a career in academia, the easier it will be to achieve ethnic and racial diversity in our nation's college and university faculties.

APPENDIXES   NOTES   REFERENCES   INDEX

Career Choice Survey

1. Below are fields in which college graduates are frequently employed. Please check at least one box in EACH COLUMN to indicate:

A. The career(s) you were interested in when you entered college. (Check *all* that apply.)

B. The career(s) you are considering now, even if you have not completely made up your mind. (Check *all* you are considering.)

C. Of all those you marked in B, pick the *one* career you are most likely to end up in. (Check only *one*.)

A B C

❑ ❑ ❑ Allied health professions (pharmacist, optometrist, therapist, technician)
❑ ❑ ❑ Architecture, design, urban planning
❑ ❑ ❑ Business, management, industry
❑ ❑ ❑ Clergy
❑ ❑ ❑ Communications, media, advertising
❑ ❑ ❑ Computer analyst or programmer (nonacademic)
❑ ❑ ❑ Dentist (including orthodontist or oral surgeon)
❑ ❑ ❑ Engineering
❑ ❑ ❑ Environment, natural resources management
❑ ❑ ❑ Fine/performing arts
❑ ❑ ❑ Government, public policy, politics
❑ ❑ ❑ Health care administration
❑ ❑ ❑ Homemaker (full-time)
❑ ❑ ❑ Human/social services
❑ ❑ ❑ Journalism, writing
❑ ❑ ❑ Lawyer (attorney)
❑ ❑ ❑ Library, museum
❑ ❑ ❑ Military, law enforcement
❑ ❑ ❑ Nursing
❑ ❑ ❑ Psychologist—clinical (nonacademic)
❑ ❑ ❑ Physician
❑ ❑ ❑ Researcher (in a university)

❑ ❑ ❑   Researcher (not in a university)
❑ ❑ ❑   Skilled trades, crafts, farming
❑ ❑ ❑   Teaching, administration (elementary, secondary)
❑ ❑ ❑   University/college administration
❑ ❑ ❑   University/college professor
❑ ❑ ❑   Veterinarian
❑ ❑ ❑   Other
❑ ❑ ❑   Undecided

2. Within the year after you graduate, do you plan to begin the graduate education that will be necessary for your future career? (Check only *one;* if you plan to take a few years off check "no.")

Yes   ❑
No   ❑
Don't know   ❑

3. How important has each of the following been in influencing your career plans? (Check *one* in each row.)

	Important	Somewhat important	Not important	Does not apply
a. Parent(s)	❑	❑	❑	❑
b. Other family member(s)	❑	❑	❑	❑
c. Official faculty advisor	❑	❑	❑	❑
d. Other faculty	❑	❑	❑	❑
e. Graduate students	❑	❑	❑	❑
f. Friends who are students here	❑	❑	❑	❑
g. Friends who are not students here	❑	❑	❑	❑
h. Counselor(s) in the career counseling or placement center at this college	❑	❑	❑	❑
i. People at work	❑	❑	❑	❑
j. Work experience(s)	❑	❑	❑	❑

4. At any time during college did you consider the possibility of going to graduate school and becoming a college or university professor in the arts and sciences? (By "arts and sciences" we mean the **social sciences,** including anthropology, economics, history, political science, psychology, sociology; the **humanities,** including archeology and art history, classics, English, other language and literature, music, philosophy, religion; and the **natural sciences,** including physics, biochemistry, biophysics, statistics, chemistry, computer science, geological sciences, mathematics. **NOT** included in the "arts and sciences" are business, education, engineering, journalism, law, medicine, and social work.) (Check only *one.*)

I never thought of it.   ❑ [SKIP to Q.8]
I thought about it, but I never considered it seriously.   ❑ [SKIP to Q.8]
I considered it seriously, but decided against it.   ❑ [SKIP to Q.8]
I probably will go, but not next year.   ❑ [Go on to Q.5]
I definitely plan to go, but not right after I graduate.   ❑ [Go on to Q.5]
I definitely plan to go right after I graduate.   ❑ [Go on to Q.5]

5. As a college or university professor, which of the broad subject areas included in the arts and sciences would you specialize in? (Check only *one*.)

❑ Physical sciences (e.g., astronomy, chemistry, geology, physics)
❑ Mathematics/computer science
❑ Biological sciences (e.g., biology, biochemistry, biophysics, botany, marine science, microbiology)
❑ Humanities (e.g., art, English, language, literature, music, philosophy)
❑ Social sciences (e.g., anthropology, economics, history, political science, psychology, sociology)

6. When you enter a graduate program in the arts and sciences, what is your final degree likely to be? (Check only *one*.)

❑ MA
❑ Ph.D.
❑ Don't know

7. If you do NOT receive financial assistance will you abandon your plans to become a college or university professor?

❑ No
❑ Yes
❑ Don't know

8. Were either of your parents teachers at any of the following schools? (Check *all* that apply.)

Mother	*Father*	
❑	❑	Teacher at a college or university
❑	❑	Teacher at a junior/senior high school
❑	❑	Teacher at an elementary school

9. For each of the following, do you think it would be harder or easier for members of an underrepresented racial/ethnic minority: (check one in each *row*)

	Harder	Easier	Wouldn't make any difference	Don't know
a. To get into a Ph.D. program in the arts and sciences	❑	❑	❑	❑
b. To get a job as a professor	❑	❑	❑	❑
c. To have a successful career as a professor	❑	❑	❑	❑

10. Which of the following reasons would make a career as a college professor APPEALING to you—whether or not you have ever considered it as a career. (Check *all* that apply.)

❑ The opportunity to teach undergraduates
❑ To live and work in the world of ideas
❑ Academic knowledge can be used to improve public policy
❑ The opportunity to mentor minority students

263

❑ Academia is relatively liberal and tolerant
❑ Professors are under less pressure than doctors or lawyers
❑ Living in an academic community would be attractive
❑ I got really involved in the subject of my major
❑ I would get a lot of satisfaction from doing research
❑ As a minority professor I would be of service to my ethnic community
❑ Nobody can tell professors what to teach or study
❑ Once you get tenure, you have great security
❑ Professors have a flexible work schedule

11. Which of the following reasons would make a career as a college professor UNAP-PEALING to you—whether or not you have ever considered it as a career choice. (Check *all* that apply.)

❑ Other jobs offer greater financial returns.
❑ Academia is too competitive.
❑ I don't think I have the ability.
❑ Academic life is too remote from the real world.
❑ Getting a Ph.D. takes too long.
❑ Getting a Ph.D. costs too much.
❑ It is hard getting a job in academia.
❑ There is too much emphasis on research and publications rather than teaching.
❑ It is very hard to get tenure.
❑ I don't want to be a student any more.
❑ Some very good teachers don't get tenure.
❑ Other jobs have more prestige.
❑ It means teaching too many poorly prepared undergraduates.
❑ Other jobs give me greater opportunity to help improve the lives of members of minority groups.
❑ One would have to devote too much time and energy to this work—I want to be able to spend more time with my family and friends.
❑ The politics within academia seems very nasty.
❑ I am too much in debt to consider a Ph.D.

12. How would your parents feel if you decided to become a college professor? (Check only *one*.)

They would be pleased.   ❑
They would be upset.   ❑
They would support me in whatever I choose to do.   ❑
They would not care one way or another.   ❑
Don't know.   ❑

13. In which of the following broad categories is your current major? (Check only *one* unless you have a double major.)

❑ Physical sciences (e.g., astronomy, chemistry, geology, physics)
❑ Mathematics/computer science
❑ Biological sciences (e.g., biology, biochemistry, botany, marine science, microbiology)

264

- ❏ Humanities (e.g., art, English, language, music, philosophy)
- ❏ Social sciences (e.g., anthropology, economics, history, political science, psychology, sociology, women's studies)
- ❏ Ethnic studies (e.g., Africana studies)
- ❏ Business
- ❏ Education
- ❏ Engineering
- ❏ Nursing
- ❏ Other (please specify:_____)

14. How many credits (or units) toward your BA did you take at this college? (Check only *one*.)

- ❏ All
- ❏ More than half
- ❏ Half
- ❏ Less than half

15. Since entering this college have you:

	Yes	No
Joined a fraternity or sorority	❏	❏
Had a part-time job while attending school	❏	❏
Worked full-time while attending school	❏	❏
Participated in a study abroad program	❏	❏
Participated in an internship program aimed at preparing you for a particular occupation	❏	❏
Participated in a program for racial/ethnic minorities aimed at encouraging you to become college teachers	❏	❏
Participated in a program for racial/ethnic minorities aimed at increasing your interest in math and science	❏	❏
Participated in campus protest/demonstrations	❏	❏
Run for or been elected to a student office	❏	❏
Been engaged in student journalism	❏	❏
Taken remedial courses	❏	❏
Enrolled in an ethnic studies course	❏	❏
Enrolled in a women's studies course	❏	❏
Attended a racial/cultural awareness event or workshop	❏	❏
Participated in a racial/ethnic student organization	❏	❏
Worked on a professor's research project	❏	❏
Served as a teaching assistant to a professor or graduate student	❏	❏
Participated in research as part of a course	❏	❏
Had an off-campus job working in research	❏	❏
Participated in a summer research training program	❏	❏
Conducted a research project on my own (e.g., senior thesis)	❏	❏
Attended a lecture by an outside speaker	❏	❏
Attended a classical music concert on campus	❏	❏
Attended an on-campus theatrical or dance performance	❏	❏
Performed volunteer work	❏	❏
Participated in intercollegiate football or basketball	❏	❏
Participated in other intercollegiate sport	❏	❏

Had as a close friend a student on this campus who is:

	Yes	No
African American	❏	❏
Asian American	❏	❏
Caucasian American	❏	❏
Latino/Latina	❏	❏
Foreign	❏	❏

Felt harassed because of my ethnic background by:

	Yes	No
Student(s)	❏	❏
Faculty	❏	❏
Administrator(s)	❏	❏
Campus security	❏	❏
Other	❏	❏

Felt harassed because of my gender by:

	Yes	No
Student(s)	❏	❏
Faculty	❏	❏
Administrator(s)	❏	❏
Campus security	❏	❏
Other	❏	❏

16. We are interested in the type of interaction(s) that you have had on this campus with instructors of varying ethnic background. For each of the following type of instructor mark all that apply.

A. *African American/black* instructor(s)

	Male instructor	Female instructor
Taught one of my classes	❏	❏
Influenced my choice of major	❏	❏
Received career advice from	❏	❏
Showed that somebody like me can become a college professor	❏	❏
Urged me to consider the career of college professor	❏	❏
Socialized with me outside of class	❏	❏
Served as an important role model	❏	❏

B. *Asian* instructor(s)

	Male instructor	Female instructor
Taught one of my classes	❏	❏
Influenced my choice of major	❏	❏
Received career advice from	❏	❏
Showed that somebody like me can become a college professor	❏	❏
Urged me to consider the career of college professor	❏	❏
Socialized with me outside of class	❏	❏
Served as an important role model	❏	❏

	Male instructor	Female instructor
C. *Caucasian* instructor(s)		
Taught one of my classes	❑	❑
Influenced my choice of major	❑	❑
Received career advice from	❑	❑
Showed that somebody like me can become a college professor	❑	❑
Urged me to consider the career of college professor	❑	❑
Socialized with me outside of class	❑	❑
Served as an important role model	❑	❑

	Male instructor	Female instructor
D. *Latino/Latina* instructor(s)		
Taught one of my classes	❑	❑
Influenced my choice of major	❑	❑
Received career advice from	❑	❑
Showed that somebody like me can become a college professor	❑	❑
Urged me to consider the career of college professor	❑	❑
Socialized with me outside of class	❑	❑
Served as an important role model	❑	❑

17. Do you agree or disagree with each of the following statements:

	Agree	Disagree	Don't know
a. Most professors on this campus care primarily about their research and very little about undergraduate students.	❑	❑	❑
b. In most of the classes I have taken at this college the instructor has been able to identify me by name.	❑	❑	❑
c. Too many courses at this college are taught by graduate students.	❑	❑	❑
d. Most instructors I have had at this school have been good teachers.	❑	❑	❑
e. On this campus, more students are interested in partying and having a good time than in learning.	❑	❑	❑
f. Most of the friends I have at this college I would consider to be intellectuals.	❑	❑	❑
g. In hiring faculty, this school should give more weight to the candidate's racial/ethnic background.	❑	❑	❑
h. Most instructors I have had at this school are generally available outside of class.	❑	❑	❑
i. I wish the faculty at this college would give me more feedback on my performance.	❑	❑	❑

j. There are special programs at this school that
   encourage racial/ethnic minority students to become
   college or university professors.   ❑   ❑   ❑

18. Why did you choose this college? (Check *all* that apply.)

❑   It has a very good academic reputation.
❑   The social life is famous.
❑   Its size enables me to get a very good education.
❑   The urban/rural location appealed to me.
❑   The student body is diverse.
❑   I couldn't get into the school(s) I really wanted to.
❑   I heard that the faculty really cares about students.
❑   It's said to be a good place from which to get into a good arts and sciences
     graduate program.
❑   It's said to be a good place from which to get into a good professional school.
❑   I expected to find a lot of serious students like myself here.
❑   The friends you make here will help in your career.
❑   It was a school I could afford to go to.

19. Overall, how satisfied have you been with your undergraduate education at this college?

Very satisfied   ❑
Generally satisfied   ❑
Ambivalent   ❑
Generally dissatisfied ❑
Very dissatisfied   ❑

20. Which of the following best describes where you are currently living?

❑   Fraternity, sorority (or equivalent)
❑   Campus housing
❑   Off-campus room, apartment, house
❑   With my parents (or other relative)

21. Which of the following best describes your undergraduate grade point average?

❑   A (3.75–4.0)
❑   A–, B+ (3.25–3.74)
❑   B (2.75–3.24)
❑   B–, C+ (2.25–2.74)
❑   C or less (less than 2.25)

22a. In general, comparing yourself with *all* people your age, how would you rate your academic ability?

22b. In general, comparing yourself with *seniors at this college,* how would you rate your academic ability? (Mark *one* in each column.)

a   b

❑   ❑   Among the highest 10%
❑   ❑   Above average
❑   ❑   Average
❑   ❑   Below average
❑   ❑   Among the lowest 10%

23. Did you take the SAT test when you were in high school?

    ❑   No [If no, SKIP to Q.26]
    ❑   Yes

24. Please indicate the highest score you received on the SAT verbal test:

    ❑   700 or higher
    ❑   600–699
    ❑   500–599
    ❑   400–499
    ❑   Less than 400

25. Please indicate the highest score you received on the SAT quantitative test:

    ❑   700 or higher
    ❑   600–699
    ❑   500–599
    ❑   400–499
    ❑   Less than 400

26. Which of the following best describes your high school grade point average? (Check only one.)

    ❑   A (3.75–4.0) (93–100)
    ❑   A−, B+ (3.25–3.74) (87–92)
    ❑   B (2.75–3.24) (83–86)
    ❑   B−, C+ (2.25–2.74) (77–82)
    ❑   C or less (less than 2.25) (less than 77)

27. Which of the following describes the high school you attended? (Check *all* that apply.)

❑   Public
❑   Private (nonreligious)
❑   Private (religious)
❑   More than 80% of the graduating class was Caucasian
❑   More than 80% of the graduating class was non-Caucasian
❑   Almost all students who graduated went on to college
❑   You had to take a test to be admitted to this high school

28. Please indicate your parents' highest educational attainment. (Check only *one* in each column.)

	Mother	Father
8th grade or less	❏	❏
Part high school	❏	❏
High school graduate	❏	❏
High school graduate plus vocational training	❏	❏
Part college	❏	❏
College graduate	❏	❏
Graduate or professional degree beyond the bachelor's	❏	❏

29. When you were in high school were your parent(s):

- ❏ Living together
- ❏ Divorced/separated
- ❏ Widowed
- ❏ Both parents deceased

30. When you were in high school was your family:

- ❏ Poor
- ❏ Lower middle class
- ❏ Middle class
- ❏ Upper middle class
- ❏ Wealthy

31. What is your best estimate of your parent(s)' total income from all sources before taxes in 1994? (Consider only the parent(s) with whom you were living during high school.)

- ❏ Under $20,000
- ❏ $20,000–$39,999
- ❏ $40,000–$59,999
- ❏ $60,000–$99,999
- ❏ $100,000–$149,999
- ❏ $150,000 and over

32. Do you consider your racial/ethnic background to be: (check all that apply)

African American/black	❏
Caribbean/black	❏
Chinese	❏
Korean	❏
Japanese	❏
Vietnamese	❏
Pacific Islander	❏
Indian	❏

Pakistani ❑
Puerto Rican ❑
Cuban ❑
Mexican American/Chicano ❑
Other Latino/Latina ❑
Caucasian/white ❑
Native American/Alaskan Native ❑

33. What is your gender?

Female ❑
Male ❑

34. What is your citizenship status?

Citizen, by birth ❑
Citizen, naturalized ❑
Foreign ❑

35. Were your parent(s) born in the United States?

	Yes	No
Mother	❑	❑
Father	❑	❑

36a. In which religion were you reared?

36b. What is your current religious preference?

a	b	
❑	❑	Catholic
❑	❑	Islamic
❑	❑	Jewish
❑	❑	Protestant
❑	❑	Other
❑	❑	None

37. How would you characterize your political views? (Check only *one*.)

Far left ❑
Liberal ❑
Middle-of-the-road ❑
Conservative ❑
Far right ❑
Liberal on some issues, conservative on others ❑
Have no set political views ❑

38. What is your age?

20 or younger ❑
21–22 ❑
23–24 ❑
25–29 ❑
30 or older ❑

39. How many siblings do you have—

a. that are older? (Mark one.)
  ❑ None
  ❑ One
  ❑ Two
  ❑ Three or more

b. that are younger? (Mark one.)
  ❑ None
  ❑ One
  ❑ Two
  ❑ Three or more

c. Are you a twin?
  ❑ No
  ❑ Yes

40. Which of the following describe your life when you were growing up? (Mark one in each row.)

	Yes	No
My mother was a full-time homemaker.	❑	❑
I had to do chores.	❑	❑
I was expected to earn money myself for expensive things I wanted but didn't really need.	❑	❑
My mother and/or father was politically active.	❑	❑
My mother and/or father did volunteer work in the community.	❑	❑
I was always expected to go to college.	❑	❑
My mother and/or father believed in strict discipline for children.	❑	❑
I visited a foreign country with my parent(s).	❑	❑
My mother and/or father frequently read to me.	❑	❑
My parent(s) took me to see theater or dance.	❑	❑
My parent(s) took me to the opera or to classical concerts.	❑	❑
My parent(s) took me to the movies.	❑	❑
Gender equality was very important to my parents.	❑	❑
My mother and/or father used to help me with my homework.	❑	❑
My parent(s) had an active role in my college selection.	❑	❑
I was fighting a lot with my mother and/or father.	❑	❑
My parent(s) limited the amount of TV I could watch.	❑	❑
High achievement is very important to my parent(s).	❑	❑
My parent(s) have always expected me to get married and have children.	❑	❑
My parent(s) wanted me to go to college near home.	❑	❑

All or most of my friends went to college.   ❏   ❏
I was afraid to tell my parent(s) if I got a bad grade in school.   ❏   ❏
My parent(s) had more traditional values than I did.   ❏   ❏
My parent(s) tried to influence my choice of friends.   ❏   ❏
The language spoken in my home was English.   ❏   ❏

Thank you very much for your participation!

Career Choice Survey

Directions

Your responses will be read by an optical mark reader. Your careful observance of these few simple rules will be most appreciated.
- Use *only* black lead *pencil* no. 2.
- Make heavy black marks that will fill the oval.
- Erase clearly any answer you may wish to change.
- Make no stray markings of any kind.

EXAMPLE

Will marks made with ball-point or felt-tip marker be properly read?
Yes ○ No ●

1. Below are fields in which college graduates are frequently employed. Please follow the directions for EACH COLUMN to indicate:

A. The career(s) you were interested in when you entered college. (Mark *all* that apply.)

B. The career(s) you have in mind now, even if you have not completely made up your mind. (Mark *all* you are considering.)

C. Of all those you marked in B, pick the *one* career you are most likely to end up in. (Mark only *one*.)

A	B	C	
○	○	○	Allied health professions (pharmacist, optometrist, therapist, technician, dentist, health care administrator)
○	○	○	Architecture, design, urban planning
○	○	○	Business, management, industry
○	○	○	Communications, media, advertising
○	○	○	Computer analyst or programmer (nonacademic)
○	○	○	Engineering
○	○	○	Environment, natural resources management
○	○	○	Fine/performing arts
○	○	○	Government, public policy, politics
○	○	○	Human/social services
○	○	○	Journalism, writing
○	○	○	Lawyer (attorney)
○	○	○	Library, museum
○	○	○	Psychologist—clinical (nonacademic)
○	○	○	Physician
○	○	○	Researcher (in a university)
○	○	○	Researcher (not in a university)

○ ○ ○ Teaching, administration (elementary, secondary)
○ ○ ○ University/college administration
○ ○ ○ University/college professor
○ ○ ○ Other
○ ○ ○ Undecided

2. Within the year after you graduate, do you plan to begin the graduate education that will be necessary for your future career? (Mark only *one;* if you plan to take a few years off mark "no.")

Yes	○
No	○
Don't know	○
No graduate education is necessary	○

3. At any time during college did you consider the possibility of going to graduate school and becoming a college or university professor in the arts and sciences? (Mark only *one.*)

NOTE: NOT included in the "arts and sciences" are business, education, engineering, journalism, law, medicine, and social work.

I never thought of it.	○ [SKIP to Q.6]
I thought about it, but I never considered it seriously.	○ [SKIP to Q.6]
I considered it seriously, but decided against it.	○ [SKIP to Q.6]
I probably will go, but not next year.	○ [Go on to Q.4]
I definitely plan to go, but not next year.	○ [Go on to Q.4]
I definitely plan to go next year.	○ [Go on to Q.4]

4. As a college or university professor, which of the broad subject areas included in the arts and sciences would you specialize in? (Mark only *one.*)

○ Physical sciences (e.g., astronomy, chemistry, geology, physics)
○ Mathematics/computer science
○ Biological sciences (e.g., biology, biochemistry, biophysics, botany, marine science, microbiology)
○ Humanities (e.g., archeology, art, art history, classics, English, language, literature, music, philosophy, religion)
○ Social sciences (e.g., anthropology, economics, history, political science, psychology, sociology)
○ Other

5. When you enter a graduate program in the arts and sciences, what is your final degree likely to be? (Mark only *one.*)

○ MA/MS
○ Ph.D.
○ Don't know

6. How important has each of the following been in influencing your career plans? (Mark *one* in each row.)

	Important	Somewhat important	Not important	Does not apply
a. Parent(s)	O	O	O	O
b. Official faculty advisor	O	O	O	O
c. Other faculty	O	O	O	O
d. Graduate students	O	O	O	O
e. Friends who are students here	O	O	O	O
f. Friends who are not students here	O	O	O	O
g. Counselor(s) in the career counseling or placement center at this college	O	O	O	O
h. Work experiences	O	O	O	O

7. Which of the following reasons would make a career as a college professor APPEALING to you—whether or not you have ever considered it as a career. (Mark *all* that apply.)

- O The opportunity to teach undergraduates
- O To live and work in the world of ideas
- O Academic knowledge can be used to improve public policy
- O The opportunity to mentor minority students
- O Academia is relatively liberal and tolerant
- O Professors are under less pressure than doctors or lawyers
- O Living in an academic community would be attractive
- O I got really involved in the subject of my major
- O I would get a lot of satisfaction from doing research
- O Professors have a lot of time off

8. Which of the following reasons would make a career as a college professor UNAPPEALING to you—whether or not you have ever considered it as a career choice. (Mark *all* that apply.)

- O Other jobs offer greater financial rewards.
- O Academia is very competitive.
- O I don't think I have the ability.
- O Getting a Ph.D. takes too long.
- O It is hard getting a job in academia.
- O There is too much emphasis on research and publications rather than teaching.
- O It is very hard to get tenure.
- O I don't want to be a student any more.
- O Other jobs have more prestige.
- O I am in too much debt to consider a Ph.D.

9. Do you think people of your ethnic/racial background would face discrimination in:

	Yes	No	Don't know
a. Getting into a Ph.D. program	O	O	O
b. Getting a job as a professor	O	O	O

10. In which of the following broad categories is your current major? (Mark *all* that apply.)

- O Physical sciences (e.g., astronomy, chemistry, geology, physics)
- O Mathematics/computer science
- O Biological sciences (e.g., biology, biochemistry, biophysics, botany, marine science, microbiology)
- O Humanities (e.g., archeology, art, art history, classics, English, language, literature, music, philosophy, religion)
- O Social sciences (e.g., anthropology, economics, history, political science, psychology, sociology)
- O Ethnic studies (e.g., Africana studies)
- O Other

11. Upon graduation, how many credits (or units) towards your BA/BS will you have taken at this college? (Mark only *one*.)

- ❑ All
- ❑ Half or more
- ❑ Less than half

12. Since entering this college have you:

	Yes	No
Had a part-time job while attending school	O	O
Participated in an intercollegiate sport	O	O
Participated in campus protest/demonstrations	O	O
Participated in a racial/ethnic student organization	O	O
Participated in a program aimed at encouraging you to become a college professor	O	O
Participated in a program aimed at increasing your interest in math and science	O	O
Served as a *research assistant* on a professor's or graduate student's research project	O	O
Served as a *teaching assistant* to a professor or graduate student	O	O
Participated in a summer research training program	O	O
Had an off-campus job working in research	O	O
Conducted a research project on your own (e.g., senior thesis)	O	O
Been urged by a faculty member to become a college professor	O	O

13. Compared to other students at this campus:

- O I spend *more* time than average socializing
- O I spend about the average time socializing
- O I spend *less* time than average socializing

14. Indicate which of the following you have ever taken a class with and/or has served as an important role model to you: (mark *all* that apply)

	Taken a class with	Served as an important role model
African American male instructor	O	O
African American female instructor	O	O
Asian male instructor	O	O
Asian female instructor	O	O
Caucasian male instructor	O	O
Caucasian female instructor	O	O
Latino instructor	O	O
Latina instructor	O	O

15. What do you mean by a role model? (Mark *all* that apply.)

Someone I would like to model my entire life after	❏
Someone I would like my personal life to be like	❏
Someone I would like my professional life to be like	❏
Someone who possesses traits that I admire	❏
Someone who is a very good teacher	❏
Someone who is very knowledgeable	❏
Someone who really cares about helping others	❏
Someone who has mentored me	❏

16. Do you agree or disagree with each of the following statements:

	Agree	Disagree	Don't know
a. Most professors on this campus care primarily about their research and very little about undergraduate students.	O	O	O
b. In most of the classes I have taken at this college the instructor has been able to identify me by name.	O	O	O
c. Too many courses at this college are taught by graduate students.	O	O	O
d. Most instructors I have had at this school have been good teachers.	O	O	O
e. In hiring faculty, this school should give more weight to the candidate's racial/ethnic background.	O	O	O
f. Most instructors I have had at this school are generally available outside of class.	O	O	O
g. This college is known as a good place from which to get into a good arts and sciences graduate school.	O	O	O
h. An important reason why I chose this college was that I expected to find a lot of serious students like myself here.	O	O	O
i. Some faculty members at this college have made my undergraduate experience more difficult because of my racial/ethnic background.	O	O	O

17. Does this college offer special programs to encourage students from racial/ethnic minorities to pursue any of the following advanced degrees:

	Yes	No	Don't know
Ph.D.	O	O	O
MD	O	O	O
Law	O	O	O
MBA	O	O	O

18. Overall, how satisfied have you been with your undergraduate education at this college?

Very satisfied	O
Generally satisfied	O
Ambivalent	O
Generally dissatisfied	O
Very dissatisfied	O

19. Which of the following best describes where you are currently living?

- O With my parents (or other relative)
- O Fraternity, sorority (or equivalent)
- O Campus housing
- O Off-campus housing

20. Which of the following best describes your undergraduate grade point average?

- O A (3.75–4.0)
- O A– (3.50–3.74)
- O B+ (3.25–3.49)
- O B (2.75–3.24)
- O B–, C+ (2.25–2.74)
- O C or less (less than 2.25)

21a. In general, comparing yourself with *all* people your age, how would you rate your academic ability? (Mark only *one.*)

21b. In general, comparing yourself with *seniors at this college,* how would you rate your academic ability? (Mark only *one.*)

a	b	
O	O	Among the highest 10%
O	O	Above average
O	O	Average
O	O	Below average
O	O	Among the lowest 10%

22. Did you take the SAT test when you were in high school?

- O No [If no, SKIP to Q.25]
- O Yes

23. Please indicate the highest score you received on the SAT *verbal* test:

      ○   700 or higher
      ○   600–699
      ○   500–599
      ○   400–499
      ○   Less than 400

24. Please indicate the highest score you received on the SAT *math* test:

      ○   700 or higher
      ○   600–699
      ○   500–599
      ○   400–499
      ○   Less than 400

25. Please indicate your parents' highest educational attainment. (Mark only *one* in each column.)

	Mother	Father
High school or less	○	○
Part college	○	○
College graduate	○	○
Graduate or professional degree beyond the bachelor's	○	○

26. Has either of your parents been a teacher at a college or university?

      Yes ○
      No   ○

27. When you were in high school was your family:

      ○   Lower class
      ○   Lower middle class
      ○   Middle class
      ○   Upper middle class
      ○   Upper class

28. What is your best estimate of your parent(s)' total income from all sources before taxes in 1994? (Consider only the parent(s) with whom you were living during high school.)

      ○   Under $20,000
      ○ $20,000–$39,999
      ○ $40,000–$59,999
      ○ $60,000–$99,999
      ○ $100,000–$149,999
      ○ $150,000 and over

29. When you were growing up:

	Yes	No
a. Did your parents believe in strict discipline for children?	O	O
b. Did your parents have more traditional values than you?	O	O

30. Do you consider your racial/ethnic background to be: (mark all that apply)

African American/black	O
Caribbean/black	O
Caucasian/white	O
Native American/Alaskan Native	O

Asian:

Chinese	O
Indian	O
Japanese	O
Korean	O
Pacific Islander	O
Pakistani	O
Vietnamese	O
Other Asian	O

Latino/Latina:

Cuban	O
Mexican American/Chicano	O
Puerto Rican	O
Other Latino/Latina	O

31. What is your gender?

Female	O
Male	O

32. What is your citizenship status?

U.S. citizen, by birth	O
U.S. citizen, naturalized	O
Foreign	O

33. Were your parent(s) born in the United States?

	Yes	No
Mother	O	O
Father	O	O

34. What was the main language spoken in your home when you were growing up?

O	English
O	Another language plus English
O	A language other than English

35. What is your religious preference?

- O   Catholic
- O   Jewish
- O   Protestant
- O   Other
- O   None

36. How would you characterize your political views? (Mark only *one*.)

Far left   O
Liberal   O
Moderate   O
Conservative   O
Far right   O
Not interested in politics   O

37. What is your age?

22 or younger   O
23–29   O
30 or older   O

38. How many brothers and sisters do you have?

- O   None
- O   One
- O   Two
- O   Three
- O   Four
- O   Five
- O   Six or more

Thank you for your cooperation!

Table B3.1 Distribution of final occupational choice for the total sample and total sample adjusted for the fact that the telephone survey offered only ten occupational choices

Occupational choice	Sample (%)	Adjusted sample (%)
Allied health	4	5
Architecture	1	1
Business	12	11
Communications	3	4
Computer Analyst	1	2
Engineering	1	1
Environment	2	3
Fine/performing arts	4	4
Government	5	4
Human/social services	5	5
Journalism/writing	3	4
Lawyer	9	9
Library, museum	1	1
Psychologist	2	3
Physician	15	14
Professor or univ. researcher	10	9
Researcher (not in univ.)	3	3
Teacher (elementary and secondary)	8	7
University admninistrator	—	—
Other	6	6
Undecided	5	5
Total	101	101
N of cases	28,867	28,867

Note: Dash = less than 1 percent.

283

Table B4.1 Socioeconomic indicators, by ethnicity (percent)

SES indicator	Total	Whites	African Americans	Asians	Latinos
Mother's education					
High school	19	15	25	26	46
Part college	16	15	23	13	19
College graduate	32	34	25	36	18
Graduate/professional degree	33	36	27	25	17
Total	100	100	100	100	100
Father's education					
High school	16	12	32	18	39
Part college	10	10	19	9	13
College graduate	23	23	19	25	20
Graduate/professional degree	51	55	30	49	28
Total	100	100	100	101	100
Family SES					
Lower class	4	2	14	6	16
Lower middle class	12	9	25	14	25
Middle class	36	35	42	38	34
Upper middle class	42	47	18	36	22
Upper class	6	7	1	6	3
Total	100	100	100	100	100
Parents' income					
Under $20,000	6	4	14	8	16
$20,000–$39,999	14	12	27	18	27
$40,000–$59,999	18	17	22	20	21
$60,000–$99,999	29	31	23	23	20
$100,000–$149,999	16	18	10	15	9
$150,000 or higher	16	18	5	16	7
Total	99	100	101	100	100

Note: When variables are dichotomized (education less than college graduate and college graduate or more; family SES less than upper middle class and upper middle class or higher; and parents' income less than $60,000 and $60,000 or higher) each ethnic group significantly different from whites at $p < .05$ (chi-square in SUDAAN).

Table B5.1 Odds ratios from multinomial logistic regression models predicting
selection of one of the five leading occupations as first choice.
A: Whites. B: African Americans. C: Asians. D: Latinos.

A. Whites

Type of ratio	Business	Law	Medicine	Teaching	Other
SES index	1.000	.981	1.243	.863	.934
Combined SAT	.980	1.071	.849	.786*	.904
School type					
Liberal arts	.724	.847	.733	1.010	1.292
State	.178*	.742	.421*	.930	.625
Freshman aspiration					
Business	7.363*	.757	1.192	.485	.933
Law	.732	9.616*	.731	1.019	.862
Medicine	.763	.617	14.460*	.598	.523*
College professor	.262*	.285*	.374*	.311*	.345*
Elementary/secondary					
teaching	.933	.822	.654	7.249*	.968
College GPA	.722	.776	1.699	.753	.715
College major					
Physical sciences	.205*	.000*	1.677	.203*	.745
Mathematics/computer					
science	.941	.135*	.298	2.158	1.153
Biological sciences	.329*	.345	3.830*	.506	1.024
Humanities	.448*	.571	.514	.712	.590*
Social sciences	.874	1.223	.800	.578	.751
Influence on career plans					
Parents	1.096	1.100	.975	1.093	1.034
Graduate students	.759	.700	.597*	.689	.966
Work experiences	1.705*	1.248	2.261*	2.074*	1.675*
College professor appealing					
Teach undergraduates	.374*	.608	.359*	1.143	.463*
Research	.232*	.337*	.357*	.255*	.263*
College professor					
unappealing					
Lacks financial rewards	3.017*	2.587*	1.242	.494*	1.149
Takes too much time	3.733*	1.576	1.692	2.593*	2.671*
Politically conservative	2.339*	1.634*	1.671*	1.191	1.198
Discrimination index	.989	1.284	1.230	1.355	1.089
Career orientation index	.843	1.120	1.146	.780	.628*
Percent freshman interested					
in college teaching	.939*	.972	.981	.961*	.977
Satisfaction with					
undergraduate education	1.154	1.222	1.077	.747	.853

Table B5.1 (continued)

Type of ratio	Business	Law	Medicine	Teaching	Other
Participated in college professor program	1.010	1.440	.926	.827	.966
Participated in summer research training program	.813	.807	1.304	.750	.592*
Conducted own research project	.544*	.733	.919	.762	.856
Academic role model	.762	.579	.464*	.991	.877
Faculty contact index	.599*	.659*	.620*	.863	.631*
Academic self-confidence	1.029	1.239	1.342	.626*	.917

Note: College professor is the omitted category on the dependent variable; Ivy League is the omitted category on school type; "other" is the omitted category on major.

  * $p < .05$

Table B5.1 (continued)
B. African Americans

Type of ratio	Business	Law	Medicine	Teaching	Other
SES index	1.133	1.146	1.265	.815	.980
Combined SAT	.996	.837	.933	.786	.956
School type					
Liberal arts	.912	1.533	.308	2.780	1.591
State	.227*	.482	.280*	1.362	.577
HBCUs	.334	.410	.115*	1.391	.571
Freshman aspiration					
Business	18.079*	2.295	1.808	2.602	1.715
Law	2.228*	16.451*	.634	.728	1.381
Medicine	.259*	.379*	28.121*	.379	.289*
College professor	.518	.235*	.521	.380*	.341*
Elementary/secondary					
teaching	.589	.896	.357	8.199*	.859
College GPA	.374	.827	1.911	.789	.818
College major					
Physical sciences	.142	1.260	2.487	1.019	1.339
Mathematics/computer	3.054	.942	.315	4.164	1.225
science					
Biological sciences	.244	.038*	2.832	.271	.685
Humanities	.155*	.229*	.345	.530	.297*
Social sciences	.392*	.508	.313*	.515	.475*
Influence on career plans					
Parents	1.368	1.388	1.882*	1.477	1.396
Graduate students	.573	.516*	.623	.379*	.563*
Work experiences	3.557*	1.732*	2.458*	2.612*	2.142*
College professor appealing					
Teach undergraduates	.281*	.491*	.397*	.725	.441*
Research	.374*	.358*	.328*	.283*	.457*
College professor					
unappealing					
Lacks financial rewards	2.393*	3.130*	3.345*	.772	1.861*
Takes too much time	2.829*	1.996*	.674	2.106*	1.990*
Politically conservative	1.816	1.514	1.829	1.311	1.774*
Discrimination index	.729	.949	.841	1.091	.851
Career orientation index	.916	.954	1.632	.863	.811
Percent freshman interested					
in college teaching	.987	1.005	1.025	.994	.987
Satisfaction with					
undergraduate education	1.041	1.088	1.547	.762	1.018
Participated in college					
professor program	.142*	.231*	.512	.460	.325*

Table B5.1 (continued)

Type of ratio	Business	Law	Medicine	Teaching	Other
Participated in summer research training program	.488	.610	.683	.406	.814
Conducted own research project	.244*	.397*	.297*	.259*	.561
Academic role model	.531	.884	1.054	.612	.476
Faculty contact index	1.002	.977	1.053	1.151	.924
Academic self-confidence	.739	.950	.631*	.533*	.771

Note: College professor is the omitted category on the dependent variable; Ivy League is the omitted category on school type; "other" is the omitted category on major.

 * $p < .05$

Table B5.1 (continued)
C. Asians

Type of ratio	Business	Law	Medicine	Teaching	Other
SES index	.954	.985	.981	1.142	.989
Combined SAT	1.127	.956	1.319*	.771	.903
School type					
Liberal arts	1.844	2.111	.726	2.880	2.194*
State	.384	.944	.833	1.505	.799
Freshman aspiration					
Business	8.859*	1.702	.934	1.285	1.482
Law	1.426	8.219*	.689	1.239	1.442
Medicine	1.422	1.223	14.008*	.780	1.135
College professor	.281*	.282*	.264*	.255*	.253*
Elementary/secondary					
teaching	.576	.485	1.129	6.471*	.910
College GPA	.449	1.192	2.122	.535	.497
College major					
Physical sciences	.180*	1.051	1.849	1.271	.651
Mathematics/computer					
science	1.017	.604	.332	1.272	.563
Biological sciences	.234*	.082*	2.696	.460	.640
Humanities	.262*	1.363	.452	.720	.569
Social sciences	1.036	2.435	.513	.600	.578
Influence on career plans					
Parents	1.247	2.189*	1.668*	1.117	1.491
Graduate students	.441*	.561	.441*	.568	.678
Work experiences	1.469	.837	1.347	1.058	1.158
College professor appealing					
Teach undergraduates	.252*	.633	.542	1.102	.441*
Research	.197*	.170*	.218*	.225*	.337*
College professor					
unappealing					
Lacks financial rewards	4.038*	2.003	1.709	.516	.958
Takes too much time	3.034*	.935	.978	1.703	1.687
Politically conservative	1.149	.808	1.205	.764	.880
Discrimination index	.777	1.207	1.077	.880	.953
Career orientation index	.627	.809	1.080	.723	.798
Percent freshman interested					
in college teaching	.961	.983	.988	.996	.988
Satisfaction with					
undergraduate education	1.045	1.206	1.407	1.188	1.069
Participated in college					
professor program	6.734*	2.791	1.481	11.561*	1.784

Table B5.1 (continued)

Type of ratio	Business	Law	Medicine	Teaching	Other
Participated in summer research training program	.482	.843	1.701	.085*	.456*
Conducted own research project	.804	.785	.759	1.244	.825
Academic role model	.863	.883	1.365	.605	.864
Faculty contact index	.483*	.525*	.559*	.502*	.528*
Academic self-confidence	.685	1.083	.809	.419*	.612*

Note: College professor is the omitted category on the dependent variable; Ivy League is the omitted category on school type; "other" is the omitted category on major.

* $p < .05$

Table B5.1 (continued)
D. Latinos

Type of ratio	Business	Law	Medicine	Teaching	Other
SES index	1.103	1.147	1.138	1.090	1.164
Combined SAT	1.077	1.011	.945	.908	.944
School type					
Liberal arts	1.783	1.001	1.200	4.375*	1.847
State	.356*	1.131	.788	5.427*	1.711
Freshman aspiration					
Business	5.757*	.550	1.006	.450	.830
Law	1.203	12.394*	1.444	1.144	1.215
Medicine	1.424	2.216	26.454*	.988	1.605
College professor	.178*	.567	.203*	.275*	.380*
Elementary/secondary					
teaching	.758	.668	.957	5.729*	.967
College GPA	.824	2.150	6.191*	.460	1.120
College major					
Physical sciences	1.713	2.914	2.180	3.838	1.434
Mathematics/computer					
science	.562	.227	.257	.629	.913
Biological sciences	.167*	.097*	2.183	.831	.439
Humanities	.265*	.561	.419	.917	.638
Social sciences	.549	1.141	.352*	1.091	1.076
Influence on career plans					
Parents	.962	1.351	1.299	1.024	.775
Graduate students	.891	.887	.732	.814	.692
Work experiences	1.813*	1.603	1.901*	2.055*	1.813*
College professor appealing					
Teach undergraduates	.488	.522	1.071	1.250	.498*
Research	.369*	.381*	.555	.391*	.462*
College professor					
unappealing					
Lacks financial rewards	1.277	1.710	.544	.337*	.656
Takes too much time	3.940*	1.934	1.859	4.255*	3.527*
Politically conservative	2.176*	1.492	1.309	1.141	1.217
Discrimination index	1.282	1.478	1.260	1.187	1.217
Career orientation index	.869	1.562	1.422	1.442	1.092
Percent freshman interested					
in college teaching	1.002	1.049	1.056*	1.025	1.015
Satisfaction with					
undergraduate education	.795	.929	1.034	.611*	.762
Participated in college					
professor program	.538	.577	.927	.381	.275*

Table B5.1 (continued)

Type of ratio	Business	Law	Medicine	Teaching	Other
Participated in summer research training program	.266	.383	2.649	.231	1.089
Conducted own research project	.744	1.143	.664	.815	.903
Academic role model	.600	1.071	.467	.620	.753
Faculty contact index	.818	.621*	.500*	.715	.713*
Academic self-confidence	.851	.668	.747	.576	.643*

Note: College professor is the omitted category on the dependent variable; Ivy League is the omitted category on school type; "other" is the omitted category on major.

* $p < .05$

Table B5.2 OLS regression of GPA on ethnicity

Ethnicity	A	B	C	D
Black	−.304		−.207	
	(.016)		(.017)	
African American		−.268		−.180
		(.017)		(.017)
Caribbean		−.229		−.157
		(.030)		(.029)
Asian	−.063		−.069	
	(.015)		(.015)	
Chinese		−.025		−.030
		(.023)		(.022)
Indian		.010		−.027
		(.036)		(.037)
Korean		−.079		−.102
		(.025)		(.025)
Other		−.078		−.067
		(.022)		(.021)
Latino	−.189		−.122	
	(.017)		(.017)	
Chicano		−.177		−.099
		(.023)		(.022)
Puerto Rican		−.182		−.113
		(.035)		(.035)
Other		−.121		−.082
		(.024)		(.024)
SAT			.077	.078
			(.006)	(.006)
R^2	.07	.07	.14	.13

Notes: $p < .05$ indicated by boldface.

In this OLS regression on GPA we use dummy variables for each of the three minority groups (see Column A of this table).

Models include dummy variables for institution and field of major. (Whenever grades are included in regression analysis we control for school by using a series of dummy variables for each school because different schools may have different distributions of grades. By controlling for school we make sure that any effect of GPA is not an artifact of what school the student attends. We also control for field of major by lumping together all the natural sciences and math as one group and social sciences and humanities as another. The reason for this is that grades are generally lower in the sciences.)

Models C and D include a control for combined SAT score.

Numbers in parentheses are standard errors.

Table B5.3   OLS regression on GPA for ethnicity and other variables

Factor	A	B	C
Intercept	3.559	2.425	2.666
African Americans	**−.295**	**−.182**	**−.175**
	(.022)	(.022)	(.025)
Asians	−.028	−.046	.007
	(.019)	(.019)	(.026)
Latinos	**−.164**	**−.087**	**−.065**
	(.022)	(.021)	(.024)
SAT		**.081**	**.027**
		(.006)	(.005)
Classmate self-confidence			**.237**
			(.010)
Interest in academia as freshman			**.033**
			(.015)
Social sciences and humanities index			**.040**
			(.014)
Parents' influence			**−.022**
			(.009)
Discrimination index			−.009
			(.010)
Role model			**.032**
			(.016)
Occupational orientation index			**.023**
			(.009)
SES			**.018**
			(.005)
Faculty contact			**.348**
			(.052)
Left/liberal			**.034**
			(.014)
Part-time job			**−.053**
			(.015)
Athletics			**−.054**
			(.016)
Professor program			.032
			(.029)
Women			**.091**
			(.013)
Both parents born outside U.S.			−.003
			(.025)
English only spoken in home			−.001
			(.026)

Table B5.3 (continued)

Factor	A	B	C
Strict parents			−.022
			(.014)
Traditional parents			−.011
			(.014)
Subculture index			−.019
			(.011)
R^2	.09	.16	.43

Notes: p < .05 indicated by boldface; standard errors are in parentheses.
All models control for academic institution.

Table B8.1 Odds ratios from logistic regression model predicting medicine as first-choice occupation

Factor	Model 1	Model 2
Ivy League schools	1.589*	1.290
African Americans		2.206*
Asians		2.838*
Latinos		1.687*
Freshman interest in medicine		35.077*
SES index		1.140*
Combined SAT		.967
College GPA		3.114*
Academic self-confidence		1.256*

* *p* < .05

Table B8.2 Logistic regression of African American underperformance at liberal arts schools

Liberal arts schools	**−1.25**	**−1.309**
	0.298	*0.296*
Combined SAT		**0.195**
		0.049

Notes: Significant effects (*p* < .05) in bold; standard errors in italics.
Models control for institution (using mean GPA at each of the liberal arts schools) and major field of study.

Table B8.3 OLS regression of influences on two indicators of self-confidence (2.8 GPA or higher)

Factor	Compared to age cohort		Compared to classmates	
	A	B	C	D
Ivy League schools				
Intercept	2.882	−.512	1.973	−3.895
African American	**−.279**	−.013	**−.276**	**.177**
	(.048)	(.053)	(.057)	(.054)
Asian	**−.137**	**−.196**	−.042	**−.104**
	(.039)	(.036)	(.052)	(.045)
Latino	**−.133**	.085	**−.372**	−.031
	.043	.048	.055	.046
Grades	—	**.364**	—	**1.109**
	—	(.053)	—	(.062)
Combined SAT	—	**.149**	—	**.138**
	—	(.020)	—	(.020)
R^2	.06	.22	.05	.37
State universities				
Intercept	2.362	−1.280	2.358	−2.48
African American	**−.233**	.020	**−.252**	**.080**
	(.049)	(.045)	(.051)	(.043)
Asian	**−.238**	**−.195**	**−.183**	**−.095**
	(.040)	(.033)	(.043)	(.033)
Latino	**−.204**	.001	**−.181**	.037
	(.041)	(.039)	(.055)	(.044)
Grades	—	**.556**	—	**.935**
	—	(.040)	—	(.041)
Combined SAT	—	**.148**	—	**.131**
	—	(.010)	—	(.010)
R^2	.06	.32	.04	.40
Liberal arts colleges				
Intercept	2.810	−.207	1.797	−3.707
African American	**−.500**	**−.196**	**−.316**	**.173**
	(.071)	(.075)	(.065)	(.061)
Asian	**−.214**	**−.192**	−.079	.012
	(.044)	(.042)	(.052)	(.044)
Latino	**−.346**	**−.144**	**−.258**	.060
	(.057)	(.054)	(.065)	(.058)
Grades	—	**.292**	—	**1.110**
	—	(.058)	—	(.061)
Combined SAT	—	**.143**	—	**.118**
	—	(.017)	—	(.018)
R^2	.12	.23	.02	.33

Notes: Dummy variables for institution were included in each regression, but are not reported in the table. Numbers in parentheses are standard errors.

Coefficient significant at $p < .05$ indicated by boldface.

Table B8.4 Grades by type of school (percent)

Grade	Liberal arts colleges sample	Ivy League sample	State universities		HBCUs	
			Sample	Adjusted	Sample	Adjusted
A	8	13	16	10	14	6
A−	26	31	24	15	19	8
B+	31	28	32	20	25	11
B	28	22	25	15	36	16
B− or less	7	5	2	40	7	59
Total	100	99	99	100	101	100

Note: "Adjusted" columns include the students who were excluded from the study because they had lower than 2.8 GPAs at the end of their junior year.

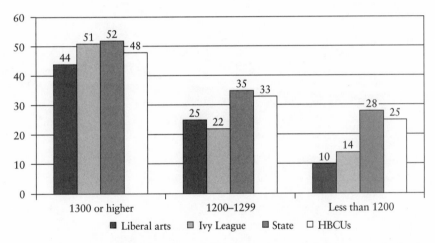

Figure B8.1 Percentage of students with GPA of A− or above, by type of school, controlling for SAT scores

Table B8.5   Logistic regression of influence of type of school and academic self-confidence on African Americans' persistence in decision to become a university professor (GPA of 2.8 or higher)

Factor	A	B
Elite schools	**−.719**	−.574
	(.337)	(.353)
Academic self-confidence	—	**.471**
	—	(.239)
Constant	−.879	−1.900
R^2	.02	.04

Notes: Academic self-confidence compared to classmates.
$p < .05$ indicated by boldface; standard errors are in parentheses.

Table B8.6 Variables measuring interest in college professor, by ethnicity and by school type (percent)

Variable	Total		Whites		African Americans		Asians		Latinos	
	Range	Mean	Range	Mean	Range	Mean	Range	Mean	Range	Mean
% professor as most likely										
Total	2 to 19	10 (34)	1 to 23	11 (30)	2 to 19	8 (24)	2 to 18	7 (22)	2 to 27	12 (19)
Liberal arts colleges	2 to 19	11 (13)	1 to 23	12 (13)	3 to 11	7 (6)	4 to 12	7 (6)	3 to 15	7 (5)
Ivy League universities	3 to 18	10 (8)	2 to 19	11 (8)	2 to 19	7 (7)	3 to 18	8 (8)	2 to 27	15 (8)
State universities	5 to 16	10 (9)	4 to 18	10 (9)	6 to 14	9 (7)	2 to 13	7 (8)	8 to 16	13 (6)
HBCUs	9 to 13	11 (4)	—	—	9 to 13	11 (4)	—	—	—	—
% interested in professor as freshman										
Total	14 to 52	32	12 to 60	35	11 to 42	22	20 to 53	32	3 to 45	30
Liberal arts colleges	19 to 49	34	19 to 54	37	15 to 42	27	20 to 53	31	3 to 33	25
Ivy League universities	26 to 52	36	25 to 60	39	11 to 25	21	26 to 44	34	31 to 45	36
State universities	14 to 35	29	12 to 37	29	14 to 25	20	21 to 42	32	10 to 40	27
HBCUs	20 to 30	24	—	—	20 to 30	24	—	—	—	—
% professor most likely/ % professor as freshman										
Total	9 to 62	33	5 to 58	32	12 to 76	38	5 to 48	24	6 to 100	45
Liberal arts colleges	9 to 51	32	5 to 58	33	15 to 50	26	9 to 44	25	13 to 100	41
Ivy League universities	12 to 47	27	7 to 48	27	12 to 76	32	8 to 41	21	6 to 73	42
State universities	17 to 46	34	13 to 49	36	26 to 67	46	5 to 48	25	38 to 80	53
HBCUs	30 to 62	48	—	—	30 to 62	48	—	—	—	—
% recruits										
Total	0 to 7	3	0 to 8	3	0 to 12	4	0 to 7	2	0 to 16	5
Liberal arts colleges	0 to 7	3	0 to 7	3	0 to 3	1	0 to 5	2	0 to 9	3
Ivy League universities	1 to 3	2	0 to 4	2	0 to 12	4	1 to 5	3	2 to 14	5
State universities	1 to 7	4	1 to 8	4	2 to 8	5	0 to 7	2	3 to 16	7
HBCUs	1 to 5	4	—	—	1 to 5	4	—	—	—	—

Note: Values in parentheses are number of schools used to compute statistics.

The purpose of this appendix is to provide brief descriptions in as non-technical language as possible of the primary methods used in this book and some of the problems involved. We hope that these descriptions will be help nonspecialist readers understand the basic logic of these methods. Some of the methodological issues are discussed in the text and foot-notes. Some of the methods, however, cannot be described without the use of mathematical formulas; these will be found here.

SOURCES OF ERROR IN SURVEYS

Sampling error. Many surveys are samples of large populations (for example, a presidential poll may utilize a sample representative of all registered voters who are likely to vote), and one goal of such a survey is to make generalizations from the sample to the population at large. In order to do so one needs a random sample drawn from that population. The population of students that we wanted to describe in this study were high-achieving minority group students and a control sample of high-achieving white students. Taking a true random sample of such students would have involved first selecting a random sample of colleges and universities. We did not have the resources to follow this procedure. We therefore arbitrarily selected a set of schools in each of four categories that we believed would have high-achieving students enrolled. Our selection was heavily biased in favor of elite private universities (the Ivy League schools) and selective liberal arts colleges. We selected these schools because we thought that a significant majority of high-achieving minority students attend schools such as these. We also had an arbitrarily selected sample of state universities and HBCUs. Within each of these schools we interviewed only high-achieving students (those with GPAs of

2.8 or higher who were majoring in an arts and sciences subject). Therefore, given that our sample is not a random sample, we cannot make generalizations to a population. We can only assume that the students we interviewed are representative of the population of high-achieving minority students and that if we did have a truly random sample of such students they would have similar career aspirations and attitudes as those we interviewed.

Even in random-sample surveys there is the potential that the sample will not be representative of the population. There are many reasons for this, including errors in the sample design and response bias for surveys, with a failure of all members of the sample to complete the interviews. Even for well-designed samples with no response bias, parameter estimates from a sample can still differ from the true population parameter by chance. The probability of this occurring is determined primarily by the size of the sample.

In the case of our survey we can only use the data we collected to generalize to the population of students in our sample categories at the schools included in the sample. Since we only completed interviews with 76 percent of the students included in our sample, there is some chance that the 24 percent of students whom we failed to interview could be significantly different from those we did interview. We did find some evidence showing that the respondents to the mail survey did indeed differ on some significant variables from the nonrespondents to the mail survey. We utilized a telephone survey to interview a sample of these nonrespondents. For the telephone survey, however, we completed interviews with slightly less than 50 percent of those in the sample. Because a large majority of the failure to completes were a result of faulty phone numbers rather than refusals, we have made the assumption that the completed telephone interviews represent a random sample of nonrespondents to the phone survey. To the extent that this assumption is incorrect there could be errors in generalizing from our achieved sample to the population of students at the schools included in our sample.

As we point out in the body of this book, when one conducts tests of significance on survey data and uses, for example, a .05 level of significance, this means that it is possible simply by chance for a relationship to exist in 5 percent of the correlations or cross-tabulations that may appear to be statistically significant when in fact they are not. When one is doing hundreds of tests of statistical significance and finds only a few of them to be significant, the analyst must be very cautious in giving meaning to these findings, as they could be a result of chance.

Measurement error. In social surveys researchers use questions asked of individuals as indicators of variables, or concepts, that they are interested in. In all surveys there is the possibility that the indicators used are not adequate measures of these variables. There is one particular case in our research where there is possibly significant measurement error. We were interested in knowing what the occupational interests of students were when they entered college. We did not, however, have the time or the resources to conduct a longitudinal study in which we would first interview a sample of freshmen and then reinterview them in their senior year. Instead, we must depend on the students' retrospective memory of what their occupational interests were when they were freshmen. To the extent that the students do not adequately report what these interests actually were, significant measurement error has been introduced into the survey.

We employ many concepts in this survey. For some of them the reader can see a relatively clear connection (face validity) between the indicator and the concept; for others, the connection is less clear. But even for those with good face validity, there is a possibility of measurement error. Thus, for example, we measure the concept "academic self-confidence" by asking the students to compare their academic ability with "all people your age" and with "seniors at this college" (see Appendix A, mail questionnaire, Q21). To interpret answers given to these questions as indicators of academic self-confidence has significant face validity. Nonetheless, were other measures of the concept employed we might have come up with different results.

For some of our concepts there is a much less direct relationship between the indicator and the concept. Take, for example, our use of the term "occupational orientation" as an example. By "occupational orientation" we meant that students with such an orientation saw college as primarily a way to prepare for a specific occupation. Students who did not have an occupational orientation were more likely to see college as a way of gaining a broad liberal arts education and the analytical skills that come with such an education. We used three indicators of occupational orientation. The first was the extent to which the students socialized (mail questionnaire, Q13). Students who said that they spent less time

303

than average socializing were considered to have an occupational orientation. The second indicator was whether or not the student mentioned only one occupation that they were interested in as a freshman. Students who mentioned a single occupation as freshmen were considered to have a higher occupational orientation than students who mentioned more than one. The third indicator was whether the student mentioned only one occupation they were interested in as seniors. We added these three indicators together in order to form a measure, or index, of occupational orientation. To the extent that these indicators fail to adequately measure the underlying concept we were interested in, error has been introduced into the analysis of the survey and the conclusions reached.

Normative responding. A potential source of error in surveys that is frequently not given the attention it deserves is the possibility that respondents will answer a question in ways they think they are supposed to feel or behave rather than the actual ways in which they feel or behave. A clear example of this, from surveys of voting behavior, are questions on whether or not the respondent is registered to vote. Respondents, particularly those with high levels of education, know that the social norm is that they "should" be registered to vote. It has been shown in empirical research that a significant portion of respondents will tell interviewers that they are registered to vote when they are not in fact registered (S. Cole 1976).

Clerical errors. Projects such as ours involve the collection and processing of massive amounts of data. At every stage of the process it is possible for inadvertent errors to be made. Frequently, for example, errors are made in coding responses. For the mail survey used in this project, the responses were read by an optical scanner, minimizing the possibility of coding errors. Nonetheless, some respondents may have made errors in filling out the questionnaire, which were recorded by the optical scanner. It is also possible that errors could have been made in applying the complex weighting formula we used (see the next section). And it is certainly possible that in the many thousands of pages of computer analysis that were produced inadvertent errors could have been made in programming or in moving data from computer output to the tables and figures presented in this book. Given the tremendous amount of work that went into completing this project, and all the steps involved, it would be surprising if some errors were not made. In order to guard against this we repeated our analyses several times, especially when figures turned up that didn't look "right." Despite all the care that was taken to prevent errors, however, it is of course possible that some got past us.

Self-reports. Researchers often ask respondents to provide important data about themselves. Depending on the type of data the respondent is asked to provide, there is more or less uncertainty as to the accuracy of the self-reports. (See our earlier discussion of normative responding.)

In this study the two most significant variables that are self-reported are grade point average (GPA) and score on the Scholastic Aptitude Test (SAT). Although it is possible that students may have reported higher values for these variables than what they actually achieved, we have evidence that leads us to believe that the self-reports of both GPA and SAT in this survey are accurate. For one school we had the distribution of actual GPAs. Comparing the actual distribution with the self-reported distribution for this school we could see that the two figures were virtually identical. As for SAT scores, our study included an "institutional questionnaire" in which an administrator at each school was asked to provide data on the school. One piece of data requested was the mean combined SAT scores of students enrolling in fall of 1992, the year in which most of our students enrolled. Only 19 of the 34 schools provided us with the data. When we compared the means provided us by the schools and the means computed from the student self-reports the self-reports were an average of 24 points higher. This small difference is well within the possible error, or "overlap," in the computation of our SAT index. Thus we may conclude that very little, if any, bias was introduced into this study by self-reported data from the questionnaires.

Given all the possible sources of error in conducting research such as that reported here, it is wise not to take small observed differences too seriously. For this reason, we did not use decimal points in reporting survey data because we felt that the use of decimals would give the impression that the data is more accurate than it actually is. We also tried not to give too much weight to small percentage differences or regression coefficients. We attempted to look for differences large enough to be considered substantively significant. Frequently in surveys of this type, as a result of the large sample size small differences become statistically significant. In this report we tried not to emphasize statistically significant differences that are relatively small in size. In fact, to de-emphasize the importance of statistical significance we only reported when an observed result is significant at the .05 level even if in many of the cases the result was significant at the $p < .01$ or $p < .001$ levels. We did so in order to counteract the incorrect tendency to use the extent to which a relationship is significant as an indicator of the strength of the relationship or its substantive size.

WEIGHTING THE DATA

The sample weights were designed to represent the relevant population of the 34 schools included in the study. They were not designed to represent the universe of institutions of higher education in the United States. The weights were constructed on a spreadsheet with the cases being levels of stratification based on 34 schools, 4 races, and 2 majors (for Asians only).

This prescribes an original need for 132 weights (less than $34 \times 4 \times 2$ because only African Americans were sampled at the HBCUs). The necessary number of weights almost doubles when mail and telephone respondents are considered (as explained below).

The elements used in the weighting were the following:

Pop$_i$: the size of the eligible population in each stratum (obtained from the school registrars)
Sam$_i$: the sample size from each stratum
Resp$_i$: the number of respondents from this sample
Mail$_i$: the number of these respondents who responded to the original mail questionnaire
Phone$_i$: the number of the respondents who did not originally respond, but were captured with the (shorter) telephone questionnaire.

Using this raw material, the sample weights were made in two steps. First the respondents were weighted to sum to the total population, taking school, race, and major (for Asians) as the criteria on which the sample population was originally stratified, so that—in principle at least—the weights would be a function of the ratio of the population in the stratum and the respondents there:

$$\text{Weight} = \frac{\text{Pop}_i}{\text{Resp}_i}$$

This would suffice if everyone in the sample responded, but of course not all did. And those who did responded in two different ways, some to the original mail questionnaire, others to the follow-up telephone interview (and recall that the latter survey was less detailed than the former).

The telephone interviews we assumed reflected all nonrespondents to the mail questionnaire and the mail respondents represented all the rest (those who filled out the mail questionnaire). This tended to have the effect of slightly lowering the weights for mail respondents and substantially raising the weights for telephone respondents. For each of the school, race, field stratum we had to adjust all the telephone respondents by an X_i, where $Sample_i = Mail_i + Phone_iX_i$.

$$X_i = \frac{Sample_i - Mail_i}{Phone_i}$$

Also, we had to adjust everyone by the ratio of respondents to the sample in each stratum, since we were now including nonrespondents in our coverage. So

$$WGTMail = WGT_i \frac{Respondents_i}{Sample_i}$$

$$WGTPhone = WGT_i \frac{Respondent_i}{Sample} \left(\frac{Sample_i - Mail_i}{Phone_i} \right)$$

In order to make the respondents sum to the total population size again, one need only multiply all the weights by the same ratio Σ Pop/Σ Resp (or 29804/7612).

There were a small number of respondents whose race we did not know, so they could not be included in the weighting procedure in any straightforward way. We declared all their weights to be equal to 1.0 and kept them in the data analyses. The weights for everyone else were in the end adjusted to keep the totals adding up to the sample size and the population size respectively.

TYPES OF REGRESSION ANALYSIS EMPLOYED

Three main types of outcome variables are examined in this book: binary, multinomial (more than two categories), and continuous. Each requires a different technique for multivariate analyses. As is customary, predictors of a binary, or dichotomous, dependent variable, such as selection of medicine as most likely occupation, are evaluated using logistic regression; predictors of a multinomial variable, such as top five occupational choices, are evaluated using multinomial logistic regression; and predictors of a continuous variable, such as GPA, are evaluated using ordinary least square regression.

The aim of each of these techniques is to predict the value of a dependent *(Y)* variable based on the value of an independent variable(s) *(X)*. To do this we use the raw data to find the functional relationship between X and Y: the equation is $Y = a + bX$ for one independent variable model, or $Y = a + b_1X_1 + b_2X_2$ . . . in the case of a multivariate model. In the simple two-variable situation the equation describes a line that will best fit each case as plotted in a two-dimensional scattergram, with a being the place where the line crosses the Y axis and b representing the slope of the line (or the change in Y for each change in X). The line is computed so the average squared distance from each point in the scattergram to the line is minimized. With no knowledge of X, or if there is no relationship between Y and X (e.g., if $b = 0$ in the two-variable equation), our best predictor of Y would be the mean of Y. But since we have information on X, and moreover because we believe that X and Y are not independent (in fact, we believe that there is a causal relationship and thus the value of Y depends to some extent on the value of X), the overall mean of Y is not our best guess. Instead we need to factor in the influence of the relevant independent variables. The different regression techniques provide us with parameter estimates *(b)* for each independent variable, which tells us the functional relationship between the independent variable(s) and the dependent variable.

Ordinary least square (OLS) regression. With a continuous dependent (outcome) variable we attempt to minimize the squared error between our observed value and our predicted value, hence the term "least square regression." As previously stated, if two variables are related but we predict an outcome based only on the mean value of the dependent variable, we would have more error than if we picked the mean value of Y at each value of X. One can think of OLS regression as computing a mean value of Y for each value of X and then attempting to draw a line through those mean points. This then minimizes the prediction error from each of the raw data points.

This line is represented by the functional relationship in the above equation. For each independent variable we get a parameter estimate and the statistical significance of that estimate—that is, the probability that the influence of a particular independent variable on the dependent variable (with all other independent variables controlled) is due to chance. This estimate tells us the unit change in Y for each unit change in X. Thus if the parameter estimate *(b)* for X is 10, each unit increase in X results in a 10-unit increase in Y. In the preceding example, to compute how many units Y increases with a 2-unit increase in X, we multiply 2 by 10. As opposed to other regression techniques, computing the predicted value of Y in OLS is fairly straightforward: we multiply the mean values of each X by the parameter estimate (*b* in the above equation) of each X, and sum these products along with the constant term (*a* in the above equation) to get the predicted value of Y.

For an excellent technical discussion of linear regression see Neter, Wasserman, and Kutner 1989.

Logistic regression analysis. When predicting dichotomous dependent variables (such as choosing to be a doctor or not), we use logistic regression. Using regression analysis on such dependent variables involves violating two assumptions of the method. The most obvious to a user is that expected values should be sensible, within the possible range of the dependent variable. Regression analysis can predict values of a dichotomous variable above 100 percent and below 0 percent. The second violated assumption is that the error terms are normally distributed, a problem that leads to inefficient estimates of the effect parameters (βs).

To solve these problems logistic regression addresses a transformation of the probability of an event, the natural logarithm of the odds of the event:

$$\text{logit}_i = \log_e\left(\frac{p_i}{1-p_i}\right)$$

This logit is obviously something that is not known for any case in advance of the analysis, since all one really knows is whether case *i* does or does not have the trait being studied (mathematically represented as a 1 or a 0, respectively). What the logistic procedure does is set the logits on the left side of a regression equation. The right side of the equation looks like a regular regression equation: there is an intercept, α, and a series of effects multiplied by the independent variables.

Putting this in algebraic form, we get:

$$\log_e\left(\frac{p_i}{1-p_i}\right) = \text{logit}_i = \alpha + \Sigma\beta X_{ji}$$

There is no error term in this equation; the right-hand side of the equation predicts 100 percent of the variance in the left-hand side. The logits then are something like predicted Ys in regression. This formulation is predicting a dependent variable, which can vary from negative to positive infinity and can never imply a probability greater then 1.0 or less than 0.0. Toward the two ends of the possible probabilities, small differences in p are seen as increasingly large differences in logits. Thus logistic regression sees moving from 1 percent of a population choosing Y to 2 percent as a greater change than moving from, say, 50 percent to 51 percent.

The most common problem with logistic regression is neither its appropriateness or the practical doing of it, but in putting its findings into a form that can make sense in English sentences. Most users turn to one of two strategies: they either convert the logits into odds and report "odds ratios," or they convert the logits back to probabilities, as we have done. This conversion is made by exponentiating the logits to get the probabilities predicted by the logistic regression:

$$p_i = \frac{e^{\log it}}{1+e^{\log it}} = \frac{1}{1+e^{-\log it}}$$

For a clear description of logistic regression see Bowen and Bok (1998), Appendix B, pp. 342–344. For an excellent technical discussion of regression using categorical data, see Long (1997) and Agresti (1990).

Multinomial logistic regression. Multinomial logistic regression is an extension of logistic regression. The difference is that the multinomial technique allows us to compute probabilities for more than one category on the dependent variable; it is not limited to a binary, dependent variable. However, multinomial logistic regression is really no more than binary logistic regression performed one less time than the number of categories on the dependent variable. (See Long 1997 for a technical discussion of binary and multinomial logistic regression.) So, for example, if the outcome variable has six categories, the multinomial procedure computes five complete regression models; the sixth category is the comparison group.

In the logistic regression models that we have run throughout this book we computed the probability of selecting a particular occupation (e.g., doctor) compared to the selection of all other occupations combined. The advantage of multinomial logistic regression is that it allows us to compute the probability of selecting academia (or any other comparison group that we might choose) over medicine, or academia over business, or law, or teaching, and so on, without having to compute a different logistic model for each outcome comparison. It allows us to compute all of the required models in one step and gives us an indication of how accurately all of the independent variables in our model predict the several categories of our dependent variable. Substantively the difference between logistic and multinomial logistic regression is that the former only allows us to look at what variables influence the selection of academia as an occupation when compared to only one other category. The multinomial technique allows us to look at what variables influence the selection of academia as an occupation compared with several other categories—in our case, specific other occupations. Throughout this book these other occupations are medicine, law, business, teaching, and "all others."

The interpretation of logistic parameter estimates requires additional transformations to make sense of the estimates not necessary in OLS. But once these transformations are made we are able to discuss both the direct and the relative effects of the independent variables in the model, though in the various logistic regression techniques we talk about the odds ratio as opposed to the unit increase. We have not reported odds ratios in this book because in almost all of the cases in which we use logistic regression techniques we start with a relationship between a particular independent variable and a dependent variable and try to understand that relationship by seeing what other variables have to be controlled to reduce the initial relationship to statistical insignificance. These other control variables then indicate the reasons why the independent variable had its effect on the dependent variable.

Computing predicted probabilities from multinomial regression models. As previously noted, multinomial logistic regression is powerful in its ability to look at multiple categories of the dependent variable as a system; thus we are not forced to assume, as we do in logistic regression, that all the people who do not select academia are alike. Instead, we can look at the effects of an independent variable on the selection of academia over, for example, medicine, business, and law individually. Although the resulting regression coefficients provide a great deal of information, it is easier to see the effects of various independent variables by graphing the predicted probabilities generated from the multinomial model.

To get these predicted probabilities we multiply the regression coefficients from the multinomial model by the respective mean values for the model independent variables and thus generate an overall mean log odds ratio. (We used the software program CLARIFY to obtain the predicted probabilities reported in this book.) The model used in our project resulted in five regression models (one for each outcome minus the omitted category) and thus resulted in five overall mean log odds ratios. We then converted these ratios, through exponentiation, to predicted probabilities. Since the sum of all predicted probabilities equals one, we added the predicted probabilities from the five regression models and subtracted this total from one to get the predicted probability for the omitted group (academia).

We used these multinomial models to assess the effect of predictor variables after controlling for all other variables that we believe contribute to occupational choice. To show these controlled effects we manipulated the value of an independent variable (say, GPA) while controlling for all other predictor variables at their respective means. This allowed us to see the change in interest (as measured by predicted probabilities) in business, law, medicine, academia, and all other occupations, moving from the lowest level of GPA to the highest level of GPA, with all other variables set equal to their means.

Treatment of missing data in regression models. In any large survey such as ours it is typical to have missing data on many or all of the variables. Sometimes the amount of missing data on a particular variable is substantial. In our survey this was especially true for those variables not included on the telephone survey. Since the total weighted N for this study is approximately 29,000 but the weighted N for those who answered the mail survey was about 20,000, this means that for any variable that was not included on the phone survey there were approximately 10,000 weighted missing cases. In addition, missing cases occurred in other types of variables for other reasons. There were, for example, some cases of missing SAT scores because some students did not remember or chose not to report their SAT scores and some schools did not require SAT results.

Because regression analyses are based on correlation matrices, there are two ways in which the missing data problem is typically treated. The first is to delete all cases for which there is missing data on any of the variables included in the model ("listwise" deletion). This is considered to be the most conservative and statistically legitimate way to handle missing cases. Since our multinomial logistic regression model contained over 30 variables and many had a large number of cases with missing data, this approach would have meant that our final models would have been based on only a fraction of the cases included in the survey. For this reason listwise deletion was not practical for these large multinomial models.

The second way to handle missing data is called "pairwise" deletion. In this method the correlation coefficient for any two variables in the initial correlation matrix on which the regression analysis is to be based is computed on the basis of the available data. This is essentially equivalent to assuming that all of the missing cases would be the mean for the particular independent variable. (Obviously we cannot include cases on which there is missing data on the dependent variable.)

We chose to use neither of these two techniques for our missing data; instead, for the multinomial logistic regression model we used a method called "imputation," which we believe is superior to pairwise deletion. For all but a few variables with missing data, we computed a regression equation using the available data in order to predict the score on the missing variable. (We did not do this for the dependent variable or the school type variable.) We imputed the values using the ordinary least square (OLS) regression imputation procedure in the statistical software package STATA. As independent variables we used those included in the multinomial model reported in Appendix B, Table B5.3, except that we used only one model to impute the value for all four ethnic groups with ethnicity included as an additional predictor variable. For each imputed variable we deleted that variable as a predictor and substituted it as the dependent variable. The impute command in STATA saves out the predicted value of the variable for each case missing a value on that predicted variable. Since many of our independent variables are nominal and the OLS procedure predicts continuous variables, we recoded the values so that cases below the midway point were coded down and cases at or above the midway point were coded up. Thus, a predicted value of 1.49 was recoded as 1, while a predicted value of 1.5 was recoded as 2.

We compared the means after imputation to the means prior to imputation and found no substantial differences between the two. To the extent that the available data are able to yield an accurate prediction of the missing data, this method is superior to the pairwise deletion method. If all of the available data told us nothing about the missing data, this technique would be equivalent to the pairwise deletion method.

USING STATA AND SUDDAN TO ESTIMATE LINEAR AND LOGISTIC REGRESSIONS AND CORRESPONDING PARAMETERS

In order to compute descriptive statistics that will accurately describe our population of students, we had to weight the data. When estimating multivariate causal models there are advantages and disadvantages of using weighted as opposed to unweighted data (Winship and Radbill 1994).[1] We decided to use weighted data for all of the analyses in our study. This meant that we had to use a program that would take the weights into account in computing parameter estimates and tests of significance. Both STATA and SUDDAN do this. In the simplest of terms what these programs do in computing tests of significance is to use the number of cases from the unweighted data and compute the variance based on the weighted data. Both STATA and SUDDAN use essentially the same techniques in doing this. The STATA manual describes these techniques more clearly than does the SUDDAN manual; for those interested in exactly how tests of significance are computed on weighted data we advise you to read the excellent description provided in the STATA manual (see esp. pp. 427–430).

Because the weighted number of cases is not the number actually used by either SUDDAN or STATA to calculate the standard errors and compute tests of significance, these weighted numbers are not very meaningful except as descriptions of, for example, how many students in the population of the 34 schools were in a particular category. We have therefore not reported number of cases in the tables and figures.

COMPUTING THE DATA FOR TABLE B3.1

In Table B3.1 we estimate what the distribution for the entire sample would have been on final choice occupation, if we had included all nineteen occupations instead of ten on the telephone survey. The following procedures were used:

314

1. Our best estimate of the proportion of telephone respondents who would have selected one of the missing occupations is the proportion who selected this occupation among the mail respondents. Using the total size of the telephone sample and the percentages for the missing occupations from the mail survey we computed the number of cases among the telephone respondents who would have selected each of the missing occupations.
2. We subtracted the number of students estimated to have selected one of the missing occupations from the total N for the telephone survey.
3. We calculated new cell Ns for the occupations that were included in the telephone survey using the smaller total N as computed from step 2 but the same percentages as in the original distribution for the telephone survey.
4. We then added the number of cases for each occupation from the mail survey to the new estimated numbers for the telephone survey. We computed new percentages for each occupation from this distribution. This is the "adjusted" column reported in Table B3.1.

One can see from Table B3.1 that if the telephone respondents would have had the same probability of selecting the nine missing occupations as the mail respondents, the effect of having only ten of the twenty occupations on the telephone survey was minimal and had no substantive effect on the conclusions of this study.

COMPUTING THE DATA FOR TABLES 9.1 AND 9.2

The estimates that we report in Table 9.1 are based on our analysis of the 1990 census. There are, however, multiple sources of data on educational attainment. One of the best is the annual *Digest of Educational Statistics* published by the National Center for Education Statistics (NCES). We examined the NCES data for the number of college degrees granted in a given year to people in each of our four ethnic groups. The 1995 digest provides data on the number of bachelor's degrees conferred by institutions of higher education in the year 1991–92 (the year closest to the census estimate). When we compared the estimates we made on the basis of the 1990 census with the NCES data we found some discrepancies.

Based on the 1990 census we estimated that 882,000 whites between the ages of 25 and 29 would have received college degrees, the NCES data for 1991–92 shows that 937,000 degrees were granted to people who were white. This discrepancy is a result of the procedure we are using (i.e., using the percentages from the 35–39-year-old cohort and multiplying that by the number of people in the 25–29-year-old cohort). Computing the number for whites based on the actual 35–39 birth cohort produces a figure of 917,777. Remember, cohort sizes differ, and even in 1990 the 25–29 age cohort of whites is smaller than the 35–39 cohort.

There are no significant discrepancies between the estimates made for Hispanics and Asians using the two different sources. The 1990 census data led us to estimate that 47,000 Latinos aged 25–29 would receive a college degree each year in the coming ten years. This is greater than the 41,000 bachelor's degrees granted to Latinos in 1991–92 as reported by the NCES. The census estimate for Asians in the 25–29-year-old group who will have earned a college degree in each year is 51,000. The NCES data show 47,000 college degrees granted to people of Asian or Pacific Islander origins for 1991–92. For both Latinos and Asians the NCES figures are lower than the census figures. This difference is probably accounted for by the fact that some Latinos and Asians entered the country with college degrees obtained in their homeland and because we projected figures based on a larger birth cohort whereas the NCES reported actual numbers of degrees awarded in a given year.

We found a problem when we compared the two sources for African Americans. Here the census data indicated that there would be 63,000 African Americans aged 25 to 29 who would earn college degrees in each of the coming ten years; the NCES digest for 1995, however, reported a total of 72,000 degrees granted to black, non-Hispanics in 1991–92.[2] Thus, the census data led to the estimate that 19 percent of African American high school graduates aged 35–39 would have received college degrees, while the NCES data yield 22 percent. We were unable to determine the reasons for this difference. The discrepancy is not a function of cohort size used, since among African Americans the 25–29 cohort is larger than the 35–39 cohort. Given this difference, we did an alternative calculation of Rows 6 through 9 of Table 9.1 using the higher NCES figure. We found that replacing the lower census estimate with the higher NCES number resulted in no substantial change in the estimate of African Americans who want to be college professors when they graduate from college.

We found one additional source of data on the number of African Americans receiving college degrees in 1994: a work by Michael Nettles, Laura Perna, and Kimberly Edelin (1997), based on what the authors refer to as Integrated Postsecondary Education Data System (IPEDS). Nettles and his coauthors report that in 1994, 23,434 African Americans received college degrees from HBCUs (28 percent of the total), and that in 1995, 61,208 African Americans received college degrees from predominantly white schools. If we add and round these numbers we come up with an estimate of 85,000 college degrees granted to African Americans in the 1994–95 period.[3] The NCES reported that in 1993–94 84,000 African Americans received a bachelor's degree. The correspondence between these two figures gives credence to the NCES data.

Once again, our estimate of the number of African Americans receiving college degrees based on census data are lower than figures obtained from the NCES. The last year of data we have from the NCES is for 1995–96; according to the NCES 91,000 African Americans received bachelor's degrees that year.[4] The NCES data from 1991 to 1995–96 indicate a fairly significant increase in the number of bachelor's degrees granted to African Americans during this period. If we assume that those figures continued to rise from 1995–96 through 1998 it is possible that approximately 100,000 African Americans obtained B.A. degrees in 1998.

CLASSIFICATION OF FIELDS AS ARTS AND SCIENCES

The NCES *Digest of Educational Statistics* (1995, Table 257) classifies the following fields as being within the undergraduate arts and sciences:

Area, ethnic, and cultural studies
Biological/life sciences
Communications
Communications technologies
Computer and information science
English language and literature
Foreign languages and literatures
Law and legal studies
Liberal arts and scienences, general studies, and humanities
Mathematics
Multi- or interdisciplinary studies

Philosophy and religion
Physical sciences and science technologies
Psychology
Social sciences and history
Visual and performing arts

The same source—the NCES *Digest of Educational Statistics* (1995, Table 263) classified these same fields as being within the arts and sciences for doctoral studies.

All other fields were classified as being non–arts and sciences.

I. THE PROBLEM

1. In general, there are so few Native American students and faculty members in the universities and colleges we studied that we were unable to treat them as a separate group. Our study focuses on African Americans and Latinos. We also studied Asian students because of concern about the appropriate representation of Asian faculty members in the humanities and social sciences.

2. For a summary of this literature see Pascarella and Terenzini (1991), Chapters 10 and 11. Three of the most widely cited studies conducted by sociologists are Blau and Duncan (1967), Featherman and Hauser (1976), and Jencks et al. (1972). Economists have also conducted many studies demonstrating the connection between education and income.

3. A sophisticated discussion of the scope and limits of the educational advantages of diversity may be found in Klitgaard (1985), pp. 72–75.

4. Although Asians are not in general underrepresented on the faculties of research universities, they are overrepresented in the natural sciences and substantially underrepresented in the social sciences and humanities. For this reason we decided to include Asian students in our study, along with African American, Latino, and a large control group of white students.

5. In the philosophy and sociology of science this is called "stand point" epistemology. This view holds that only members of particular groups can fully understand their problems.

6. A set-aside is a position or series of positions reserved exclusively for minority candidates.

7. Many of the elite colleges that give preference to students from underrepresented racial or ethnic groups also give preferences to students with other characteristics. For example, according to Bowen and Bok (1998) a "legacy" (a student who has a parent who has graduated from the school) has about the same chance of being admitted as an African American applicant to the schools in the Bowen and Bok sample. Of course, this statistic alone needs to be informed by information on the qualifications of legacies. Bowen and Bok found for the schools they studied that students who are on coaches' recruiting lists ("jocks") have the highest probability (ca. 80 percent) of being admitted.

8. These data indicate that the proportion of Asian students and faculty members is relatively close; but, as we have noted, there are significant differences in the distribution of Asians among academic fields. Asian faculty members are more likely to teach in the natural sciences and mathematics, but are underrepresented in the social sciences and humanities. Another problem is that Asian students are substantially overrepresented in elite schools. Thus, although 6 percent of all students are Asian, 18 percent of seniors in the Ivy League schools and 10 percent of seniors in the select liberal arts colleges were Asian.

9. Some of these schools may be historically black colleges or universities (HBCUs), in which the proportion of African American faculty is usually quite high. Thus the proportion of African American faculty members in predominantly white educational institutions is probably less than the figures indicated here.

10. Most of the studies of occupational choice were conducted as many as forty years ago. This topic has not been a focus of attention of social scientists in recent years. When we cite findings from old studies, there is always the question of whether or not those findings are still relevant given the changes in social and economic conditions that have occurred since the studies were completed. We try to remain sensitive to this issue, and our own study represents a test of the extent to which variables found to be important in the past are still important today.

11. S. Cole and Meyer (1985), in a study of the demand for new assistant professors in physics, found that demand peaked in 1966 and had very substantially diminished by 1976. The demand for professors in other areas may have had different time patterns.

12. Ehrenberg (1992) reports on many studies that examine factors influencing the supply of academics, but these do not include studies that directly measure demand.

13. In order to conduct such a study one would have to collect data on the number of students entering and completing graduate study (relatively easy to collect from NCES and other sources) and on the demand for professors (relatively difficult to collect). S. Cole and Meyer (1985) determined demand by examining lists of faculty members in universities having Ph.D. programs in physics and counting the number of new instructors listed. This had to be done in year-to-year comparisons and was extremely time consuming.

14. From the point of view of understanding occupational choice of college students, the most important study that could be done would be one showing how real levels of demand influence occupational choice.

15. Of course in the early 1960s there would have been so few high-achieving African Americans and Latinos enrolled in college that it probably would have been impossible to have conducted a study like the one we report on in this book. Baird (1973) reports that 18.4 percent of a random sample of college graduates in 1971 said that they planned to enroll in an arts and sciences graduate program in the year after graduation. But many of these students could have been seeking master's degrees and not have had the intention of becoming a college professor.

16. It is unclear as to whether the sample utilized by Astin was a truly random sample. It also appears that the response rate to Astin's questionnaire was substantially below what social scientists consider adequate.

17. Given the authors' training this study uses a sociological perspective in analyzing this problem. Economists who study occupational choice tend to emphasize the anticipated rewards students feel they can obtain from entering different careers. More sophisticated economists, however, take into account sociological factors, and as a result their work is compatible with the approach taken here. See for example Freeman (1971) and Ehrenberg (1992).

18. Pascarella and Terenzini (1991), in an informative didactic methodological appendix, discuss in detail some methodological problems encountered in trying to assess the impact of college on students.

19. For a full discussion of this decision and its consequences for our study see Chapter 2.

20. Our study was conducted before the Educational Testing Service (ETS) added an "analytic" test to the existing verbal and quantitative exams (the analytic test has since been abandoned for a "writing" test). It was also conducted before SAT scores were "renormed," raising the average combined score to 1000.

21. For an interesting history of the SAT see Part I of Nicholas Lemann's *The Big Test* (1999).

22. In most of these studies the freshman GPA is used as the dependent variable.

23. Klitgaard (1985), in a thorough study of the predictors of both academic success and success in later life, reluctantly came to the conclusion that SAT scores are the best predictors available of both. Some argue that although SAT scores may be the best *available* predictor, they still are a relatively weak one. A correlation of .70, however, suggests that SAT scores may not be as weak a predictor of GPA as these critics believe.

24. The fact that Steele claims to have explained only the underperformance phenomenon and not the large original difference in SAT scores is sometimes overlooked by discussants of his work.

25. One reader of an earlier draft of this book felt that Steele's theory is a type of "blaming the victim" theory. He argued that what harms the performance of African Americans is not their own fear of negative stereotypes but the belief in the validity of the stereotypes by whites, who, in their roles as professors, admissions officers, and the like, act on such beliefs.

26. Although there were no gender differences in the proportion of men and women wanting to be college professors, there were some gender differences in our data set. One of the more interesting of these is a gap in academic self-confidence between men and women (women being less self-confident) even when GPA is controlled. Melissa Bolyard is currently analyzing these gender differences.

27. Certainly we do not mean to imply that there is anything wrong with random samples. But in a sample such as ours, which heavily overrepresents minority students, we might find different results than in a random sample, in which minority students would make up only a small fraction of the sample.

28. These studies are quite dated. We do not know the extent to which their findings would still be true. In this study we do look at the effect of concern with finances on selecting various occupations.

29. One significant problem in survey research (discussed at greater length in

the first section of Appendix C) is what is called "normative responding." This is the tendency of respondents to tell the researcher what the respondent thinks he or she is supposed to believe as opposed to what the respondent actually believes. There may be some tendency for students to deny that financial considerations are very important to them. This is certainly true for students wanting to be physicians. These students are aware that if medical schools think that their primary motivation in becoming a physician is to maximize income, they are likely to be rejected. In qualitative interviews Fiorentine and Cole (1992) found a greater interest in monetary rewards among aspiring physicians (especially men) than could be ascertained from survey data. Another potential problem is that students in general and minority students in particular may not have adequate knowledge of the likely earnings of the main occupations that compete for talented minorities. There is little doubt that in comparing college professors with physicians, partners in large law firms, and senior executives, even successful professors earn less money. But the *average* earnings of professors might not be significantly less, and may even be higher, than the *average* earnings of all of the major competing occupations, with the exception of medicine.

30. See the recent memoir by Thomas Sowell (*A Personal Odyssey,* 2001) as an example of how African American cultural attitudes toward studying and saving for education made it very difficult for him to attain his education.

31. For just one example see Hanushek 1996.

32. The fact that it is always impossible to control for all the input characteristics that might influence an outcome causes the serious methodological problem of what is called "uncontrolled selectivity" (Lieberson 1985). In an important paper Dale and Krueger (1999) use a method to eliminate selectivity in the data used by Bowen and Bok (1998) to support the effectiveness of race-sensitive admissions policies. The Berg and Krueger paper leads to the conclusion that some of Bowen and Bok's conclusions concerning the positive consequences of race-sensitive admissions are invalid.

33. See Astin 1993, pp. 438–441. The multiple R tells how well all of the independent variables together can explain the dependent variable. The higher the multiple R, the more able one would be to predict a particular individual's score on the dependent variable by knowing that person's scores on all of the independent variables used in the regression equation. Squaring a multiple R reveals how much of the total variation in the dependent variable is explained by all of the independent variables in the regression equation.

34. The advent of grade inflation may have changed conditions, so that the Davis theory will no longer apply in explaining the career choices of contemporary college graduates. However, in Chapter 8, where we examine the Davis theory as a possible explanation of career choice among the students in our sample, we point out that the equal distribution of grades among different schools is unnecessary for the Davis theory to be correct. What is essential is that students compare themselves with classmates rather than with their age cohort at other schools.

35. There were some significant measurement problems, however, that Davis faced in his analysis. Most important, Davis had no measure of the students' academic ability. He had to assume that students attending the highest-quality schools

had the highest level of ability. He measured school quality by the number of National Merit Scholar finalists and semifinalists attending each school. But he was unable to distinguish ability levels among those students attending schools of a given quality. Also, his measure of academic self-confidence is not direct, but rather was obtained from responses to whether students felt they had a "flair" for a particular subject.

36. They do find, however, that tuition cost has an independent effect on later earnings. This effect, however, may also be a result of uncontrolled selectivity because Dale and Kreuger failed to match students by the cost of schools they applied to and were accepted and rejected by.

37. The same role model argument with regard to race and ethnicity was used by those in favor of racial preferences in briefs presented to the Supreme Court in the Bakke case. No data were presented to show whether the race or ethnicity of the role model actually made a difference.

38. As just one of many examples, Addis quotes an article that appeared in the *Washington Post* on January 20, 1992, in which a member of Congress is quoted as follows: "The current statistics for minority higher education are discouraging . . . the lack of African-American role models has been cited in study after study as one of the prime reasons our youngsters do not pursue college educations and certain career options like science and engineering" (quoted in Addis 1996, p. 1378).

39. The last part of the Addis article deals with the use of the concept of role model in many legal cases. In virtually all of the cases he cites the claims being made for the desirability of same-ethnicity role models are subject to empirical verification. It is only when one frames the importance of role models as symbols of cultural acceptance that it becomes difficult to evaluate the argument with empirical data, although it probably would be possible to design a study that would test the legitimacy of the symbolic argument.

2. OBTAINING THE DATA

1. At the less selective schools, we restricted our sample to students who had a GPA of 2.8 or higher at the end of their junior year. The reasons for this are discussed later in this chapter.

2. See any one of the recent reports of the Cooperative Institutional Research Program (CIRP), conducted by Alexander Astin and the Higher Education Research Institute at UCLA, on surveys of freshmen entering college.

3. The research also indicates that initial career choice as freshmen is the strongest influence on career choice as seniors. In the case of academia, past studies have shown that the proportion selecting academia at the end of the senior year is usually greater than the proportion expressing an interest in the career in freshman year, the reason likely being that high school students are generally not familiar with the occupation of university professor.

4. As explained later, some of this difference is attributable to the way in which we measured occupational choice.

5. From the point of view of the sponsors of this research it was important to

learn how many minority group members would receive Ph.D.s and enter academia; but it may be even more important for them to learn how many of these Ph.D.s have the type of qualifications that would meet minimum hiring standards at the more selective colleges and universities. Certainly the students who are likely to meet such standards would be most likely to be found among the highest-achieving undergraduates.

6. This theory was discussed in Chapter 1. Throughout the book it should be kept in mind that the logic of the "fit hypothesis," frequently put forth by opponents of affirmative action (Sowell 1993), is similar to the logic of the frog pond hypothesis (J. Davis 1966). If one is correct, then the other is also likely to be correct.

7. The percentage of applicants who are admitted is only one indicator of selectivity, given the high degree of variation in the quality of the applicant pool at different schools. Even if the percentage admitted is relatively high (for example, 45 percent at one of the Ivy League schools), the institution may well be extremely selective if the great majority of the applicants have very high academic qualifications (as was the case with the Ivy League school just mentioned). Nevertheless, such a school would clearly not be as selective as other schools where a lower percentage of applicants are admitted but where mean SAT scores are higher. When we chose our sample of institutions, we were able to do no more than make assumptions about their selectivity; information generated by the survey permitted us to develop a more sophisticated hierarchy of selectivity. Ultimately we decided to use as our measure of selectivity the mean combined SAT score of graduating students included in our survey.

8. There is not necessarily a correlation between being outstanding in research and being a poor teacher. However, even if research stars are not poor teachers, they usually spend most of their time and effort on research rather than teaching.

9. Given the lack of agreement on how to evaluate teaching, the fact that so-called teacher evaluation surveys are for the most part nothing more than popularity contests, and the norm of closed classrooms, it is not surprising that teaching does not count more in promotion, tenure, and hiring. At some schools that require departments to include a teaching evaluation as part of a tenure or promotion file, the procedure is usually perfunctory with virtually no one designated an inadequate teacher. How teaching could be effectively evaluated is a difficult topic, beyond the scope of our study; but we believe that a necessary component of such an evaluation must include colleague observation and that universities should make teaching as visible as their faculties' publications. Universities should also pay more attention to training Ph.D. candidates how to teach than is currently the practice at most schools.

10. Steele's theory was discussed briefly in Chapter 1; data relevant to the theory are presented in Chapter 5 and Chapter 8.

11. There is substantial disagreement about the extent of "institutionalized" racism at predominantly white schools. Many minority faculty members have expressed the view that racism is endemic, while many white faculty members believe that both faculty and administration (students are usually not discussed) at pre-

dominantly white schools are liberals who have sympathetic views toward minority students.

12. The percentage of African American faculty at one of our Ivy League institutions is 6 percent and significantly lower at others; at one of our HBCUs it is 35 percent and at another, 60 percent. If, as is sometimes claimed, the reason for the underrepresentation of minority faculty at predominantly white schools—particularly the elite schools—is the failure on the part of these schools to make an adequate effort to hire minority faculty, one might wonder why at even many HBCUs the majority of faculty is white. If there were indeed a large enough pool of African American academics, it would seem that the proportion of faculty at HBCUs who are African American would be higher.

13. For detailed discussion of the admissions process at selective schools see Klitgaard (1985), Bowen and Bok (1998), and Shulman and Bowen (2000).

14. Opponents of race sensitive admissions might agree with this statement but argue that currently it is not illegal to admit on the basis of qualifications other than SAT scores and GPAs, but it is illegal to use race as an admission criterion.

15. We have "oversampled" in quotes because the selection of schools that we included in our study is completely nonrandom, but selected for theoretical reasons rather than to represent all schools in the country.

16. No school (in all four school types) that was asked to participate in the survey refused.

17. We had to include this many liberal arts colleges in the sample because of the small number of minorities enrolled in each. As it is, the number of African Americans and Latinos is the smallest in this category of school. Adding more schools would have resulted in diminishing returns, as the schools not included in our sample had even fewer minority students graduating.

18. All of these schools, with the exception of Tufts, which is slightly larger and sometimes not classified as a liberal arts college, were in the top twenty-five liberal arts colleges as rated by *U.S. News and World Report* (2000). One of the *U.S. News* top ten, Haverford, was used in our pretest. Our sample included all the top ten liberal arts colleges in the 2000 evaluation except for Wellesley.

19. We did not include any single-sex schools. This would have meant introducing yet another variable into the design; and our resources did not permit us to include a sufficient number of women's colleges to make meaningful analysis possible. Given the small number of colleges that remain women's colleges and their relatively small size, it is doubtful that it would even be possible to obtain a large enough sample of minority students suitable for conducting multivariate statistical analysis.

20. One reader of an earlier draft of this book pointed out that he would not classify students with a B− average at any school as being high-achieving. We chose a cutoff point of 2.8 for these schools in an attempt to capture virtually all students who might be interested in a career in academia.

21. Including even small samples of students with GPAs of less than 2.8 at the thirteen less selective institutions, however, would have significantly increased our sample size and increased the already substantial costs of conducting this research.

22. It is possible to produce estimated mean scores by assuming that each student achieved a score at the midpoint of the category that he or she checked off. We make these calculations occasionally in the text.

23. All the students in our sample took the SAT examination before the "renormalization" of the test that occurred in the mid-1990s. SAT scores had been declining since the 1970s, and the Educational Testing Service (ETS), which produces the SAT, had been under some pressure to help explain this decline. (There is a large literature debating the reasons for the decline: see R. Rothstein 1998; Murray and Herrnstein 1992.) Until the mid-1990s the grading of the SAT had been based on the performance of around 10,000 students who first took the exam in 1941. The median correct on each of the two tests by this group was designated 500. This was useful for making comparisons of performance over time, but made it easy to see a decline in performance. The ETS simply decided to renorm the test every year, with the median correct by test takers in each year designated as 500. From then on, the median was always 500, even though a 500 might indicate substantially different numbers of correct answers from year to year. This eliminated the problem of declining scores by fiat, but made it impossible to compare scores over time without the use of some complex formulas issued by the ETS, enabling one to convert a renormed score each year into a score prior to renorming. To compare the scores of our students with current students, one would have to adjust for this difference.

24. This estimate is confirmed by staff of The College Board (personal communication) and by Professor Michael T. Nettles, Executive Director of The Frederick D. Patterson Research Institute of the United Negro College Fund.

25. The survey design was also aided by studies done by the Consortium for Financing Higher Education (COFHE), a group of 31 elite private universities and liberal arts colleges that conducts research of use to its members.

26. The results are available in Barber and Cole (1996b). While we were doing this study we were asked by Brown University and the Leadership Alliance (a group of private research universities and HBCUs that work to further the education of primarily African American students) to conduct a focus-group study of minority and white graduate students. At the time we did the research, the Alliance was located at Brown and headed by Brown's president at the time, Vartan Gregorian. These focus groups were also transcribed and analyzed; the results are available in Barber and Cole (1996a).

27. As in the main survey our sample was restricted to arts and sciences graduates and at Maryland to students with a GPA of 2.8 or higher.

28. In comparing the results of the pretest and the final survey we found that on questions appearing in both, the marginals (distribution of responses to the questions) were quite similar. Also, correlations between particular variables were very similar for the pretest and final survey data.

29. The size of these samples differed at different types of school. For details on how the sample was selected see Appendix C.

30. A substantial portion of African American and Latino students attending our elite schools were on full or partial scholarships. Many of these schools have a

"need blind" admissions policy. This means that they make admissions decisions without regard to the student's ability to pay; only after the admissions decision is made do these institutions try to work out a financial package (in many cases including full scholarships) that enable the admitted students to attend. Other elite schools offer minority members admitted as students full scholarships even if they come from upper-middle-class families who could well afford to pay the tuition and other fees. This is currently an issue of debate among the most selective schools.

31. Remember that these numbers are for one graduating cohort, not all the minority students currently enrolled.

32. At the two small liberal arts colleges that declined to release student phone numbers, the response rates were indeed somewhat lower than the norm including the phone follow-up—63 percent at one and 66 percent at the other.

33. For this type of research 75 percent is a relatively high standard. The response rates, particularly for African Americans, achieved by Alexander Astin in many of the studies carried out by the UCLA Higher Education Research Institute (HERI) are substantially lower (Astin and Astin 1992). In fact, the Astin CIRP study is not based on a random sample. For a critique of the sampling strategy used for the CIRP see Lerner and Nagai (1991).

34. In surveys such as the one we conducted it is quite possible that there is self-selection in who returns the questionnaire and that the self-selected respondents may differ in important ways from the nonrespondents. This problem is usually ignored because there is not much that can be done to estimate the characteristics of the nonrespondents.

35. Andrea Tyree, professor of sociology at Stony Brook, in consultation with the authors, did the weighting. The details of how the weighting was done are presented in Appendix C.

36. Later in this chapter we discuss how we classified the students by ethnicity.

37. Because we ran virtually all of the analyses on weighted data, this presented a problem in conducting tests of statistical significance. We used two statistical programs, which allowed us to conduct tests of significance on weighted data using the actual number of cases in the computation. These were STATA and SUDDAN. The latter program was specifically developed in order to analyze weighted data sets. For the number of weighted and unweighted cases broken down by school and ethnicity see Table 2.4.

38. For the exact wording of this question see Appendix A, Mail Questionnaire, Q. 30.

39. The probable reason for this is that "Latino" is an ethnic rather than a racial category.

40. It is difficult to be altogether consistent or to make altogether satisfactory choices when it comes to terminology in the area of race and ethnicity. We use the category "African American" for two reasons: first, it is one of the categories used by many of the schools that supplied us with data on their students (though some use "black"); second, it is the term currently preferred by Americans of African descent. All the students in our sample are U.S. citizens or permanent resident aliens,

and it was not practical for us to differentiate between black students whose parents are native-born Americans and those whose parents came to this country from Caribbean countries.

41. Keep in mind throughout the entire analysis that what we call an ethnic group is in fact an empirical grouping of people from different cultures. This includes the majority group, whites.

42. We did this because we did not have enough Native American/Alaskan Natives to analyze them as a separate group.

43. Percentages do not always add up to 100 because of rounding. In this book we generally do not use decimal places for survey data, both for simplicity of presentation and because using decimal places gives an impression of a degree of accuracy that is not warranted by most survey data. We use the convention of rounding to the nearest whole number and in the case of .5, rounding to the nearest even number. In the case of .5, SUDDAN (the program we used for most of the quantitative analysis) uses the convention of rounding up to the next highest number. Throughout the report, the reader may find very slight discrepancies in some of the numbers reported due either to weighting or to rounding.

44. In fact we ended up combining two of the careers: "University/college professor" and "Researcher (in a university)" and treated them as representing an interest in "academia." Also, on the telephone survey, given the difficulty of reading a long list of careers and having the students select from among them, we limited the number of career choices to what previous analysis of the pretest data had indicated were the ten most popular. The effect that this had on the results will be discussed in Chapter 3 and the relevant section of Appendix C. In fact, as pointed out in Chapter 3, a substantial majority of the students we interviewed were interested in only a handful of careers.

45. Using the multiple-choice method to measure freshman career interest retroactively reduces the probability of error in this measurement. If a student can list several occupations he or she is less likely to be influenced by current occupational interests than if forced to list only one.

46. For the exact wording of this question, see Appendix A, Mail Questionnaire, Q. 1.

47. The problem of determining causality in quantitative research is discussed at length in many methods texts in sociology, including S. Cole (1976), Hirschi and Selvin (1967), and Rosenberg (1968).

48. It will not escape the reader that data on freshman interest in various careers were collected at the same time as final-choice career data were collected: in the senior year. Thus, there is a legitimate question of whether the freshman choice actually precedes in time the senior choice. It is possible that those students who end up being interested in academia were more likely to indicate this as a freshman interest even if this was not really true when they were freshmen. There is no way for us to determine the veracity of their statements about their attitudes as freshmen. One of the many assumptions on which our analysis is based is that retrospective questions such as this provide roughly accurate measures of the students' freshmen occupational interests. There is disagreement in the literature on the extent to which such retrospective measures are accurate. Part of this disagreement is

based upon the unwise decision to ask students to indicate only one occupational interest as freshmen. In Chapter 4 we discuss reasons why we believe the retrospective question provides a roughly accurate measure of freshman career interest.

3. ETHNIC DIFFERENCES IN OCCUPATIONAL CHOICES

1. This chapter deals only with ethnic differences in occupational choice. The ways in which occupational choice varies by social characteristics other than ethnicity are discussed in following chapters.

2. J. Davis (1966) reported that in four annual follow-ups in his study of career aspirations, career choice as a senior was a generally accurate predicator of what the student would be doing at least in the years immediately following graduation.

3. The statistics on occupational choice were very slightly influenced by the fact that the telephone survey had only ten occupational choices on it, rather than the twenty on the mail survey. In Appendix B, Table B3.1 gives an estimate of what the distribution of occupational choices would have been if not for this methodological problem. The reader will see that there is no more than a one percentage point change in the proportion selecting any particular occupation. (Appendix C describes how this estimate was computed.)

4. In Table 3.1 the ordering of occupations that have the same percentages displayed was determined by unshown decimal points. Whenever we refer to the proportion of students selecting "University professor" (or "academia") we are in fact referring to the sum of those selecting the survey choices "University/college professor" and "Researcher (in a university)." In order to estimate how different the distribution of occupational choices displayed in Table 3.1 was for each ethnic group we computed a *D*, or index of dissimilarity, for the distribution between each pair. *D* indicates what proportion of, let us say, African Americans would have to change their occupational choices if they were to have the same distribution as that of whites. The distribution of the choices of the four groups are generally similar, with the largest differences being between Asians and the other ethnic groups (data not shown). Throughout our analysis we found that Asians generally stood out as being the most different of the four ethnic groups. This is in large part a result of the very strong commitment of Asian students to the medical field.

5. There is one exception. The fifth most frequently chosen occupation for Asian students is allied health. Given the exceptionally high interest of Asian students in medicine, it is possible that some of these students who selected allied health did not have high enough grades to get into medical school. In fact, among those Asians selecting physician as their first choice, 50 percent have A or A− GPAs and only 21 percent have B or lower GPAs, whereas among those Asians selecting allied health as their first choice, 24 percent had A or A− GPAs and 52 percent B or lower GPAs.

6. This is pretty much how Herrnstein and Murray (1994) characterized the social stratification system of the United States at the end of the twentieth century. Most of the high-achieving students would enter a relatively small number of occupations. This presents some serious problems for the sectors of society that are not attractive to high-achieving students. And as we point out later, when we

show that one fifth of Ivy League graduates want to enter a single occupation—medicine—the question of whether elite schools should try to influence the occupations their students enter is one that must be considered. The fact that the Council of Ivy Group Presidents sponsored this study implies that they believe it is legitimate for schools to try to influence the selection of at least some occupations for at least some of their graduates. The first part of the Herrnstein and Murray book, in which the authors analyze how social stratification in the United States has changed over the twentieth century from a system based on the family into which one is born into one more heavily based on cognitive skills, has been ignored because many readers strongly object to the analyses in the later parts of the book, where the authors note what they believe to be genetically determined differences in IQ between blacks and whites.

7. In Chapter 4 we explore some possible explanations of this ethnic difference.

8. There is some possibility that the proportion expressing an interest in professor was influenced upward by the students' knowledge that our survey was focused on this choice of career (indicated by the cover letters sent out with the questionnaire). However, students who answered the telephone survey were not told that there was a special interest in college professor as career choice; they were told of only a general interest in occupational choice. Students contacted by phone were slightly more likely to say they were interested in the career of professor than the students answering the mail survey. This is true even when we adjust for the fact that there were fewer occupations listed in the phone survey. True, students answering the telephone survey had been sent three copies of the mail survey before they were called. But we believe that they were less likely to have been influenced by the wording of the cover letter than those who answered the mail survey.

9. In order to get into medical school, it is necessary to take at least ten semesters of specified science courses; a year of mathematics (generally calculus); a year of introductory biology; two years of chemistry (organic and inorganic); and a year of physics. If a student has not taken these courses, as well as the Medical College Admission Test (MCAT), the standardized test administered by the Association of American Medical Colleges that premedical students must take in order to have their application to medical school considered, he or she knows that it is impossible to become a physician. The MCAT is usually taken by students in August of their junior year in college, because it is offered only in August and April. Most of the students we interviewed who said they were interested in being physicians had already received their MCAT scores and had some idea about their chances of getting into medical school.

10. For example, some of the students at Columbia University's School of General Studies have a BA degree and have decided to return to school to take pre-med courses.

11. Indeed, only 10 percent of those selecting physician as their most likely occupation did not have this as a freshman year choice.

12. Applicants to most law schools are required to take the LSAT, an examination administered by the Law Services, a not-for-profit organization associated with the Consortium of Law Schools.

13. Later we indicate ways of measuring commitment to the one field the student is most likely to enter.

14. Increasingly school systems are allowing college graduates to begin teaching even if they do not have all the necessary course requirements, allowing them to complete these requirements while they are in service.

15. R. G. Ehrenberg (1992), p. 843, presents data showing that there has been a gradual increase in the interval between graduation and the taking of Graduate Record Examinations (GREs) between 1976 and 1985. This indicates that at least in that period there was a tendency for students hoping to enter a Ph.D. program not to enter such a program directly after graduating from college.

16. We report data on allied health because this was the fifth most popular occupation among Asians.

17. African Americans and Latinos who select schoolteaching as their final career choice are much more likely than Asians and whites to say that they will go directly on to graduate education. This may indicate a higher commitment to this occupation on the part of African Americans and Latinos. Or perhaps more of the whites and Asians intend to teach in private schools, which usually are less likely to require credentials and education courses.

18. In this part of the analysis we examine only the ten occupations that are most frequently selected as final choice careers (see Table 3.1).

19. We conducted the same analysis on freshman year interests as on senior year interests and obtained similar results.

20. If students were interested in both the column and the row occupation as seniors but selected some other occupation as their most likely final choice, they are excluded from this analysis. It is possible, and even likely, that a student selecting the particular pair of occupations indicated by a given cell in Table 3.10 could also have selected three, four, or even more occupations of interest; technically it would be possible to compare combinations of three, four, and even more occupations. Unfortunately, our data set is not large enough to allow for anything other than pairwise comparisons. But the exclusion of occupations not in the pair has no influence over which member of the pair "wins out" in the final selection because each cell includes only those students who end up in their final selection choosing either of the two occupations.

21. For ease of presentation (and at the expense of some redundancy) we present both halves of the matrix.

22. In his 1993 monograph *The Cost of Talent,* Derek Bok found that high-achieving college students were not going into teaching. Certainly the increase in demand for teachers in recent years has had an influence on the attractiveness of that job, and of course an increase in the number of talented students who enter elementary and secondary school teaching would be beneficial for those school systems and might lead to the better academic preparation of all students, not just minority students.

23. In Table 3.11 we should be cautious in drawing conclusions from the data for the minority groups, as in some cells the number of cases on which the percentages are based is small. If the number of unweighted cases in a particular cell is too

small, the percentages will neither be stable nor a reliable indicator of strength (and we have left blank those cells where the number of cases were too small to examine a meaningful percentage).

24. As pointed out earlier, given the substantial number of requirements to get into medical school, by the time they reach their senior year premedical students have a greater investment in their careers than do students pursuing most other occupations. This is not true for students intending to enter Ph.D. programs in some of the natural sciences—for example, chemistry. In order to be accredited, however, an undergraduate chemistry program must require its students to take in excess of 60 credits of chemistry and related subjects. It is in the social sciences and the humanities, in which the majority of students major, where students have relatively little invested in their careers by the time they reach their senior year.

4. INFLUENCES ON INITIAL OCCUPATIONAL CHOICE

1. Recall that we determined freshman interests by a question asked in the senior year. For potential problems with such questions and reasons why we believe they are at least roughly accurate here, see Chapter 2.

2. As is shown in Chapter 3, when students select careers as freshmen, academia is the most frequent choice of Latinos and whites, the second most frequent choice of Asians (significantly behind physician), and the fourth most frequent choice for African Americans.

3. The percent given here for the total sample may on first examination seem at odds with the numbers given for each of the four ethnic groups. But this figure is based upon weighted data in which white students represent the overwhelming majority of students. Given that both African American and Latino students are less likely to be "persisters" but are equally likely as whites and Asians to select academia as a final-choice career, these data indicate that both African American and Latinos are more likely to be "recruits" than Asians and whites.

4. This logic of causal analysis is explained in detail in Hyman (1955) and S. Cole (1976).

5. Nationwide, about one fifth of African American students attend HBCUs (Ehrenberg and Rothstein 1994); a slightly higher portion of African Americans graduate from HBCUs (Nettles 1997).

6. For the reasons why we believed this to be a plausible hypothesis see Chapter 1.

7. Table B4.1 in Appendix B shows the relationship between each of the four SES indicators and ethnicity.

8. In the pretest, we asked separately for father and mother whether the parent is (or has been) a professor or a teacher at a lower level. The data indicate that having a mother who is a college professor has a slightly stronger influence on the initial career decision than having a father who is a college professor. Having parents who are teachers at lower levels has no effect. (For a description of the pretest see Chapter 2.)

9. Students expressing an interest in journalism have the same mean.

10. We did some analysis of the influences on the number of freshman occu-

pational choices. We found that higher SES students, students with higher SAT scores, those with high scores on an index of "occupational orientation" (defined in Chapter 5), and those not attending HBCUs made more choices than their counterparts.

11. These differences are statistically significant. There is no meaningful difference between the number of choices made by Asians and Latinos and those made by whites.

12. The concept of "effective scope" was introduced by Paul F. Lazarsfeld in the 1940s. One way in which he measured it was by the distance on the radio dial between stations people listened to. He found that SES was correlated with effective scope. People with low SES tended to listen to a narrower portion of the radio band than those with higher SES.

13. As we pointed out in Chapter 1, with the exception of physician, this is not so much because the average income of college professors is so much less than the average income of other competing occupational groups, but because people at the top of these competing occupational groups earn much more than even the best-paid professors. Also, the focus groups and qualitative interviews suggested that students perceived the financial rewards of academia as lower than those of other competing occupations.

14. See Chapter 6 for the effect of interest in financial rewards on the selection as a final-choice career of academia and the four other major competing occupations (medicine, law, business, and teaching).

15. Hamilton and Hargens (1993) show that there has been little change in the distribution of faculty political self-identifications from 1969 to 1984 and that the more selective institutions have higher proportions of faculty who identify as liberal-left than do less selective institutions.

16. Although at the time the final draft of this book was being written the American economy was in a recession and many "new economy" companies had gone bankrupt, when the students filled out the questionnaire in the fall of 1995 and the spring of 1996 the information technology field was in an unprecedented economic expansion. It is also likely that despite the recession that the job opportunities for natural science and math majors remain better than those for social science and humanities majors.

17. When we add up the differences for all three groups, we get an 11 point difference between African Americans and whites rather than a 12 point difference. This is due to rounding error. Rounding error also explains why adding the proportions of whites in all three groups results in a total of 33, whereas the total without rounding is 34.

18. A logistic regression is usually used when the dependent variable is a dichotomy (e.g., professor most likely career/some other career most likely). For a brief discussion of this method see Appendix C.

5. THE INFLUENCE OF ACADEMIC PERFORMANCE

1. GPAs are self-reported by the students in either the fall or the spring semester of their senior year.

2. Even in these situations, where we report results only for academia, the data are drawn from the multinomial model, which shows how the variable influences all five top occupations. We have not reported the irrelevant data for the other four occupations. The reasons why we use a multinomial rather than a logistic regression model are discussed in Appendix C.

3. This finding is actually stronger than it looks, given that our sample heavily overrepresented elite schools, where almost all students receive GPAs of B− or better; and in the nonelite schools we only sampled students who had a GPA of 2.8 or higher. If we had a more nearly random sample of schools and had not used the GPA 2.8 cutoff point, the relationship between GPA and selection of academia as a most likely career would surely be even stronger.

4. Later in the chapter we show the influence of GPA on the probability of selecting the four occupations that compete most strongly with academia for talent.

5. Because different colleges in our sample have different grading practices and students in some majors, such as some of the social sciences and the humanities, have on average higher GPAs than students in the sciences and math, when GPA is used as a dependent variable it is necessary to control for school and field of major. (For a discussion of how these controls are actually applied see Appendix C.) Of course, in a cross-tabulation such as that presented in Figure 5.2 school and field of major cannot be controlled. In order to make sure that the results displayed in Figure 5.2 were not substantially influenced by these uncontrolled variables we reran the analysis as an ordinary least squares (OLS) regression, which enabled us to control for school and field of major (data not shown). Controlling for these variables had no effect on the substantive conclusions we draw from Figure 5.2. In this book, whenever GPA is used as a dependent variable, school and field of major are controlled.

6. As explained earlier, the "elite" schools in our sample are the Ivy League and the selective liberal arts colleges. The nonelite schools are the HBCUs and the state universities.

7. Although virtually all politicians and a majority of the educational establishment believe that the quality of American education (K–12) has deteriorated over the last forty years (Steinberg 1996; Ravitch 2000), others have presented convincing arguments that the data usually used to support this conclusion are inadequate and that existing data suggest that current students may actually know more than students of the past (R. Rothstein 1998; Murray and Herrnstein 1992). But whether or not there has been a decline in standards, all agree that the current educational system is in need of change and improvement. They disagree over what type of change and how to attain the improvement.

8. Recruits are students who do not express an interest in academia as freshmen but then as seniors select academia as their most likely career.

9. The predicted probabilities for GPA are computed using a multinomial regression equation (with college professor as the comparison category) with only one independent variable, GPA. See Appendix C for an explanation of how we used regression coefficients from multinomial logistic regression equations in order to compute predicted probabilities.

10. As explained in Chapter 6, the extent of parental influence is not statisti-

cally significant for Latinos or whites. We believe that Latino parents do not put the same type of pressure on their children as do Asian and African American parents because Latino parents (particularly mothers) have lower educational levels than do Asian and African American (see Table B4.1), and the mere fact of their children's getting a college degree is probably more gratifying to Latino parents than it is to the parents of the other two minorities. There also may be differences in Latino culture that influence how parents treat their children. The parents of white students probably have a much broader idea of what constitutes "getting ahead" than do the parents of minority students. Since the parents of most white students in our sample are upper middle class (see Table B4.1), they are more likely to take the attitude that their children should pursue whatever career will give them the most personal satisfaction. This is, however, speculation, and more work should be done on how parents influence the occupational choices of minority students.

11. The full model is presented in Table B5.1B.

12. Variables that hide the effect of another variable are called "suppressor" variables because they suppress a relationship that exists but is not visible when looked at in a simple two-variable analysis. Readers who are interested in this question can discover the suppressor variable(s) by examining the full regression model presented in Table B5.1A.

13. To be fair we should mention that admission to the police force had nothing to do with this student's GPA but was based on his score on a test administered by the police department. The general point, however, still stands: except for a few elite law schools students do not have to have either high GPAs or high LSATs in order to be admitted to law school.

14. Clearly this is not the case for GPA. We would not devote so much space to presenting an erroneous analysis.

15. In fact, in this example, family status is not the reason why men publish more than women. This means that when family status is controlled, gender continues to be significant, with men outpublishing women in every category of the family status variable (see J. R. Cole and S. Cole 1973; J. R. Cole 1979).

16. A more accurate measure would be the ratio of the percentage for the lowest grades to that for the highest grades. This is essentially the "odds ratio" (see Appendix C) computed by the regression equation. However, the percentage differences are easier to understand, and in this case the substantive conclusions would be the same if we used ratios instead of the absolute size of the percentage difference.

17. Interestingly, SAT scores were strongly correlated with answers given to the question in which students were asked to compare themselves to their age cohort. Given the fact that they took the SATs at least four years prior to the administration of our survey, this indicates the great importance of standardized tests such as the SAT in the formation of students' self-conception (Lemann 1999). Of course, to study this issue adequately we would have to have data on other variables, such as high school GPA and SES, which might make the relationship between SAT scores and a student's later academic self-conception spurious.

18. In Chapter 8 we discuss in more detail the importance of low grades in in-

fluencing self-confidence, which as we have shown here has a strong effect on choice of academia as a career.

19. On July 5, 2001, it was announced in the *Chronicle of Higher Education* that the University of California was going to be making significant changes in its admissions system. The verbal and quantitative (SAT I) tests would no longer be required for admission; instead, applicants would have to take five of the SAT II exams (examinations testing specific subjects such as history, requiring a written essay, etc.). The University of California was also going to put more emphasis on high school grades, guaranteeing admission to all students in the top 4 percent of their high school classes and to all students in the top 12 percent of their high school classes who first completed an associate's degree at one of the state's community colleges. One of the stated purposes of these changes is to increase the racial and ethnic diversity of the student body. Chancellor Richard Atkinson claims that these changes are not an attempt to get around Proposition 209, which made the use of racial preferences in admissions illegal.

20. Robert Klitgaard, in *Choosing Elites* (1985), examines a great deal of evidence, considers the goals of colleges and universities, and comes to the conclusion (a conclusion he was hoping not to come to) that scores on standardized tests such as the SAT, and high school grades to a lesser extent, are the best predictors not only of how well students will do in college but how well they will do in later life.

21. This debate has been going on for the past thirty years and will most likely continue for a long time unless the Supreme Court were to make a broad ruling on whether or not the use of racial preferences in admissions to college is constitutional. There is a possibility that two cases involving the University of Michigan will end up being decided in the Supreme Court. In one of these cases, involving the law school, the lower court ruled affirmative action illegal; but this ruling was recently overturned by the appeals court, and plaintiffs say they will take the case to the Supreme Court. The other, involving race-sensitive admissions in the college, at the time of this writing is still in the appeals court.

22. The ETS produces and markets the SAT as well as many other standardized tests, including the Graduate Record Examination (GRE). It has a large staff of highly qualified researchers who conduct studies on testing. Since the ETS produces these tests, some might see the studies produced by their research staff as suffering from a conflict of interest. However, we have found the ETS reports we have read to be very well done, with no evidence of bias. Klitgaard, a professor at the Kennedy School of Government, with no connection to the ETS, reaches conclusions very similar to those of Ramist et al.

23. See our discussion of the importance of the restriction of range problem in Chapter 2.

24. For the equations and calculations used to reach this conclusion see Klitgaard (1985), Appendix 1. It might be pointed out that one might alternatively add 240 points to the combined SAT scores of white students.

25. Our data show approximately the same-size gap between the SAT scores of African Americans and those of whites attending Ivy League schools. Bowen and Bok (1998) report similar results. Perhaps the most important research yet con-

ducted that attempts to explain the SAT gap between African Americans and whites is presented in Jencks and Phillips (1998).

26. If this logic is correct, it should mean that the regression coefficient for SAT predicting GPA of African Americans and Latinos (other variables held constant) should be higher for both elite schools looked at separately and nonelite schools looked at separately than it would be for all schools. This is indeed what we observe. For African Americans the coefficient for SAT in the equation including all schools is .033. In the elite schools it is .072; and in the nonelite schools, .039. For Latinos the coefficient for SAT in the equation including all schools is .051. In the elite schools it is .082, and for the nonelite schools it is .063. These are relatively small differences, but they are in the direction expected, if our interpretation of the data is correct. We thank Gary Field for suggesting we look at the data this way.

27. This measurement is obtained because among those African Americans with SAT scores of 1300 or above at the liberal arts colleges only 12 percent receive GPAs of A or A−. The reasons why African Americans do so poorly in the liberal arts colleges will be discussed at length in Chapter 8.

28. The normal way in which this is done is through the use of regression models. We have run such a model in which we not only show the extent of underperformance of the three ethnic groups, but of subgroups within the Asian and Latino categories where enough cases exist. In the regression model we also control for individual schools and field of major—thus making sure that the underperformance is not a result of differing grading policies among schools or in different grade distributions among the various fields of major. This model is presented in Appendix B as Table B5.2. In the text we use tables that we believe are easier to understand and make the point quite clearly.

29. It is of course possible that differences in SAT scores among the ethnic groups in the 1300+ category could explain some of the underperformance. However, since we found the same type of underperformance when we used the regression model, which does not have this problem, this gives us confidence that these results are roughly indicative of the underperformance phenomenon in our data. (It was necessary to collapse categories at the top of the SAT distribution because there were not enough African Americans and Latinos in the 1400+ category to lead to stable results.)

30. Of course it is possible that there are other differences between the elite and the state universities that could explain the difference in level of underperformance. In fact, at the liberal arts colleges there are many reasons why African Americans do not do as well as white students. These reasons are discussed in Chapter 8.

31. We studied the extent of underperformance for the minority groups in a regression model and found the same substantive results as are observed in Table 5.5.

32. College and Beyond is a large data set collected by the Andrew W. Mellon foundation. Foundation president William Bowen, with Derek Bok, used these data to write *The Shape of the River* (1998), a defense of affirmative action; and, with James Shulman, a book on athletics (2000). Other papers are being written using these data, including Dale and Krueger (1999), cited earlier.

33. The primary reasons for this are that there are some background variables on which African Americans and whites differ but do not affect college GPA and there are very few variables on which they differ that would affect GPA but not SAT scores.

34. A paper by Steele and Aronson (1998) reports some of the same experiments and some additional ones.

35. Many interesting questions are suggested by both Steele's theory and his experiments. We suggest only one. Presumably the primary mechanism through which stereotype threat operates is through test anxiety experienced by the individual (although Steele to our knowledge never explicitly states this). Steele recognizes that all people may experience some individual test anxiety, but he claims that a stereotyped group must carry, in addition, anxiety arising from the stereotype threat. Assuming substantial individual variation in the experience of test anxiety, there may be some members of a nonstereotyped group who experience even greater anxiety than members of a stereotyped group. In other words, controlling for the total amount of test anxiety felt by individuals (which we believe could be physiologically measured) should eliminate performance differences (when ability is also controlled).

36. This is essentially the same logic used in arguing that underperformance is evidence against bias in the SAT examination.

37. Since we have no data on actual discrimination, the items in both the main survey and pretest measure perceived discrimination.

38. Only four of the items are statistically significant: whether the student had to do chores (negative), whether parent(s) frequently read to the student (positive), whether the student was afraid to report a bad grade (negative), and whether the student perceived the parents to be more traditional than him- or herself (negative). Using only these statistically significant items in the equation suggests that they have little influence on the underperformance of African Americans.

39. Substantively the difference between the two coefficients is relatively small. The adjusted R square for the model with all twenty-four family background variables included is quite small. This is not surprising, given that most of the variables do not have statistically significant correlations with college GPA. Because this analysis is based on the pretest, in which the number of minority students was quite small and the response rate relatively low, we do not report numbers from this survey, but only use the data as suggestions for further research.

40. Qualitative support for this hypothesis may be found in Sowell (2001).

41. In a larger sample this difference might have been statistically significant for African Americans also.

42. The interactions for Asians and Latinos were significant at the $p < .06$ level.

43. Given the difficulty of collecting adequate data in the social sciences—data that contain clear operationalizations of all important concepts—we believe it is worth using rough, "indirect" measures in an experimental way, even if later more precise measures should prove the original conclusions wrong. The use of these measures at least provides hypotheses for other scholars to test when better data become available.

44. In 1991, 45 percent of all African American applicants to American medical schools were admitted; 54 percent of white applicants were admitted. Given the desire of most American medical schools to admit African Americans and given that most of them have affirmative action plans it is unlikely that this difference in acceptance rate is a result of discrimination. Rather it suggests that self-selection is not working as well among African Americans as among whites. This fits in with data presented in this chapter showing that for African Americans GPA is not correlated with selection of medicine as a first-choice career. (In 1991, 51 percent of Asian applicants and 55 percent of Latino applicants were admitted.)

45. This theory will be analyzed in more detail in Chapter 8 on school effects.

6. ATTITUDES TOWARD ACADEMIA

1. The one exception is that African Americans as freshmen are less likely than white students to be interested in a career as a university professor. The reasons for this were explained in Chapter 4.

2. It should be pointed out that in Tables 6.1 and 6.2 we are simply reporting the proportion of students who indicated a particular aspect of academia would be appealing or unappealing to them. These data tell us nothing about causality. Later, when we consider how answers to each item actually correlate with the decision to become a professor, we discover that some of the items mentioned by many students have no causal influence on their decision. Thus, the first part of this chapter is strictly descriptive. It tells us the proportion of students saying that each aspect would be appealing or unappealing to them. It is only when we get to the data in Table 6.3 that we begin the causal part of our analysis.

3. In Chapter 2 we discussed the problem of establishing causality in this data set. The relationship between attitudes toward academia and selecting academia as a career is a good example of that difficulty. We have no way of establishing that the attitudes of the students preceded their final occupational choice. It is possible that some of the students may first have decided to become professors and that this occupational selection may then have influenced how they answered the questions on the appealing and unappealing aspects of academia. In fact, for some of the items, we have reason to believe that this is exactly what happened. The only basis on which we can consider these attitudes causes of occupational choice is by adopting the assumption that students consider the benefits and debits of particular careers prior to making their final choice.

4. One possible reason why this item had no causal effect for the three minorities was a restriction of range on the independent variable.

5. Unlike law school, it does not make much difference what medical school one gets into. Perhaps this is because law school graduates are hired by big law firms in part on the basis of the prestige of the law school from which they graduated. What medical school a doctor graduates from has little influence on his or her career.

6. Since the emphasis in this book is on understanding the career choices of minority students, we did not think it necessary to do the work needed to specify exactly which variable(s) were "washing out" the effect of concern with financial re-

wards for white students. We leave this to further research. Also, since our model was aimed at explaining why students are interested in academia, it is not the best model to understand the reasons why students' concern with financial rewards may influence their choice of occupations other than academia.

7. ROLE MODELS, INTERACTION WITH FACULTY, AND CAREER ASPIRATIONS

1. This use of the concept of role model is very close to what Adeno Addis (1996) refers to as role models as a tool in the "politics of recognition." For a full discussion see Chapter 1.

2. Actually the influence of same-gender, same-race teachers and role models are two analytically separate questions. Either one may or may not be effective in achieving specific goals. In this chapter we confine our analysis to the impact of same-gender and same-race role models on a series of dependent variables, most importantly, interest in becoming an academic. We do not examine the question of the impact of same-gender, same-race teachers.

3. We analyze only the data on role models; the data on taking a class with certain types of instructors did not yield any interesting results. The questions on role models were not included in the telephone survey; thus, all the analysis presented here is based only on those students who answered the mail questionnaire.

4. This is quite a large difference and indicates (along with other data presented in this book) that research is needed to better understand the problems that Asian students have in college.

5. For males a same-gender role model would be any male role model irrespective of race or ethnicity; similarly, for females a same-gender role model would be any female role model irrespective of race or ethnicity.

6. The results for white females miss being significant by one point (they are significant at the .06 level, and the results for African American males are significant at the .11 level).

7. These numbers are slightly different from those reported in Chapter 3 because they were computed only for mail survey respondents, the only respondents for whom we have role model data.

8. There was a minor problem in using this technique in estimating proportions for African American males. Of those African American males who did not have a same-gender role model (only 15 weighted cases) none selected academia as a most likely career. Since we had one empty cell, the program would not compute a test of statistical significance. We computed the test "by hand," so to speak, and found the relationship between same-gender role models for African American males to be insignificant, primarily because of the very small number of cases who did not have a same-gender role model.

9. Since all the students included in the same-gender, same-race, and same-gender–same-race sections of the table, the proportion of those having any of these types of role model or not who want to be professors should average out to the same proportion as those reporting having any role model. In all cases they do.

10. Data reported on below show that the gender and ethnicity of role models

340

also had no effect on selecting other occupations studied in the survey or other outcome measures such as GPA, likelihood of going on with graduate work and satisfaction with school.

11. The students could check off as many of the items as they wanted.

12. The exceptions were African American males, Latinas, and white males.

13. In the analyses reported here and later in the chapter we looked only at whether a student had a professor as a role model. When we examined the effects of same-gender, same-race, and same-gender–same-race role models, the number of statistically significant coefficients were no greater than what we would expect to have found by chance. And some of these were negative.

14. On the questionnaire we asked the students separately about their official faculty advisor and "other" faculty members. Since we found no meaningful difference in the way in which these two variables acted we combined them and created an index of faculty influence. Students who said that either type of faculty member had been "important" in influencing their career plans were counted as having been influenced by faculty.

15. The other two exceptions are African Americans at state universities, the ethnic group that had the highest level of faculty contact at this type of school; and Asians at these same schools, who have the lowest level of faculty contact. It is hard to speculate on the reasons for this.

8. THE INFLUENCE OF SCHOOL CHARACTERISTICS

1. In some state universities ethnic diversity of the student body has progressed so far that white students may be less than half of the students enrolled. Even in these situations, however, whites would still be the largest single racial group, and African Americans would generally be in a minority of no more than 5 to 10 percent.

2. Thirteen such schools were in our sample. The selective liberal arts colleges that were not included had very small numbers of minority students (in some cases they had none). Many liberal arts colleges find it difficult to recruit high-achieving minority members in competition with the larger private elite schools. In fact, the past president of one highly selective liberal arts college told us that his school had essentially given up its attempt to attract significant numbers of minority students (personal communication).

3. See Chapter 2 for an explanation of why in cross-school comparisons we control for GPA and only look at students with GPAs of 2.8 or higher.

4. See Fuller (1989) for a description of how she collected her data. We believe her methodology to be sound and followed a similar strategy in our own study.

5. There are currently groups within the medical community who are working to find ways to attract more minority students to select medicine as a career. This points to the problem of competition for talent among different sectors of the society, and what role, if any, institutions of higher education should play in this competition.

6. As we discuss in Chapter 10, on policy implications, administrators of Ivy League schools (and presumably some other highly selective elite schools) must

consider whether it is desirable to have such a heavy concentration of their graduates enter one occupation.

7. In Table B8.1 we present a logistic regression model that looks at the effects of these variables.

8. The unadjusted data are the proportion of African Americans having GPAs of A or A− at each type of school without controlling for any other variables.

9. The regression equation used to compute Figure 8.2 may be found in Table B8.2.

10. The *absolute* level of satisfaction of African American students is not lower at the liberal arts colleges; but the level of satisfaction *relative* to white students is. In fact the absolute level of satisfaction for African American students is about the same at all three predominantly white types of school.

11. Responses to this question were not significantly correlated with selection of academia as a first-choice career among any of the ethnic groups.

12. The fact that type of school is statistically significant for African Americans is not due to the inclusion of the HBCUs. Even when students attending HBCUs were left out of the analysis, there was a statistically significant difference between the liberal arts schools and the other predominantly white schools.

13. In the case of persistence with an interest in a career in academia there is no difference between the liberal arts colleges and the Ivy League schools.

14. African American students are also more likely to persist with plans to be a physician if they attend a state university or an HBCU than if they attend a liberal arts college.

15. Asians and Latinos are also less likely to persist with plans to be a physician if they attend a liberal arts college rather than an Ivy League school. It might be argued that this is not necessarily a result of a difficult environment for African Americans, but rather the lower degree of emphasis at these schools on occupational orientation. However, since white students at the liberal arts colleges are no less likely than white students at the Ivy League schools to persist with an interest in medicine, this hypothesis is unlikely to be true. Medicine is a prestigious and relatively high-paying occupation. If African Americans who want to be doctors do not persist in that ambition it is usually because they have not done well academically, and we expect that this is what is happening at the liberal arts colleges.

16. Unfortunately, because of the small number of liberal arts colleges and restricted range on the number of African American students attending these colleges, we were unable to perform an empirical test of this hypothesis.

17. The influence of school type on the decision of African Americans to go directly on is significant $p < .05$.

18. We are aware that our measure of occupational orientation is at best indirect. Prior to the analysis we did not see that this might be an important variable (an inevitable problem in survey research). Nevertheless, such measurement techniques as we use here are or should be used in all survey research. It is better to have a rough measure of a concept than no measure. Also the fact that the index correlates with the dependent variable is some validation that it probably measures something close to what we mean by "occupational orientation."

19. Davis classified lawyer, physician, and academia as high-achievement ca-

reers. Business and education were among the low-achievement careers. Davis's sample was a true random sample of colleges and was not limited to arts and sciences students.

20. Some believe that the higher distribution of grades is greater at the elite schools because there has been more grade inflation at these schools. In Figure B8.1 we show the distribution of grades by type of school when SAT scores are controlled. These data suggest that the reason why the grade distribution at the elite schools is higher is because they have better students. When SAT scores are controlled, the students at the nonelite schools receive higher GPAs than those at the elite schools. There has been a good deal of debate over whether there has been grade inflation and, if so, whether it has been greater at the elite schools. See Sabot and Wakeman-Linn (1991) and Adelman (1997).

21. It is probable that there are uncontrolled SAT differences between the African Americans attending the Ivy League and those attending the liberal arts colleges. The former tend to attract African American students with the highest SAT scores. However, in an OLS regression on GPA, controlling for school type, ethnicity, SAT scores, individual institutions, and field of major, school type remains statistically significant (data not shown).

22. William Bowen and Derek Bok (1998) claim to find no empirical support for the "fit" hypothesis in the dependent variables they examined in their study of the effects of race-sensitive admissions policies. Our data, using different dependent variables, are more consistent with the fit hypothesis.

23. There is no school in our sample that has a mean SAT score of 1400, although many of them could if they choose to weight SAT scores more in their admission decisions. The schools in our survey with the highest SAT scores had mean scores between 1350 and 1400 (prior to renormalization).

24. Some may argue that this is not the only way for the very elite schools to admit African Americans. They might argue that the SAT test should no longer be required or that the emphasis placed on it should be reduced. The University of California is trying to deal with this problem by requiring its students to take the SAT II tests instead of the SAT I tests. The former are in specific subjects, such as history or a language. The SAT I measures more abstract reasoning ability (where African Americans are most likely to do worse than whites). Students who were born speaking a foreign language, such as many Latinos and some Asians, would theoretically get a boost using this technique because it is thought that they will do very well on the language part of the SAT II test. Of course, even if this policy were adopted and it raised the relative scores of Latinos and Asians, it would do nothing for African American students, the group that is in the greatest need of help. It is probable that using the SAT II tests instead of the SAT I tests will not have a significant impact on increasing racial diversity (without the use of racial preferences). This is because Latinos, for example, who were brought up speaking Spanish may still have a hard time on a language test that does not measure ability to speak colloquial Spanish. It is also possible that white and Asian students' scores on all of the SAT II tests will be substantially higher than those of African Americans and Latinos. Some critics of the recent change in the admissions policies at the University of California have argued that they represent a thinly veiled attempt to get

around Proposition 209, which makes the use of racial preferences in educational admissions illegal in the state of California. Another proposal to increase racial diversity without the use of racial preferences is to weight high school GPA more than SAT scores. But the high school GPAs of white and Asian students are significantly higher than those of African American and Latino students (Steinberg 1996). Still others argue that preferences should be given to students who come from underprivileged SES backgrounds. This (as far as we know) is not currently illegal, although some might argue that this preference scheme also violates the equal protection clause of the Fourteenth Amendment. Thomas Kane (1998) has convincingly argued that this would not work, as there are many more poor whites than there are poor African Americans and Latinos. Robert Klitgaard (1985) collected a great deal of data to see how predictive various admissions criteria are of both academic success and achievement in later life. He concluded, contrary to what he expected, that SAT scores are the best predictor of both. He noted that if elite colleges admit students with SAT scores lower than students they reject they obviously will lower the quality of the student body.

25. What would be needed is data showing that diversity has positive consequences on the students attending a school. This issue is at the heart of some legal cases pending before the courts, particularly appeals currently being prepared for two recent cases concerning the use of racial preferences in admissions at the University of Michigan. In our opinion so far there is no clear-cut evidence demonstrating that diversity (meaning having, let us say, a higher number of African American students enrolled) has any meaningful influence on the other students attending the university. Some data presented to the court are the result of asking students whether or not they *thought* that they benefited from having different types of students in their classes. In our opinion such survey evidence is of limited or no value. The question calls for a normative response; and even if we assume that the students actually believe that diversity has had beneficial effects on them, beliefs are frequently not reflected in reality. If all social scientists had to do to determine what the consequences of some social arrangement were is to ask the participants, our job would be much easier than it is. The data we present later in fact show that race sensitive admissions policies likely have at least some negative educational consequences on those they are intended to help.

26. Thomas Kane's 1998 study, like all the others we are familiar with by economists who deal with this question, uses national random sample data sets. These data sets are inadequate to answer the question of what effect attending an elite school has on any outcome variable, because there are so few students in a national random sample who attend an elite school. The economists who conduct these studies are usually forced to define the top 20 percent of schools as "elite." The Bowen and Bok (1998) data set, however, does have a sample of truly elite schools (one very similar to ours).

27. The data sets used by economists who have made these studies are so large that very small effects can be statistically significant. There probably are studies that express the effect in terms of dollars rather than regression coefficients, but we are not familiar with them.

28. This conclusion contradicts some of those reached by Bowen and Bok (1998). But, as we pointed out earlier, Dale and Krueger (1999) have shown that the "selectivity" effect reported in Bowen and Bok is an artifact of uncontrolled selectivity.

29. The Davis (frog pond) hypothesis is only true for African Americans. Among the other three ethnic groups type of school has no meaningful influence on persistence.

30. We should point out that the effect of school was just barely significant at the .05 level and that the coefficient did not have to be reduced very much for it to become insignificant. This analysis is based on a relatively small number of cases: those African Americans (22 percent of all African Americans) in our study who as freshmen expressed an interest in academia. Given the importance of the fit hypothesis it would be highly desirable to replicate this study and other relevant studies on larger samples.

31. As Henry Rosovsky (1990), the former dean of Harvard's School of Arts and Sciences, points out, giving students who are qualified a preference over other students who might be slightly more qualified in order to obtain ethnic diversity is no different than giving preferences to students who are "legacies," "jocks," or concert violinists. Bowen and Bok (1998) and Klitgaard (1985) make similar points. And in fact, we believe, according to Claude Steele's theory, students who are members of identifiable subgroups such as "jocks" and "legacies" might suffer (at least to a limited extent) the same type of stereotype threat as that faced by minority students and consequently underperform academically in certain situations. When SAT scores and ethnicity are controlled along with all other variables we could find that influence grades, athletes still underperform (the coefficient is small but statistically significant), although the degree of their underperformance was not as much as that suffered by African Americans. If some of the athletes are African American we could have some uncontrolled interaction influencing this equation that should be looked at. (We are unable to identify legacies.)

32. Robert K. Merton, in lectures at Columbia University, analyzed this phenomenon as the "haunting presence of functionally irrelevant statuses." For an application to the position of women in academia see J. Cole (1979).

33. We had considerable difficulty in using schools as the unit of analysis. First, we had too few cases, because only 24 schools provided adequate institutional data. Second, in many of the schools there were too few students in the sample for us to construct a valid dependent variable (we used only those schools where at least twenty minority group members responded to our questionnaire). At all the state universities, the number of African Americans in our sample are especially small, and at all but two of them, the same is true of the Latino figures. These small numbers explain why there are so few African Americans and Latinos in the arts and sciences pipeline (see Chapter 9).

34. It must be kept in mind, however, that the number of minority students at many of these schools (even those having twenty or more such students) was relatively small, and the percentages computed therefore might not be very stable.

9. THE PIPELINE INTO ACADEMIA

1. There were minor differences in the proportion of each group wanting to be university professors, but these differences were not statistically significant and could have been a result of sampling error.

2. This calculation excludes UCLA, which did not provide us with adequate information to compute the proportion of students who had higher than 2.8 GPAs. Thus it is based on eight of the nine state universities in our sample.

3. This number represents *all* African Americans at the nine state universities who met our sampling criteria, not the total number who filled out and returned our questionnaire.

4. Even with so many schools in our sample, African Americans and Latinos at liberal arts colleges were the smallest subsamples that we analyzed. It would not have been fruitful to add more of these schools to our sample since the selective liberal arts colleges not already in our sample had very few minority students.

5. Recall that for the liberal arts colleges and the Ivy League schools we included *all* African American and Latino graduates and did not use a GPA cutoff point (see Chapter 2 for a full explanation).

6. For an analysis of the minority pipeline in the 1970s see Astin (1982). Astin included Native Americans but did not include Asians in his study. His study is much more detailed than that presented here and tries to examine the causes of why there are so few minorities in the academic pipeline. He does not, however, project percentages into numbers emerging in any given year; and for the specific purpose of our study, the method we have adopted provides more relevant data. The Astin study contains many policy recommendations, some controversial, that still may be relevant to institutions of higher education interested in increasing the number of minority Ph.D.s in the arts and sciences.

7. For our analysis of census data we used the 1 in 100 Public Use Microdata Sample of the 1990 U.S. Census and the March 1998 Supplement of the Current Population Survey. The NCES digests for 1995 through 1998 provided us with data on the number of Ph.D.s granted by American institutions of higher education 1991 through 1995, years close to 1990 and 1998, the years for the census data we used. We used data from our survey because it was the best way available to us to estimate two of the parameters we were interested in.

8. In most cases we rounded numbers to the nearest thousand. In making estimates for African Americans we encountered substantial differences in using different data sources that we did not encounter in making estimates for the other ethnic groups. We discuss these difficulties below. But let us point out here that it is widely believed that the census underrepresents African Americans. Therefore it is possible that our estimate of 429,000 for an average cohort between the ages of 25 and 29 may be too small. Using only individuals included in Row 1 of Table 9.1 (this excludes people for whom racial data were not available or those in other racial groups) we see that 11 percent of the population between the ages of 25 and 29 were African American.

9. To make it quite clear what we are doing in Rows 2 through 6, the *percentages* presented are based upon the 35–39-year-old cohort, but to obtain the *num-*

bers in each cell we multiplied the percentage for the 35–39-year-old cohort by the total number we obtained for the 25–29-year-old cohort.

10. Bowen and Bok (1998) show that even at highly selective schools, for which the dropout rate is generally lower, African Americans had higher dropout rates than white students.

11. By "terminal" associate degrees we mean those who earn an associate degree and by the age of 39 have not completed a BA degree.

12. This may indicate a change from the 1970s, as Astin reports that minority students are much more likely than white students to attend two-year community colleges. Of course, it is possible that higher proportions of college dropouts among minority groups (included in Row 4 of Table 9.1) may drop out of two-year colleges.

13. There are some discrepancies between data computed from the census and those obtained from the NCES for the number of African American college graduates. We discuss these discrepancies in Appendix C.

14. The percentages in the table may not add up to exactly 100 percent due to rounding.

15. It is possible that a small number of students with undergraduate engineering degrees may enroll in Ph.D. programs in one of the physical sciences or in math or computer science.

16. Examination of the NCES data for other years indicates that this figure is relatively stable from year to year; for this reason, we used the 1992–93 estimate for both Table 9.1 and Table 9.2.

17. For a list of the majors classified as being in the arts and sciences and those classified as not fitting in this category see Appendix C.

18. We are of course aware that there may occasionally be a "late bloomer"—a student who does relatively poorly in college and performs at a much higher level later on. Unfortunately the number of late bloomers is not very high. For an estimate of the proportion among scientists see S. Cole and Meyer (1985) and S. Cole (1992, Ch. 9).

19. See Appendix C for a list of those fields classified as being within the arts and sciences and those fields classified as being outside of the arts and sciences.

20. NCES data significantly underestimate the numbers of Latino and Asians who hold a Ph.D. because the data do not include all those people who immigrated to this country who had obtained a Ph.D. prior to immigration. This becomes relevant later, when we use census data to estimate the numbers of Latino and Asians who have Ph.D.s.

21. Figures on the proportion of Ph.D.s in the arts and sciences obtained from the 1990 census yield higher estimates than those obtained from the 1992–93 NCES data. Since we believe the NCES data to be less problematic, we used the estimates on the proportion of Ph.D.s obtained from the NCES. The NCES, however, does not tell us where the Ph.D.s were employed. Therefore, the only estimate of the proportion of arts and sciences Ph.D.s working in academia that is available is that from the census.

22. A significant minority of these Ph.D.s could have been employed in administrative positions in colleges and universities.

23. The majority of the rest of the arts and sciences Ph.D.s were employed in business and government.

24. Actually since the dropout rate for African Americans is higher than for white students, the total proportion of arts and sciences students who are African American is probably higher than 7 percent.

25. We do not address here the important question as to whether the total number of people with Ph.D.s in arts and sciences fields who will take jobs in academia will be enough to fill demand. There is a large literature on this topic, and the question is well beyond the scope of our project. We should only point out here that estimates of shortages made in the past have not turned out to be correct. In most fields in the arts and sciences the current job market for Ph.D.s is poor. We should also point out that the figures given in Row 12 of Table 9.1 indicate how many Ph.D.s will enter academic work in a given year. They do not tell us the pool of eligible candidates for jobs in academia. This pool is undoubtedly substantially larger than the numbers indicated in Row 12. One reason is that at any given point the pool of eligibles will include recipients of Ph.D.s granted over a number of years who have not yet found or taken a job in academia. This is likely to be particularly true for white recipients of Ph.D.s. It may also be useful to emphasize again here what we have said in Chapter 1: although the job market in general for academics may be poor, the market for minority Ph.D.s may be substantially better. This is certainly true as long as schools continue to make use of racial preferences in faculty hiring.

26. We have also shown in Chapter 8 that African American graduates of elite schools (the selective liberal arts colleges and the Ivy League) are, when grades are controlled, slightly less likely than graduates of state universities and HBCUs to select university professor as their first-choice career.

27. To be more precise, the proportion of white students is slightly higher than 50 percent and the proportions of both African American and Latino is slightly lower than 50 percent.

28. These figures cannot be explained by the fact that there are many Asian nonresident aliens who receive Ph.D.s in the United States, as the NCES has a separate category for nonresident aliens.

29. These were the most recent data available to us at the time this analysis was conducted.

30. This assumption is supported by looking at the size of the white cohort between the ages of 35 and 39 in the 1998 CPS. This number is 3,230,000, a number in line with our estimate from the 1990 census.

31. When we computed these tables the last year we had available for the NCES statistics was 1994–95. Since then we have obtained the latest edition of the NCES Digest of Educational Statistics (1998) and compared the number of Ph.D.s received by each ethnic group in 1994–95 with those obtained in 1995–96. There were virtually no changes in these figures from the earlier year to the later year; therefore we have maintained the figures for 1994–95.

32. Although Mickelson and Oliver (1991) do not deny that there is a shortage of African Americans coming out of the Ph.D. pipeline, they do argue that some of the more prestigious schools are prejudiced in their hiring practices of African

American Ph.D.s who earn their degrees from some of the less prestigious schools. Whether or not this is true, the data in Tables 9.1 through 9.3 show that there are so few African Americans coming through the pipeline that one need not resort to a 'prejudice' argument to explain the shortage of African American faculty at all institutions of higher education. Even some HBCUs have only a minority of their faculty who are African American.

33. Although between 1990 and 1998 there has been a significant increase in educational attainment for all the groups, Mexican Americans and Puerto Ricans still have educational attainment levels that more closely resemble those of African Americans than whites.

34. We ignore here the difficult question of the qualifications of minority Ph.D.s when compared to white Ph.D.s. The data presented in this chapter indicate that even if all minority Ph.D.s were highly qualified there would not be enough of them to achieve the goal of increasing ethnic diversity among our faculties at institutions of higher education.

10. POLICY RECOMMENDATIONS

1. The reason for this is that of all students who get high grades at college (A or A−) a substantial portion of them become either doctors or college professors.

2. We were able to conduct this preliminary evaluation because there were many schools in our sample that had MMUF programs. We did not have the resources or the time to conduct a full evaluation of the MMUF program. A majority of the funds used to conduct the research reported in this book was supplied by the Andrew W. Mellon Foundation.

APPENDIX C

1. The Winship and Radbill article was written before programs like SUDDAN and the latest version of STATA became available. Some of the problems discussed in this article are no longer relevant given the availability of these programs.

2. The difference between the two sources cannot be accounted for by degrees granted to blacks who are not American citizens because the NCES has a special category for nonresident aliens.

3. It is not clear whether the IPEDS includes foreign nationals (such as citizens of West Indian countries) who might have obtained college degrees in the United States. But in general the data Nettles et al. report is very close to those reported by the NCES for 1993–94.

4. There also appears to be a significant discrepancy between our census estimates in Table 9.2 for the number of white college graduates in 1998 (823,000) and the number of degrees the NCES reports were granted to whites in 1995–96 (905,000). This also seems to be a result of the fact that we applied percentages from the 35–39-year-old cohort to the 25–29-year-old cohort. Applying the 35–39-year-old cohort percentage for whites to the number of whites in that cohort produces an estimate of slightly more than one million bachelor's degrees granted to white students. The number of whites in the 25–29-year-old cohort who have B.A.

degrees is probably somewhere between the census estimate indicated in Table 9.2 and the NCES figure. But we are not particularly concerned with this discrepancy, because we are primarily interested in estimating the number of minorities who will exit the Ph.D. pipeline. If the NCES data are in fact more accurate than the census estimates for whites, this would mean that the number of white Ph.D.s attempting to obtain a job in academia in one of the arts and sciences would be even greater than what we have indicated in Row 12 of Table 9.2.

Addis, Adeno. 1996. "Role Models and the Politics of Recognition." *University of Pennsylvania Law Review* 144: 1377–1468.

Adelman, Clifford. 1995. "A's Aren't That Easy." *New York Times,* May 17, p. A21.

—— 1997. "Diversity: Walk the Walk and Drop the Talk." *Change,* July–August, pp. 34–45.

Agresti, Alan. 1990. *Categorical Data Analysis.* New York: John Wiley.

Allen, Walter R., Edgar G. Epps, and Nesha Z. Haniff, eds. 1991. *College in Black and White: African American Students in Predominantly White and in Historically Black Public Universities.* Albany: State University of New York Press.

Allen, Walter R., and Nesha Z. Haniff. 1991. "Race, Gender and Academic Performance in US Higher Education." In Walter R. Allen, Edgar G. Epps, and Nesha Z. Haniff, eds., *College in Black and White: African American Students in Predominantly White and in Historically Black Public Universities.* Albany: State University of New York Press.

Archibold, Randal C. 1998. "Just Because the Grades Are Up, Are Princeton Students Smarter?" *New York Times,* February 18, p. A1.

Association of American Medical Colleges. 1991. "Facts: Applicants, Matriculants, and Graduates, 1991–1997." Prepared by the Section for Student Services, October 21, 1991. Washington, D.C.: Association of American Medical Colleges.

Astin, Alexander. 1962. "Influences on the Student's Motivation to Seek advanced Training: Another Look." *Journal of Educational Psychology* 53: 303–309.

—— 1963. "Undergraduate Institutions and the Production of Scientists." *Science* 141: 334–338.

—— 1968. "Undergraduate Achievement and Institutional Excellence." *Science* 161: 661–667.

—— 1977. *Four Critical Years.* San Francisco: Jossey-Bass.

—— 1982. *Minorities in American Higher Education.* San Francisco: Jossey-Bass.

—— 1993. *What Matters in College: Four Critical Years Revisited.* San Francisco: Jossey-Bass.

Astin, Alexander, and Robert J. Panos. 1969. *The Educational and Vocational De-

velopment of College Students. Washington, D.C.: American Council on Education.

Astin, Alexander W., and Helen S. Astin. 1992. *Undergraduate Science Education: The Impact of Different College Environments on the Educational Pipeline in Sciences.* Higher Education Research Institute, UCLA.

Baird, Leonard. 1973. *The Graduates: A Report on the Plans and Characteristics of College Seniors.* Princeton, N.J.: Educational Testing Service.

——— 1976. "Who Goes to Graduate School and How They Get There." In Joseph Katz and Rodney Hartnett, eds., *Scholars in the Making: The Development of Graduate and Professional Students.* Cambridge, Mass.: Ballinger.

Barber, Elinor G., and Stephen Cole. 1996a. *The Graduate School Experience of Minority Students.* Report prepared for the Leadership Alliance.

——— 1996b. "The Career Choices of High Achieving Minority College Graduates: A Report of Focus Groups." Manuscript.

Becker, Gary S. 1957. *The Economics of Discrimination.* Chicago: University of Chicago Press.

——— 1975. *Human Capital: A Theoretical and Empirical Analysis with Special Reference to Education.* 2d ed. New York: National Bureau of Economic Research.

Bizzari, Janice. 1995. "Women, Role Models, Mentors, and Careers." *Educational Horizons:* 145–152.

Blau, Peter, and Otis Dudley Duncan. 1967. *The American Occupational Structure.* New York: Free Press.

Bok, Derek. 1993. *The Cost of Talent: How Executives and Professionals Are Paid and How It Affects America.* New York: Free Press.

Bowen, William G., and Derek Bok. 1998. *The Shape of the River: Long-Term Consequences of Considering Race in College and University Admissions.* Princeton, N.J.: Princeton University Press.

Bowen, William G., and Neil L. Rudenstine. 1992. *In Pursuit of the Ph.D.* Princeton, N.J: Princeton University Press.

Bowen, William G., and Julie Ann Sosa. 1989. *Prospects for Faculty in the Arts and Sciences.* Princeton, N.J.: Princeton University Press.

Chait, Richard, and Cathy Trower. 2001. "Professors at the Color Line." *New York Times,* September 15, p. A23, col. 1.

Clark, Burton R. 1970. *The Distinctive College.* Chicago: Aldine.

Cole, Jonathan R. 1979. *Fair Science: Women in the Scientific Community.* New York: Free Press.

Cole, Jonathan R., and Stephen Cole. 1973. *Social Stratification in Science.* Chicago: University of Chicago Press.

Cole, Stephen. 1976. *The Sociological Method.* 2d ed., revised and enlarged. Chicago: Rand-McNally.

——— 1986. "Sex Discrimination and Admission to Medical School, 1929–1984." *American Journal of Sociology* 92: 549–567.

——— 1992. *Making Science: Between Nature and Society.* Cambridge, Mass.: Harvard University Press.

Cole, Stephen, and Gary S. Meyer. 1985. "Little Science, Big Science Revisited." *Scientometrics* 7: 443–458.

Cole, Stephen R., and Robert Fiorentine. 1991. "Discrimination Against Women in Science: The Confusion of Outcome with Process." In Harriet Zuckerman, Jonathan R. Cole, and Jon Bruer, eds., *The Outer Circle: Women in the Scientific Community*. New York: W. W. Norton.

Coleman, James S. 1960. "The Adolescent Sub-Culture and Academic Achievement." *American Journal of Sociology* 65: 337–347.

Collins, Randall. 1979. *The Credential Society: An Historical Sociology of Education and Stratification*. Orlando, Fla.: Academic Press.

Constantine, Jill. 1995. "The Effect of Attending Historically Black Colleges and Universities on Future Wages of Black Students." *Industrial and Labor Relations Review* 48: 531–546.

Dale, Stacy Berg, and Alan B. Krueger. 1999. "Estimating the Payoff to Attending a More Selective College: An Application of Selection on Observables and Unobservables." National Bureau of Economic Research, Working Paper 7322.

Davis, James A. 1964. *Great Aspirations: The Graduate School Plans of American College Seniors*. Chicago: Aldine.

———— 1965. *Undergraduate Career Decisions*. Chicago: Aldine.

———— 1966. "The Campus as a Frog Pond." *American Journal of Sociology* 72: 17–31.

Davis, Robert. 1991. "Social Support Networks and Undergraduate Student Academic-Success-Related Outcomes: A Comparison of Black Students on Black and White Campuses." In Walter R. Allen, Edgar G. Epps, and Nesha Z. Haniff, eds., *College in Black and White: African American Students in Predominantly White and in Historically Black Public Universities*. Albany: State University of New York Press.

Douvan, Elizabeth. 1976. "The Role Models in Women's Professional Development." *Psychology of Women Quarterly* 1: 5–20.

Ehrenberg, Ronald G. 1992. "The Flow of New Doctorates." *Journal of Economic Literature* 30: 830–875.

———— 1995. "Role Models in Education." *Industrial and Labor Relations Review* 48: 482–485.

Ehrenberg, Ronald G., Daniel D. Goldhaber, and Dominic J. Brewer. 1995. "Do Teachers' Race, Gender, and Ethnicity Matter? Evidence from the National Educational Longitudinal Study of 1988." *Industrial and Labor Relations Review* 48: 547–561.

Ely, Jane Alice. 1998. "Interest in Mathematics and Science among Students Having High Mathematical Ability." Ph.D. diss., SUNY at Stony Brook.

Evans, Mark O. 1992. "An Estimate of Race and Gender Role-Model Effects in Teaching High School Economics." *Journal of Economic Edcuation* 23 (Summer): 209–219.

Feagin, Joe R., Hernan Vera, and Nikitah Imani. 1996. *The Agony of Education: Black Students in White Colleges and Universities*. New York: Routledge.

Featherman, David, and Robert Hauser. 1976. *Opportunity and Change*. Orlando, Fla.: Academic Press.

Feldman, Kenneth, and Theodore M. Newcomb. 1969. *The Impact of College on Students*. San Francisco: Jossey-Bass.

Fiorentine, Robert. 1987. "Men, Women and the Premed Persistence Gap: A Normative Alternatives Approach." *American Journal of Sociology* 92: 1118–1139.

——— 1988. "Increasing Similarity in the Values and Life Plans of Male and Female College Students: Evidence and Implications." *Sex Roles* 18: 143–158.

Fiorentine, Robert, and Stephen Cole. 1992. "Why Fewer Women Become Physicians: Explaining the Premed Persistence Gap." *Sociological Forum* 7: 469–495.

Fleming, Jacqueline. 1984. *Blacks in College: A Comparative Study of Students' Success in Black and in White Institutions.* San Francisco: Jossey-Bass.

Fordham, Signithia. 1988. "Racelessness as a Factor in Black Students' School Success: Pragmatic Strategy or Pyrrhic Victory." *Harvard Education Review* 58: 54–83.

——— 1996. *Blacked Out: Dilemmas of Race, Identity, and Success at Capitol High.* Chicago: University of Chicago Press.

Freeman, Richard B. 1971. *The Market for College-Trained Manpower.* Cambridge, Mass.: Harvard University Press.

Fuller, Carol. 1989. *Undergraduate Origins of Women and Men 1970–1982 Graduates Who Received Doctorates between 1970–1986.* Ann Arbor: Great Lakes Colleges Association.

Hamilton, Richard, and Hargens, Lowell. 1993. "The Politics of the Professors: Self-Indentifications, 1969–1984." *Social Forces* 71 (3): 603–627.

Hanushek, Eric. 1996. "School Resources and School Performance." In Gary Burtless, ed., *Does Money Matter?* Washington, D.C.: Brookings Institution.

Herrnstein, Richard, and Charles Murray. 1994. *The Bell Curve: Intelligence and Class Structure in American Life.* New York: Free Press.

Hirschi, Travis, and Hanan C. Selvin. 1967. *Delinquency Research: An Appraisal of Analytic Methods.* New York: Free Press.

Holland, John. 1957. "Undergraduate Origins of American Scientists." *Science* 126: 433–437.

Hsia, Jayjia. 1988. *Asian Americans in Higher Education and at Work.* Hillsdale, N.J.: Lawrence Earlbaum.

Hyman, Herbert H. 1955. *Survey Design and Analysis.* New York: Free Press.

Institute for the Study of Social Change. 1991. *The Diversity Project.* Berkeley: University of California at Berkeley.

Jackson, Kenneth W., and L. Alex Swan. 1991. "Institutional and Individual Factors Affecting Black Undergraduate Student Performance: Campus Race and Student Gender." In Walter R. Allen, Edgar G. Epps, and Nesha Z. Haniff, eds., *College in Black and White: African American Students in Predominantly White and in Historically Black Public Universities.* New York: State University of New York Press.

Jacobs, Jerry. 1989. *Revolving Doors: Sex Segregation and Women's Careers.* Stanford, Calif.: Stanford University Press.

Jencks, Christopher. 1998. "Racial Bias in Testing." In Christopher Jencks and Meredith Phillips, eds., *The Black-White Test Score Gap.* Washington, D.C.: Brookings Institution.

Jencks, Christopher, and Meredith Phillips, eds. 1998. *The Black-White Test Score Gap.* Washington, D.C.: The Brookings Institution.

Jencks, Christopher, et al. 1972. *Inequality: A Reassessment of the Effect of Family and Schooling in America.* New York: Basic Books.

Kamens, David. 1971. "The College 'Charter' and College Size: Effects on Occupational Choice and College Attrition." *Sociology of Education* 44: 270–296.

——— 1977. "Legitimizing Myths and Educational Organization: The Relationship between Organizational Ideology and Formal Structure." *American Sociological Review* 42: 209–219.

Kane, Thomas. 1998. "Racial and Ethnic Preferences in College Admissions." In Christopher Jencks and Meredith Phillips, eds., *The Black-White Test Score Gap.* Washington, D.C.: Brookings Institution.

Kanter, Rosabeth. 1977. *Men and Women of the Corporation.* New York: Basic Books.

Klitgaard, Robert. 1985. *Choosing Elites.* New York: Basic Books.

Knapp, Robert H., and Hubert B. Goodrich. 1952. *Origins of American Scientists: A Study Made under the Direction of the Faculty of Wesleyan University.* Chicago: University of Chicago Press, for Wesleyan University.

Knapp, Robert H., and Joseph J. Greenbaum. 1953. *The Younger American Scholar: His Collegiate Origins.* Chicago: University of Chicago Press.

Ladd, Everett C., and Seymour Martin Lipset. 1975. *The Divided Academy: Professors and Politics.* New York: McGraw-Hill.

Lazarsfeld, Paul F., and Wagner Thielens, Jr. 1957. *The Academic Mind.* New York: Free Press.

Lemann, Nicolas. 1999. *The Big Test: The Secret History of the American Meritocracy.* New York: Farrar, Straus, and Giroux.

Lerner, Robert, and Althea K. Nagai. 1991. "A Critique of the Expert Report of Patricia Gurin in *Gratz v. Bollinger.*" Prepared for the Center for Equal Opportunity, Washington, D.C.

Lieberson, Stanley. 1985. *Making It Count.* Berkeley: University of California Press.

Long, J. Scott. 1997. *Regression Models for Categorical and Limited Dependent Variables.* Thousand Oaks, Calif.: Sage.

Maccoby, Eleanor, and Carol Nagy Jacklin. 1975. *The Psychology of Sex Differences.* Stanford: Stanford University Press.

McCaughey, Robert. 1994. *Scholars and Teachers: The Faculties of Select Liberal Arts Colleges and Their Place in American Higher Learning.* New York: Andrew W. Mellon Foundation.

Merton, Robert K. 1957. "Continuities in the Theory of Reference Groups and Social Structure." In *Social Theory and Social Structure.* Glencoe, Ill.: Free Press.

Merton, Robert K., and Alice Rossi. 1957. "Contributions to the Theory of Reference Groups." In Robert K. Merton, *Social Theory and Social Structure.* Glencoe, Ill.: Free Press.

Mickelson, Roslyn Arlen, and Melvin L. Oliver. 1991. "The Demographic Fallacy of the Black Academic: Does Quality Rise to the Top?" In Walter R. Allen, Edgar G. Epps, and Nesha Z. Haniff, eds., *College in Black and White: African*

American Students in Predominantly White and in Historically Black Public Universities. New York: State University of New York Press.

Murray, Charles, and Richard Herrnstein. 1992. "What's Really Behind the SAT-Score Decline." *Public Interest* 106: 32–56.

NCES [National Center for Educational Statistics]. 1995–1998. *Digest of Educational Statistics.* Washington, D.C.: United States Department of Education.

Neter, John, William Wasserman, and Michael H. Kutner. 1989. *Applied Linear Regresion Models.* 2d ed. Homewood, Ill.: Irwin.

Nettles, Michael T. 1991. "Racial Similarities and Differences in the Predictors of College Student Achievement." In Walter R. Allen, Edgar G. Epps, and Nesha Z. Hanif, eds., *College in Black and White: African American Students in Predominantly White and in Historically Black Universities.* Albany: State University of New York Press.

Nettles, Michael, Laura W. Perna, and Kimberly C. Edelin. 1997. *The Role of Affirmative Action in Expanding Student Access at Selective Colleges and Universities.* Frederick D. Patterson Research Institute of UNCF, University of Michigan.

Nettles, Michael T., A. Thoeny, and E. Gosman. 1986. "Comparative and Predictive Analyses of Black and White Students' College Achievement and Experience." *Journal of Higher Education* 57: 289–318.

Oppenheimer, Valerie K. [1970] 1976. *The Female Labor Force in the United States: Factors Governing Its Growth and Changing Composition.* Westport, Conn.: Greenwood.

Pascarella, Ernest, John Smart, Corinna Ethington, and Michael Nettles. 1987. "The Influence of College on Self-Concept: A Consideration of Race and Gender Differences." *American Educational Research Journal* 24: 49–77.

Pascarella, Ernest, John Smart, and J. Stoecker. 1989. "College Race and the Early Status Attainment of Black Students." *Journal of Higher Education* 60: 82–107.

Pascarella, Ernest, and Patrick Terenzini. 1991. *How College Affects Students: Findings and Insights from Twenty Years of Research.* San Francisco: Jossey-Bass.

Phelan, Thomas W. 1979. "Undergraduate Orientations Towards Scientific and Scholarly Careers." *American Educational Research Journal* 16: 411–422.

Phillips, Meredith, Jeanne Brooks-Gunn, Greg J. Duncan, Pamela Klebanov, and Jonathan Crane. 1998. "Family Background, Parenting Practices, and the Black-White Test Score Gap." In Christopher Jencks and Meredith Phillips, eds., *The Black-White Test Score Gap.* Washington, D.C.: Brookings Institution.

Portes, Alejandro, and Kenneth Wilson. 1976. "Black-White Differences in Educational Attainment." *American Sociological Review* 41: 414–431.

Ramist, Leonard, Charles Lewis, and Laura McCamley-Jenkins. 1994. *Student Group Differences in Predicting College Grades: Sex, Language, and Ethnic Groups.* College Board Report Number 93-1. Princeton, N.J.: College Board.

Ravitch, Diane. 2000. *Left Back: A Century of Failed School Reforms.* New York: Simon & Schuster.

Rosen, Harvey S., and Brandice J. Canes. 1995. "Following in her Footsteps? Faculty Gender Composition and Women's Choices of College Majors." *Industrial and Labor Relations* 48: 486–505.

Rosenberg, Morris. [1957] 1980. *Occupations and Values.* New York: Arno Press.

——— 1968. *The Logic of Survey Analysis.* New York: Basic Books.

Rosovsky, Henry. 1990. *The University: An Owner's Manual.* New York: W. W. Norton.

Rothstein, Donna S. 1995. "Do Female Faculty Influence Female Students' Educational and Labor Market Attainments?" *Industrial and Labor Relations Review* 48: 515–530.

Rothstein, Donna S., and Ronald G. Ehrenberg. 1994. "Do Historically Black Institutions of Higher Education Confer Unique Advantages on Black Students: An Initial Analysis." In Ronald G. Ehrenberg, ed., *Choices and Consequences: Contemporary Policy Issues in Education.* Ithaca, N.Y.: ILR Press.

Rothstein, Richard. 1998. *The Way We Were? The Myths and Realities of America's Student Achievement.* New York: Century Foundation Press.

Sabot, Richard, and John Wakeman-Linn. 1991. "Grade Inflation and Course Choice." *Journal of Economic Perspectives* 5: 159–170.

Sacks, Peter. 1996. *Generation X Goes to College: An Eye-Opening Account of Teaching in Postmodern America.* Chicago: Open Court.

——— 1999. *Standardized Minds: The High Price of America's Testing Culture and What We Can Do to Change It.* Cambridge, Mass.: Perseus Books.

Shulman, James, and William G. Bowen. 2000. *The Game of Life.* Princeton, N.J.: Princeton University Press.

Smelser, Neal. 1993. "The Politics of Ambivalence: Diversity in the Research Universities." In Jonathan R. Cole, Elinor G. Barber, and Stephen R. Graubard, eds., *The Research University in a Time of Discontent.* Baltimore: Johns Hopkins University Press.

Solnick, Sara J. 1995. "Changes in Women's Majors from Entrance to Graduation at Women's and Co-educational Colleges." *Industrial and Labor Relations Review* 48: 505–514.

Sowell, Thomas. 1972. *Black Education: Myths and Tragedies.* New York: McKay.

——— 1993. *Inside American Education: The Decline, the Deception, the Dogmas.* New York: Free Press.

——— 2001. *A Personal Odyssey.* New York: Touchstone.

Speizer, Jeanne J. 1981. "Role Models, Mentors, and Sponsors: The Elusive Concepts." *SIGNS* 6 (2): 692–712.

Steele, Claude. 1997. "A Threat in the Air: How Stereotypes Shape Intellectual Identity and Performance." *American Psychologist* 52: 613–629.

Steele, Claude, and Joshua Aronson. 1998. "Stereotype Threat and the Test Performance of Academically Successful African Americans." In Christopher Jencks and Meredith Phillips, eds., *The Black-White Test Score Gap.* Washington, D.C.: Brookings Institution.

Steele, Shelby. 1994. "A Negative Vote on Affirmative Action." In Nicholas Mills, ed., *Debating Affirmative Action: Race, Gender, Ethnicity, and the Politics of Inclusion.* New York: Delta.

Steinberg, Laurence. 1996. *Beyond the Classroom: Why School Reform Has Failed and What Parents Need to Do.* New York: Touchstone.

Stolzenberg, Ross M. 1994. "Educational Continuation by College Graduates." *American Journal of Sociology* 99: 1042–1077.

Stouffer, Samuel, et al. 1949. *The American Soldier: Adjustment during Army Life.* Princeton, N.J.: Princeton University Press.

Thomas, Gail E. 1991. "Assessing the College Major Selection Process for Black Students." In Walter R. Allen, Edgar G. Epps, and Nesha Z. Haniff, eds., *College in Black and White: African American Students in Predominantly White and in Historically Black Public Universities.* Albany: State University of New York Press.

Thomas, Gail E., and S. Hill. 1987. "Evaluating the Payoffs of College Investments for Black, White, and Hispanic Students." Report no. 344. Baltimore: Johns Hopkins University, Center for Social Organization of Schools.

Trow, Martin. 1976. "Elite Higher Education: An Endangered Species." *Minerva* 14: 355–376.

Vars, Frederick E., and William G. Bowen. 1998. "Scholastic Aptitude Test Scores, Race, and Academic Performance in Selective Colleges and Universities." In Christopher Jencks and Meredith Phillips, eds., *The Black-White Test Gap.* Washington, D.C.: Brookings Institution.

Winship, Christopher, and Larry Radbill. 1994. "Sampling Weights and Regression Analysis." *Sociological Methods and Research* 23: 230–257.

Wood, Thomas E., and Malcolm J. Sherman. 2001. *Race and Higher Education: Why Justice Powell's Diversity Rationale Preferences in Higher Education Must Be Rejected.* Princeton, N.J.: National Association of Scholars.